D0747260

Political Movements and Violence in Central Ameri...

This book offers an in-depth analysis of the confrontation between popular movements and repressive regimes in Central America for the three decades beginning in 1960, particularly in El Salvador and Guatemala. Examining both urban and rural groups as well as both nonviolent social movements and revolutionary movements, this study has two primary theoretical objectives. The first seeks to clarify the impact of state violence on contentious political movements. Under what conditions will escalating repression provoke challengers to even greater activity and perhaps even to the use of violence themselves or, conversely, intimidate them back into passivity? The second defends the utility of the political process model for studying contentious movements, indeed, finds in this model the key to resolving the repression-protest paradox. The study is based on the most thorough set of events data on contentious political activities collected for Latin American countries.

Charles D. Brockett received a Ph.D. in political science from the University of North Carolina at Chapel Hill in 1974. He is the author of *Land, Power, and Poverty: Agrarian Transformation and Political Conflict in Central America*, which was selected as a *Choice* "Outstanding Academic Book" of 1988. He is also the author of numerous articles published in scholarly journals and edited volumes, including the *American Political Science Review* and *Latin American Research Review*. In recognition of his work, he has received Fulbright awards for participation in the South America Today program in 1995, for lecturing/research in Guatemala in 2000, and for research in Mexico in 2004; the John B. Stephenson Fellowship from the Appalachian College Association; and a National Endowment for the Humanities Summer Stipend. He is currently Biehl Professor of International Studies, Department of Political Science, at Sewanee: The University of the South.

Cambridge Studies in Contentious Politics

Editors

Jack A. Goldstone   *George Mason University*
Doug McAdam   *Stanford University* and *Center for Advanced Study in the Behavioral Sciences*
Sidney Tarrow   *Cornell University*
Charles Tilly   *Columbia University*

Ronald Aminzade et al., *Silence and Voice in the Study of Contentious Politics*
Doug McAdam, Sidney Tarrow, and Charles Tilly, *Dynamics of Contention*
Jack A. Goldstone, ed., *States, Parties, and Social Movements*
Charles Tilly, *The Politics of Contentious Violence*
Charles Tilly, *Contention and Democracy in Europe, 1650–2000*
Elisabeth Wood   *Yale University*

Political Movements and Violence in Central America

CHARLES D. BROCKETT

Sewanee: The University of the South

CAMBRIDGE
UNIVERSITY PRESS

CAMBRIDGE UNIVERSITY PRESS
Cambridge, New York, Melbourne, Madrid, Cape Town, Singapore, São Paulo

Cambridge University Press
40 West 20th Street, New York, NY 10011-4211, USA

www.cambridge.org
Information on this title: www.cambridge.org/9780521840835

First published 2005

Printed in the United States of America

A catalog record for this book is available from the British Library.

Library of Congress Cataloging in Publication Data
Brockett, Charles D., 1946–
Political movements and violence in Central America / Charles D. Brockett.
    p.   cm. – (Cambridge studies in contentious politics)
Includes bibliographical references and index.
ISBN 0-521-84083-X – ISBN 0-521-60055-3 (pb.)
1. El Salvador – Politics and government – 1979–1992.   2. El Salvador – Politics and
government – 1944–1979.   3. Guatemala – Politics and government – 1945–1985
4. Guatemala – Politics and government – 1985–   5. Social movements.
6. Political violence.   7. Political persecution.   I. Title.   II. Series.
III. Series: Political economy of institutions and decisions
F1488.3.B73   2005
972.8405′3–dc22   2004045926

ISBN-13   978-0-521-84083-5 hardback
ISBN-10   0-521-84083-X hardback

ISBN-13   978-0-521-60055-2 paperback
ISBN-10   0-521-60055-3 paperback

Contents

Figures, Tables, and Maps

Figures

ix

Tables

Maps

Abbreviations and Acronyms

El Salvador

AES	Asociación de Estudiantes de Secundaria
AGEMHA	Asociación General de Empleados del Ministerio de Hacienda
AGEUS	Asociación General de Estudiantes Universitarios Salvadoreños
ANDA	Asociación Nacional de Acueductos y Alcantarillado
ANDES	Asociación Nacional de Educadores Salvadoreños
ARENA	Alianza Republicana Nacionalista
ARS	Acción Revolucionaria Salvadoreña
BPR	Bloque Popular Revolucionario
CCS	Comité Coordinación de Sindicatos
COACES	Confederación de Asociaciones Cooperativas
CODEFAM	Comité de Familiares de Presos, Desparacidos y Asesinados Políticos
CUTS	Confederación Unificada de Trabajadores Salvadoreños
CVES	Comisión de la Verdad para El Salvador
ERP	Ejército Revolucionario del Pueblo
FAPU	Frente de Acción Popular Unificada
FARN	Fuerzas Armadas de Resistencia Nacional
FDR	Frente Democrático Revolucionario

FECCAS	Federación Cristiana de Campesinos Salvadoreños
FENASTRAS	Federación Nacional Sindical de Trabajadores Salvadoreños
FESINCONTANS	Federación de Sindicatos de Construcción, Transportes y Similares
FMLN	Frente Farabundo Martí de Liberación Nacional
FNOC	Frente Nacional de Orientación Cívica
FPL	Fuerzas Populares de Liberación
FSR	Federación Sindical Revolucionaria
FTC	Federación de Trabajadores del Campo
FUAR	Frente Unido de AcciÚn Revolucionaria
FUNPROCOOP	Fundación para la Promoción de Cooperativos
FUSS	Federación Unitaria Sindical de El Salvador
IUDOP	Instituto Universitario de Opinión Pública
LP-28	Ligas Populares 28 de Febrero
MNR	Movimiento Nacional Revolucionario
MUSYGES	Movimiento Unitario Sindical y Gremial de El Salvador
ORDEN	Organización Democrática Nacionalista
PCN	Partido de Conciliación Nacional
PCS	Partido Comunista de El Salvador
PDC	Partido Demócrata Cristiano
PRTC	Partido Revolucionario de los Trabajadores Centroamericanos
SJ	Soccoro Jurídico
TL	Tutele Legal
UCA	Universidad Centroamericana "José Simeón Cañas"
UCS	Unión Comunal Salvadoraña
UDN	Unión Democrática Nacionalista
UNADES	Unión Nacional de Damnificados
UNO	Unión Nacional Opositora
UNOC	Unidad Nacional Obrero Campesina

Abbreviations and Acronyms

UNTS	Unión Nacional de Trabajadores Salvadoreños
UPD	Unidad Popular Democrática
UPT	Unión de Pueblo de Tugurios
UR-19	Universitarios Revolucionarios 19 de Julio
UTC	Unión de Trabajadores del Campo

Guatemala

AEU	Asociación de Estudiantes Universitarios
ANC	Asociación Nacional Campesino
ANN	Alianza Nueva Nación
CEH	Comisión para el Esclaracimiento Histórico
CERJ	Consejo de Comunidades Etnicas "Runujel Junam"
CETE	Comité de Emergencia de los Trabajadores del Estado/Consejo de Entidades de Trabajadors del Estado
CGTG	Confederación General de Trabajadores de Guatemala
CIRMA	Centro de Investigaciones Regionales de Mesoamérica
CNC	Confederación Nacional Campesina
CNCG	Confederación Nacional Campesina de Guatemala
CNT	Confederación Nacional de Trabajadores
CNUS	Comité Nacional de Unidad Sindical
CONAVIGUA	Coordinadora Nacional de Viudas de Guatemala
CONDEG	Consejo Nacional de Desplazados de Guatemala
CUC	Comité de Unidad Campesina
CUSG	Confederación de Unidad Sindical de Guatemala
DC	Partido Democracia Cristiana Guatemalteca
EGP	Ejército Guerrillero de los Pobres
EOS	Escuela de Orientación Sindical
FAR	Fuerzas Armadas Rebeldes (earliest)
FAR	Fuerzas Armadas Revolucionarias (after 1968)

FAS	Federación Autónoma Sindical
FASGUA	Federación Autónoma Sindical de Guatemala
FCG	Federación Campesina de Guatemala
FDNG	Frente Democrático Nueva Guatemala
FERG	Frente Estudiantil Robin García
FUEGO	Frente Unido Estudiantil Guatemalteco Organizado
FUR	Frente Unido de la Revolución
GAM	Grupo de Apoyo Mutuo
INTA	Instituto Nacional de Transformación Agraria
JOC	Juventud Obrera Católica
JPT	Juventud Patriótica del Trabajo
MLN	Movimiento de Liberación Nacional
MR-13	Movimiento Revolucionario 13 de Noviembre
MRP-Ixim	Movimiento Revolucionario Popular-Ixim
ORPA	Organización del Pueblo en Armas
PAC	Patrullos de Autodefensa Civil
PGT	Partido Guatemalteco del Trabajo
PID	Partido Institucional Democrático
PODER	Participación Organizada de Estudiantes Revolucionarios
PR	Partido Revolucionario
STUSC	Sindicato de Trabajadores de la Universidad de San Carlos
UNSITRAGUA	Unión Sindical de Trabajadores de Guatemala
URNG	Unidad Revolucionaria Nacional Guatemalteca

Others

AAAS	American Association for the Advancement of Science
AIFLD	American Institute for Free Labor Development
ATC	Asociación de los Trabajadores del Campo

Abbreviations and Acronyms

CIIDH	International Center for Human Rights Investigations
FSLN	Frente Sandinista de Liberación Nacional
IMF	International Monetary Fund
MPU	Movimiento Popular Unido
OAS	Organization of American States
ORIT	Inter-American Regional Organization of Workers (AFL-CIO)
PRI	Partido Revolucionario Institucional
UMWA	United Mine Workers of America
UNAG	Unión Nacional de Agricultores y Ganaderos
UNC	Unión Nacional de Campesinos
UPANacional	Unión de Pequeñas Agricultores Nacional
USAID	U.S. Agency for International Development

Acknowledgments

As I finished work on an earlier book on agrarian transformation and political conflict in Central America, I realized that the study was incomplete concerning the social actors that brought the two themes together. Fortunately, I soon had the opportunity to address that deficiency as a participant in a National Endowment for the Humanities Summer Seminar on social movements offered by Sidney Tarrow at Cornell University. Not only was the seminar under his guidance a vibrant intellectual experience, but it also set in motion the research program that, after many years, has resulted in this book. My debt to Sid Tarrow goes further, including also his advice and encouragement on several articles undertaken at the earlier stages of this journey. A second editor of the series in which this book appears, Charles Tilly, read an earlier draft of the manuscript and provided a number of useful suggestion for revision. As the reader will soon learn throughout the following pages, my intellectual debt to Tarrow and Tilly, along with the third editor of this series, Doug McAdam, is substantial. It is a delight to have my work appear under their editorship.

I gratefully acknowledge receipt of a John B. Stephenson Fellowship from the Appalachian College Association (and especially the support of Clarence Minkle, graduate dean at the University of Tennessee), as well as an earlier James Still Fellowship that afforded me a summer of library research at the University of Kentucky. The Stephenson Fellowship provided me with a semester's research leave that I spent at the University of North Carolina, Chapel Hill, furthering my study of the literature on contentious movements. While there, I benefited from status as a visiting researcher at the Institute of Latin American Studies and the generous assistance of the institute's director, Jonathan Hartlyn. Lars Schoultz was more than generous, turning over for my use both his faculty office and his library carrel.

I also enjoyed the opportunity to discuss common interests with other UNC faculty, notably Charles Kurzman, Tony Oberschall, and Christian Smith.

I spent the first half of 2000 in Guatemala on a Fulbright Fellowship for both research and lecturing. My big thanks for the experience to my students at Rafael Landívar University in Guatemala City, as well as to deans David Son Turnil and Rosa Tuck. The Fulbright also gave me the opportunity to undertake research at the Centro de Investigaciones Regionales Mesoamérica (CIRMA) in Antigua, as I did again the following summer. My deepest gratitude to everyone associated with this marvelous research facility, from director Tani Adams, to the library's benefactors, and especially to the many wonderful staff people upon whose assistance I depended. A side trip to San Salvador was also taken; my appreciation also to the library staff at the Universidad Centroamericana "José Simeón Cañas."

Over the years of this project, I have received financial support for a number of research trips from my home institution, Sewanee: The University of the South. Much of this book was written during a sabbatical spent in Río Caribe, Venezuela, and most of the rest over a summer in Colima, Mexico, both made possible by university support. I am also grateful to the residents of both communities whose kindness made our stays such a pleasure. University support (as well as a National Endowment for the Humanities Summer Stipend) also funded research at the U.S. National Archives on U.S. policy toward Guatemala and with the very important collection of government documents on U.S. policy collected by the National Security Archives located at George Washington University. University support has been critical over the years through Sewanee's competent and collegial Print Services Office, most especially from Tammy Scissom and Minnie Raymond.

This study makes substantial use of the International Center for Human Rights Investigations/American Association for the Advancement of Science (CIIDH/AAAS) database on human rights violations in Guatemala; my thanks to Patrick Ball for his assistance, as well as to him and his colleagues for undertaking this important project and making it so accessible to others. My deepest appreciation also goes to the many Central American researchers and activists upon whose efforts I draw. I am humbled by their efforts undertaken in the face of risk; indeed, a tragic number of them have been killed for seeking truth.

Elements of this research have been presented over the years in conference papers and journal articles. The resulting book has been greatly improved by the suggestions from numerous panelists, audience members,

Acknowledgments

journal editors, and referees. It has been particularly strengthened by the insightful suggestions from the reviewers secured by Cambridge University Press to review an earlier version of this manuscript. Among many, I wish to thank Robert Jackson, editor of *Sociological Forum*, for his good advice; Ken Sharpe, who drew my attention some years ago to the importance of the Salvadoran protest cycle of the mid-1980s; James Scott, for his generous reading of a much earlier attempt at what grew into Chapter 5; and Stephanie McSpirit for our work together.

Lewis Bateman, Cambridge's Senior Editor for Political Science and History has been supportive of this project from our first contact, for which I am most grateful. My thanks also to the book's production editor, Ernie Haim, and copy editor, Barry Ross, for their most competent assistance.

Most importantly, Heather Tosteson has shared many of these experiences with me, greatly enhancing them all. The process of sharing our manuscripts has been for me an extraordinarily enjoyable and rewarding intellectual experience. I freely admit that I have gotten the better of the exchange. In appreciation, it is to her that this book is dedicated.

Political Movements and Violence in Central America

1

Introduction

Progressive activists grew more assertive in Central America during the 1960s, mobilizing groups around their shared grievances and struggling through collective action to create a better life for themselves and others. Normally initiated by students, teachers, and other professional groups, these efforts were joined by urban labor organizations, which by the 1970s were frequently in the forefront of the broader social movements that had emerged. Organizing in the countryside invariably has faced greater constraints in Central America, but here, too, peasant movements grew and on notable occasions played important roles in furthering the demands of popular (i.e., non-elite) movements.

Across the region, these movements faced great odds, from the intransigence of economic elites to harassment and intimidation by both public and private security forces. They also were attacked violently by agents of the state. As nonviolent mass movements grew in size and contentiousness – often paralleled by the rise of armed groups fighting for their revolutionary cause – states became more repressive, less so in Costa Rica and Honduras, much more so in Nicaragua, and horrifically so in El Salvador and Guatemala. Yet, even in the face of virulent state terrorism, some committed and courageous activists continued on; and whenever repression slackened, popular movements reappeared.

This confrontation between committed popular movements and state violence is most striking in the cases of El Salvador and Guatemala, which are the primary focus of this study. The two countries are tragically well known for their high level of political violence – around 200,000 killed in Guatemala in the three decades up to 1996 (CEH 1999,

1:73)[1] and more than 80,000 in El Salvador for the period of 1980–1991 (Seligson and McElhinny 1996, 224), overwhelmingly noncombatants killed by the state (and its allied death squads) in both countries.[2] What are less well known are the persistent contentious but nonviolent activities by dedicated popular forces, such as marches, strikes, factory and farm occupations, and sit-ins at public offices, not only prior to the escalation of regime violence but even in the face of it. This was true in both countries even in the mid-1980s, following extraordinary levels of state terror earlier in the decade and in the midst of civil war.

These developments resonate with a number of important controversies in social science. It is my hope that this study of Central American contentious movements will make an important contribution to our understanding of such issues as the following:

- *Grievances:* Are socioeconomic grievances such a constant among the disadvantaged that, as many scholars assume, they are relatively unimportant for explaining the emergence of popular movements and the intensity of their collective political activities? Or, as will be argued here, are new socioeconomic grievances often critical to understanding why even the poor and powerless sometimes undertake risky contentious efforts to redress the wrongs they believe they have suffered?
- *False consciousness:* To what extent is "consciousness raising" a precondition for the successful mobilization of popular forces? What is the role of higher status political allies and other support groups (or- "outside agitators" from the elite's perspective) in the mass mobilization process?
- *Political opportunities:* To what extent is the opening of greater political opportunities a precondition for the emergence of mass contentious movements and for their growth and persistence? For success in their objectives? If the relationship between contention and opportunities (or constraints/threats) is conditioned by other factors, what generalizations can be made about these interrelationships?

---

[1] The report of the Comisión para el Esclaracimiento Histórico (CEH), the Guatemalan truth commission, is available in twelve print volumes as well as on CD. The latter may be obtained from the American Association for the Advancement of Science at http://www.aaas.org.

[2] The report of the Salvadoran truth commission, the Comisión de la Verdad para El Salvador, can be downloaded from the U.S. Institute for Peace at http://www.usip.org/library/tc/doc/reports/el_salvador/tc_es_03151993_toc.html.

- *Revolutionary movements:* Are the relationships among the variables that explain the emergence and trajectory of social movements different when nonviolent social movements transform into, or are incorporated by, armed revolutionary movements? How important is the role of the revolutionary leadership to this transformation? How important is repression by the state?
- *Repression-protest paradox:* More specifically, why is it that under some conditions repression has the unintended consequence of spurring even greater popular challenges to state authority? Clearly, at other times repression does succeed in its objective of reducing popular protest and even eliminating contentious movements themselves. Is it possible to resolve in a consistent way this repression-protest paradox?
- *Protest Cycle:* Is the protest cycle (or cycle of contention) merely a descriptive summary of the changing level of collective action? Or might the cycle of contention be the analytic key to resolving the repression-protest paradox?
- *Role of emotion:* Finally, how helpful is the inclusion of emotion as a crucial component of individual and group motivation to answering these questions?

As a preface to our consideration of these questions in the Central American context, consider the following two vignettes. The first comes from Guatemala, the second from El Salvador. One concerns rural movements, the other urban. In one case, repression smashes a nonviolent popular movement; in the other, popular resistance persists in the face of great risk. Combined, they bring to life the central themes of this study.

Rural Contention and Repression in Guatemala

Among the most dreadful aspects of the years of mass contention and state violence in Central America were the many massacres of unarmed civilians in El Salvador and Guatemala outside of combat situations, usually including women and children. This was especially true in Guatemala, whose truth commission detailed 601 massacres occurring between 1978 and 1985 (CEH 1999, 3:257). The first sizeable massacre – one that shook the nation and international observers – took place on May 29, 1978 in the indigenous town of Panzós in the department of Alta Verapaz when fifty-three unarmed Q'eqchi' Maya were shot down and another forty-seven were injured

(CEH 1999, 6:13–24).[3] The town plaza was filled that day with an estimated seven hundred peasants from the surrounding area protesting their treatment at the hands of landowning elites and their friends in local government and the military. Tensions had been escalating in the region for several years as peasants protested again and again this assault on their access to land, to both their economic security and way of life.

The roots of this conflict went far back. As the Guatemalan coffee export economy expanded, up to three-quarters of the land in the entire department ended up in the hands of German planters by the latter part of the nineteenth century. The indigenous population was left with little recourse but to provide the necessary cheap labor as a resident workforce. These German lands were expropriated during WWII and then – along with other large holdings – were redistributed to peasants in the Panzós area in the early 1950s through an agrarian reform implemented by the progressive Jacobo Arbenz government. When Arbenz was overthrown by a U.S.-engineered coup in 1954, prereform owners got their lands back and the nationalized farms were distributed over the following years to the well-connected. The construction of new roads and the discoveries of oil, copper, and nickel deposits in the region made the area more attractive to entrepreneurs. Competitors to peasants for land with the know-how, resources, and connections secured title to parcel after parcel. A prime example was the mayor of Panzós himself. Elected in the 1950s as the candidate of the ruling party of the counterrevolution (the Movimiento de Liberación Nacional, MLN), he stayed in power into the 1970s, using his political base to become one of the largest landowners in the area.[4]

The demonstration in Panzós on the day of the 1978 massacre was the latest in a series of protests occurring in the area across the past decade. For example, conflicting land claims were the point of a demonstration in June 1970 by hundreds of peasants in one Panzós area town (IMP77 June 20, 1970),[5] as well as of many other efforts in the following years. Greatly expanding the arena of their protest, in 1975 Alta Verapaz peasants from towns in the municipalities (which are like U.S. counties) of both Panzós and Chisec managed to get their denunciations read on the floor of the national

---

[3] For further discussion of the region and the massacre, as well as the exhumation of the bodies and the subsequent burial ceremony that broke the silence within the community over the 1978 tragedy, see Sanford 2003, 53–58, 63–75.

[4] CEH (1999 6:13–24). Also see Aguilera Peralta 1979; Carter 1969; IWGIA 1978.

[5] For an explanation of this and other identification codes, see the beginning of the Bibliography section.

congress. Before the nation, they charged local landlords with threatening to dispossess them at gunpoint of lands they had worked for many years (IPV Apr. 2, 1975, 320). In August 1977, peasants met to denounce the abuse of authority by the mayor of Panzós, charging him with using threats and jailings in the interest of the local oligarchy to prevent them from organizing (IPV, Aug. 19, 1977, 194). A few months later, peasant representatives claimed that 10,000 residents under threat of eviction would resist, if necessary with machetes, sticks, and stones (IPV Oct. 10, 1977, 320).

Similar denunciations were made by peasants from the municipality of Cahabón, located about twenty winding miles to the north of Panzós. Local landlords using their political connections had obtained formal titles to the land claimed by peasants and in 1972 began attempts to remove them by armed threats and burning down their homes. Through the national labor organization, the Federación Autónoma Sindical de Guatemala (FASGUA), which was providing legal assistance to the peasants, their representatives succeeded in 1973 in gaining an audience with President Carlos Arana Osorio and believed the problem settled. But it only worsened (IPV Feb. 8, 1975, 250). In November 1974, the landlords struck with force. Through their contacts at the Confederación Nacional Campesina (CNC), peasants charged landlords with shooting two community residents, beating six others, and having three more arrested (IPV Dec. 4, 1974, 128). In January 1975, residents brought in representatives from FASGUA to discuss the situation, but the meeting was broken up by a squad of soldiers who forced the FASGUA representatives out of town. The hundreds of children waiting for their parents scattered during the attack by the soldiers; three weeks later, fifteen were still reported as missing (IPV Feb. 8, 1975, 250).

A similar story was told by peasants from the Tucurú area, located some thirty-five miles to the west of Panzós. Representatives of 115 families who had been working on the *finca* (farm) La Esperanza for about fifty years visited Guatemala City newspaper offices in both December 1976 and February 1977 to tell their story and gain support for their position. After the finca was expropriated from its German owner during WWII, these families continued working their same plots as a cooperative on about half the finca. Sometime during the late 1950s/early 1960s, the finca was reportedly "given" to its current owner. The peasants continued farming their plots while working for the new owner. But due to the low wages he paid, around 1976 they decided to stop working for him – but with the intention of staying on "their" land. He, though, intended to evict them from "his" land. The peasants had traveled to the capital, but "since we are indigenous," they complained, "nobody in the government wants to attend to us" (IPV Mar. 24, 1977, 117). The conflict continued up to the eve of the Panzós massacre. At one point in April 1977, the local military commissioner led an assault of 300 men on the cooperative, ravaging member's fields. Through FASGUA in February 1978, the peasants denounced the landlord for burning their crops and their homes, running cattle through their fields, and for being behind the disappearance of one of their members the year before, when he traveled to the department capital to secure assistance, as well as for the failed kidnapping of two others and the beating of yet two more.[6]

The large landowners of the area were so disturbed by the pace of peasant organizing and their activities that in May 1978 they met with the governor, asking for military protection for citizens "threatened" by peasant actions. Soon thereafter, a military contingent was moved into the town of Panzós in anticipation of the upcoming demonstration. The military commander in the region believed the peasant organizations were linked to communist guerrillas, as undoubtedly other elites believed as well (CEH 1999, 6:15). Indeed, it was true that armed revolutionaries were beginning to organize in the region. Probably the more important "outside agitators" at this time, though, were the advisers from the national labor movement. Both groups of outside activists saw fertile grounds for their organizing: Poor peasants, mistreated for decades because they were powerless and indigenous, now faced new and serious threats to their economic security. In addition, intermittent repression from private and public elites was now threatening their physical security, adding to their grievances.

In the months prior to the Panzós massacre, tensions in Alta Verapaz also were escalating because of labor conflicts in the region. In October 1977, workers went on strike for a week at the important Chixoy hydroelectric project, located about twenty miles south of the departmental capital of Cobán.[7] Another large group at Chixoy went on strike for a few days in March 1978 and then in early April marched to Cobán, where they were joined by striking mining workers from Oxec, who also had marched in from the countryside from about 15 miles north of Panzós.

---

[6] IPV (Mar. 24, 1977, 117; Mar. 25, 1977, 24; Dec. 8, 1976, 135); IPSET13 (FASGUA Feb. 20, 1978). Similarly, at the end of 1975 and again in early 1976 representatives of thousands of peasant families in the nearby municipalities of both Cahabón and Chisec journeyed to the capital to publicize the evictions and threats occurring in their areas, as well as four recent murders by landowners (IPSET5 campesinos Dec. 2, 1975; Jan. 20, 1976), IPV (Feb. 2, 1976, 263–264).

[7] This was also the site of the Río Negro massacre to be discussed in Chapter 2.

Improving life for miners had proved particularly difficult. An earlier organizational effort in 1974 had been met by a wave of firings at a number of companies. At the huge Oxec copper mine operated by the multinational Guatemalan Mining Corporation, for example, some 136 miners went on a hunger strike protesting purported violations of the labor code concerning working conditions and salaries. Forty were fired. Frustrated by the lack of response by management and the courts to their petitions, in the spring of 1978 Oxec miners went on strike for fifteen days. Joining the Chixoy workers in Cobán in April, the two groups totaled around 1,500 marchers. Instead of disbanding after their demonstration, they settled in the central plaza, occupying it for eight days. Both groups won concessions from management. But commentators later saw a connection between these protests and the tragedy a little over a month later in Panzós.[8]

Not so successful was the other major unionizing effort in the area. At Calzado Cobán, a business located in San Cristóbal Verapaz about twenty miles down the road from the department capital, the struggle had been long and difficult. An initial organizing meeting held in June 1975 attended by some six-hundred workers and supporters, including a local priest and assisting lawyer, was met the next day at the plant with the firing of twenty-four workers, including two of their leaders. Unionizing efforts continued but a few weeks after the Panzós massacre two dozen more workers were fired and management succeeded in busting their union.[9]

How many of these Alta Verapaz peasants and workers continued their activism in the months and years ahead, perhaps to the point of supporting or even joining the armed revolutionaries, is impossible to say. Clearly, some did continue, but under growing risks. For example, peasants in the community of Baldio Pombaac in Panzós continued to press their claims to contended lands, but they were warned in April 1979 by a local landlord that the agrarian reform agency, the Instituto Nacional de Transformación Agraria (INTA), was "in favor of the landlords" and that President "General Lucas gave permission to the landlords to kill" (IPSET5 campesino Apr. 17, 1979). In the four years after the Panzós massacre, at least 310 selective killings by the military occurred in the valley where Panzós is located, many of the victims identified by Guatemala's truth commission as community leaders, especially those concerned with land conflicts. Also among the dead

---

[8] IMP12 (Nov. 4, 1977); IPSET8 (Companias mineras); IMP17 (July 4, 1974); IMP25 (Apr. 6, 1978); ASIES (1995, 3:514–519).
[9] IPSET5 (Calzado Coban); ASIES (1995, 3:516).

7

were Amalia, Elvira, and Faustina Caal, ages five, four, and three, little girls murdered at home by soldiers right in front of their parents in January 1981.[10] No further demonstrations occurred in the Panzós area through the years of armed conflict that dragged on until 1996 (CEH 1999, 6:19).[11]

Urban Contention and Repression in El Salvador

Public school teachers have been significant participants in the contentious politics of El Salvador since the mid-1960s. Teachers created one of the interest groups most important to the politics of the late 1960s/early 1970s. They then provided crucial leadership to the multisector mass organizations that dominated the contentious political activities of the last half of the 1970s, as well as to the armed revolutionary movement that fought the civil war of the 1980s. Hundreds of teacher-activists were among the thousands of victims of the state terror that traumatized El Salvador in the early 1980s. Many of the surviving teacher-activists who did not join the revolutionary armies were later central to the resurgence of an important nonviolent contentious movement in the mid-1980s, even while the civil war continued.

After unsuccessful strike attempts in 1965 and 1967, the newly formed Asociación Nacional de Educadores Salvadoreños (ANDES) went on full strike in early 1968. Lasting 54 days, in the end the teachers won many of their demands. Strikers held a number of demonstrations and marches, occupied the Ministry of Education, and spurred the mobilization of broad sectors of society in their support. The "elected" but military government often responded with harassment and sometimes with violence – at least four protestors were killed. This repression was said to be critical in developing the "revolutionary consciousness" of those teachers who were later to join the Fuerzas Populares de Liberación (FPL), including the FPL's number two in command up to 1983 (Melida Anaya Montes) and its top commander from 1983 on (Salvador Sánchez Céren).[12]

Conflict between ANDES and the government was again central to Salvadoran politics throughout much of 1971. Teachers pressured the government during the first half of the year for passage of an education

---

[10] CEH (1999, 8:23). A listing of all of the documented dead and disappeared in Alta Verapaz is found between pages 21 and 86.

[11] Alta Verapaz ranked fourth among Guatemala's twenty-two departments in the total number of massacres of civilians during the 1962–1995 period, with 9 percent of the country total (CEH 1999, 6:257). It ranked third in total human rights violations for the same period, again with 9 percent of the country total (CEH 1999, 2:328).

[12] Harnecker 1993, 38–41.

reform sponsored by ANDES. Tactics included brief work stoppages and demonstrations extending throughout the country. When the government finally acted in July, it passed a law disliked by teachers. A major strike then ensued. Two weeks later only about forty percent of the nation's teachers were working. Lasting through August, the strike was supported by almost daily marches. Some were broken up by authorities, especially a teacher and student torchlight parade on July 16 that was attacked by some 200 security agents who injured and arrested many. In the end, teachers accepted less than desired, turning their hopes now to the February 1972 presidential elections (UCA 1971).

A broad center-left coalition gathered behind the candidacy of José Napoleón Duarte of the Partido Demócrata Cristiano (PDC). Duarte appeared to be leading the results when the military regime handed the victory through fraud to its own candidate. A general strike called by Duarte was unable to deter the regime; neither was a coup attempt from within the military a month later. Teachers were among the major activists behind the center-left coalition's efforts and major targets of the repression that followed. For many, more contentious forms of struggle now appeared the only viable direction, a conclusion reinforced by fraud again with the 1977 presidential elections which brought in an even more repressive military president. For the rest of the decade the most important outlet for teachers' political activities was not institutional politics but multisector mass organizations focused on contentious activities.

ANDES was one of the groups involved in the formation in spring 1974 of the first of the mass organizations. Through the Frente de Acción Popular Unificada (FAPU), teachers were brought together with organized groups of peasants, students, and workers, as well as the communist party and religious workers. The following year, ANDES again was involved with the formation of a second mass organization, the Bloque Popular Revolucionario (BPR). It was these organizations, and especially the BPR, that were the core of the contentious movements that dominated Salvadoran politics in the last years of the 1970s and going into 1980. Revolutionary in their objectives (and covertly tied to the armed left), part of the genius of the mass organizations was their dramatic nonviolent contentious repertoire.

In addition to numerous marches and other demonstrations, a frequent tactic of the mass organizations was to occupy buildings, especially those of the government, churches, and foreign embassies. Usually done to dramatize grievances, sometimes occupants were held as bargaining chips (and protection) in negotiations with authorities. As the popular movements grew in size and contentiousness in the later 1970s, government violence escalated as well and on a number of occasions activists were murdered, sometimes in isolation but then increasingly in groups of growing size during government attacks on protesters. By mid-1979, teachers claimed that more than thirty of their activists had been murdered. Yet, their activism continued. For example, a September march by several thousand teachers in defiance of a government ban protested the murder of one of their leaders.[13]

Such popular activism was largely responsible for a coup on October 15, 1979 led by progressive junior military officers. Reaching out to civilian counterparts, they hoped that their new reform government could stop the polarization and the violence. But the violence continued, in part from some of the armed left but most especially from the hard right. The mass organizations continued their nonviolent efforts into 1980, but the escalating violence took its toll. For example, in mid-February 1980 fifty ANDES militants seized the Education Ministry, taking one hundred to two hundred hostages. ANDES also had brief strikes in April and June, largely to protest the intensifying repression – but without success.[14] It was during this time that state terrorism closed all of the remaining space for nonviolent political activity in El Salvador. Except for an occasional denouncement of the violence, no further political activity by ANDES is recorded for the next several years by the sources consulted for this study. In one of these denouncements, coming on Teachers' Day, June 14, 1981, ANDES made public the names of 211 teachers that it claimed had been killed since October 15, 1979 and of another 20 who were in prison (ECA #393: 703).

During 1980 El Salvador moved toward civil war, one certainly fully underway by the time of the guerrillas' misnamed "final offensive" of January 1981, as the war continued for another 11 years. Yet, incredibly, nonviolent mass mobilization resumed during the mid-1980s, albeit primarily in the capital. Despite the massive violence directed at the popular sector during 1980–1983, despite the continuing intermittent killing of activists through the rest of the decade, and despite the larger context of an on going civil war, organizations such as ANDES slowly and courageously resumed their contentious activities.

Public employee unions led the way with a few strikes in San Salvador in late 1983 and a growing number in 1984. ANDES returned to action with

[13] ECA (#372:1002); *NY Times* (Sept. 16, 1979, 6).
[14] *NY Times* (Feb. 19, 1980, 6; June 6, 1980, 3); *El Imparcial* (Feb. 19, 1980, 1); ECA (#379:506).

its economic concerns, testing the situation with a one-day work stoppage in March 1985, followed by another for three days in May and then two more in the fall, as well as others in 1986 and 1987.[15] Street demonstrations returned more slowly, as seen, for example, with the symbolic May First march commemorating International Labor Day. Clearly too risky in the early 1980s, the annual observation returned in 1984 when some 2,500 brave individuals marched. The following year, the march grew to ten to fifteen thousand demonstrators and in 1986 to somewhere between twenty-five and fifty thousand participants.[16] Emboldened by this resurgence on the one hand and driven by economic crisis on the other, more contentious forms of activity returned as well. For example, ANDES seized an education office in July 1987 – reportedly holding a hostage for a time – in order to press both its economic demands and to dramatize charges of corruption against the education minister (ECA #465: 494).

More terrible events still lay ahead for mass movements that would recall the worst days of the early 1980s. On October 31, 1989, a union headquarters was bombed, killing ten people and injuring another three dozen. Then on November 15, the military murdered six Jesuit priests affiliated with the Universidad Centroamericana (as well as their housekeeper and her daughter), several of whom had long been among the most powerful voices for nonviolent and progressive change in the country. In between, the Frente Farabundo Martí de Liberación Nacional (FMLN) unleashed its largest and most successful offensive since January 1981, bringing the war right into the streets of the capital.[17] With the increasing repression that came with the FMLN offensive and then its withdrawal, the mass movement was paralyzed for several months. However, on May 1, 1990 the combined opposition mounted the largest demonstration of the past decade as some eighty thousand marched, calling for a peaceful settlement of the war (Solis 1990, 471). Seemingly still beyond reach at this point, that settlement finally came with the signing of a peace accord on January 16, 1992.

Contentious Movements and Political Violence

Central American events of recent decades show human behavior at both its most courageous and its most barbaric. The opposing phenomena of

---

[15] ECA (#439:418; #441:546; #443:725; #445:853; #456:910; #463:357, 364).

[16] ECA (#428:446; #429:583; #441:546; #451:457, 472); NY Times (May 2, 1986, 3).

[17] ECA (#492:867); *NY Times* (Nov. 1, 1989, 7); ECA (#493:1140); *NY Times* (Nov. 16, 1989, 1).

mass mobilization and of state terrorism pose some of the most profound questions that can be asked by social science. How to explain the willingness of political elites and their agents to slay thousands – tens of thousands – of their fellow human beings, even when their victims are unarmed and even when they are small children? Conversely, how do we account for ordinary people undertaking protest activities under circumstances so dangerous that even their lives are at risk? When – and why – do some support and even join revolutionary movements while others seek safety in passivity or flight?

The relationship between mass political activity and repression is the central concern of this study. It is a paradoxical relationship, as often noted in the scholarly literature: State violence crushes popular mobilization under some circumstances, but at other times similar levels of violence (or even greater) will provoke broad contentious movements rather than pacify the target population.[18] This study examines this relationship between state violence and popular political activity within cycles of contention and repression in Central America. The primary evidence will be protest and repression events data collected for El Salvador and Guatemala beginning with 1960 and extending through 1991 for the former and 1984 for the latter.

Although the regional scope of this study is narrow, substantively and theoretically its ambitions are broad. The full array of contentious political activities will be examined, from peaceful marches led by centrist political parties seeking fair and free elections and nonviolent occupations of buildings by progressive movements, across the spectrums of political activities and ideologies, to violent actions by revolutionary movements, thereby uniting within the scope of this study what are normally separate scholarly subjects and literatures.[19] Certainly, there are important normative

---

[18] A recent discussion of this paradox explicitly grounded within the study of contentious politics is Goldstone and Tilly 2001. This literature is discussed in Chapter 8.

[19] Few have followed Tilly's (1978) ambitious lead in *From Mobilization to Revolution*, neither in scope nor even in the literature that is utilized. The present study can be seen in part as a response to the challenge issued by Tilly, writing with McAdam and Tarrow, for an integrated perspective on social movements and revolution (McAdam et al. 1997; also see Goldstone 1994) – or indeed, all forms of contentious politics (McAdam et al. 2001). Also see Tilly's (1997) response to critiques of their 1997 challenge by Lichbach 1997 and Selbin 1997a. McAdam, Tarrow, and Tilly define contentious politics as "episodic, public, collective interaction among makers of claims and their objects when (a) at least one government is a claimant, an object of claims, or a party to the claims, and (b) the claims would, if realized, affect the interests of at least one of the claimants" (McAdam, Tarrow, and Tilly 2001, 5). For a good assessment of an earlier formulation by the same authors, see Goldstone 1998b.

and theoretical differences between "rule-conforming and rule-violating" (Piven and Cloward 1995) or "routine and non-routine" (Useem 1998) collective action. However, what is too often ignored by these analytic distinctions is continuity in the real world as individual activists move between different forms of contention and as the dominant mode of contentious activity within a country alters from one type to another.[20]

The analytic distinction between institutional politics and social movements is more meaningful in institutionalized democracies than it is for the majority of the world's people.[21] Political party activists in systems with weak traditions of free and fair elections are at times the most important and courageous protesters within their countries. The occasional recourse to repression in institutionalized democracies is meant to restrict nonconventional – and usually illegal and disruptive – protest. In Central America, in contrast, repression often has been directed at limiting the effectiveness of opposition political parties or, worse, at eliminating them – or even their activists – altogether.[22]

Similarly, the analytically (and for many, normatively) clear distinction between revolutionaries and nonviolent protesters misses the more complex reality. It is not just that the same individual might move back and forth between these two forms of struggle. More importantly, Central American

[20] Still, it is worth keeping in mind Piven and Cloward's point: "a riot is clearly not an electoral rally, and both the participants and the authorities know the difference" (Piven and Cloward 1995, 139).

[21] But even so, as a leading scholar of First World movements notes, "insurgencies often begin within institutions and even organized movements become rapidly involved in the political process, where they interact with interest groups, unions, parties, and the forces of order" (Tarrow 1998a, 143). Also see Meyer and Tarrow (1998, 25). Similarly, Goldstone argues: "Social movement activity and conventional political activity are different but parallel approaches to influencing political outcomes, often drawing on the same actors, targeting the same bodies, and seeking the same goals" (Goldstone 2003, 8). Burstein goes further, arguing: "Every serious attempt to distinguish between social movements and other forms of political action . . . fails. . . . We should conclude that the distinction between 'SMOs' [social movement organizations] and 'interest groups,' which seems so obvious initially, *does not exist*, in the sense that no one has developed a convincing basis – theoretical or empirical – for distinguishing consistently between the two" (Burstein 1998, 45).

[22] As McAdam, Tarrow, and Tilly point out, "there is no fundamental discontinuity between social movements and institutional politics." They note that "the same groups that pour into the streets and mount barricades may be found in lobbies, newspaper offices, and political party branches." Furthermore, "movements can cooperate with parties and interest groups; compete with them for support; or try to occupy the same political space that they do" (McAdam, Tarrow, and Tilly 1996, 27). For a good application of a political opportunities explanation of mobilization strategies, see Marks and McAdam 1999.

13

revolutionaries at times were critical to the creation of effective nonviolent mass organizations. They then attempted to integrate the strategies and activities of both the violent and nonviolent vehicles – connections not always understood by nonviolent protesters.[23] Furthermore, whether revolutionaries are allied with other organizations or not, revolutionary situations seldom develop from the activities of the revolutionaries alone but are the culmination of escalating contentious politics involving large numbers of people and organizations with reformist rather than revolutionary objectives. Conversely, as Stoll reminds us, "Instead of building up the grassroots left, guerrilla warfare usually destroys it" through the repression it provokes (Stoll 1999, 76).

Central to the argument of this study is that to understand the protest-repression dynamic, we must place it in the larger context of the grievances that fuel contentious movements, the mobilization processes and strategies that create and direct them, and the political opportunities and constraints that facilitate and suppress them. Most of the world's people do not live in institutionalized democracies. Instead, their social movements are much more likely to occur under conditions of acute grievances and high risks than is the case in the industrialized democracies. Since grievances and repression are more central to the dynamics of social movements in most of the world, they will receive more attention here than is usually the case in a literature that largely focuses on First World movements.

The Configuration of Political Opportunities

Scholars writing from a political process approach to social movements have compellingly made their case that contentious politics is as much a function of "the political realities confronting members and challengers at any given time" (McAdam 1988, 245) as it is of grievances, availability of resources, or underlying socio economic change.[24] This insight has been conceptualized as "the structure of political opportunities," a term developed by Eisinger (1973) to help explain the outcomes of the 1960s' urban protest in

---

[23] During the years of violence, this subject was a dangerous one because it jeopardized the lives of nonviolent protesters. Accordingly, it was often not discussed, but it can be now. See Chapters 3 through 5, as well as 7 and 8.

[24] See especially McAdam 1982; McAdam, Tarrow, and Tilly 1996, 1997; Tarrow 1989, 1998a; Tilly 1978; and among the many edited volumes, Costain and McFarland 1998; Giugni, McAdam, and Tilly 1998, 1999; McAdam, McCarthy, and Zald 1996; Meyer and Tarrow 1998; Morris and Mueller 1992. For a parallel construct in the field of public policy studies, see Kingdon 1984.

14

the United States.[25] The dominant definition is provided by Tarrow as those "dimensions of the political environment that provide incentives for collective action by affecting people's expectations for success or failure" (Tarrow 1998a, 76–77). As political opportunities shift in ways advantageous to challengers, mass mobilization is encouraged, challengers' political leverage increases, and the possibility of positive outcomes improves (McAdam 1982, 43).

The original word choice – "*structure* of political opportunities" – was an unfortunate one because the concept of structure does suggest, as Goodwin and Jasper point out, "factors that are relatively stable over time and outside the control of movement actors" (Goodwin and Jasper 1999, 29).[26] Although these conditions might often be true, they are not always. Political opportunities can change rapidly and significantly (as fast, for example, as a right-wing military coup can depose an elected progressive civilian government), and political opportunities also can be altered by movement activities for better (often among their objectives) or for worse. This overly structuralist connotation has been recognized: "structure" for some time now has not been used alongside "political opportunities" by its core theorists.[27] Indeed, McAdam et al. acknowledge the "overly structural" quality

[25] Goodwin and Jasper 1999 credit Robert Merton in the 1950s as the first to use the concept of an opportunity structure (see Merton 1996).

[26] This point is one of several crucial to the critique by Goodwin and Jasper of political process theory (including its political opportunity thesis), which in their view is either "tautological, trivial, inadequate, or just plain wrong," depending on how it is understood (Goodwin and Jasper 1999, 28). Their critique is the lead article in a journal mini-symposium; for their response to the commentaries on their critique, see Jasper and Goodwin 1999. They are particularly concerned by what they see as the elevation of this approach to the level of a "paradigm", one that they claim "systematically discourages investigation" of other important variables, especially cultural variables (Jasper and Goodwin 1999, 121; see also Jasper 1997, 34–39, 59). To me, however, the leading political process theorists have been characterized by openness to scholarly dialogue and self-criticism. As one example, McAdam, Tarrow, and Tilly warn: "So broad has the concept [of political opportunities] become that there is danger of its confusion with the political environment in general and with post hoc 'explanations' that find opportunities only after movements have had success" (McAdam et al. 1997, 153). In fact, in their most recent collaboration McAdam, Tarrow, and Tilly (2001) manifest an apparent agreement with many of the substantive criticisms issued by Goodwin and Jasper. Also see Lichbach 1998, which is less of a critique and more "designed to stimulate a dialogue between the two competing approaches – rational action-oriented . . . and structure-oriented . . . – to contentious politics" (Lichbach 1998, 405). He adds that whereas political process theory "is strong on structure and weak on action," rational actor theory "is strong on action and weak on structure" (p. 412).

[27] Others make the same point–for example, Goodwin and Jasper (1999, 41) and Polletta (1999, 64 n.2).

of their past work (McAdam, Tarrow, and Tilly 2001, 18) and now refer instead to the "*attribution* of opportunity and threat" (p. 43; my italics).[28]

However, as Koopmans reminds us, "not all of opportunity is agency . . . , some of it is structured" (Koopmans 1999, 102). To get at the central importance for social movement emergence and success of a set of "objective *conditions* confronting acting individuals" (Merton 1996, 154) without the problematic connotations carried by the concept of structure, my preferred alternative is "the *configuration* of political opportunities."[29] As separate dimensions, these opportunities can and do vary independently, for the overall social movement sector generally, from individual movement to movement, and for any one movement, over time.[30]

Agreement concerning these specific "dimensions of the political environment that provide incentives for collective action" (Tarrow 1998a, 76–77), though, has not been easy. Nonetheless, in his 1996 state-of-the-literature essay, McAdam offers what he calls a "highly consensual list" of four dimensions of political opportunity:[31]

1. The relative openness or closure of the institutionalized political system;
2. The stability or instability of . . . elite alignments;

---

[28] Goldstone and Tilly correctly point out that it is a mistake to treat threats as "merely the flip side of opportunity" (Goldstone and Tilly 2001, 181). They distinguish between current and anticipated "harm," that is, "costs of repression" (184–185). Repression is but one dimension of political opportunities and does have its own dynamics (p. 181) that differ from those of the other dimensions. As will be discussed thoroughly in later chapters, both current and anticipated repression (threats) create new grievances, providing perhaps enough motivation to override constricting opportunity in order to sustain existing mobilization or to spur new activities.

[29] Brockett 1991b uses the term; Diani 1996 and Schock 1999a make the move from structure to configuration more fully; Koopmans (1999, 99) comes close to doing so.

[30] Here I do not share Schock's (1999a, 371) reading of the political opportunities literature as ignoring the potential of independent variation among the separate dimensions.

[31] Yet, three years after McAdam's "consensual list" Goodwin and Jasper (1999, 33) still claim much disagreement in the literature as to "just what factors to include." Also see Amenta et al. 2002. Nonetheless, it seems to me that most of the disagreement comes from: (1) inappropriately conflating other concepts with political opportunities, such as the mobilization of resources (e.g., Kitschelt 1986) or grievances (e.g., Gould 2001 and Goodwin and Jasper's illustrations of Smith 1996a and Meyer's [1999, 89] use of his own prior [1990] work); or (2) conceptualizing as separate dimensions concerns that could be incorporated within McAdam's list without difficulty. For example, Schock 1999a adds as additional dimensions the international context (also see Jenkins and Schock 1992, among others), as well as press and information flows. Concerning international factors, in this study two are especially important: international linkages of challengers (incorporated within allies and support

3. The presence or absence of elite allies;
4. The state's capacity and propensity for repression (McAdam 1996, 26–27).[32]

These four dimensions of political opportunity will be used to structure much of the analysis undertaken by this study.[33]

The political opportunity framework originally was elaborated to explain First World cases, the two most prominent being the U.S. civil rights movement (McAdam 1982) and the Italian social movements of the same period (Tarrow 1989a); its use also has been fruitful in other First World case studies and comparative work.[34] As some scholars called attention to the lack of application of the framework to the Third World,[35] a number of studies appeared, finding the approach useful as well in the rest of the world.[36]

The configuration of political opportunities is a conceptual construct and therefore not something that can be observed as existing "out there" in

---

groups) and international linkages of regimes (incorporated within elite alignments). Press and information flows are targets of repression. There are times when repression is light enough that it does not seem to affect press coverage (e.g., Guatemala in the mid-1970s) and other times when it does, especially when state terror is turned against journalists themselves (both El Salvador and Guatemala in the early 1980s). Wickham-Crowley gives especially good coverage to the role of the mass media in revolutionary situations; see, for example, his discussion of Cuba (Wickham-Crowley 1992, 174–178).

[32] This list is an improvement over earlier efforts by McAdam, (e.g., McAdam 1988). It is close to an earlier list offered by Tarrow (1989), which includes the first three dimensions; the fourth is similar to Brockett 1991b.

[33] Amenta et al. 2002 point to the unfortunate lack of conceptual attention given to each of the individual dimensions themselves. A point well taken, effort will be made in later chapters to address this deficiency.

[34] As examples, see other works on the U.S. civil rights movement (Andrews 1997); others on Italy (Diani 1996); the Townsend Movement in the U.S. (Amenta and Zylan 1991; Amenta et al. 1992); the women's movement both in the U.S. (Costain 1992) and compared with the U.K. and Sweden (Gelb 1989); the anti-nuclear power movement (Kitschelt 1986); and the peace movement (Meyer 1990; Rochon 1988).

[35] See, for example, Boudreau 1996.

[36] As examples, see Central American peasant movements (Brockett 1991b); the Chilean protest cycle of the 1980s (Hipsher 1998); student protest in China (Crane 1994); the Zapatista uprising in Mexico (Schulz 1998); the Nicaraguan – Revolution (Cuzán 1990); seventeenth-century Ottoman villagers (Barkey and Van Rossem 1997); mass movements in the Philippines and Burma (Schock 1999a); labor in South Korea (Suh 2001); and a non-violent uprising in Thailand (Schock 1999b). Kurzman (1996), however, finds the framework unhelpful for explaining the movement that overthrew the Shah in Iran. Finally, the framework also has been incorporated into cross-sectional quantitative analysis of political violence; for examples, see Krain 1997 and Schock 1996.

society. The movement activist's understanding of its constituent dimensions is mediated by perception (which in turn is heavily influenced by social factors), giving an important subjective and cultural dimension to all contentious politics.[37] However, it would be poor movement activists who did not attempt to rise as best they could above their own perceptual biases, paying close and constant attention to any possible shifts in political opportunities. The probability of state violence or the dependability of support from higher-status allies or the intensity of elite fragmentation are for activists their "objective" context. As analysts, we want to know how accurately activists perceive their context and how strategically they respond to what they (in interaction with others) perceive. But we also want to understand the determinants not only of action but also of its consequences.[38] As important as are perception and cultural interpretation,[39] the "power shifts that are most defensibly conceived of as political opportunities should not be confused with the collective processes by which these changes are interpreted and framed" (McAdam 1996, 25–26).[40]

A dramatic example for this point is provided by the many young radical-movement activists who died in El Salvador in the late fall of 1979. Misperceiving the social reality before them and believing that the revolutionary victory enjoyed in Nicaragua a few months earlier was now imminent in their own country, they (along with the violent right) intentionally sabotaged a key opportunity for significant reform and social peace

---

[37] For Jasper and Goodwin, cultural aspects are downplayed in political process theory and represent another manifestation of its structural bias: "The main blind spot we see among process theorists is a failure to recognize or incorporate the insights of the cultural constructionism since the late 1970s" (Jasper and Goodwin 1999, 120). They add: "Good sociology, if it is to get a solid purchase on explaining social life, must balance agency and structure, conscious intentions and unintended consequences, individuals and the constraints they face" (p. 122).

[38] My assumption is that while the *attribution* of opportunities and threats is crucial for understanding the decision to act, "objective *conditions* confronting acting individuals" (Merton 1996, 154) remain crucial for explaining success in movement emergence, persistence, and achievement of policy goals. Certainly, there is an interaction between movement activities and political opportunities. But the impact of activities on opportunity will depend substantially on qualities of the latter that are independent of the former. Scholars should be concerned with understanding both the subjective and objective sides of social movements, which is what I take to be Goodwin and Jasper's point at this general level.

[39] Goodwin and Jasper (1999, 33).

[40] McAdam acknowledges that at times it "is extremely hard to separate these objective shifts in political opportunities from the subjective processes of social construction and collective attribution that render them meaningful" (McAdam 1994, 39).

18

in El Salvador. However, rather than their movement growing into the successful revolutionary insurrection they imagined leading, they lost their lives to the early stages of what would become a long, terrible, and inconclusive civil war. Although it is important to understand why the insurrectionists acted as they did, it is also important to understand the objective conditions they misperceived that led to the failure of their objectives and to their own deaths.

Doubts about the utility of the political process model for answering such questions have recently been raised even by the key theorists of the model itself. In their most recent collaboration, McAdam, Tarrow, and Tilly point out four "major defects" in the model "as a tool for the analysis of contentious politics" (McAdam et al. 2001, 43). Perhaps the most important of the defects they identify is the model's focus "on static, rather than dynamic relationships" (McAdam et al. 2001, 43). Their response is to move beyond the political process model to the specification of causal mechanisms "that recur in a wide variety of contention" (p. 37).[41]

My reaction is that their turn in this direction is a significant contribution, but one that is most powerful when still rooted within their earlier political process model. Furthermore, I find the "major defects" in their prior work that they point out to be overstated. Which is to say, McAdam et al. 2001 notwithstanding, a major purpose of this study is to demonstrate the continuing analytic utility of the political process model. Nonetheless, this study will follow their lead in identifying the causal mechanisms at work in the contentious politics examined here; especially useful is their specification of the mechanisms of social appropriation (pp. 44–48), brokerage (pp. 120–121, 142–143), and certification/decertification (pp. 121–122, 145–147).

The other "defects" are really more about the limits of the work that has been done with the model rather than with the inherent shortcomings of the political process model itself. First, it is said that the model "works best when centered on individual social movements and less well for broader episodes of contention" (McAdam et al. 2001, 42). Indeed, most research has been on individual movements. In contrast, this study will show that the model is especially useful for understanding broader episodes of contention. Second,

---

[41] In a more recent work, Tilly (2003) has done the same for collective violence, identifying the causal mechanisms and processes (many of them the same) that explain the outbreak of a wide array of different forms of collective violence.

the authors point out that the model "focused inordinately on the *origins* of contention rather than on its later phases" (p. 42). Instead, this study will demonstrate that the political process model is especially useful for understanding the *trajectories* of contentious movements and their *outcomes*. Third, it is correct, as the authors note, that the political process model had its "genesis in the relatively open politics of the American 'sixties'" and that this led to an overemphasis on opportunities as opposed to threats, the expansion of resources over their deficits (p. 42). But it does not follow that the model lacks utility for the understanding of contentious politics under different conditions.

Indeed, there are good reasons to believe that the opening and contraction of political opportunities is more central to the mobilization and success of Third World contentious movements than it is for those in the First World.[42] Changing political opportunities are critical for politically marginal groups, which is a much larger share of both society and of the universe of movements in the Third World than in the First World. Mainstream movements in institutionalized democracies face different constraints than do those of the politically marginal anywhere.[43] Furthermore, the First World is characterized by the institutionalized quality of its democracies, which means that political opportunities fluctuate within a limited scope compared to most of the rest of the world where gaining securely institutionalized political access and eliminating state violence often are still unrealized objectives of mass mobilization rather than the context within which popular forces act.[44]

---

[42] Munck points out, "We could say that in Latin America the window of opportunity for potential social movements is both smaller and remains open for less time than in Western Europe" (Munck 1990, 30). Good collections of essays on social movements in Latin America are provided by Eckstein 2001; Escobar and Alvarez 1992; and Alvarez, Dagnino, and Escobar 1998.

[43] For an earlier effort in this direction, contrasting movements of "crisis" and of "affluence," see Kerbo 1982; also see Jasper (1997, 8–9) and Goodwin and Jasper (1999, 34).

[44] Rochon's study of the mobilization of European peace movements in the early 1980s is a good example of this point. Referring to preexisting organizations, Rochon notes, "These organizations had all the resources, social and political, that a resource mobilization theorist could deem important. What they lacked was an audience" (Rochon 1988, 23). The same point can be made about political opportunity. Later, he adds, "What is normally lacking is an aggrieved population, ready to embrace proposals for change" (p. 212). Fluctuating political opportunities, then, should be of less importance to the *emergence* of mainstream movements in institutionalized democracies. Nonetheless, political opportunities remain an important variable for explaining the *degree of success* in reaching their objectives.

Summarizing, I am distinguishing four types of movements. The importance of changing political opportunities to movement emergence, and especially growth and persistence, is hypothesized to be in the following order:

- marginal groups in noninstitutionalized democracies
- mainstream groups in noninstitutionalized democracies
- marginal groups in institutionalized democracies
- mainstream groups in institutionalized democracies.

The order between the second and third types is less fixed, though, depending on where the group would fall on a mainstream-marginal continuum and the regime on an institutionalized-noninstitutionalized continuum.

It would be difficult to hold to the *strongest* formulation of the "political opportunities thesis" – that a positive change in the configuration of political opportunities is *necessary* for *all* successful social movement mobilization, given the existence of contrary examples cited by critics. Nonetheless, I still do argue for a *strong* thesis: that change in political opportunities is necessary for the successful emergence and persistence of *most* social movements. The cases of El Salvador and Guatemala provide ample documentation for the strong thesis, as later chapters will demonstrate.

Why We Do What We Do

Contentious politics is about human behavior. Any meaningful explanation of contentious movements, then, includes a social-psychological dimension, even if only implicitly. When scholars are explicit, they often rely on some variant of a rational actor model, with much attention focused on the apparent paradox that collective action is said to be often individually "irrational." Derived from economist Mancur Olson's (1965) seminal work on the relationships between public goods, free riding, and selective incentives in motivating collective action,[45] the "Rebel's Dilemma" is, as phrased by Lichbach: "Unless the free rider problem is overcome (e.g., by selective incentives), ... a rational person will ordinarily not rebel"

---

[45] For a critical review of Olson and other formal models of collective action, see Oliver 1993. As she notes, "The 'rational actor' still has a place in these models but now shares the stage with the adaptive learner, the target of influence, the probabilistic decision-maker, and the inscrutable person who is willing to make a particular contribution for reasons known only to himself" (Oliver 1993, 293).

(Lichbach 1995b, 10).[46] However, as useful as the individualistic (and largely materialistic) rationality of economics has been for the social sciences, it remains too incomplete of a conception of human motivation to adequately account for much contentious activity occurring under conditions of high risk.

More useful have been expanded rational actor models that broaden the scope of its assumptions. For example, individual rationality should be distinguished from collective rationality, as Muller, Opp, and their associates stress.[47] This distinction is empirical as well as analytic – non-elites can recognize and do act on the basis of this difference. Opp (1989, 77) states the point well: "average citizens may adopt a collectivist conception of rationality because they recognize that what is individually rational is collectively irrational – that if people like themselves were individually rational free riders, the likelihood of success of protest action would be very small, and that, therefore, it is collectively rational for all to protest despite the fact that the objective probability of a single individual influencing the outcome is negligible."[48]

Even more broadly, the community-based existence of both rural and urban non-elites dissolves much of the free-rider problem. Risk-avoiding free riders, who enjoy collective goods with no contribution of their own, create a collective action problem for large potential groups. Even "mass" mobilization, though, begins within discrete communities. As an example, Moore finds peasant rebellion to be a two step process from his assessment of the relevant literature. Large-scale rebellions tie together much

---

[46] Lichbach's encyclopedic *The Rebel's Dilemma* (1995b) is a masterful examination of the possible resolutions of the dilemma – with examples drawn from around the world and across the centuries – providing a virtual instruction manual of strategies available to organizers (or governments) who would mobilize (or squelch) contentious movements. But, as it stays within the limits of a rational actor model, in the end it is a limited portrayal of what motivates contentious politics or, as Tilly (1997, 108–109) notes, much of what is important about contentious politics.

[47] See, for example, Finkel, Muller, and Opp 1989; Muller, Finkel, and Dietz 1991; Muller and Opp 1986; Opp 1989; and Opp and Roehl 1990. The thrust of this work is to posit a second type of rational choice model: the public goods model. In their work, this expanded model fares better empirically than the conventional private interest model (e.g., Muller, Finkel, and Dietz 1991). Other studies concur: See, for example, the study by Parks and Vu (1994) contrasting native-born and Vietnamese-born subjects living in the U.S. in their differing responses to a social dilemma game.

[48] From another perspective, though, the finding is unexceptional. As Turner and Killian note, "Children are routinely introduced to this kind of rationality in grade school civics.... 'What would happen if everyone thought that way?'" (Turner and Killian 1987, 333).

smaller movements where "people are mobilized in the context of the social networks in which they live their daily lives" (Moore 1995b, 431).[49] Within these networks, "micromobilization processes" unfold,[50] involving a variety of nonmaterial incentives and sanctions. These processes can facilitate individual participation in protest activities, a participation that might appear irrational from an individualist private interest perspective. Calhoun makes the point well, observing that traditional communities "give people the 'interests' for which they will risk their lives – families, friends, customary crafts, and ways of life" (Calhoun 1988, 150).[51]

The essential point, then, is this: Solidarity and principle are motivational forces just as important under many conditions as private self-interest. Individuals are related through familial and friendship ties, as well as membership in groups. These relationships can "generate a sense of common identity, shared fate, and a general commitment to defend the group," as Fireman and Gamson (1979, 21) point out. Such bonds of solidarity can be important motivators for collective action, especially when shared understandings of principles such as "justice, equity, or right" lend legitimacy to that action (p. 26). This critical role of social networks, solidarity, and shared principles for mass movements is a major theme of Chapters 3 through 5.

How far rational actor models can be stretched to incorporate these important motivational forces beyond private interest and still be meaningful is not a controversy to be settled here.[52] Certainly, though, a third challenge

---

[49] This point is well portrayed by Popkin's (1979, 1988) work on Vietnam. Also see Moore 1995b; Taylor 1988; and Wilson and Orum (1976, 198). Elaborating the process even further, Petersen 2001 elaborates three stages taking rebels from neutrality to membership in a rebel army.

[50] See Opp and Roehl 1990.

[51] Along related lines, see the essay in the same edited volume by Taylor (1988), as well as Calhoun (1982, 136). Also relevant is Oliver's finding that in small groups where individual efforts do make a difference, some act because "If I don't do it, nobody else will." (Oliver 1984, 602).

[52] For example, both Muller and Opp place themselves within a rational choice framework, albeit a greatly expanded one based on "value-expectancy" models; see, in particular, Opp 1989 and Muller 1979. Other leading examples of expanded rational actor models are Lichbach 1995b and Oberschall 1994, 1995. More recently, Calvert 2000 argues that expressive-identity motivations can be understood within a rational choice framework. Others in contrast, such as Fireman and Gamson (1979, 20), argue that such an expansion of the model "is to destroy the raison d'être of the selective incentive argument by reducing it to a useless tautology" (Fireman and Gamson 1979, 20) while Mansbridge (1990, 20) argues that if self-interest is understood to encompass any motive then the model is "vacuous" (Mansbridge 1990, 20). Koopmans 2001 provides a good discussion of such alternatives and a helpful resolution for altruistic movements.

goes beyond the widest scope of any rational actor model. The role of emotion in motivating collective action has been an "especially notable 'silence'" (Amizade and McAdam 2001, 14) until very recently, probably as a reaction to the earlier literature, which portrayed mass collective action as irrational (e.g., the "mob").[53] Honoring the rationality of mass behavior is indeed important but should not be achieved at the expense of a better account of human (elite and non-elite) behavior.[54] To be concrete and relevant to the main concerns of this study, a violent attack by state agents against a member of a group (such as a parent, a close friend, a village elder, or factory union leader) might provoke antiregime activity from other group members, not necessarily out of self-defense but out of rage and a desire for revenge (as well as justice) – even when to do so jeopardizes the most fundamental self-interest of self-preservation.[55]

Rational actor theory would not be so influential unless it had strong explanatory power. But beyond the industrialized democracies out where most of the world's people live, contentious politics often occurs in situations of acute grievances (as certainly it does at times in the First World) and carries high risks, even to life itself. Behavioral models that originated to explain consumer choices do not take us very far in understanding the responses of parents whose children are chronically hungry and ill when others in town squander abundant wealth, or when one's children or parents are raped or murdered before one's eyes.[56] Under conditions

[53] Turner and Killan note: "For a while it seemed that the feelings associated with expressive tendencies... were about to be banished from analyses of crowds and social movements" (Turner and Killan 1987, 104). Scheff goes further, finding a strong "taboo against emotions... in modern social science" (Scheff 1992, 105). Also see Snow and Oliver (1995, 589).

[54] As Marcus, Neuman, and MacKuen point out: "To idealize rational choice and to vilify the affective domain is to misunderstand how the brain works. The various challenges confronting human judgment require the active engagement and interaction of both mental faculties, just as it does the contributions of the left and right hemispheres of the brain" (Marcus, Neuman, and MacKuen 2000, 2).

[55] Miller and Vidmar explain: "The response to a crime like murder involves far more than just the perception that the act has challenged the group's values; it confronts essential belief systems – an impersonal objective order has been disturbed. The affective reaction in these instances is strong, and a compelling need to see the moral order set right is aroused" (Miller and Vidmar 1981, 156). For further discussion, see the essay by Hogan and Emler in the same volume.

[56] In his 1997 Presidential Address to the American Sociological Association, Smelser points out that "the traditions of rational choice apply best to situations in which *relative* freedom of choice reigns" (Smelser 1998, 13).

of acute grievances and high risks, contentious movements are fueled and constrained by hope and fear, by love and rage, and underneath, far too often, by grief.[57]

The motivational role of emotion is now receiving increased attention in the social sciences. In psychology, for example, a 1999 review of research finds "evidence for the ubiquity of emotion, with the influence of emotion extending to all aspects of cognition and behavior" (Cacioppo and Gardner 1999, 195).[58] In sociology, the long-term efforts of scholars such as Calhoun (1982), Lofland (1985), and Scheff (1983, 1990, 1994)[59] have been joined recently by others arguing for the importance of emotion, including explicitly for the study of social movements[60] and contentious politics.[61] Political science has lagged behind, with notable exceptions such as Marcus and associates.[62] However, in recent studies Fernández (2000) argues that the "politics of affection" and the "politics of passion" are central to understanding Cuban political history,[63] while Petersen (2003) places emotions at the center of his explanation of ethnic violence in Eastern Europe as does Wood (2003) with peasant support for the revolutionary movement in El Salvador. Finally, in philosophy, Elster (1999) brilliantly integrates the

---

[57] Based on her studies of communist Poland, Flam argues that a successful opposition movement in repressive societies requires the construction of "a contrasting ethical system," an effort that is "an outcome as much of emotional as of cognitive-organizational processes" (Flam 1996, 104).

[58] Also see Kitayama and Niedenthal (1994,3), who claim that "Emotion and motivation have come back to the center stage of psychological inquiry."

[59] The American Sociological Association has had a formal section on the Sociology of Emotion since 1986. A 1989 review of the sociological literature, though, found little attention had yet been given to emotion as an independent or mediating variable, that is, to its role in motivation (Thoits 1989).

[60] See, especially, Jasper 1997 and 1998, as well as Goodwin, Jasper, and Polletta 2001.

[61] Aminzade and McAdam, in an essay on emotions and contentious politics, acknowledge that the mainstream literature had downplayed "the mobilization of emotions as a necessary and exceedingly important component of any significant instance of collective action" (Aminzade and McAdam 2001, 14).

[62] See Marcus 2000 as well as Marcus, Neuman, and MacKuen (2000, 2), the latter of which notes: "Drawing on extensive sources in neuroscience, physiology, and experimental psychology, our research has led us to conceptualize affect and reason not as oppositional but as complementary, as two functional mental faculties in a delicate, interactive, highly functional dynamic balance."

[63] Fernández argues, "One of the weaknesses of traditional approaches to politics since the advent of modernity is that they do not take into consideration the emotional and the informal in everyday social relations and how they relate to the political" (Fernández 2000, 22).

social sciences with the humanities to demonstrate why emotions matter.[64] Appeal to such multidisciplinary work is one base for the argument here that the role of emotion is critical for understanding contentious politics, especially in high-risk situations like the Central American cases. Indeed, one purpose of this study is to demonstrate that significant attention to the role of emotion can be easily integrated with an analytical approach based on the political process model.[65]

Direct experience also provides support for the role of emotions. Some of my own actions under strong cross-pressured conditions are unintelligible without understanding the dynamic relationship between my emotional responses and my value system.[66] Sometimes I have acted consciously following my emotions and values contrary to what others understood to be my own (even broadly) understood self-interest.[67] These were not "heroic" acts but instead examples from the everyday social dimension of complex human lives that do find their true heroic expression with individuals acting under conditions of high risk. As authors such as Frank (1988, 1990) and especially Monroe (1991a; Monroe et al. 1991) demonstrate,[68] examples of rescuer behavior at significant risk to one's own life, even of people previously unknown to the rescuer, are noble evidence for the limitations

[64] "Most simply," Elster claims, "emotions matter because if we did not have them nothing else would matter. Creatures without emotion would have no reason for living nor, for that matter, for committing suicide. Emotions are the stuff of life" (Elster 1999, 403).

[65] As Polletta and Amenta point out in their essay that concludes *Passionate Politics: Emotions and Social Movements*, some of the authors in this edited volume see their work as modifying the political process model while others challenge its key assumptions. They provide a good concise discussion of the relevant issues (Polletta and Amenta 2001, 304–308).

[66] Fine and Sandstrom point out: "People feel their ideologies deeply and sincerely, just as their feelings lead to ideological choices. Ideology is linked to emotion recursively – both causing and being caused by affect" (Fine and Sandstrom 1993, 29).

[67] Whether we can really know through introspection the determinants of our choices, though, introduces a further complexity, but one that seems more trouble for rational actor models than for the position I am taking here. See Nisbett and Wilson 1977. An additional difficulty, as well discussed by Elster 1999, are the "alchemies of the mind" by which we unconsciously transmute our motives (interests, reasons, passions) into ones that are more acceptable to us.

[68] As Elster shows, Frank is unduly cautious in his qualifications of rational actor theory (Elster 1999, 355). Monroe goes much further with her evidence of behavior motivated by a belief that all people are connected by bonds of a common humanity. In a more recent work, Monroe 2001 argues that rational choice is a theory under stress, proposing that it be replaced by a theory of perspective on self and other.

of rational actor theory.[69] More concretely, listen to the testimony of one Guatemalan union activist explaining his continuing efforts during the worst years of that country's state terrorism during the first half of the 1980s. Commenting on the murder of his sister-in-law, one of forty-four labor leaders to be disappeared from two meetings in 1980 never to reappear alive, Angel explains, "The loss presented a challenge to the family about continuing with the union. We decided we had to continue the struggle. I don't think it's a question of valor or spontaneity but rather that the work had to go on. Our commitment, and particularly my commitment, had to continue within the labor movement and in mass movement activities. So that's what we did. We continued to be active, although obviously we had to reflect about the need for personal security" (quoted in Reed and Brandow 1996, 41).

Since some rational choice models have been expanded to include altruistic preferences,[70] they probably could be expanded further still to include affect, because affect is an indicator of preferences. I am untroubled by this move, although it seems then to have the model merely saying, as Jasper points out, "that people usually have some idea of what they want, and act to attain it" (Jasper 1997, 25). My more fundamental critique is the assumption, still held in the most expanded value expectancy model, that even in their contentious behavior people "cognitively process information about the likely benefits and costs of various courses of action and then make a conscious choice about their behavior," as nicely characterized by Snow and Oliver (1995, 583).[71] I also reject the

---

[69] Rational actor advocates can acknowledge rescuer behavior but dismiss it as so infrequent to not matter theoretically (e.g., Tullock 1995, 117). Frank, though, contends that "Acts of heroism occur very frequently" (Frank 1988, 213). Furthermore, Tullock's dismissal misses the everyday examples of self-sacrifice that certainly are frequent. As Frank points out, "We often bear costs in the name of fairness; and we often act selflessly in the context of love relationships" (Frank 1988, 213). If such social behavior were not an important part of our humanity, it is improbable that contentious movements under conditions of high risk would exist.

[70] See, for example, Opp (1989, 9).

[71] Also see Aminzade and McAdam 2001, 17 for a similar point. This is where I find even the best of the rational choice attempts to handle emotion to fall short–for example, in this statement by Oberschall: "Too much has been made of the incompatibility of rational choice with emotion and sentiment. No one maintains that people do not feel emotions, and sometimes very strong ones, in crowds, as they do in many other situations and choices. What is claimed is that the chooser weighs benefits and costs regardless of the kind and intensity of the emotions experienced" (Oberschall 1994, 80). Also see Oberschall (1995, 33–38). Tilly makes a related critique of such claims, though from an emphasis on interactive

frequent corollary assumption that if behavior is not cognitively determined, it is irrational.[72]

Emotions have been downgraded in studies of collective action in large part, I suspect, because sympathetic analysts did not want to obscure the justness of protestors' causes, such as civil rights, peace, social justice, and environmental protection.[73] It is perhaps not surprising that those of us for whom the intellect is the primary tool of our trade give it privileged position and therefore are prone to confuse the nonrational with the irrational.[74] There might also be a gender-bias in this confusion.[75] Again, I appeal to experience: It is clear that some of the worst decisions that I have made resulted when I was oblivious to, denied, or ignored my emotional responses. Certainly, other bad choices were made because emotions were not also screened by logical analysis. But "rational" action uninformed by emotion is just as likely to be irrational as would be the reverse. The best decisions – especially in areas of great importance to me – occur when I integrate both sources of information.[76] We humans, then, have two systems of mental processes, interconnected yet performing separate tasks.[77] To include the emotional dimension of contentious politics does

processes rather than emotions, noting, "Within contentious politics, actions that observers and participants retroactively interpret as consequences of deliberate individual choice almost always turn out to result from interactive processes" (Tilly 2001, 39).

[72] Similarly, Monroe, Barton, and Lingemann argue that rescuer behavior not only "constitutes a significant theoretical challenge to the fundamental assumption of self-interest which lies at the heart of the theory of rational action" but furthermore that "Behavior is more than the product of conscious choice." The rescuers they studied "insisted that they simply saw no other option available to them. . . . The rescuers thus suggest that certain behaviors arise spontaneously, resulting from deep-seated dispositions which form one's central identity" (Monroe, Barton, and Klingemann 1991, 340–341).

[73] Others make the same point–for example, Snow and Oliver (1995, 589–590).

[74] Turner and Killian (1987, 105), observe that "To regard the intrusion of emotion into thought processes as irrational and inevitably dysfunctional reflects a distorted view of human nature."

[75] Ferree claims, "The separation of reason from emotion is not value-neutral; emotionality is denigrated, along with the persons of whom it is thought to be characteristic: women and the 'lower orders' of men" (Ferree 1992, 42). For this and additional reasons, also see Aminzade and McAdam (2001, 23–24).

[76] For a different approach to integrating reason and emotion, see Brams's (1997) attempt at a game theory modeling of emotions.

[77] See Issacs (1998, 5). Kitayama and Niedenthal (1994, 6) point out: "Recent advances in neuroscience indicate that the brain substrates involved in the processing of emotion are highly integrated with those that participate in memory, learning, and other cognitive processes."

not undermine protestors' rationality but rather acknowledges their full humanity.[78]

What is emotion? It can be understood as "a set of adaptive functions of acting or responding to stimuli, that are both prewired or 'prepared' by biological evolution and yet at the same time, shaped, elaborated, and finely 'configured' by learning – especially by social and cultural learning" (Kitayama and Niedenthal 1994, 6). There are relatively few primary emotions, those that are "acute, structurally distinct, . . . have specific eliciting conditions," and "have unique information processing effects" (p. 7). Our emotions – such as joy, grief, fear, and anger – provide evaluations (affect) and arousal (pp. 6–7). Affective evaluations are our source of information about the significance and meaning of inner and outer events; each is a message "that by its quality informs us of the meaning of the event evoking it and by its intensity informs us how important the event is to us" (Isaacs 1998, 6, 18).[79]

In contentious politics, emotions play an important role for both nonelites and elites in motivating their actions. For non-elites, emotional responses are what turn objective circumstances into grievances and an important part of what determines whether grievances will generate mobilization, at what intensity, and how long it will persist in the face of a lack of governmental responsiveness and perhaps even repression. Similarly, under conditions of high grievances but political passivity due to overwhelming repression, why some people immediately resume political activity when repression ends while others remain passive long beyond the end of danger can not be reduced to rational calculations of self-interest but must also include differential emotional reactions to repression.[80] It is also true that some contentious activity is more expressive than instrumental in its motivation.

---

[78] Central to Frank's (1988, 1990) critique of rational choice models is the observation that "Being motivated by emotion is often an advantage" because "there are many problems that purely self-interested persons simply cannot solve" (Frank 1988, 255). A prime example is a relationship that requires trust.

[79] According to Bruner, "Everybody agrees, I think, that there is both evidence for as well as adaptive advantages to fast, direct affective arousal that can preadapt and then steer subsequent cognitive processing. Everybody also agrees that too much or too preemptive such preattentive triggering risks biasing attendant cognitive processing into maladaptive error and psychological tunnel vision" (Bruner 1994, 273).

[80] A particularly good introduction to the "culture of fear" created by systematic state terror is the volume edited by Corradi, Fagen, and Garretón (1992).

Mobilization involves ties between people and occurs through groups. The group solidarity discussed earlier that overcomes the free-rider paradox is at least as much emotional as it is cognitive. As Elster notes, "Emotions are the most important bond or glue that links us to others" (Elster 1999, 403). These emotional allegiances and experiences then help propel the group into protest activities.[81] Effective groups usually have effective leaders. Charisma is not a personality characteristic of the leader but rather "springs from leaders' skillful, deliberate manipulations of feeling and display rules" (Thoits 1989: 333). The secret of charisma, then, is "the emotional, not the cognitive, content of the message" (Scheff 1994, 118).

When the social order that elites support and the privileged position that elites enjoy is threatened, their responses come not just from rational calculations of self-interest but also from anger, shame, and fear. Scheff, for example, diagnoses the anger – and even rage – that sometimes leads to violent behavior by those with power against those with little power as a mechanism to cover the shame felt when those socially "beneath" them show disrespect toward elites and their authority (Scheff 1994, 68–69). Consequently, much of both sides of the mass-elite interaction in contentious politics includes an important emotional dimension, especially the protest repression dynamic, as will be demonstrated throughout this study.

Overview of the Book

The substantive focus of this study is the interaction between contentious political activities and political violence. The primary cases to be examined are El Salvador and Guatemala. Of the five countries of Central America, these two have suffered from higher levels of domestic political violence and over a longer period of time than the others and also have featured higher levels of contentious mobilization over longer periods of time. This is certainly true when they are compared to Honduras and Costa Rica, but it is also true when compared to Nicaragua.

Except for the peak of antidictator activity directed against Anastasio Somoza in the last years of the 1970s, Nicaragua has not manifested the levels of sustained popular protest reached in El Salvador and Guatemala.

---

[81] This sentence paraphrases Jasper (1997, 113). Similarly, Turner and Killian (1987, 105) point out: "On the group level the display of emotions serves to unify and empower the crowd, whatever its objective or the form of coordination may be." Emotional contagion, Hatfield, Cacioppo, and Rapson 1994 argue, is well established by psychological research and historical evidence.

Some might believe that this was due in part to repression by the radical Frente Sandinista de Liberación Nacional (FSLN) during its rule throughout the 1980s. However, while there was harassment of the opposition, murder was not an instrument of Sandinista policy. Even under the prior Somoza dictatorship, high levels of violence were specific to periods of intense insurrectional activity, whereas in El Salvador and Guatemala, high levels of violence also were employed against nonviolent movements outside of insurrectional situations. Finally, the Nicaraguan case is compounded by a war that lasted throughout the 1980s. Although in part a civil war, the opposition was substantially organized and heavily financed by the United States, and therefore it is more accurately understood as at least as much an international war as a domestic conflict.

For all of these reasons, then, El Salvador and Guatemala provide better cases for the analysis of the relationships between contentious movements and political violence. At the same time, because the Central American countries do share many common characteristics and yet a range of differences as well, the others provide useful comparative checks for generalizations based on these two cases. Costa Rica, Honduras, and especially Nicaragua, then, will be used throughout this study for analytic but not descriptive purposes.[82]

Protest events data have been collected by the author for both El Salvador and Guatemala, primarily from domestic sources. These data begin with 1960 for both countries and continues through 1984 for Guatemala and 1991 for El Salvador. For both theoretical and practical reasons, the data are most thorough for 1974–1980 for Guatemala and 1979–1991 for El Salvador. In addition, political violence data have been obtained for largely the same periods, again from domestic sources. Each of these four sets of data is a far superior approximation of the reality they seek to measure than those used in most quantitative analyses of protest and political violence – certainly for those utilizing Third World cases.

Part One: From Grievances to Contentious Movements

Chapter 2 initiates Part One of the book, analyzing the role of grievances in propelling the contentious movements under examination. Although

---

[82] The approach, then, is similar to della Porta (1995), utilizing a few critical cases, avoiding the idiosyncrasies of a single case study or the grossness of an aggregate study (della Porta 1995, 15).

stressed by traditional approaches to the study of collective behavior, the importance of motivational factors was downplayed in the 1970s and 1980s in favor of both the mobilization of resources and the fluctuation of political opportunities. With the addition of framing processes to the political process model in the mid-1980s, grievances and their social construction partially returned to the scholarly agenda.[83] However, a principal argument to be developed in this study is that a full understanding of the emergence, trajectory, and outcome of contentious movements requires a fuller integration of grievances into our work. This is most especially true for mass mobilization under conditions of substantial risk, which is the situation much of the time in much of the world and certainly has been in El Salvador and Guatemala.

Chapters 3, 4, and 5 look at the key groups through which popular forces in Central America have been mobilized for political action. Urban groups and movements are examined in Chapter 3 for El Salvador and Chapter 4 for Guatemala, with the peasantry for both in Chapter 5. El Salvador and Guatemala are both excellent examples of why the origins of revolutionary situations should not be studied separately from social movements. Armed revolutionary organizations do not make revolutions alone but rather in conjunction with other contentious movements, often with intimate connections between them. The evidence reported here shows that the revolutionary leadership was more important to the nonviolent mass mobilization of the 1970s in both countries than usually understood at the time or as conventionally portrayed in the scholarly literature. This is true whether the subject is students, teachers, or workers. It is most certainly true for peasant mobilization. Chapter 5 on the peasantry has a strong theoretical component, examining the issues of "false consciousness" and the role of outside organizers, especially religious and revolutionary activists, in the "consciousness raising" purported to be often necessary for mass mobilization.

Part Two: Opportunity, Contention, and Repression

Part Two of the book begins with Chapter 6, which is a descriptive chapter, laying out the cycles of contention for the two countries beginning with 1960. Evidence is presented from the events databases on fluctuations across the decades of different forms of mass contentious political activities

---

[83] Benford and Snow 2000; Snow et al. 1986; Snow and Benford 1988.

covering the full spectrum, including violent actions by revolutionary organizations.

Chapters 7 and 8 demonstrate that the relative openness or closure of the institutionalized political system, the stability or instability of elite alignments, and the capacity and propensity of the state for repression have been key aspects of the political realities facing contentious challengers in these Central American cases. These dimensions of the configuration of political opportunities, along with the presence of elite allies, have been crucial determinants of the success of contentious movements, including their emergence, persistence, and outcomes, as Chapter 7 demonstrates for Guatemala and Chapter 8 for El Salvador and then for the rest of Central America.

Chapters 9 and 10 then turn fully to the relationship between mass contention and state repression. Drawing on the case material from the prior chapters and quantitative evidence from the contention and political violence databases, a comprehensive explanation for the protest-repression paradox is elaborated and defended.

Chapter 11 concludes this study, both summarizing and extending its core argument.

PART ONE

From Grievances to Contentious Movements

2

The Social Construction of Grievances

Traditional approaches to the study of collective action – be it union organizing in the cities or revolutionary mobilization in the countryside – stressed levels of discontent, or grievances, as the central explanatory factor. In the 1970s and 1980s, however, the importance of motivational factors was downplayed in favor of the mobilization of resources and then the fluctuation of political opportunities and constraints.[1] These later analytical perspectives have greatly enriched our understanding of collective action, correcting the exaggerated attention given to grievances in the earlier "traditional" model, as well as its frequent unfortunate assumption about the social disconnectedness of participants.

There certainly can be analytic utility to holding one dimension of collective action constant, such as grievances, in order to gain a better understanding of another dimension, such as the mobilization of resources. It is seriously misleading, however, to maintain that discontent is a secondary source of collective action or that discontent is a constant among underprivileged populations and therefore is not useful for explaining movement emergence.[2] To the contrary, the principal argument of this chapter is that a full understanding of the causes, course, and consequences of contentious politics requires an integration of the older concern for grievances with

---

[1] In contrast, during the same period the "new social movement" approach was more influential in Western Europe. For comparative overviews of each of these approaches, see Klandermans 1986; Klandermans and Tarrow 1988; and Tarrow 1988.

[2] Implicit in many studies, the latter assertion is made explicit by some, such as Jenkins and Perrow 1977 and McCarthy and Zald 1977. In a subsequent work, Jenkins 1985 insightfully discusses the importance of the perception of discontent but still identifies it as a secondary factor in the explanation of insurgency.

attention to resources, frames, opportunities, and mechanisms.[3] This is most especially true for understanding collective action under conditions of significant risk, which is the situation much of the time in much of the world.

Over the last two decades, some authors have called for renewed theoretical and empirical attention to grievances in a more unified perspective on social mobilization.[4] However, few case studies actually achieve this objective, and when they do their focus is usually movements that are not made up of the disadvantaged.[5] A major exception – and an important contribution to our understanding of the role of grievances in social mobilization – is Snow et al. 1998. What is often missed in discussions of the poor and powerless is how resourcefully they construct lives for themselves under the difficult circumstances they face and therefore a life with meaning and integrity to them. To those with little to lose, what they do have and the daily routines that are associated with them are of great value, and therefore their possible loss or disruption is a great threat.[6] Focusing explicitly on the disadvantaged, Snow et al. portray the source of grievances as the actual or threatened disruption of these taken-for-granted routines and at-

---

[3] For a similar argument, see Schock 1996.

[4] See, for example, Aminzade 1984; Kerbo 1982; Klandermans 1984; Klandermans and Tarrow 1988; McAdam 1988; Opp 1988; Walsh 1981; and Webb et al. 1983. The political process model also expanded to incorporate "framing processes" (Benford and Snow 2000; Snow and Benford 1988; also see McAdam 1996; Tarrow 1998a). However, interest here is often greater in the *process* of framing than with the underlying grievances themselves.

[5] A frequently cited example is Law and Walsh's study of a short-lived organization whose grievances were not directed against elites and whose membership was not drawn from the poor. In their concluding statement about the relative role of grievances and structural factors, they claim that new grievances are critical to understanding the mobilization of higher status groups, because they already have substantial resources. The poor, however, "are more likely to experience widespread, serious and chronic discontent" and therefore research properly focuses on "organizational- and societal-level variables" to explain their mobilization (Law and Walsh 1983, 135). Other commonly cited examples of integration are Useem 1980 and Walsh 1981, both of which are cases set in the United States. Some leading scholars offer models that attempt to draw together individual motivation with some degree of political opportunity, notably Gurr and Duvall 1973; Muller 1979; and Tilly 1978, but the formulations of the first two lean heavily toward motivation while that of the third toward opportunity (as also noted by Zimmerman 1980). Also see Gurr 1993. The importance of grievances for understanding the mobilization of nonmarginal groups is a theme picked up again by Jasper 1997 and Goodwin and Jasper 1999; also see Kerbo 1982.

[6] "People will, in short, resist the disruption of the communities and ideas within which they are oriented to the world," as Calhoun (1982, 234) demonstrates in what remains one of the best theoretically informed portrayals of the importance to collective action of discontent and of social bonds.

titudes of everyday life (the "quotidian").[7] The authors identify both socio economic and sociopolitical disruptions of the quotidian, each of which will be integrated into a broader framework in this chapter.[8] Similarly, McAdam and Sewell highlight the role of "transformative events," whose key feature is "that they come to be interpreted as *significantly disrupting, altering, or violating the taken-for-granted assumptions governing routine political and social relations* . . . by increasing this sense of uncertainty, such events also fuel a dramatic escalation in the mobilization of emotion by all parties to the conflict. The increase in perceived threat typically heightens fear and anger on the part of movement opponents, while 'rising expectations' expands hope and anger among insurgents" (McAdam and Sewell 2001, 110).

The different types of actors who have been involved in Central American contentious politics in recent decades are numerous and therefore the scope of grievances included in the analysis here is necessarily broad. At a very general level, this study assumes that most participants in nonrevolutionary movements are motivated by specific grievances. These are often socioeconomic in nature but might include sociopolitical issues as well. For those relatively few who move on to active participation in revolutionary movements or for the greater number who give such movements some degree of support, state violence is often the most salient grievance

---

[7] Jasper provides a similar analysis in his discussion of "ontological security and risk aversion" (Jasper 1997, 121–126), part of which "involves what might be termed *dignity*, a serenity and pride that come from confidence in one's place, whether that place is one's social role or physical surroundings." Mobilization is often provoked by "moral shocks" that disrupt this security.

[8] Snow et al. 1998 place their discussion of grievances in the context of the long-standing controversy between *breakdown* and *solidarity* theories of collective action. Breakdown theorists unfortunately have conflated the importance of grievances with an argument about collective action involving largely the disaffiliated and dislocated. Solidarity theorists (i.e., most of those with a resource mobilization and/or political opportunities perspective) have convincingly demonstrated the error of the disaffiliated assumption but generally have skipped over serious consideration of the importance given to grievances. Useem – one of the leading breakdown theorists – makes the good point that breakdown theory was formulated to cover nonroutine forms of "collective action such as riots, rebellions, and civil violence" and therefore is poorly tested when analysts look at less contentious activities (Useem 1998, 215). However, he still defends the assumption that it is the more disaffiliated and dislocated who are more likely to participate in collective action. Although Useem makes a good case for the U.S. urban riots of the 1960s, solidarity theorists have provided too much evidence for the importance of preexisting social networks to participants in even nonroutine forms of contentious activity. Some of their evidence – as well as ample evidence from Central America – will be provided in the next two chapters. For one of the better assessments of the two theories, see Turner and Killian (1987, 388–392).

explaining this radicalization of their contention. Their prior grievances remain, continuing to provide motivation for collective action, but do not in themselves explain the revolutionary involvement. Which is to say, it is often a mistake to try to explain revolutionary participation and support in terms of the grievances that might have motivated prior nonrevolutionary activity.[9]

The Problem of Determining Who Does What and Why

Admittedly, attempts to specify linkages between grievances and contentious movements present huge problems. Although socially constructed, grievances are experienced by individuals. Yet, outside of a few, largely First World cases, we have little survey data on movement participants and their motivations.[10] Even when objective conditions appear miserable enough to the outside observer to be assumed a constant stimulus to mobilization, the conditions must first be experienced as a source of discontent by potential challengers. Yet, as McAdam reminds us, "the link between objective conditions and action is seldom straightforward" (McAdam 1982, 34). Such considerations lead straight to controversies concerning "hegemonic ideologies," "false consciousness," and the role of "consciousness-raising" agents. Do subordinate groups internalize the masks and roles forced on them by their oppression? Do they eventually accept their suffering as inevitable and legitimate? These issues will be amply explored in Chapter 5.

The important point for this chapter is that objective conditions are seldom constant and neither are grievance levels. Furthermore, both improving, as well as deteriorating, conditions can generate grievances and popular mobilization. Some participants might be motivated more by their individual circumstances, others more by comparisons to relevant reference groups. Socioeconomic concerns might be most pressing for some, sociopolitical matters for others. The behavior of some activists might be motivated more by abstract principals, while others more by strong emotions. The

---

[9] For a good statement along similar lines, see Seligson (1996, 154–155).

[10] Notable exceptions are Anderson and Seligson 1994 and McElhinny and Seligson 2001. Even if there were more survey data on movement participants, there would remain all of the classic problems of survey research, such as costs, questionnaire construction, sample representativeness, possibility of dissembling answers, the complex linkages between attitudes and behavior, and even whether an individual truly knows his or her own motivations.

particular configuration of grievances of any individual participant might vary from one point in time to another. Movements are made up by thousands of such individuals. The analyst wants to find simplicity, like the Wall Street reporter at the end of the day "explaining" the day's stock market dynamics in terms of one or two "causes."

Mass movements are not so simple; neither are individual contentious events. As a concrete example, take a composite large march in Guatemala in the late 1970s: We find peasants protesting the disruption of their way of life by land-grabbing elites, industrial workers protesting a decline in their own living standard, public employees concerned about a socioeconomic position that has not matched their expectations (nor perhaps that of some of their university classmates), political party activists protesting contracting political space, well-organized unionists demonstrating in solidarity with colleagues at a local factory where the owner is trying to bust the nascent union-organizing effort, and long-time political activists advocating social justice for the entire *pueblo* itself. In addition to their specific concerns, each group is irate and apprehensive about a recent increase in selective repression. Finally, we find others drawn by the excitement of the event itself (invariably younger males), perhaps even the adrenaline rush of a possible confrontation with authority.

This study of the relationship between grievances and opportunities in contentious politics is guided by the following assumptions. A *grievance* is a claim that one's discontent is the product of an injustice that must be corrected. Grievances have three dimensions: cognitive, moral, and emotional.[11] First, there is the cognitive awareness of the situation that is the source of one's discontent. This awareness can be either self-regarding (i.e., one's situation in itself) or other-regarding (i.e., dissatisfaction in relationship to others).[12] One important cognitive aspect is the attribution of responsibility for that situation. As Javeline 2003 points out, attribution need not be accurate, but the more specific the better for mobilization.[13]

---

[11] This categorization appears standard, see for example, Jasper 1997; Knoke 1990; and Smith 1996a. More generally, Oberschall finds culture itself characterized by the same three dimensions (Oberschall 1995, 201).

[12] This distinction follows Lichbach. As he points out, the self-regarding assumption fits a rational actor model while other-regarding corresponds to a deprivation model (Lichbach 1989, 456–461).

[13] "An aggrieved individual who attributes blame specifically but incorrectly is still a more likely protester than the aggrieved individual who attributes blame unspecifically due to a thoughtful and accurate assessment" (Javeline 2003, 108).

Second, collective action is normative. It is motivated not solely by deprivation but also by "righteous indignation" (Lupsha 1971, 102), by a "sense of injustice" (Moore, 1978). To alter an important observation by Scott, grievances must be understood not just in terms of frustrated needs but also in terms of violations of basic "standards of justice and equity" (Scott 1977, 236). As an example, Anderson found "a search for justice" as the most frequent response given by Costa Rican and Nicaraguan peasants in her survey of their reasons for political activity (Anderson 1990, 103).

Third, grievances are fundamentally emotional in nature. Emotional response by its "intensity informs us how important the event is to us" (Isaacs, 1998, 6, 18). Without emotion, there are no preferences and therefore there are no grievances. In addition, the very physiological responses themselves at least in part determine what individuals do with their grievances. Anger provides energy for action, especially necessary in the face of high-risk situations, while the bodily sensations of fear encourage one to turn away from action. Emotions are often amplified within group settings where they also might be transformed. Collins speaks of the development of "emotional energy" in the latter case: "the transmutation of the initiating emotion into something else. This is the emotion which makes up solidarity, and which makes the individual feel stronger as a member of the group" (Collins 2001, 29).

Making sense of one's emotional responses to unjust situations or improper treatment is worked out not just individually but very much in interaction with others. This social construction of grievances is captured well by the literature on collective action frames. Snow and Benford (1988) identify three core framing tasks: diagnostic, prognostic, and motivational framing.[14] As they have explained, "Collective action frames are constructed in part as movement adherents negotiate a shared understanding of some problematic condition or situation they define as in need of change, make attributions regarding who or what is to blame, articulate an alternative set of arrangements, and urge others to act in concert to affect change" (Benford and Snow 2000). Especially important is the formulation of an "injustice frame," which, according to Gamson et al., "provides a rationale

---

[14] As with the framing literature more generally, this important essay overstresses the cognitive dimension of frame resonance, giving insufficient attention to the emotional dimension. Goodwin and Jasper (1999, 46–51) make a similar point. For an application of the framing approach to the U.S. labor movement in the late nineteenth century, see Babb 1996, and to late twentieth-century Italy, Diani 1996, which insightfully links successful framing strategies to different configurations of political opportunities.

for acting on the hostility or anger that participants may feel" (Gamson et al. 1982, 123).[15]

Grievances are divided below between those that are socioeconomic in origin and those that are more sociopolitical. Greater attention is given in this chapter to socioeconomic grievances. Although different types of sociopolitical grievances will be identified here, their extended treatment will be delayed to later chapters. Brief separate attention also will be given to the ideological and the affective dimensions of contentious politics.

Socioeconomic Grievances

Most attention to grievances focuses on socioeconomic factors, often in the mistaken attempt to identify *the* cause of the collective action of the group examined. To the contrary, it will be argued here that grievances are multidimensional. Their configuration can shift in different ways over time even for members of the same type of group, depending on the impact of other factors. For example, there is a significant literature on the grievances of peasants. Considerable attention is paid to whether the more important cause of group discontent is landlessness, unequal landownership patterns, or income inequality.[16] Or the focus has been on which type of peasant is most likely to become involved in contentious movements, especially in revolutionary movements. Is it the middle peasant, the wage laborer, the sharecropper, the squatter, or the plantation worker? Or perhaps it is not the peasant's specific tenancy status but rather a threat to subsistence?[17]

Again, because there are virtually no survey data on movement participants, the analyst does the best one can with the available aggregate data to test hypotheses about individual behavior. As an example of the problems this creates, take the assumption that peasant participation in Central

---

[15] "An *injustice frame* is an interpretation of what is happening that supports the conclusion that an authority system is violating the shared moral principles of the participants" (Gamson et al. 1982, 123). Also see Turner and Killian's discussion of "the sense of injustice as emergent norm" (Turner and Killian 1987, 242–245) and Aminzade and McAdam (2001, 30–31) on the emotional component of "cognitive liberation."

[16] The landlessness hypothesis is argued in Prosterman and Riedinger 1987, unequal landownership distributions that leave many peasants with farms too small to support themselves in Midlarsky 1988, and national income inequality in Muller and Seligson 1987. For an evaluation, see Brockett 1992.

[17] Compare the classic works of Paige 1975, Popkin 1979, Scott 1976, and Wolf 1969. The conclusion? "What these studies seem to show is that there is no single cause or variable that best explains [peasant] rebellion" (Magagna 1991, 22).

American revolutionary movements is motivated by deteriorating economic circumstances, with sharecroppers and squatters the most likely to support the revolutionary cause. National economic trends apply equally to both the revolutionary and nonrevolutionary peasant. Regional data can be collected (albeit with the same ecological fallacy problem), correlating zones of higher and lower peasant revolutionary activity with economic trends and the relative prevalence of different types of peasants, as done impressively by Wickham-Crowley 1992.

However, any relationships discovered might be spurious. Zones of deteriorating economic security are often more marginal areas. They are often further from larger markets, have poorer quality soils, and are mountainous. These also are the areas where squatters and more traditional forms of tenancy are found (i.e., sharecropping as compared to wage labor) and are often the sources of migratory labor. They also are often areas more inaccessible to authorities and their armies. Therefore, they are often more attractive to revolutionaries than other areas, especially in the incubatory stage of their movements.[18] Counterinsurgency operations invariably harm peasants, some of whom then join the guerrillas out of a mix of indignation and hope for protection. Part of their joining the revolutionaries probably also include socioeconomic motivations. But nothing in this mode of analysis can establish that the socioeconomic grievances of the now revolutionary peasants are stronger than those of nonrevolutionary peasants living in regions of the country less harmed by counterinsurgency operations.[19] Both McClintock and Wood make the point effectively for El Salvador. McClintock points out that the northern guerrilla strongholds of Chalatenango and Morazán were neither the poorest departments in the country nor the location of the greatest peasant dislocation due to expanding commercial agriculture (which was instead the Pacific coastal zone) (McClintock 1998, 168–170). She clinches the point through her interview with guerrilla leader Joaquín Villalobos.[20] In one of the few studies of peasant support for revolutionary movements that is based on interviewing peasants themselves,

---

[18] Wickham-Crowley finds a fairly strong association for the location of Latin American revolutionary movements in "areas with rebellious histories" (Wickham-Crowley 1992, 137), a theme reiterated in Selbin 1997b.

[19] Snow et al. make a similar point for studies of the homeless, which are usually based on aggregate data, overlooking "the different effects that disruption might have on different segments of a population" (Snow et al. 1998, 6 n.3).

[20] Also see the discussion of Laqueur 1976 by Oberschall (1995, 53), as well as Grenier (1999, 84).

Wood also finds that what distinguishes areas of support from nonsupport is not their socioeconomic characteristics but rather two "path-dependent" variables: local past patterns of repression and proximity to insurgent forces (Wood 2003, 237–238).

Similarly for Guatemala, the Ejército Guerrillero de los Pobres (EGP) was incubated in the far north of the country. Mario Payeras, one of the top EGP commanders, criticized this choice after he broke with the group. The EGP located in this region precisely because it was so remote but underestimated "the very social backwardness of a marginal area of the capitalist system" (quoted in Stoll 1999, 138). Isolation brought safety for the guerrillas but also a limited supply of readily available converts (until counterinsurgency operations in the area escalated).[21] Meanwhile, Rodrigo Asturias ("Gaspar Ilom"), the leader of the Organización del Pueblo en Armas (ORPA), also emphasizes difficult terrain as a primary reason for the location of ORPA's center of operations (Harneker 1984, 315).

We are not in a position, then, where we can establish empirically which regions in a country have the greatest peasant *attitudinal* support for contentious movements but at best where there is the most *active* support. To say the obvious, active support will be greatest for insurgent movements in the regions where the movements are actually located; most likely, the larger the guerrilla presence, the greater the active support. But what is seldom noted is that attitudinal support for the revolutionaries actually could be relatively low in the overall peasant population of that region or perhaps even declining at the same time that active support is increasing.[22]

The evidence of this study is that there is usually not any one shared grievance that explains the contentious activity of members of the same group. All the more mixed are the grievances motivating the diverse

---

[21] As Payeras continues, "The immediate consequence of this backwardness translated into slow rhythms of accumulation of forces and huge difficulties, particularly in the formation and reproduction of cadres" (quoted in Stoll 1999, 138). Similarly for Cuba, although the guerrilla stronghold of Oriente Province ranks at the top of Wickham-Crowley's (1992, 96) crucial indicator of the prevalence of squatters, it also was as far as one could get from the center of state control in Havana, a region "marginal to both law enforcement and material progress" (p. 132). At the same time, it was still close to one of Castro's major sources of resources, the urban center of Santiago. Finally, there is the example of Ché Guevara himself, choosing to ignite his Bolivian "revolution" not in the region that had the most of the "right" type of peasant but rather again in an area remote from the center of state control (pp. 116–117).

[22] These problems are missed in Paige's (1983) attempt to demonstrate how well a class conflict model explains the support gained by the Guatemalan revolutionaries in the early 1980s.

45

participants in larger movements. And this mix might very well change across time. This complexity enriches the importance of grievances, even as it makes analysis more problematic. Concerning socioeconomic grievances during Central America's contentious decades, they are divided here between long-standing deprivation and new threats to economic security.

Long-Standing Deprivations

Long-standing deprivations are like those assumed in the grievances-are-constant literature. Since they have been long-standing prior to mobilization, in themselves they cannot explain movement emergence. However, the interaction between long-standing deprivation and other variables often is important for understanding the trajectory of collective action and its outcomes. Long-standing deprivation is analytically distinct from a suddenly imposed grievance that arises at the point when economic security (and the rights and norms that protect it) is lost. Nonetheless, if the loss is not rectified, with the passage of time such a grievance analytically becomes a long-standing deprivation. Examples of long-standing grievances in Central America include the following:

- A Salvadoran peasant activist interviewed by Wood in April 1992 explained that his years of activism were "born out of social resentment, that's how to understand it. I am an unskilled farm worker, my father never gave me anything. I worked for the rich, it was heavy labor. I felt rage, resentment. It was a hard life, sometimes I would cry with resentment when I couldn't finish the assigned task" (Wood 2001, 273).
- In March 1977, around two hundred Guatemalan peasants marched from their homes in the highlands of Momostenango to the presidential palace in hopes of gaining support in their conflict with landlords over national lands they had been farming for years. As one explained, "While the owners of large farms live tranquilly in their luxurious mansions without even working their lands, hundreds of peasants that live in the countryside, working the land throughout our lives, die without knowing what it means to be owners of one inch of land" (IPV 3/13/1977, 156).
- In June 1954, ten years of increasingly radical but constitutional reform came to an end in Guatemala with the U.S.-driven overthrow of the Jacobo Arbenz government (a suddenly imposed grievance at this point). As mass movements slowly began to reassert themselves in

the years that followed, their rhetoric was often cast in terms of regaining what had been lost, even after the passage of more than two decades. Primary sites of contention were industries, *fincas* (farms), and agricultural mills that had the most militant unions during the reform years and in peasant communities that had gained – and then lost – the most from the Arbenz agrarian reform.[23] Protesters' experiences during the reform years and their memories of that period were resources to be drawn on that gave contentious politics in Guatemala a different complexion from that in the rest of Central America, as did the emotional depth of their feeling of deprivation.[24] Writing in 1970, Adams noted that to understand the then contemporary situation, one had to go back to "the 'sociological awakening' [of the reform period] that could not be forgotten within the generation, the fact that organizing had been learned, and the awareness that the United States had intervened at the international level to stop the organization process" (Adams 1970, 193).

New Threats to Economic Security

Unlike long-standing grievances, new threats to economic security do explain the emergence of new contentious movements of the disadvantaged, along with variables such as new resources or better opportunities. Threats to subsistence routines are identified by Snow et al. 1998, for example, as a powerful source of new grievances, following in the path laid out by the influential works on "the moral economy" by Thompson 1971 and Scott 1976. Their insights are expanded here into a more general concern for economic security.

In premarket peasant communities, economic security could be no more than a right to subsistence, and, therefore, analytically they are the same.[25] For poorer peasant families, they remain the same after the introduction of

---

[23] Wickham-Crowley notes, for example, that the Guatemalan revolutionaries of the 1960s organized most successfully in areas of Communist Party (PGT) success prior to 1954 organizing banana workers (Wickham-Crowley 1992, 147).

[24] LeGrande provides a similar explanation for Colombia, where settlers dispossessed by elites maintained "memory of the injustices they had undergone" but without acting on this until circumstances changed (LeGrande 1986, 91).

[25] Among studies besides those of Scott 1976 and Wolf 1969 finding support for a link between peasant rebellion and threats to subsistence, see Jenkins 1983b for Russia; McClintock 1998 for Peru (but not El Salvador); and Wickham-Crowley 1992 for several Latin American cases.

market forces.[26] However, with higher levels of economic development, although the desire for economic security remains (as well as associated moral claims), threats to that security are experienced at levels higher than subsistence. Therefore, the better analytic focus is threat to *economic security*, not to *subsistence*.[27] With economic security as the focus, much of the scholarly debate over which type of peasant is most likely to become contentious dissolves. The answer is, it depends. In some cases, the type of peasant whose economic security is most threatened might be smallholders, in others it might be sharecroppers and migratory laborers or the latter two plus squatters.[28] Sometimes, it might even be plantation workers, as examples in this study will show for Guatemala. Furthermore, an analytic focus on types of peasants precludes comparison with urban workers. But economic security is a shared concern across the urban/rural divide.

In Central America in the decades following WWII, certainly the most important threat to rural economic security that generated grievances and contentious movements was the forced eviction of peasants from the lands upon which they had built their homes and raised their crops, in many cases for decades or even generations.[29] Usually, these evictions were at the hands of rural elites, but sometimes they were caused by government projects. In a few cases, they were the consequence of conflicts between rival peasant communities themselves. As the percentage of peasants able to support themselves on their own land has declined, rural wages have become increasingly important.

Another significant source of grievances has been the failure of wages to keep up with inflation, both in the countryside and in the cities. This was especially true in Central America in the critical decade of the 1970s. Rising inflation, as well as contracting economies, hit the poor hard. They also can be a serious blow to the expectations of groups that are not so poor. Frustrated rising expectations was once offered as a theoretical explanation that tried to cover the behavior of too many disparate contentious groups.

---

[26] For a congruent claim that "premarket peasant norms are consistent with self-interested behavior," see Campos and Root (1995, 98).

[27] For parallel discussions see Roeder 1984 and Tutino 1986.

[28] The relevant examples are, respectively, Wolf 1969 on Mexico; Paige 1975 and 1983 (respectively on Vietnam and Guatemala); and Wickham-Crowley 1992 on Cuba and Nicaragua.

[29] As Chirot and Ragin note: "What infuriates peasants (and not just peasants) is a new and sudden imposition or demand that strikes many people at once and that is a break with accepted rules and customs" (Chirot and Ragin 1975, 429).

Nonetheless, frustrated rising economic expectations does explain the contentious activity of some groups some of the time.[30]

Land Dispossession by Elites   As commercial agricultural possibilities expanded in the postwar period for both large export-oriented estates and family farms producing for growing urban markets, peasants throughout Central America found themselves in competition with wealthier and more powerful interests. Sometimes the competition was financial; these new profit-making possibilities attracted affluent urban groups to speculative agriculture, thereby increasing the demand for land. As land values increased, poor rural people found themselves priced out of land markets. On many occasions, however, the competition was settled by force as peasants were dispossessed of land to which they had long enjoyed use, either because the peasants believed that they held legitimate possession or through some type of sharecropping arrangement. These evictions were widespread in each of the Central American countries, though less so in Costa Rica.[31]

---

[30]   The classic work using frustrated rising expectations as the explanation for contentious movements is Davies 1962. This explanation is one example of the more general relative deprivation approach. Originally perceived as promising, especially with the publication of Gurr 1970, relative deprivation models soon encountered a withering barrage of attacks for empirical, methodological, and normative reasons. Although there are good reasons to believe that relative deprivation is *one* source of discontent, the problem is the assumption that this should be *the* explanation of what motivates contentious activity. No sooner had Gurr's *Why Men Rebel* been published then its claim for the preeminence of relative deprivation as the source of protest was contradicted by Muller's (1972) empirical study of Waterloo, Iowa, which finds that low trust in authorities and high belief in use of violence are more powerful variables for at least this case (Brush 1996, 529). Brush's analysis of some five hundred evaluations of *Why Men Rebel* that were published through 1985 provides fascinating variations in disciplinary reactions and trends. Positive evaluations by political scientists (40% of total evaluations) dropped from 75% in the early period to about 50% later, and those by sociologists (30% of total) dropped from 45% to 20%, but interestingly the psychologists (15%) remained at 80% favorable evaluations (Brush 1996, 536). Unfortunately, many "tests" of relative deprivation models, both the supportive and the critical, make inferences from aggregate national data, including cross-national work by both Gurr (e.g., Gurr and Duvall 1973) and Muller (Muller and Weede 1990, 1994). Although convenient and suggestive, such data are not a valid measure of individual motivation. For a sampling of commentaries on relative deprivation models from a variety of concerns, see Aya 1979; Barnes et al. 1979; Finkel and Rule 1986; Gurney and Tierney 1982; Jenkins and Perrow 1977; Jenkins and Schock 1992; Lindstrom and Moore 1995; Martin and Murray 1984; Muller 1979; Nardin 1971; Snow and Oliver 1995; and Useem 1980.

[31]   See Booth 1991; Brockett 1998; and Williams 1986. Colombia is a parallel example, "Colombia thus provides an excellent example of the expansion of export agriculture into public land areas and the accompanying conflicts between peasant settlers and land entrepreneurs for control over frontier resources" (LeGrande 1986, xv).

Further aggravating tightening land markets for the peasantry was its population growth, which exploded during the same period. Underlying the mobilization of the Central American peasantry, then, was the further integration of the countryside with the international market and the transformation of the rural class structure, as analysts such as Skocpol (1979, 14–33) would have us note. Suggestive of the numerous cases are the following examples:

- Death threats were made in 1975 against Guatemalan peasants in Santo Domingo Suchitepéquez for protesting against their dispossession by local landlords from lands that they had been working for many years.[32]
- At least two different peasant delegations were in Guatemala City at the same time in December 1975 to denounce their evictions from their lands in the country's Atlantic zone. Around four thousand peasants had been pushed off of banana company lands in Izabal that they had been working for more than thirty years by company forest guards who claimed the land for their own use and that of their associates. The other delegation represented eight hundred families in Buena Vista who also had been evicted, leaving them without land upon which to live or grow their food.[33]
- Guatemalan peasants in the Chiquimulilla area of Santa Rosa protested in 1977 that their *milpas* (corn and bean patch) and fruit trees had been destroyed on lands that they had worked for forty years in order to put in a sugar mill, with no compensation to them.[34]

Land Dispossession by the State   When peasants are dispossessed of their land by private elites, they often turn to government agencies – sometimes repeatedly – for assistance before they turn to contentious action. When it is the government itself that is the threat to their economic security, peasants should be more easily mobilized for collective action by groups advocating their cause. Examples of land dispossession by the state that had especially significant consequences include the following:

- Major centers of Salvadoran contentious politics outside of the capital in the 1970s were Aguilares and Suchitoto. A large hydroelectric

---

[32] IPV (July 25, 1975, 37). See a similar 1977 story for peasants in San Juan Sacatepequez (IPV Mar. 30, 1977, 97). In the latter case, they gained assistance from the legal aid program run by the national law school.

[33] IPSET (Bandegua Dec. 15, 1975).

[34] IPV (Oct. 24, 1977, 198).

project (Cerron Grande) was built to their north, and as the lake behind the dam grew, many peasants were displaced from their lands, aggravating land markets already tightening because of spreading sugar cultivation. Their locations close to San Salvador (about twenty-five and thirty miles, respectively) facilitated organizational support from the capital for the peasant cause. The Aguilares effort in particular is fairly well known because it was the site for an important experimental project by religious workers and was the focus of careful studies by members of the team (to be discussed further in the Chapter 5). The area also was subject to much repression, notably the March 1977 assassination of a central and popular member of the religious team, Father Rutilio Grande, along with its military occupation.[35]

- In 1975, work began in Guatemala on what was then Central America's largest hydroelectric plant, located in the Chixoy watershed in the department of Baja Verapaz. When the dam was ready to fill in 1978 the eight hundred Achí Mayas of Río Negro, living in what they claimed to be the best organized and most prosperous town in the region, did not want to move. Not only did they not like the relocation plan they were offered, but this also was the ancestral land upon which their people had lived for some four hundred years. About the same time, the Comité de Unidad Campesina (CUC) entered the area, offering its help and then the next year connected community leaders with the Ejército Guerrillero de los Pobres had just established a presence in the area.[36] Soon the army declared the guerrillas to be behind the community's refusal to move. On February 13, 1982, fifty-five men and nineteen women from the community were executed by the Civil Patrol of a nearby town. On March 13, 1982, the soldiers and the same Civil Patrolers entered Río Negro. Finding no men present, they charged that the missing must be off in the mountains with the guerrillas. Raping young females and ransacking homes first, these state agents then murdered everyone they captured: 77 women and 107 children. Towns where the survivors took refuge were then subjected to the same: 79 peasants killed and 15 women disappeared on May 14 in Los Encuentros; 92 people more killed on September 14 at

---

[35] The story of both the Aguilares experiment and of Grande's life and work are told in Cardenal 1987. Aguilares is a major subject in Montes's (1980) study of agrarian El Salvador of the 1970s. Also see Cabarrús 1983a, 1983b and Carranza 1977.

[36] Earlier efforts at revolutionary organizing in the area began in the early 1960s (Macías 1996, 114–117).

Agua Fría. The dam was filled. Today twelve families live in Río Negro in extreme poverty.[37]

Land Conflicts Between Peasant Communities   Although land conflicts between different peasant communities are analytically distinct from those where the agents of their distress are private elites or the state, these conflicts still can be potent causes of peasant discontent. Additional grievances could be generated by how local officials do or do not handle these conflicts. Victims might also give their support to contentious groups that offer them help.[38]

- People living in the mountains above the Sansare region of El Progreso, Guatemala came down for the fourth time in 1977 (as they had in previous years), destroying the crops of villagers and setting forest fires. Both sides claimed the land in question. Although some villagers claimed land rights going back two hundred years, about one hundred peasants gave up in May and pulled out of their community.[39]
- In June 1977, peasants of one community drove those of another off of contested land in the Santa Cruz Barillas area of Huehuetenango, Guatemala. After police arrested some of the leaders of the action, the police station was attacked by the same group, who freed the captives and injured the police chief and a deputy in the process.[40]

Declining Rural Incomes   As the number and percentage of landless and near-landless in Central America increased, be it from land evictions or population pressures, these peasants joined those whose economic security

---

[37] CEH (1999 6:45–56); also see IPV (Aug. 10, 1978, 136), Stoll (1999, 295 n.24). Twenty percent of the entire Achí ethnic group were killed in this violence, for a total of some 4,400 deaths recorded by the Guatemalan truth commission. The Achí is one of the commission's four cases for charging the Guatemalan military with genocide (CEH 1999 3:360–377). For coverage of the exhumation of the Río Negro victims and the attempt to prosecute those responsible, see Sanford (2003, 282–285).

[38] This is one of the major differences between the story told by Nobel Prize winner Rigoberta Mechú (Burgos-Debray 1984) and Stoll's (1999) controversial attempt to verify that story. Instead of land conflicts between her father and *ladino* elites as Menchú relates the story, Stoll finds instead the major conflict was with his in-laws. Indeed, Stoll claims that the in-laws were the ones responsible for his arrest on two occasions over their conflicting land claims (p. 32). Altogether, Stoll finds five different indigenous groups in conflict for the same land (p. 36).

[39] IPV (May 4, 1977, 209); IPV (May 5, 1977, 202); IMSET (conflicto Jalapa Apr. 29, 1977, 10).

[40] IPV (June 6, 1977, 154).

Table 2.1 *El Salvador: Change in Real Minimum Wage, 1971–1981**

	1971	1975	1979	1980	1981	Change
Agriculture						
general	2.25	2.06	2.19	1.87	1.14	−49%
coffee**	3.00	3.65	5.97	4.77	3.10	+3%
cotton**	2.63	3.32	3.38	2.70	1.75	−33%
sugar**	3.00	3.65	3.59	2.87	1.86	−38%
Urban***	3.35	4.22	3.80	3.70	2.40	−28%

Notes: * Colones per hour in 1971 prices.
** Combines separate wage scales for harvesting and processing.
*** Combines separate wage scales for industry/service and commerce.
Source: Official data reported in Lindo-Fuentes (1981, 901).

was already dependent on steady employment at an adequate wage. But agricultural wages in the region always had been low, usually below any reasonable meaning of a minimum wage. With the agricultural workforce rapidly expanding and landowners remaining reluctant to pay a living wage, agricultural workers often have found their incomes declining, especially during times of inflation like the 1970s.

Rural wages in El Salvador declined in real terms in the last half of the 1970s, the period during which peasant mobilization in the country was at a peak never before reached nor ever again after. Table 2.1 demonstrates again the importance of looking at specific groups instead of general categories.[41] Peasants employed in the coffee sector clearly fared much better than those in the other sectors, and therefore it is not surprising that they virtually never appear in the case material on Salvadoran contentious movements of this period. Their inclusion in one aggregate figure for all rural workers would diminish the economic squeeze actually experienced by those working with other crops. Workers in each of the three major crops enjoyed real minimum wage increases in the first half of the decade, but then real wages in cotton fell by 19 percent in the second half of the decade (1975 to 1980) and by 21 percent in sugar, whereas coffee real wages did not decline until the last year of the decade, maintaining an increase of 31 percent for 1975–1980. For general agricultural laborers, the decline in their real wage began with the decade, falling 49 percent across the entire ten-year period. It should be

---

[41] The source table (Lindo-Fuentes 1981, 900), which is from official figures, provides data for both harvesters and mill workers for each of the three crops. The differences are minor, so the two categories are combined here.

noted that the region around Aguilares, a major site of peasant mobilization during this period, was heavily planted in sugar on large estates, with three large mills operating in the area (Carranza 1977).

In addition, the incomes of the landless in El Salvador declined when measured against the average for all rural groups by 24 percent from 1971 to 1975 – while the relative share of the largest landowners increased by 23 percent (Montes 1980, 132). Landlessness itself among the economically active agriculture population in El Salvador climbed from approximately 28 percent in 1961 to 38 percent in 1971 (Seligson 1995, 62).

- In the mid and later 1970s, a Guatemalan peasant movement of historic importance spread (at first covertly), especially in indigenous villages. Many Mayan cultivators in southern El Quiché had enjoyed increasing prosperity for some fifteen to twenty years prior to the inflation of the 1970s, especially as a result of working with cooperatives (which provided better technical advice and markets for both agricultural and artisanal production). However, the inflation of the 1970s, especially for fertilizer, hit both pocketbooks and expectations. This discontent was one source of the energy behind the organizing efforts of the Comité de Unidad Campesina (CUC) and for the receptivity it enjoyed.[42]

Declining Urban Incomes   Generally, the 1960s going into the 1970s was a good time economically for Central America. But, as with the rest of the world, inflation began mounting after the oil shock of 1973. The inflation of this period was especially relevant with public employees as their wages failed to keep up with inflation during the second half of the decade. This is significant because public employees are among the best organized non-elite groups and are among the most educated of any groups. Their numbers are relatively large, given that they are concentrated in a few cities, most especially in a nation's capital. Furthermore, they have one of the strongest power capabilities of any non-elite group: They keep critical services going, such as utilities, hospitals, banks, schools, and the judicial system.

The urban minimum wage in El Salvador increased in real terms during the first half of the 1970s (see Table 2.1), but it then began to fall. The real wage declined from 1975 to 1979 by 10 percent, dropped again in 1980,

---

[42] Fernández (1988, 5); Le Bot (1995, 181).

Table 2.2 *El Salvador: Change in Real Minimum Public
Sector Salaries, 1971–1981**

	1971	1975	1981	Change
Adviser, First Class	950	655	312	−67%
Adviser, Fifth Class	494	360	141	−71%
Official, First Class	444	331	123	−72%
Driver	216	182	117	−45%
Custodian	134	122	100	−25%

Notes: *Colones in 1971 prices.
Source: Official data reported in Lindo-Fuentes (1981, 901).

and especially in 1981, for a total decline for 1976–1981 of 43 percent.[43]
The decline for Salvadoran public sector employees, however, began earlier
and was even more severe. Table 2.2 gives the maximum real salary for five
occupational categories, based on figures from three ministries and the
president's office. The decline in real salaries across the 1971–1981 period
for the three professional categories (top three rows) was especially severe,
averaging a 70 percent drop. Starting from a much lower base, drivers
and custodians at these public agencies (the last two rows) also suffered
significant declines in real salaries, dropping 45 and 25 percent, respectively.
It is important to note that declining real salaries were already occurring
by 1975 for each of the five occupational categories.[44]

Once the civil war broke out in El Salvador in 1980, the situation only
worsened. Investment dried up and factories closed down. FMLN economic
sabotage of the electrical and transportation infrastructure was heavy across
the decade. Each year, the economy contracted yet inflation often was severe. In 1987, for example, inflation ran at around 40 percent and some 50
percent of the employable population was unemployed or underemployed
(NY Times Feb. 16, 1987, 7).

Sociopolitical Grievances

Less attention will be given to sociopolitical grievances in this chapter because they can be better analyzed in the context of changes in political
opportunities, the subject of Chapters 7 through 10. The intent here is to

---

[43] Based on official figures, the source table (Lindo-Fuentes 1981, 900) provides data separately for commerce and for industry/service. The differences are minor, so they are
combined here.
[44] Lindo-Fuentes (1981, 901).

complete the typology of the different types of grievances that have been important to contentious politics in Central America. As with the socioeconomic grievances, sociopolitical grievances can be either long-standing or recent, can be either largely self-referential or in reference to other individuals and groups. The most important of these have been the following: the closing of political access, the lack of state responsiveness, intimidation and harassment by the state, state violence, and frustrated rising expectations.

Closing of Political Access

Political freedoms need to be respected by the state in order for individuals and groups to pursue any social, economic, and political interests that require activity in public space. Rights to assembly and speech must be honored as well as rights to participate in fair and free institutionalized mechanisms for selecting government officials and rights to petition those officials. The failure to respect and protect these rights – and especially new limitations on them – are potent sources of sociopolitical grievances. Examples from Central America are numerous and at the heart of later chapters. The fraud in the Salvadoran election of 1972 that was portrayed in the introduction to Chapter 1 and the repression that followed is a paramount example.

Lack of State Responsiveness

As individuals and groups act on their socioeconomic grievances, they often seek the assistance of state actors. The request – or demand – might be to enforce existing laws or regulations. It might be to investigate their plight or to come to their assistance in some other manner. The failure of the state to respond, to respond with less vigor than expected or desired, or to respond with less vigor than in the past can create a new socio political grievance reinforcing the original socioeconomic grievance.

- Resident workers in Guatemala on a San Marcos finca claimed in June 1975 that they had not been paid for nine consecutive two-week pay periods. Their children, they declared, were eating leaves and immature plantains and drinking and dirty water, and their clothes were disintegrating off their backs. The increasingly indignant workers took their plight to local, then regional, and then national labor inspectors, but with no response.[45]

[45] IMPSET 5 (campesinos June 15, 1975).

56

State Harassment and Intimidation

The lack of state responsiveness is bad enough. Unfortunately, when popular groups mobilize, too often they also face harassment and intimidation by political officials. Grievances pile on top of grievances. A group organizes around an economic concern, finds lack of government responsiveness, and then with more pressure on its part is met by state harassment and intimidation.

- In August 1976, the six hundred peasant members of a Guatemalan community organization in San Andrés Sajcabajá, El Quiché, denounced their town's conservative mayor for the harassment directed against them just for having organized. Among other charges, they claim he sent the local military police both to break up their general assembly meeting and to intimidate them and that he also was behind the jailing of their community president on a frame-up charge.[46]

State Violence

The most terrible source of sociopolitical grievances, though, occurs when the state commits violence against its citizens. The very institution that is supposed to protect citizens instead tortures, injures, and kills them. State violence represses mass movements. But sometimes it also inadvertently propels them to renewed contentious action. Enough examples already have been given to suffice for the present.

Frustrated Rising Expectations

These various forms of closing political opportunities create new sociopolitical grievances. But how these grievances are experienced will vary for different groups, for example, mainstream groups compared to those that are in the most disadvantaged social categories. Frustrated rising sociopolitical expectations largely refer to a third group between the other two.[47]

As the economic situation of individuals and groups improves, people often desire a corresponding improvement in their social status and better opportunities for meaningful political participation. If the social and

---

[46] IPV (Aug. 15, 1976, 314).
[47] This is one of three types of relative deprivation identified by Gurr, that is, "capabilities remain relatively static while expectations increase or intensify" (Gurr 1970, 46).

political systems are rigid and do not accommodate these desires, then these aspirations have been frustrated and new grievances are generated, perhaps sufficiently for at least some people to become involved in movements for political change. Increased education for new generations often accentuates this type of discontent if it is not accompanied by higher-status opportunities. Frustrated rising expectations would be a conventional explanation–for example, for the sociopolitical grievances driving the economically ascendant middle class in eighteenth-and nineteenth-century Europe that faced sociopolitical systems still controlled by a narrow elite – as well as for their twentieth-century Latin American counterparts.

- Critical to rural mobilization in Guatemala in the later part of the 1970s was the Comité de Unidad Campesina (CUC). Almost all of its founders, as well as the activist cadre that soon developed, were indigenous Mayas from families of village leaders, most of them with enough land for themselves and their children. Its leadership was educated, either through religious and cultural study groups within their home region or, for many, away from home on scholarships for secondary and even university education. They were, as Earle notes, "the group most involved with the priests, most prosperous, most Spanish speaking, and most acculturated" (Earle 2001, 295). They had organized to advance their communities economically and they had organized to advance them politically. Their primary political vehicle had been the Partido Democracia Cristiana (DC), the victim of the military regime's fraud in 1974 (see Chapter 7). And, despite their upward mobility in other respects, these indigenous leaders continued to confront a racist system pervading the larger society. Although not the only source of the grievances behind CUC, the failure of the Guatemalan social and political systems to make room for the aspirations of this critical set of Maya actors certainly was crucial to the emergence of one of the most important contentious groups of the later 1970s – and historically, perhaps the most important.[48]
- Among the Ixil-Maya of Cotzal in the remote northwestern highlands of Guatemala, "the first men to welcome the guerrillas were relatively well-off political activists," according to Stoll (1999, 116). Similarly, in the Ixcán lowlands even further to the north, the guerrillas recruited

---

[48] See Le Bot (1995, 134–179) and Grandin (1997, 15–16). Le Bot gives primacy to grievances related to racial discrimination for CUC's original activists (p. 168).

among the "rather successful, Catholic-financed cooperatives." Consequently, Stoll generalizes that instead of coming from the ranks of the destitute, "revolutionary peasants tend to come from better-off strata, whose rising expectations collide with inflexible power structures" (p. 116).

Accidents

Snow et al. identify "accidents that throw a community's routines into doubt and/or that threaten a community's existence" as one of the threats to the quotidian (Snow et al. 1998, 6), following Walsh's (1981) discussion of "suddenly imposed grievances."[49] To be a grievance, as they and Walsh note, the accident must be attributable to human negligence or error. But "acts of God" can also lead to politicized grievances, as illustrated in significant ways in Central America. Major earthquakes in Nicaragua in 1972, Guatemala in 1976, and El Salvador in 1986 were directly connected to subsequent contentious politics. It was not just that governments were overwhelmed by the destruction and unable to meet the immense human need created by the earthquakes or that government corruption siphoned off far too much of the desperately needed relief funds. More centrally, movement activists argued that these "natural" events were also political because they differentially affected the population.[50] Homes of the rich withstood the shocks. It was the weak structures of the poor that tumbled, burying under the rubble the children and the parents of the impoverished, not of the wealthy.

- The colossal earthquake that struck Guatemala in February 1976 disproportionately hit the poor. The region most directly affected was the western highlands, primarily populated by the indigenous, the poorest segment of the country. Some 27,000 deaths were estimated and another 77,000 injuries. As many as a quarter of a million homes were destroyed, leaving about one million people homeless.[51] Many of the communities hit worst by the earthquake had some history of organization and even contention going back to the Arbenz agrarian reform of the 1950s. Perhaps the most important example is the municipality of San Martin Jilotepeque, where in the town bearing that name

---

[49] Walsh 1981 conceptualizes "suddenly imposed grievances" in the context of Three Mile Island's threatened nuclear meltdown in the United States.

[50] For Guatemala in 1976, for example, see Fernández (1988, 7) and Jonas (1991, 24).

[51] CEH (1999 1:160); IPV (May 22, 1977, 177).

all 1,400 homes were destroyed. Located in the northern part of the department of Chimaltenango, this region had been "a focal point of intense social conflict" since the overthrow of Arbenz.[52] The 1976 earthquake, then, severely aggravated already long-standing deprivation and grievances. In addition, the devastation of the earthquake also brought to the impacted areas a growing number of relief workers and development-oriented organizations, both domestic and especially international, as well as the military through its reconstruction program. As a consequence, peasant organization throughout the zone increased – but so, too, did conflict. Revolutionaries had been intermittently organizing in the area since 1976. When authorities arrested two local youths in September 1979 for distributing communist literature, neighbors stormed the police station and secured their freedom under threats of burning the station down. At this point, state violence in the region escalated, as it did throughout Guatemala. In August 1980, two peasant leaders disappeared, and in November the mayor and one of his sons were kidnapped by the military, leaving behind two other sons injured.[53] And then came the holocaust. Of all of the municipalities in Guatemala, San Martín Jilotepeque had the highest documented death toll for the years of violence examined in this study, even surpassing Guatemala City itself – a total of 3,658 deaths and disappearances recorded at the hands of the state – very few of whom would have been insurgents.[54]

- In El Salvador, the earthquake that hit on October 10, 1986 was centered right in the capital. Over 1,200 people were killed, more than 10,000 injured, and total damages were estimated at more than a billion dollars. Tens of thousands of homes were destroyed, leaving some

[52] REMHI (1999, 186). Indeed, 1,500 peasants from the area were bold enough to protest the loss of their reform parcels at the time in June 1955, and the following year some of them temporarily occupied the same lands; see ASIES (1995 3:47); IPSET9 (desarrollo de la comunidad); NY Times (June 17, 1956, 4).

[53] Castro Torres (1978, 470); IPV (Apr. 26, 1979, 298; Sept. 17, 1979, 207; Nov. 23, 1980, 136); IPSET7 (CNT); CEH (1999, 2:130). Mayors of nine of Chimaltenango's sixteen municipalities were killed during the early 1980s (CEH 1999, 4:170).

[54] These are recorded deaths; actual deaths could have been several times higher. These figures come from the author's calculations using the database compiled by CIIDH/AAAS 2001. See the Appendix to Chapter 7 for further explanation. The municipality of Rabinal in Baja Verapaz was next in the total number of recorded deaths and disappearances at 3,474, followed by Chajul at 3,442, Guatemala at 3,439, and Nebaj at 2,616. Both Chajul and Nebaj are located in northern El Quiché in the Ixil Triangle, the zone of perhaps the worst state terrorism in terms of the percentage of the population victimized.

200,000 homeless people, primarily among the poor who went from living in small adobe and bamboo houses to canvas and cardboard hovels. Factories and offices also were damaged, and unemployment in San Salvador climbed 9 percent to 35 percent. Although promises of relief were prompt, the ability of the government to deliver was overwhelmed and discontent grew. Invariably found in the contentious movements of the rest of the decade were organizations of the homeless, such as the Unión Nacional de Damnificados (UNADES).[55]

The Ideological Dimension

Much of contentious politics is fueled by specific grievances. These are given a shared interpretation through collective action frames. For many movement participants, these frames will lack the cognitive elaboration and coherence that are associated with ideological thought.[56] But the activism of some is also motivated (and justified) by a more general and principled opposition, one that is not necessarily even tied to their own material self-interest or to specific sociopolitical grievances. Instead, their opposition is ideologically driven. Although a small minority most of the time, this is an important group because it usually includes the most committed activists, especially the political entrepreneurs that help to create movements in the first place and keep them going. This ideological dimension of contentious politics will be part of what is examined in the next three chapters.

The Expressive Dimension

All political activity includes some expressive element, even if not recognized by the actor (or by some theoretical approaches). Contentious politics includes the expression of identity and is in large part emotionally based. There also is catharsis in activity, and indeed, this is one of the reasons for activity itself.[57] But the mix of the expressive dimension, the ideological, and specific grievances varies between individuals and for the same individual in

---

[55] ECA (#457:1037–1039).

[56] Here, too, emotion has its role: "Ideology expresses the transformations of feelings, known through images and metaphors, into beliefs about the social system" (Fine and Sandstrom 1993, 29).

[57] A good example of this point is Law and Walsh 1983. Writing from within an expanded rational choice model, Opp notes, "We call this kind of reward the *catharsis value* of protest" (Opp 1989, 59).

different situations.[58] In some contentious activity, the expressive dimension is minor. On other occasions, though, it predominates.[59] Here are two very different kinds of examples:

- Speaking of the peasant participants in the Salvadoran revolutionary cause that she interviewed and especially of their initial involvement, Wood observes: "the *assertion of agency* itself constituted part of the meaning of those acts. Participation per se expressed moral outrage, asserted a claim to dignity, and gave grounds for pride.... some campesinos acted *in order to act*: this assertion of agency (and thus a reclaiming of dignity) was itself a reason for acting – a constitutive and expressive reason. To express rage at the arbitrary and brutal violence of authorities was perceived by some campesinos as a necessary expression of being human, while not to do so was to be less than human" (Wood 2001, 268). Indeed, so important are these expressive motivations to her interviewees that Wood 2003 gives them primacy in the explanation for individual peasant support for the revolutionary cause or even active involvement in the insurgency.[60]

- The annual celebration of Guatemala's Independence Day took a tragic turn on September 14, 1977. A group of young people began shouting at the dignitaries assembled in front of the National Palace and then started throwing rocks at them, causing at least two injuries, including to the police director-general. Police responded with gunfire, which brought more rocks and then more gunfire. The celebration broke up as the crowd fled for safety. Street vandalism continued long into the night, as did the tear gas and police shooting. Officials acknowledged one dead; the press reported four; and a few days later

---

[58] Jasper 1997 provides a good discussion of the affective dimension of protest, especially the pleasurable side. Waddington et al. do as well, perhaps even as "the purpose of the activity" itself (Waddington et al. 1989, 11). However, they still maintain the more traditional distinction between rational and irrational behavior.

[59] And in rare but historically important moments, the expressive element reaches new heights. Examining accounts of key collective action periods in French history (from 1848 to 1968), Zolberg finds "intense moments of festive joy, when an immense outpouring of speech, sometimes verging on violence, coexists with an extraordinarily peaceful disposition. Minds and bodies are liberated; human beings feel that they are in direct touch with one another as well as with their inner selves.... Factions and parties appear unreal while personal networks appear strong as steel" (Zohlberg 1972, 197).

[60] Similarly, Benn argues: "Political activity may be a form of moral self-expression ... because one could not seriously claim ... to be on that side without expressing the attitude by the action most appropriate to it in the paradigm situation" [quoted by Petersen 2001, 284].

students claimed twenty-four had been killed.[61] We can rightfully reject those who would explain most contentious activity as emotional outbursts by the alienated (e.g., the traditional breakdown model)[62] or most youthful political activism as working out authority issues with one's parents. But the desire by scholars to portray contentious activity as rational has led many to ignore the problem riotous behavior can present for social movements. There is an excitement and drama to contentious activity that is the attraction for some, indeed even the edge that comes when a violent response by authorities is a possibility. It is no disrespect to the multitude of Central Americans murdered in cold blood for asserting their just causes to point out that alongside of them were others attracted, at least in part, for different reasons, such as the thrill experienced when a small band coalesces, throwing stones at the police, breaking windows, and vandalizing stores as they escape down side streets.

The Central American Comparison

The importance of grievances for understanding contentious movements is clear when the cases of El Salvador and Guatemala are placed in their regional context. Limiting the focus here to socioeconomic grievances in rural areas, one major reason why higher levels of contention were reached in El Salvador and Guatemala than in Honduras and especially Costa Rica is that grievances were more severe. On the other hand, there are limits to the explanatory power of socioeconomic grievances: The explanation for the even higher levels of contentious mobilization in Nicaragua are found elsewhere, as demonstrated in Chapter 8.

The spread of commercial agriculture had a similar impact in the rest of the region as it did in El Salvador and Guatemala. Many landholders prospered under the new opportunities, but many others, especially those with the least resources, lost access to the land that they needed for their livelihood and way of life. As White points out for the dispossession experienced in many parts of Honduras: "The evictions were the sudden, sharp deprivation which moved *campesinos* to risk their lives in organizing to counter rural elites and protest before government authorities" (White 1977, 181–182). By the late 1960s, the peasant movement in Honduras had

---

[61] IMP73 (Sept. 16, 1977; Sept. 19, 1977).
[62] For a different characterization, see Turner and Killian (1987, 5).

Table 2.3 *Central America: Indicators of Rural Economic Security*

Country	Land[1] Availability 1978/79	EAP[2] Agriculture 1979	Polarization[3] of Land Ownership	Rural Poverty 1980[4] Extreme	Total
Costa Rica	1.7	36	47.8	18.7	34.2
El Salvador	1.3	51	7.0	55.4	76.4
Guatemala	1.8	56	11.6	51.5	83.7
Honduras	3.3	63	21.0	69.7	80.2
Nicaragua	4.5	44	37.5	50.0	80.0

KEY AND SOURCES:

[1] Hectares of cropped land (arable land plus land in permanent crops) in 1978 per economically active person employed in agriculture in 1979. Calculated from IADS (1978, 16, 17).

[2] Percentage of economically active population employed in agriculture (IADS, 1978, 16).

[3] The lower the score, the higher the polarization. Percentage of all farms in small/medium holdings during 1970s (i.e., excludes smallest and largest holdings). Calculated from Brockett (1998, Table 4.1). Years and size of category (all in hectares): Costa Rica (1973), $10 \leq 200$; El Salvador (1971), $10 \leq 200$; Guatemala (1979), $7 \leq 450$; Honduras (1974), $10 \leq 200$; Nicaragua (1971), $14 \leq 140$. If Nicaragua were $7 \leq 140$, then the appropriate figure would be 50.5.

[4] Percentages (Gallardo and López, 1986, 158).

become one of the most assertive in all of Latin America (Astorga Lira 1975, 17).

Meanwhile in Nicaragua, the spread of cotton agriculture along the Pacific coast starting in the 1950s is characterized by Gould for the Chinandega region as "the agrarian bourgeoisie's massive attack on [the peasantry's] . . . standard of living and way of life" (Gould 1990, 85). Thousands of peasants were evicted from subsistence plots on traditional haciendas, while community lands that had been open to all for wood gathering, hunting, and subsistence farming were enclosed as part of the expanding cotton plantations. Early organizational efforts were crushed by repression, but in the 1970s these villages developed into strategic bases for the successful revolution against the Somoza dictatorship.

Still, to the extent we can make the case with aggregate data, the situation in El Salvador and Guatemala was worse than elsewhere in the region. Table 2.3 provides some indication of the differences in the level of land availability and other indicators of rural inequality between the Central American countries at various points in the 1970s and presumably, therefore, some indicator of the level of rural discontent. Costa Rica drops out of the comparison. Although it is among the most land-pressured of the countries, it combines the lowest percentage of the economically active population employed in agriculture with the lowest polarization in land ownership and by far the lowest poverty levels.

The remaining four countries all rank close together in overall rural poverty levels (although extreme poverty is higher in Honduras, which also has the most people employed in agriculture). However, land is far more pressured in El Salvador and Guatemala than in Honduras and Nicaragua, and again El Salvador and Guatemala also have a much more polarized structure of land ownership. Furthermore, peasant grievances could be more easily met by land redistribution in Honduras because as late as 1974 about one-third of its land was still publicly owned. In addition, a unique opportunity to expropriate multinational banana lands opened that same year when United Brands (United Fruit) was hit by a major scandal.[63]

These sharp agrarian differences among the Central American countries were not new. Grievance levels and class tensions were already far greater in Guatemala and El Salvador because they entered the postwar period with the most exploitive and coercive rural class structures. These structural differences were due to long-standing variations between the countries in their availability of good agricultural land, rural labor, capital, and exportable crops. Consequently, any significant peasant mobilization in El Salvador and Guatemala would be experienced by elites in those countries as a serious threat to their privileged position. This is one of the most fundamental reasons for the extraordinary levels of violence directed at the peasantry of these two countries, especially during 1980–1983.

Conclusion

Two recent, excellent comparative accounts of the revolutionary movement in El Salvador (Goodwin 2001, McClintock 1998) denigrate the explanatory role of socioeconomic grievances. McClintock, for example, argues "that the correlation between areas of more severe poverty and FMLN membership was scant, and that economic variables were not emphasized by militants in their explanations of their decisions to join the FMLN. Accordingly, I contend that poverty among Salvadoran peasants during the 1970s was more of a constant than a catalyst: Peasants were not happy about their living standards; if they had been, they would have been less likely to rebel. But economic variables cannot explain when, where, or ultimately why the revolutionary movement expanded in El Salvador" (McClintock

---

[63] See Brockett 1998 for further explanation for this paragraph and the next.

1998, 159).[64] Similarly, Goodwin claims, "In contrast to analyses that focus primarily, or even exclusively, on class relations and transnational economic dependency, I shall argue that the institutional configurations and practices of Central American states best explain both the uneven development and the relative success or failure of Central America's revolutionary movements" (Goodwin 2001, 143).

In many ways, I concur. However, it is important to notice that these conclusions are specific to *revolutionary movements* and their *expansion* and *relative success*. Enlarging our focus, these revolutionary movements drew many of their participants out of preexisting *nonrevolutionary social movements*. And neither the emergence nor the trajectories of these prior social movements can be understood without reference to the socioeconomic grievances that helped to generate and fuel them. Analysts such as Goodwin and McClintock are correct in stressing the political factors – including sociopolitical grievances – that expanded small revolutionary organizations into important mass movements with significant popular support (for at least a while). Nonetheless, the socioeconomic grievances of participants that predated their revolutionary involvement undoubtedly in many cases continued to provide part of the motivation necessary to maintain contentious activity in the face of considerable risk and uncertain odds of success.

This chapter has argued that grievances do matter, not just to protesters but also to any analysis that hopes to understand the causes and course of contentious movements. But, the problem remains that in the usual absence of good survey data, the link between grievances and movements cannot be specified by aggregate data. Understanding requires instead contextual knowledge that comes with immersion by the analyst in the cases studied (with all of the reliability problems that this presents). Furthermore, individual motivation is complex. The configuration of grievances of two structurally similar individuals could be quite different and indeed for any one individual might change from one protest event to another. Practically, these difficulties mean that cross-national quantitative analysis is not well positioned to tell us much about contentious movements and the grievances that drive them.[65] It also means that the number of cases that can be included in a comparative analysis of contentious movements is probably limited.

---

[64] Wood's excellent case study of peasant support for and involvement in the Salvadoran insurgency makes the same argument (Wood 2003, 12–16, 195–200).

[65] For a parallel argument, see Snow et al. (1998, 6).

But a long distance remains for this study between connecting individual grievances to the emergence and trajectory of contentious movements. The discontent of individuals must be transformed into the shared grievances of group participants with some degree of a collective identity. Crucial to the social construction of grievances are the political activists who are featured in the following three chapters. How much success they and their movements enjoy will be determined by much more than the level of grievances. That success will depend on how shared grievances interact with the various dimensions of the configuration of political opportunities that are the subject of the rest of this book.

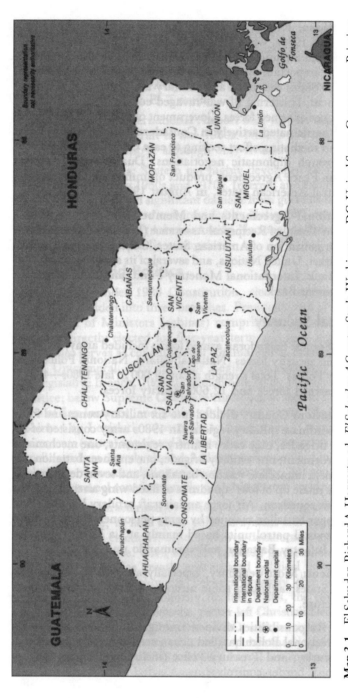

Map 3.1 El Salvador, Richard A. Haggerty, ed., *El Salvador: A Country Study*, Washington, DC: United States Government Printing Office, 1990.

3

The Emergence of Urban Contentious Movements

EL SALVADOR

Most of the time in most of the world, the poor and the powerless are not politically active and certainly not contentious when they are. Contentious movements occur infrequently, invariably enlist far less than the majority of the aggrieved population when they do, and seldom persist for long. This is especially true for the most radical expression of contention, revolutionary movements.

For radical activists (and often for scholars as well), the political quiescence of the disadvantaged is seen as self-defeating if not irrational, resulting from counterproductive values and attitudes. However, with the assistance provided by activists – be that education, training, resources, or consciousness raising – the poor and powerless can come to see their condition not as natural but as socially created, not by abstract forces but by identifiable elites who are perpetuating their own enrichment at the expense of the vast majority. With this change in understanding, the theory goes, contentious activism emerges and grows, at first motivated usually by individuals' own immediate material interests and those of their closest social affiliations. But with time and further transformation of consciousness, they might even come to understand the need for revolutionary changes in the very social order itself.

From a different standpoint, the reluctance of the disadvantaged (and other non-elites) to join the contentious causes of political activists is seldom irrational or the result of counterproductive attitudes. That activists in countries like those of Central America put their own lives and fortunes at risk should not obscure that they ask the same of anyone else who would join them and often the security and even at times the lives of their family members and neighbors who do not join. People whose economic security is precarious throughout their lifetime must develop a practical wisdom, including an acute understanding of when risk taking is and is not warranted, in order to protect what chances for security they have. From this standpoint, what needs to be explained is not why the disadvantaged fail to become contentious but rather why in limited cases they do.[1]

It is from the tension between these two perspectives that this and the next two chapters proceed. What were the steps by which normally risk-avoiding people, and especially the disadvantaged, became mobilized for contentious action in El Salvador and Guatemala, with smaller numbers becoming committed activists and even revolutionaries? Variations at the individual level are, of course, numerous, but as this chapter and the next two will show, a number of patterns emerge.

We *experience* discontent as individuals. But we almost always *act* on our grievances through groups.[2] Individuals experience the fear and terror provoked by repression, but we cannot understand whether their response will be fight or flight without placing individuals within their social networks.[3] Social movement scholarship in recent decades has given much attention to this dimension of collective action, highlighting the processes by which individuals are mobilized into and through groups, including the crucial role played by organizers themselves.[4] Not only is most contentious activity through groups, but mobilization into those groups often occurs along

[1] As Goodwin points out, "few people join or support revolutionaries – even when they are more or less in agreement with their demands or ideology – if they feel that doing so will make them more vulnerable to state violence or if they believe that they can obtain much or even some modicum of what they want, in political terms, through some routine, institutionalized, and therefore low-risk channel for political claim making.... Other things being equal, people, like electric currents, take the path of least resistance" (Goodwin 2001, 26). Also see Snow et al. 1998.

[2] Emphasizing that revolutionaries are "recruited to act, decided to act, and acted as groups rather than as individuals," Goldstone points out that group identity "leads individuals to feel outrage or distress at injuries to other members of the group, and can create severe emotional costs for actions that are inconsistent with the group's welfare- and identity-sustaining norms" (Goldstone 1994, 141, 145).

[3] For explanations of network analysis and models, along with empirical evidence, see Gamson, Fireman, and Rytina 1982; McAdam 1988; McAdam and Paulsen 1993; and Snow et al. 1980 for U.S. cases; della Porta 1992 on European revolutionaries; Gould 1991 on the Paris Commune; Opp and Gern 1993 on East Germany; and Wickham-Crowley 1992 on Latin American revolutionaries. For a sympathetic review, see Emirbayer and Goodwin 1994. In reaction to the individualistic bias of many approaches, especially rational choice models, some advocates of network analysis privilege relationships as the key social unit (e.g., Emirbayer 1997; Somers 1998). This would seem to be committing the same mistake only in reverse.

[4] The critical importance of groups to the mobilization of discontent is at the center of the resource mobilization approach to the study of social movements. Key texts for the two main

preexisting affiliation lines, giving the contentious group much more cohesiveness than it would if it were an aggregation of autonomous individuals.[5] Furthermore, relational dynamics within the contentious group can further strengthen bonds of solidarity and loyalty,[6] reinforcing commitment and courage in the face of great risks in a way that is unintelligible to individualistic models of behavior.[7]

Central American contentious movements usually have originated in the cities, particularly the capital, initiated by middle-class groups such as students, teachers, and other professionals. Middle-class activists also have provided the leadership nucleus for virtually all multisector movements that have developed in the region. Other activists have risen from the ranks of workers, beginning the difficult process of creating an assertive labor movement, often receiving assistance from the more progressive of the middle-class groups. The development of these movements in El Salvador will be examined in this chapter, for Guatemala in the next.

Given the greater domination peasants have faced, their mobilization seldom has been self-generated but rather catalyzed by outside support groups. It is here especially where the issues of "false consciousness" and the

---

variants of this approach are McCarthy and Zald 1977 and Tilly 1978. For a dissenting view by two of the foremost critics, see Turner and Killian (1987, 235–238, 388–392).

[5] As Tilly explains, "We have good reason to believe that collective action on a large scale depends heavily on commitment to subgroups within the acting population rather than directly to the enterprise as a whole" (Tilly 2001, 37). Similarly, Koopmans points to "the mobilization of *preexisting* solidarities, identities, social networks, values, and norms" as key to forging new collective movements (Koopmans 2001, 115). Petersen 2001 provides a particularly good application of these principles to a particular case (Lithuania).

[6] Fireman and Gamson include loyalty and responsibility as components of solidarity and argue that they should be thought of as "not merely as attributes of individuals but as properties of cultural codes or belief systems. Individuals exist in a climate of cultural beliefs about their obligations to those groups with which they identify and their responsibilities for contributing their shares to just causes" (Fireman and Gamson 1979, 32). In contrast, for a leading effort to explain group solidarity from a rational choice perspective, see Hechter 1987.

[7] Based on interviews and surveys with Columbia University protestors, Hirsch concludes that because of group processes individuals make decisions that they would not have made as individuals. He points out that if there is "sufficient group identification, the protesters will respond to threats as a powerful, angry group rather than as isolated, frightened individuals. . . . The sense of crisis that develops in such conflicts strengthens participants' belief that their fate is tied to that of the group. They develop a willingness to continue to participate despite the personal risks because they believe the costs of protest should be collectively shared" (Hirsch 1990, 245). Still, this is not to overlook the fascinating work within a rational choice perspective on "threshold effects," which are the aggregation of individual choices that alter group behavior – see Granovetter 1978; Moore 1995b; and Oberschall (1995, 14–15, 67–96).

"consciousness-raising" role of outside groups needs to be addressed. As the dynamics of peasant mobilization have been different from those for urban groups, these will be discussed separately in Chapter 5. Whether urban or rural, these chapters clearly establish the availability of allies and support groups as a crucial dimension of the configuration of political opportunities faced by challengers. These three chapters follow contentious movements up to around 1980, at which point space for nonviolent protest activity was violently eliminated by the state in both countries for several years. How and why nonviolent contentious movements reappeared later in the 1980s will be analyzed in later chapters.

In many circumstances, state violence has repressed these organizing efforts in Central America. At other times, though, state violence radicalized many participants, spurring even greater contentious activity, at least for a time. As the 1970s progressed, broad movements uniting popular groups from a variety of sectors became the main vehicle for this increasingly assertive contentious activity in El Salvador and Guatemala. These popular organizations also were major sources of new recruits into preexisting but small armed revolutionary movements, especially as escalating repression eliminated nonviolent opposition as a possibility.

El Salvador in particular is an excellent example of why the origins of revolutionary situations should not be studied separately from other contentious movements. Armed revolutionary organizations do not create revolutionary situations alone but rather in conjunction with other contentious movements, often with intimate connections between them.[8] Similarly, El Salvador is an excellent example of the necessity of including the role of the revolutionary leadership itself at the center of any attempt to explain why and how a revolutionary situation develops in the first place.[9] What is

---

[8] For an insightful elaboration of this argument, see Goldstone 1998b.

[9] Denardo criticizes structuralists for ignoring the crucial role of revolutionary strategy for understanding "the political struggles that are the essence of the revolutionary process after the crisis begins and from which the new regime emerges" (Denardo 1984, 15). Similarly, although McClintock is willing to concede the structuralist model might be appropriate for the classic revolutions studied by, for example, Skocpol (1979), the role of revolutionary organizations becomes more critical for understanding the revolutions of the post-WWII period (McClintock 1998, 34). Also see Berejikian 1992; Selbin 1993; Grenier 1999; Wickham-Crowley 1992. Markoff 1997 goes even further, questioning structuralist accounts of the French Revolution itself. For a good overview of various approaches to revolutionary theory, see Wickham-Crowley 1997. I must confess that my own earlier study of political conflict in Central America (Brockett 1998) woefully downplays the importance of revolutionary leaders and their organizations.

now clear is that this revolutionary leadership was more important to the contentious politics of the 1970s than often understood at the time.

Salvadoran Urban Contentious Actors

In April of 1983, Mélida Anaya Montes (alias "Ana María Gómez"), the second-ranking leader in the most important of El Salvador's armed revolutionary movements, the Fuerzas Populares de Liberación (FPL), was killed in Managua, Nicaragua. After a week of conflicting rumors, the truth emerged: Her murder had been ordered by Cayetano Carpio (alias "Marcial"), the FPL's commander since its founding. Carpio then committed suicide, ending a period of severe leadership conflict within the coalition of the five revolutionary organizations constituting the Frente Farabundo Martí para la Liberación Nacional (FMLN).[10] This bizarre ending to their lives is what is often now most remembered about Carpio and Montes. What has faded is recognition of how central the two were to each of the key stages in the development of contentious activity in El Salvador from the 1960s to their deaths – the organization of unions of workers and teachers, of the oldest and largest of the country's violent revolutionary organizations, and of broad nonviolent contentious movements. Each of these will be discussed in turn after first addressing the role of university students.

Contentious University Students

Coming into the 1960s, El Salvador had been ruled by the military since late 1931. Although some of the more recent military presidents came to office through elections, civilians generally saw the national political system as closed, especially for those located from the center to the left of the spectrum. As elsewhere throughout the Caribbean region, these advocates

---

[10] For a good discussion of the conflicts, deaths, and the aftermath, see Prisk (1991, 45–58), which is an interview with Napoleón Romero García (alias "Miguel Castellanos"). Romero García was a top FPL leader who was called upon to go to Managua to investigate the deaths of Carpio and Montes and then to travel to Cuba, the Soviet Union, and Vietnam to explain his findings. These events were critical to his decision to defect from the FMLN in 1985 after he was captured. In 1989, he was assassinated by the FMLN in an act of "revolutionary justice." El Salvador's truth commission's conclusion on this case is concise and to the point: "international humanitarian law does not permit the execution of civilians without a proper trial" (Betancur et al. 1993, 163).

of change were invigorated by the success of the Cuban revolution at the start of 1959. This impact was especially strong on students.[11]

Pressures from progressive groups through tactics such as street demonstrations were frequent in El Salvador from late 1959 through the next year. Students were especially prominent in these activities, and they also suffered when the state responded with repression. A student sit-in protesting the prior arrest of other students in August 1960, for example, was broken up by police and some were then themselves arrested. Clashes between police and student marchers the following month brought student casualties and a state of siege. Nonetheless, these pressures worked: In October, a coup brought the reformist faction of the military to power, which then shared seats on its junta with progressive civilians. The change was short-lived, though, as a counter-coup returned more conservative forces to power in January 1961. Scores of civilians were arrested in the following days, and in March the head of the student association was expelled from the country for alleged communist connections.[12]

Students then played a minor role in the national political arena until later in the 1960s. But important changes were at work. The student body of the University of El Salvador doubled in size between 1962 and 1969 while its budget quadrupled. Expansion increased the socioeconomic diversity of the student body, reinforced by the institution of a two-year basic preprofessional program in late 1969 (Webre 1979, 150).

By the late 1960s, large numbers of students (and teachers) at the national university professed radical ideologies, a common Latin American student viewpoint reinforced by the global trends of the period, from France and Mexico to even the United States. Indeed, the university at this time was "a hotbed of leftist sentiment among students and professors" (Hammond 1998, 37), and student organizations themselves have been described as "totally controlled by Marxist-Leninist groups" (Grenier 1999, 114). The best known university rector of this period, Fabio Castillo, was one of the civilian members of the October 1960 junta, a member of the Partido

---

[11] FPL leaders interviewed by Harnecker (1993, 127, 139) claim that secondary students were more important to the contentious politics of the last half of the 1970s than were university students. They informed Harnecker that the Asociación de Estudiantes de Secundaria (AES), which had reactivated in 1974, came under FPL control the following year (p. 139). The necessary information is not available, however, for separate attention here to this important actor.

[12] NY Times (Aug. 23, 1960, 5; Sept. 7, 1960, 1; Sept. 16, 1960, 3; Jan. 28, 1961, 3); Valle (1993, 47–48); and, more generally, Webre 1979 and Williams and Walter 1997.

Comunista de El Salvador (PCS), and "promoted numerous leftists to high positions within the university and ... encouraged leftist activities among the students" (McClintock 1998, 252).[13]

But ideology does not necessarily dictate strategy. The moderate Partido Demócrata Cristiano (PDC) had scored repeated victories in San Salvador mayoral elections, during the 1960s with its popular leader José Napoleón Duarte. His victory in the 1972 presidential election looked possible, especially as a coalition was formed with the smaller social democratic Movimiento Nacional Revolucionario (MNR), which provided his vice presidential running mate, Guillermo Ungo. The communist PCS also was part of this Unión Nacional Opositora (UNO) coalition through a small party it participated in, the Unión Democrática Nacionalista (UDN). Radical though they might be ideologically, university students in 1972 threw their energies and hopes into the electoral process.

As the 1970s progressed, though, many students turned away from electoral to more contentious politics, supplying many of the activists in both nonviolent and violent confrontational activities. Students also were important to peasant mobilization, bringing their progressive and activist message to the countryside.[14] Many events were critical to this behavioral radicalization, but three were key.

First, by all indications Duarte won the February 1972 presidential vote, but the military regime continued itself in power, handing the victory through fraud to its candidate, Coronel Arturo Molina.[15] A few days later, Duarte called for a general strike; although many responded, the strike failed to halt the military and then faded away. A month after the election, elements in the military attempted a counter-coup. Demonstrating substantial strength, in the end the ruling military quashed the coup attempt, coming down hard on the opposition. Over one hundred were killed, and more than two hundred were injured. Greater numbers were arrested. Martial law

[13] Later, Fabio Castillo would be one of the founders of the Partido Revolucionario de los Trabajadores Centroamericanos (PRTC), the last to form of what would be the five constituent armed movements joined together as the FMLN.

[14] As Hammond explains, "students' courses included field work in poor neighborhoods in the city and rural villages, where they offered assistance and practiced the professions they were learning" (Hammond 1998, 37).

[15] Actually, the regime probably would have continued without fraud; what was at stake was who came in first at the ballot box. The margin of victory claimed by Duarte was not enough to provide the majority necessary in a multicandidate election to avoid the national congress from deciding the victor. Most certainly, they would have picked Molina (see Webre 1979, 171).

was declared and more casualties of the repression followed. The military also occupied the University of El Salvador. Going far beyond a violation of its autonomy, the military threw out the university administration and put in its own in an indirect rule that would last for more than seven years.

As McClintock points out, "The birthplace of the revolutionary movements that were to compose the FMLN was the National University of El Salvador" (McClintock 1998, 251). The top leaders of three of the FMLN's five constituent organizations were all student activists at the University of El Salvador in the late 1960s and early 1970s, as were the second in command of two of the five, and countless others who joined the armed left. In addition, two other FMLN leaders who were from an older generation also had been student activists during their days at the university.[16] In their testimonies, many revolutionaries claim these events in early 1972 brought them to the conclusion that military intransigence precluded peaceful change in El Salvador. Armed revolutionary struggle was necessary.[17]

Second, the events of the summer of 1975 reinforced their judgment and brought many students from the next generation to the same conclusion. San Salvador newspapers in July 1975 were dominated by two very different topics: violence and Miss Universe. Following a meeting on July 4 with his top advisers, President Molina announced new measures would be taken to control the wave of crime sweeping the capital. In addition to a number of well-publicized big robberies, at the end of June the Ejército

---

[16] Joaquín Villalobos of the Ejército Revolucionario del Pueblo (ERP), Eduardo Sancho Castañeda ("Fermán Cienfuegos") of the Fuerzas Armadas de Resistencia Nacional (FARN), and Francisco Jovel ("Roberto Roca") of the Partido Revolucionario de los Trabajadores (PRTC) were all student activists at the National University in the late 1960s and early 1970s, as was the head of the Partido Comunista de El Salvador (PCS), Shafik Jorge Handal, a decade earlier. Also, university activists in the latter period were the second in command of the ERP (Ana Guadalupe Martínez Menéndez) and the PRTC (María Concepción Valladares ["Nidia Díaz"]), as well as that of the Fuerzas Populares de Liberación (FPL) in the earlier period (Mélida Anaya Montes) (McClintock 1998, 251–257). At the top of the leadership, this leaves out only Carpio (head of the FPL), who came from a poor background and then union activism.

[17] McClintock (1998, 253–255); NY Times (Jan. 3, 1983, 2). Reinforcing this domestic event was a crucial foreign one: the overthrow of Salvador Allende's elected Marxist government in Chile in September 1973. As Romero García, a FPL student organizer of the mid-1970s, explained years later, following his defection from the FMLN: "the coup in Chile reinforced our position against the traditional Communist Party. It completely annulled [their] . . . line of political thought . . . that is to say, to take advantage of the evolution of democracy in the capitalist countries in order to arrive at socialism through an accumulation of forces on the political level" (quoted in Prisk 1991, 11).

Revolucionario del Pueblo (ERP) had kidnapped a noted industrialist while another industrialist was injured in a failed kidnapping attempt on the very day of Molina's announcement.

More pleasurable was the arrival of the Miss Universe pageant to San Salvador. Events were publicized with long articles and ample photographs, day after day. Authorities grew more apprehensive, though, when an activist from the teachers' union incited a group of twenty to throw stones at a parade of the beauties. He was promptly arrested. While many Salvadorans enjoyed the pageant, taking pride in their country's selection as the host for the worldwide event, many students were offended by the lavishness of the spectacle in a country so poor. The Miss Universe pageant corresponded with the annual fair in nearby Santa Ana, which always featured its own much publicized beauty contest. Students at the local branch of the national university marched on July 25, ridiculing and protesting both contests. Four days later, they returned to the streets of Santa Ana with a larger march of some three thousand. It was broken up by police for disorderly conduct (pointing to supposedly obscene signs), detaining eleven participants overnight. The events of the next day were tragic. A student-led march of about two thousand in the capital on July 30, in protest of the events the day before in Santa Ana, as well as more generally against the government, was attacked by security forces. At least fifteen were killed, dozens more injured, and many arrested. President Molina, though, charged the marchers with a communist plot to subvert his government.[18]

The next day, in protest of the massacre, over one hundred activists from a variety of organizations occupied the National Cathedral, holding it for almost a week. It was during this occupation that activists claimed they formed the Bloque Popular Revolucionario (BPR), a coalition of leftist groups that would be the leading actor in Salvadoran contentious politics for the rest of the decade. The same day, authorities attacked another student demonstration, leaving more dead, the number ranging between one to twelve depending on sources.[19]

Third, as El Salvador moved closer to full civil war through the first half of 1980, a coalition of the leading leftist organizations and unions called

---

[18] The Salvadoran press at the time report six killed; a later Organization of American States (OAS) investigation named fifteen dead; secondary sources often give thirty-seven dead. LPG (July 1, 1975, 49; July 5, 1975, 1; July 8, 1975, 2; July 22, 1975, 12; July 30, 1975, 11; July 31, 1975, 3, 13; Aug. 1, 1975, 3). Source for the OAS is AWC/ACLU (1982, 39).

[19] NY Times (Aug. 10, 1975, 19); IDHUCA (1988, 29); Harnecker (1993, 135); LPG (Aug. 7, 1975, 3).

for a two-day general strike beginning June 24. By one estimate, 100,000 industrial workers, 30,000 teachers, another 25,000 public employees, and 100,000 rural workers responded to the call (ECA #392, 621). Two days later, strike leaders gave a press conference at the University of El Salvador, which had regained its autonomy just the June before. The university quickly had become a safe haven again for leftist groups, including, the government charged repeatedly, for armed subversives. Indeed, just two days after a reformist coup on October 15, 1979, the revolutionary ERP was said to have been on campus distributing weapons in behalf of its call for insurrection. In March 1980, a twelve-hour shootout occurred between authorities and armed groups on campus. Then on June 26, following a confrontation in a neighborhood adjoining the university and as the press conference by the strike leaders was being held, the military invaded the campus with a force of eight hundred soldiers. An estimated fifty people on campus were killed and more than double that number injured. The next day, the campus was fully occupied, suffering much damage as soldiers went from room to room searching for subversive evidence. Two and a half years later, the university still closed, a reporter described the campus as follows: "computers and filing cabinets lie smashed open, their tapes and papers strewn across office floors. Laboratories, libraries and classrooms have been ransacked, including those of the medical school, which is off the university's main campus" (NY Times January 3, 1983, 2). Even twenty years after the attack, signs of the destruction remained, most starkly in empty bombed-out buildings. For nonviolent antiregime students who had not yet been touched closely by the repression, the 1980 massacre and military occupation of the campus moved many over to the revolutionary cause.[20] As nonviolent political actors, students were dormant for the next half decade.

Teachers and Political Contention

School teachers played a critical role in the contentious politics of El Salvador, in part because of their militancy but especially because they were one of the few "national" organizations that had a truly national membership – teachers are located everywhere throughout the country.[21]

---

[20] ECA (#380, 621); ECA (#403, 343); NY Times (Oct. 18, 1979, 3; Mar. 18, 1980, 4; Mar. 19, 1980, 5; June 25, 1980, 5; Jan. 3, 1983, 2). When the university reopened in 1984, a new generation of students revived its activist tradition.

[21] Hammond (1998, 42) makes the same point.

Furthermore, teachers have social status, particularly in small towns and rural areas where they often are looked to for leadership. Through the assertion of their own interests, Salvadoran teachers created some of the most important early mobilization campaigns in the country. Later, their organization was at the heart of the multisector movement that led the mass contentious activities of the late 1970s. Teachers also supplied early on a number of leaders to El Salvador's armed left and later many militants as well.

The Asociación Nacional de Educadores Salvadoreños (ANDES) was formed on June 21, 1966, on the first anniversary of an unsuccessful strike attempt. The following year, during a period of general labor agitation, teachers participated in progressive work stoppages for several months during the fall, but the government retaliated by reassigning leaders to schools in remote rural areas. In response to these reassignments, as well as its outstanding issues, ANDES went on full strike in early 1968. The strike lasted fifity-four days, and in the end the teachers won many of their demands. In between, there were a number of demonstrations, the occupation of the Ministry of Education, and, most notably, the mobilization of broad sectors of society in support. At times, the government responded with violence and at least four protestors were killed. This repression was critical in developing the "revolutionary consciousness" of a number of teachers who were to later join the FPL. The first secretary-general of ANDES, Mélida Anaya Montes, led the organization throughout the 1966–1977 period, the last several years while covertly a top FPL leader.[22]

Conflict between ANDES and the government was again a major issue throughout much of 1971. In January, teachers presented the legislature with a proposed education reform. At the end of April, they staged a one-day strike and held demonstrations in all department capitals to push for action. In the face of continuing lack of government response, another one-day strike was held in June with a demonstration in front of the national palace, and then progressive work stoppages were held across the next three days. Finally, on July 8 the government acted, but it passed a law opposed by teachers.

What was to grow into a major strike began the same day at a few schools. Two weeks later, it was estimated that only 40 percent of the nation's teachers

---

[22] Harnecker (1993, 38–41); Valle (1993, 96–98). Salvador Sánchez Céren (alias "Leonel González") is another example of an ANDES militant also serving covertly as an FPL leader. Later, he became the FPL's commander in 1983, after the death of Carpio (McClintock 1998, 257).

were working. The strike lasted through August, with the University of El Salvador providing financial assistance to participants. Marches were held almost daily, especially in the first weeks. Some were uneventful. Others were broken up by authorities–most severely, a torchlight parade on July 16 that some two hundred security agents attacked, injuring and arresting many. In response to the attack, as well as such harassment as the arrest of one leader for possessing subversive literature, strike leaders began a hunger strike on July 18. Three days later, the homes of some leaders were broken into and ransacked. In the end, teachers accepted a government offer, though it was less than desired (UCA 1971). By the fall, hopes were focused on the February 1972 elections. Teachers were among the major activists behind the center-left coalition's efforts and major targets of the repression that followed the fraud.[23] For many, more contentious forms of struggle now appeared the only viable direction. For the rest of the decade, the most important outlet for teachers' political activities were the mass organizations and armed revolutionary movements discussed below.

Organizing Labor in El Salvador

Labor unions were prohibited in El Salvador during the General Maximiliano Hernández Martínez dictatorship of 1931–1944, and the rights of labor were only intermittently recognized for years thereafter. As the country's industrial sector developed, so, too, did its industrial work-force, followed then by organizing activity. During the 1950s and 1960s, a number of unions were formed, largely grouped into two confederations, one reformist and allied with the U.S.-backed Inter-American Regional Organization of Workers of the AFL-CIO (ORIT) and the other radical, with connections to the Partido Comunista de El Salvador (PCS). Nonetheless, the two confederations shared a nonconfrontational, gradualist orientation, focusing on concrete economic gains. From 1957 to 1966, there were only two labor strikes in the country, both prior to 1961 (Béjar 1990).

The leader of the PCS during these years was Cayetano Carpio, the only top leader of what was later to become the FMLN who actually came from a working class background. He spent some years in an orphanage after his shoemaker father died, receiving education from several religious orders. At age 14, he departed from the path leading him to the priesthood,

---

[23] ANDES documented the deaths of 258 of its members by June 23, 1982, with another 58 disappeared (McClintock 1985a, 304).

striking out on his own, traveling and working, eventually becoming a baker. In 1938, he participated in his first strike and around 1943 became the head of the bakers' union. His activism landed him in jail for over a year in the early 1950s. When he was rearrested shortly after his release because of his immediate return to activism, he went on a twenty-one-day hunger strike until he was released into exile. Following time in Guatemala, Mexico, the USSR, and China, he returned to El Salvador in 1957. In 1963, the communist party (PCS) assigned him the task of working with the labor movement. The following year, at the age of about 45, he became the head of the PCS, leading it away from the path of armed struggle that it had been intermittently attracted to following the Cuban Revolution (Harnecker 1984, 156–172; 1993, 46–52).

Labor's nonconfrontational stance changed dramatically in 1967 – there were twenty-seven strikes that year (Béjar 1990, 873). The year's first strike came in mid-January when 1,600 bus drivers halted work for three days. Crucial to their success was support from other unions through the Federación Unitaria Sindical de El Salvador (FUSS), which had been organized in 1965, especially through PCS efforts, bringing together fourteen unions. The next month saw two more strikes, both lasting just under a week, one with partial gains (IUSA) and the other with a big victory (ASEO Público). The most important strike, though, came in April during an opening created by the lame-duck period between two presidencies.[24]

What was most significant about the April 1967 strike at Fábrica de Acero was not its success but rather that victory was gained through a progressive general strike that grew day by day. The steel plant is located in Zacatecoluca, about thirty miles southeast of the capital and owned by the core elite Borgonovo family.[25] As the strike persisted, the national labor movement came to its assistance, especially FUSS. On the tenth day of the strike, supporters from all over the country gathered for a demonstration in the Zacatecoluca central plaza. In the next few days, a solidarity caravan from the capital paraded through the town and then FUSS threatened a general strike in five days if management did not settle. After a short extension of the deadline, the general strike began in progressive fashion on April 26 with some 9,000 strikers. The second day, the number grew to 22,000 and on the third 35,000. Management then settled; the strikers had won. A

---

[24] Carpio (1993, 416); Harnecker (1993, 30); Menjívar 1979; Valle (1993, 94, 414–415).

[25] In April 1977, Foreign Minister Mauricio Alfredo Borgonovo Pohl was kidnapped by the FPL. See ECA (#342, 321).

jubilant Carpio claimed another 15,000 were ready to strike on the fourth day – "the potential of a unified working class had been demonstrated with unparalleled power!" (Carpio 1993, 455).[26] The contentious year ended with Carpio on a hunger strike, in solidarity with the strike by his home union, the bakers.[27]

Labor's militancy continued: For the next five years there was an annual average of seventeen strikes. And then came the 1972 elections and the repression that followed. As labor was heavily involved in the antigovernment candidacies, the fraud and repression contributed to its radicalization but repression limited its activities. Strike levels dropped in half to an annual average of only eight from 1973 through 1976. Labor activism then intensified in the latter part of the decade as part of the broader protest cycle of that period, reaching a peak of 103 strikes in 1979 (Béjar 1990, 873). At the center of this activity was a new organization, the Confederación Unificada de Trabajadores Salvadoreños (CUTS), formed by FUSS and another, but smaller, communist federation, as well as by the larger leftist but noncommunist Federación Nacional de Sindicatos de Trabajadores Salvadoreños (FENASTRAS). At the time of its formation in October 1977, CUTS had about 26,000 members, about half coming from FENASTRAS, altogether representing about a third of the country's unionized workforce (USDS/NSA1 1979a).[28]

Labor's tactics became more militant as well toward the end of the 1970s. Striking workers increasingly occupied their plants, holding owners and managers for protection from security forces and for bargaining purposes. Demands also expanded – from employment issues to broader economic and even to political concerns. This growing militancy did not reflect increasing influence of the communist party as it would have in the 1960s but rather connections with new competitors to the PCS from its left (Véjar 1979, 516–518). This new set of activists is well illustrated by Carpio himself; indeed, as much as anyone else, he was the primary instigator of this new development.

---

[26] Another Acero strike ten years later had very different results: It was broken up and the union dissolved (Menjivar 1979, 116).

[27] Carpio 1993; Valle (1993, 93–94, 416–418).

[28] As of early 1979, about 10 percent of Salvadoran nonagricultural workers were organized in unions (76,085). The country's largest federation, with about 40,000 members, was the Federación de Sindicatos de Construcción, Transportes y Similares (FESINCONTANS), which was affiliated internationally with the U.S.-backed American Institute for Free Labor Development (AIFLD) (USDS/NSA1 1979a).

Salvadoran Revolutionary Movements

The Partido Comunista de El Salvador (PCS) dominated the far left coming into the 1970s, although it probably had only around 150 members at the time (McClintock 1998, 49). Because the PCS was illegal, many of its members participated in conventional politics through the Unión Democrática Nacionalista (UDN), one of the parties in Duarte's 1972 UNO coalition. Even before the disillusionment caused by the fraud and repression of that year, however, Carpio had decided that armed struggle was required for El Salvador, reversing his position of the 1960s.[29] Leaving the communist party in 1970, in April he formed with six other activists the Fuerzas Populares de Liberación (FPL), a Marxist-Leninist organization dedicated to a prolonged popular war strategy. Three of the other founders also came from a working-class background; in contrast, the other three were on the medical faculty at the national university. They started with a base of support from a half dozen others. The FPL's first public action came on August 22, 1972, when it set off a bomb at the Argentine embassy in protest of that country's massacre of rioting revolutionary prisoners.[30]

Following the events of 1972, FPL membership did increase; however, a number of those turning to armed struggle at that time chose instead to join a new movement, the Ejército Revolucionario del Pueblo (ERP), which had formed in 1971 (Raudales and Medrano 1994, 51). Many of ERP's members came out of the left wing of the Partido Demócrata Cristiano (PDC) rather than the communist party. They also tended to be younger, softer in their ideology, and more oriented toward insurrection in their strategy than were FPL militants. A third organization of the armed left later broke away from the ERP in 1975, when the ERP leadership murdered its best-known member, Roque Dalton, following dissension over strategy.[31] Those forming the Fuerzas Armadas de Resistencia Nacional (FARN) agreed with

---

[29] The PCS had formed a short-lived armed revolutionary group in 1963, the Frente Unido de Acción Revolucionaria (FUAR).

[30] The following year, another bomb was exploded at the Chilean embassy in response to the military's overthrow of Marxist President Salvador Allende. Another armed revolutionary group, Acción Revolucionaria Salvadoreña (ARS), had started up two years earlier. Inspired by Guatemala's Fuerzas Armadas Revolucionarias (FAR), it had taken a few actions but then was quashed by authorities (Harnecker 1993, 58, 78).

[31] One supporter of Dalton was also killed and orders given for the murder of others from his faction, though this was not carried out. The dissident faction retaliated by informing police of the location of ERP safe houses. Needless to say, it took the organization some time to recover from this internal struggle (Raudales and Medrano 1994, 133–138).

Dalton's critique of the ERP that its focus was too much on armed action and not enough on political work with the masses.[32] The violent left fragmented even further in early 1976 with the formation of the Partido Revolucionario de los Trabajadores (PRTC) out of a FARN faction. Once the PCS embraced armed struggle in 1979, there were five armed organizations fighting to bring revolution to El Salvador. The best estimate of the U.S. embassy for early 1979 was about 2,000 "hardcore insurgents," with about 800 in the FPL, 600 in FARN, and several hundred in the ERP (USDS/NSA2 1979b).

Unification of the revolutionary left was a necessity, but the process was difficult. After a series of steps, the Frente Farabundo Martí para la Liberación Nacional (FMLN) was formed in October 1980, but it was not until after Carpio's suicide in April 1983 that more effective integration was possible.[33] Throughout, the role of Cuba was critical. If Castro's immense stature were not sufficient, the support that Cuba (and the rest of the communist world) could offer was.[34] With unification came the arms that the revolutionary organizations desperately needed – one former FPL leader estimated that only one-fifth of its forces were armed in 1980 (Prisk 1991, 26). According to the memoir of one former ERP leader, shipments from Nicaragua across the Gulf of Fonseca was the major source of FMLN arms in the early 1980s (Raudales and Medrano 1994, 159–161).[35] In addition,

---

[32] For a near miss on a similar violent struggle within the FARN itself in the 1980s, see Macías (1996, 304–310).

[33] The only FMLN leader from a working-class background, firmer in his Marxist-Leninist doctrine, the head of the largest constituent organization, older than the rest, and with many more years of dedication to the revolutionary struggle behind him, Carpio believed that he should lead the FMLN with others deferring to his strategic decisions. It was when Mélida Anaya Montes, his long-time number two in the FPL, sided with others in the organizational debate within the FMLN that he covertly had her killed in Managua in April 1983 and then shortly thereafter committed suicide when the truth was discovered. Perhaps because of his role in these events and his rigidity in his dealings with other revolutionary leaders, accounts of the Salvadoran left sometimes fail to give him the credit he is due for advancing the revolutionary cause so effectively for so many years.

[34] Romero García, for one, maintains that without Castro, unification was unlikely, especially because of the reluctance of Carpio (Prisk 1991, 23).

[35] How important this support was to the viability of the FMLN is an important controversy not to be settled here. Prisk maintains a position close to that of the Reagan administration: "Given the admittedly poor internal support given to the guerrillas by the Salvadoran people, the ability to achieve this level of warfare is remarkable. . . . [it] can only be explained in terms of the great amounts of external support enjoyed by the FDR/FMLN" (Prisk 1991, 35). The Frente Democrático Revolucionario (FDR) entered into alliance with the FMLN in January 1981; for further discussion, see Chapter 10. Also see Bracamonte and Spencer

there was "the provisions of sanctuary, diplomatic and public relations support, communications, funds, and training" (Corr 1991, xvii).[36]

Revolutionary challengers might not need external assistance when the coercive capacity of the state is low. However, in a situation like El Salvador, where the armed forces remained cohesive, penetrated the country's territory, and had significant international backing, then the importance of substantial and stable international support for the revolutionary forces was critical. But dependence has its drawbacks. As the Reagan administration made its threat to the Nicaraguan revolution credible in the early 1980s, the governing Sandinistas understandably placed priority on preserving their gains and at times cut back on arms deliveries to El Salvador. Castro is generally portrayed as having been more committed to protecting the Nicaraguan revolution than he was to the success of the Salvadoran revolutionaries and as a consequence international support was not predictable, unlike the abundant support of the United States for the Salvadoran government (Prisk 1991, 82, 110).[37]

This needed support from Cuba and Nicaragua also had a price in terms of the struggles over strategy within the FMLN. The FPL believed in the necessity of the long, patient organizing work among the masses of the prolonged popular war strategy. The ERP especially, but also in contrast the FARN and PRTC, believed in the viability of creating an insurrectional situation over a shorter time frame. This latter approach dominated in the FMLN over FPL opposition, leading to the failed insurrections of the "final offensive" of January 1981 and during the March 1982 elections. The short-term insurrectional strategy of the early 1980s was favored by the Cubans and Nicaraguans, based on their interpretations of their own revolutionary triumphs. And they used the leverage of their essential support to influence the outcome of the strategic debate within the FMLN.[38]

1995. In contrast, see Montgomery (1995, 117–118). For a critical review of the position of the Reagan administration, see LeoGrande (1998, 68–69, 86–89). The U.S. embassy in El Salvador characterized Cuban support as "minimal" up to early 1979, at which point it noted growing assistance (USDS/NSA2 1979b).

[36] Edwin G. Corr was the U.S. ambassador to El Salvador in the mid-1980s. In his view, these sources of support were "More important than [the] provisions of arms" (Corr 1991, xvii). The CIA estimated in May 1980 that "more than 500 Salvadoran leftists . . . received training in Cuba since later 1978" (USDS/NSA2 1980b, 7).

[37] For a good discussion of the important role of international support groups for the Zapatista movement in Mexico, see Schulz 1998.

[38] See, for example, Prisk (1991, 22–41). The important point here is the impact of Cuba and Nicaragua, not which strategy was the wiser. Former FPL leader (and after his capture,

Throughout the 1970s, the revolutionary organizations carried out armed activities, but only intermittently until 1979. During the early years, their major violent actions were bombings as well as kidnappings of the wealthy in order to build a war chest through ransoms – the U.S. government estimated that they secured $30 million in ransom in 1977–78 and another $40 million in just 1979 (USDS/NSA2 1979b, 1980a). In addition, revolutionaries killed at least twenty-four security personnel between 1972 and the middle of 1977, along with another eighteen paramilitary personnel. All forms of violent revolutionary activity increased at the end of the decade with fifty-eight security personnel and seventy-four paramilitary killed, as well as sixteen kidnappings during the almost twenty-eight months of the Gen. Carlos Romero dictatorship lasting until October 15, 1979 (López-Vallecillos 1979, 871). Certainly, the numbers of innocent civilians killed by the two military governments beginning in 1972 totaled far more (as will be detailed in Chapter 8), which was in some measure the justification for this revolutionary violence.

At the same time, revolutionaries understood that kidnapping (and sometimes killing) the economic elite and murdering security personnel would provoke regime violence. Provoking repression was an intentional revolutionary strategy because it was believed that this would speed up the inevitable polarization that was necessary for successful revolution.[39] Among some of their major actions during this period, were the following:

- In April 1977, the Foreign Minister was kidnapped by the FPL as a "prisoner of war" and held in a "revolutionary jail as a prisoner of the people." As their announcement declared: "Revolution or Death! The armed people will triumph!"[40]
- In January 1977, a businessman was kidnapped by the ERP and later killed.

the highest ranking FMLN defector) Romero García holds the external supporters most responsible for the failures of the FMLN, claiming "The Cubans and the Sandinistas possessed by a triumphal euphoria, transmitted it to . . . and incited the FMLN. And the FMLN believed it" (quoted in Prisk 1991, 40). Romero García found the strategic training and advice of the North Vietnamese much more suited to the Salvadoran reality (pp. 28–29, 42–45, 61–67). In contrast, Lungo Unclés 1996 highlights the conditions in El Salvador that mitigated against a prolonged war strategy and the converse advantages of seizing insurrectional opportunities; also see the comments of ERP leader Joaquín Villalobos (Harnecker 1984, 175–179).

[39] As one example, see NY Times (Oct. 31, 1979, 3).

[40] Author's translation ECA (#342, 321). All events listed here are from the author's events database.

- In September 1977, the Rector of the University of El Salvador was killed by the FPL, along with two others.
- During the month of December 1978, the FARN kidnapped three people, eventually killing one of them.
- In February 1979, an ERP bomb killed fourteen police, and two by-standers, and injured twenty others.
- In May 1979, a Swiss diplomat was killed in a kidnapping attempt. The same day a businessman was kidnapped.
- In May 1979, the FPL killed the Minister of Education along with one other person.
- In June 1979, the FPL murdered two, including the mayor of Santa Tecla.
- In September 1979, the brother of President Romero was murdered by the FPL, injuring the brother's daughter as well.
- In September, 1979 the PRTC kidnapped two U.S. businessman, slaying their Salvadoran companion.

That each of these actions would provoke economic and political elites was clear. Should there have been any doubt, President Molina made it explicit following the May 1977 kidnapping of yet another elite figure and friend with a strong condemnation of leftist terrorism and promise of effective response (ECA #342, 327–330).

Contentious Mass Organizations

Rather than using violence, though, revolutionary groups during the 1970s paid more attention to developing mass organizations that could operate aboveground legally, enlisting the participation of protesters who were not yet prepared to embrace armed struggle. Through this participation, it was expected, many would be radicalized, and eventually a number of those might become revolutionary militants themselves.

Few aspects of Salvadoran politics during the 1970s and 1980s were more controversial than the possible links between the covert armed revolutionary groups and the aboveground multisector "popular organizations" (as they were commonly referred to) that were central to the contentious political activities in El Salvador during the years leading up to the civil war.[41] Much still remains to be known, but the available evidence indicates

---

[41] Good additional sources on the mass popular organizations beyond those cited below are Baloyra 1982; Lungo Unclés 1996; Montgomery 1995; and Zaid 1982.

tighter relationships than often portrayed. When a government is torturing and murdering citizens falsely accused of being subversives, it is hard to grant legitimacy to any of the government's claims about links between armed revolutionary and nonviolent protest organizations. Furthermore, substantiating any of those claims could contribute to the regime's murderous policies.[42] The analyst's dilemma, though, fades in peacetime.[43]

Origins and Organizational Links   Detailing the link between the covert and overt organizations is complicated by more than lack of information. Because there were five covert armed movements by the end of the 1970s, most desiring their ownabove ground movement, the number of organizations is challenging to track. Furthermore, the biggest popular organizations were fronts made up of a number of individual groups from different sectors. Finally, gaining affiliation of the most important of the individual groups was an object of rivalry between the covert revolutionary organizations.

Three mass organizations formed between 1974 and 1978. The first was the Frente de Acción Popular Unificada (FAPU), which appeared in spring 1974. A broad coalition centered around the Federación Cristiana de Campesinos Salvadoreños (FECCAS), it united these peasants with urban groups, including students, trade unions, teachers (ANDES), the communist party, and religious workers.[44] The idea for FAPU was born at a march held by these groups in Suchitoto on May 1, 1974, with the organization activated on June 21. The next mass organization to form was the Bloque Popular Revolucionario (BPR) in 1975, followed by the Ligas Populares 28 de Febrero (LP-28) in 1978.

The relationship between these three aboveground movements to the covert revolutionary organizations varied. LP-28 clearly was formed by the ERP. In contrast, the revolutionary dissidents who split from the ERP in 1975 to form the FARN largely came out of the aboveground FAPU (Cabarrús 1983a, 110), yet the year before as part of ERP they had played a

---

[42] As Americas Watch (1990, 170) warned concerning U.S. government labeling civilian groups as FMLN fronts when mass contention returned in the last half of the 1980s, "Placing the imprimatur of the U.S. government behind labels that are not supported by due process determinations, and which can cost persons their lives, is intolerable."

[43] To downplay this link is also to deny to the revolutionary organizations recognition of their strategic successes, especially the FPL.

[44] There were earlier antecedent organizations, such as the Frente Nacional de Orientación Cívica (FNOC), which brought together political parties with labor and student groups in early 1960.

covert role in promoting FAPU's formation (Montgomery 1995, 104). The connection between the FPL and BPR is also complex. Because it is also the most significant relationship – not only was the FPL the most important armed revolutionary organization, the BPR was by far the most important of the popular organizations – it needs to be discussed more fully.

The BPR presented itself as formed during the National Cathedral occupation following the July 30, 1975 massacre of the largely student marchers at the time of the Miss Universe pageant. The BPR also presented itself as an autonomous movement, uniting individual groups that still retained their individual identities and purposes (ANDES, UR-19, FECCAS, UTC, AES, UPT, and CCS) for common contentious actions.[45] Certainly, it often has been written about in this way.[46] But, although early August is when the BPR emerged before the public, its formation apparently already had been underway.

From its beginning, the FPL was committed to a patient strategy of creating and cooptingabove ground popular groups. Indeed, according to Carpio, the original seven FPL members were each charged with developing fifteen collaborators who could carry out the necessary organizing among the masses (Harnecker 1990a, 218). Former FPL leader Napoleón Romero García maintains that sometime in 1974 the FPL decided that it needed to increase its direct work with the masses, with the objective of creating organizations more "combative" than, for example, the "pacifist, economist" orientation of the PCS (Prisk 1991, 10). By late 1974, Mélida Anaya Montes, the head of the teachers' union (ANDES) and a member of the PCS since the 1960s, had entered covertly into the top ranks of the FPL leadership, according to FPL leaders interviewed years later by Harnecker (1993, 124). Remaining as secretary-general of ANDES, Montes was central to the organization of the BPR. A "charismatic, well-loved leader" (Romero García quoted in Prisk 1991, 49), she served as a pivotal link between the FPL and the BPR (e.g., McClintock 1998, 257), while ANDES served as a "nursery" for guerrillas (Harnecker 1993, 38–41). Facundo Guardado, both the BRP's secretary-general and a covert FPL

[45] Harnecker (1993, 135), LPG (Aug. 7, 1975, 3). For background to the rest of this paragraph, also see Carrabús (1983a, 110). Each of these groups is discussed in the paragraphs that follow, with the exception of the two least important, Unión de Pueblo de Tugurios (UPT) and Comité Coordinación de Sindicatos (CCS).

[46] Even the CIA was fooled. A 1980 assessment refers to the FPL's "gradual takeover" of the BPR, adding that "outright takeover of the BPR became a well-defined and attainable FPL objective" in 1978 (USDS/NSA2 1980a, 2).

leader, portrays ANDES as the most "combative" of the mass organizations in the early 1970s and as playing a significant ("importantisimo") role in organizing peasants and secondary students (Harnecker 1990a, 228).

Certainly, student groups were important to the BPR and the FPL. The Asociación General de Estudiantes Universitarios Salvadoreños (AGEUS) was the key student organization at the University of El Salvador. It also came under FPL control. According to Romero García, he was recruited by the FPL in 1975 from one of the study circles it covertly conducted at the university. He was given the task of developing a new student organization, which was formed as the Universitarios Revolucionarios 19 de Julio (UR-19). UR-19 gave the revolutionaries a vehicle for activities on campus, including running candidates in AGEUS elections. Some time prior to 1977, covert FPL member Medardo González Trejo (alias "Milton") was elected the head of AGEUS, with Romero García serving as his political adviser.[47] Their approach (as with the other mass organizations) was good standard organizing technique: "The first thing was to attract the masses by means of their immediate interests, the economic necessities, their platforms for recovery of their rights.... We sought to touch each person with his personal problem and mobilize him until we brought him over to our side" (quoted in Prisk 1999, 12–13). Their concern was less with ideological debate (unlike the PCS) and more on developing the "combativeness" of students.[48]

Secondary students were especially important to the BPR, being second in numbers and combativeness only to the peasants in the BPR's contentious actions (Harnecker 1993, 127, 139). The Asociación de Estudiantes de Secundaria (AES) was reactivated in 1974, and during the next year it came under FPL "control" (p. 139).

Perhaps most important to the success of the BPR, though, was the peasant group FECCAS. For some time, the FPL had been working to break away from the Christian-inspired FAPU, which was accomplished by early 1975. In areas of the country where FECCAS was weak, during this same period the Unión de Trabajadores del Campo (UTC) was organized (especially in the departments of Chalatenango, San Vicente, and Usulatán),

---

[47] Like Romero García, González was to rise to the top ranks of the FPL and FMLN leadership. See Prisk (1991, 8–19).

[48] Around 1977, Romero García was taken out of overt leadership at the university by the FPL, but he claims that "I was clandestinely to direct the student movement through the cells" until 1979 (quoted in Prisk 1991, 14).

with assistance from church workers certainly, but also from ANDES and the FPL, eventually bringing it under FPL leadership.[49]

The FPL was less successful organizing among workers directly.[50] Instead, it fared better with Comités Populares at the neighborhood level, where workers felt less at risk than at the workplace (Harnecker 1993, 146–149).[51]

At the individual level, organizational relationships, varied. Importantly, all FPL members had a BPR affiliation, and among the leadership of the various constituent groups the FPL connection was tight. According to a CIA report of May 1979, "Each of the member organizations within the BPR is directed by a leadership primarily composed of FPL members. Those who do not follow FPL guidance and direction are replaced" (USDS/NSA2 1979a).[52] Outside of the leadership, some BPR members were active in both a constituent group (e.g., ANDES) and the FPL. Others had no direct connection to the FPL personally but were aware of some linkage. Others undoubtedly did not.

Furthermore, each constituent BPR group also had a "self-defense" unit that was intended to defend participants in contentious activities from state violence. In addition, the militias had the second purpose of elevating combativeness and creating insurrectional situations. At the end of the 1970s, these units were developing into militias as the next stage in preparing the masses for armed struggle. The next stage would be incorporation into a guerrilla army.[53]

Along with their connections to the armed revolutionary organizations, the ideological orientation of the mass organizations also has been presented

---

[49] Harnecker (1993, 126–127); Prisk (1991, 17).

[50] Its key organization here was the Federación Sindical Revolucionaria (FSR).

[51] Campos 1979, the first study of the mass organizations, is strongly sympathetic to mass organizations like the BPR but highly critical of their subordination to the violent revolutionary organizations. The popular organizations, Campos writes, are "organically linked" with the revolutionary organizations and Marxist-Leninist in inspiration, not only in analysis but also in organization (Campos 1979, 924). For a related criticism concerning the peasant movements of the time by another sympathetic observer, see ECA (1987, 418–419). Similarly, in 1980 Alan Riding wrote in the *New York Times*: "By 1975 . . . the Popular Forces of Liberation's infiltration of labor and peasant groups began to pay off and a more open political mobilization began with the creation of a militant grassroots coalition called the Popular Revolutionary Bloc" (NY Times Feb. 29, 1980, 10). For a critical view of the ideological and strategic rigidity of the BPR, see Cardenal (1987, 455–456).

[52] At least by the time of this report, the CIA was aware that BPR Secretary-General Guardado was a key FPL leader.

[53] Harnecker (1993, 171–173); Leiken (1984, 117).

in contradictory fashion in the literature. Having mass memberships, individual ideological positions could be found from the center of the spectrum to the radical left. Few of their members would have had well-developed ideologies, especially among the thousands of peasant activists and secondary-level students. But the leadership was ideologically driven. Salvadoran observers sympathetic to the mass organizations characterized them in the late 1970s as Marxist-Leninist (Campos 1979) or, more specifically, the BPR and LP-28 as Marxist-Leninist but FAPU as Marxist with Leninist tendencies, and with all three calling for the establishment of a revolutionary socialist government.[54]

Contentious Activities   Despite confusions that there might have been about the identity of the popular organizations, there has been no doubt about four important facts. First, these mass organizations led Salvadoran contentious activities throughout the second half of the 1970s. From about 17,000 members in early 1978, the BPR grew to 30,000 a year later and going into 1980 had anywhere from 60,000 to 80,000 members. Estimates for the total between the three popular organizations at this time ranged from 80,000 to 100,000.[55] Second, BPR activists were noted for their high level of motivation, for their idealism, and for their willingness to sacrifice (e.g., Campos 1979, 925). Third, mass organization activists were in the front ranks of the victims of the Salvadoran repression, murdered intermittently during the late 1970s and then by the thousands in both 1980 and 1981. Fourth, relatively few of these activists had ever committed an act of political violence against other people – they were innocent victims of state terrorism.

The contentious repertoire of the mass organizations was varied. Certainly, many marches and demonstrations were held, some without incident but many with casualties. The capital was a frequent location, but they also

---

[54] As an example of the confused presentation of the BPR's ideology, the *New York Times* correspondent in El Salvador in the late 1970s, Alan Riding, got it right, characterizing the BPR as, "although practicing nonviolence, [it] has accepted armed struggle as the main instrument for revolution and is believed to be close to the" FPL (NY Times May 27, 1979 s. iv, 3). However, an unsigned dispatch in the *New York Times* that September characterized the BPR as "moderate" with "no affiliation with guerrilla groups" (Sept. 22, 1979, 4).

[55] Citing the U.S. State Department, Campos gives 1979 membership in FAPU at 8,000 to 15,000 and in LP-28, 5,000 (Campos 1979, 924). Similar figures are found in USDS/NSA2 1979b, with the BPR at more than 60,000. The *New York Times* in early 1980 gives a combined total of 100,000 (Feb. 29, 1980, 10). For the earlier estimates, see NY Times (May 3, 1978, 5; May 27, 1979 s. iv, 3).

were held in other cities, drawing on local discontent. For example, a BPR march was held in Usulatán in September 1976 protesting the regime's limited agrarian reform proposal. Marchers were primarily local students along with peasants from the wider area. When police attempted to arrest two protestors, shooting broke out from both sides, leaving one protestor dead and two injured on both sides (Cardenal 1987, 514).

Another frequent tactic was to occupy buildings. Sometimes this was done to dramatize grievances; other times occupants were held as bargaining chips (and as protection from security forces) in negotiations with authorities. Usual targets were churches, government buildings, and foreign embassies. As examples, the BPR occupied the Ministry of Labor in November 1977 in support of collective bargaining at two textile factories, as well as on-going negotiations concerning a minimum wage increase. The following February, the BPR occupied a United Nations office, holding five occupants hostage, seeking the release of "political prisoners" (NY Times Feb. 4, 1978, 5). In April 1978, the BPR occupied both the cathedral and foreign embassies to call attention to the repression of peasants in Cuscatlán (Véjar 1979, 519).

Workers and peasants backed by the mass organizations also occupied factories and farm lands. Not only did the BPR actively support strikers, beginning in 1977 it successfully penetrated the more radical unions (as did its counterpart, FAPU, though with less success), orienting them away from the communist PCS and toward a broader economic and political agenda. The BPR also had considerable success with the leftist but noncommunist FENASTRAS. Tactics also became more militant, with increasing number of plant occupations, holding owners and managers for bargaining purposes and for protection. According to U.S. embassy reports, often participating in the occupations were nonworkers from other BPR affiliates. This was particularly true during the March 1979 wave of strikes that presented an "unprecedented display of labor union power" (USDS/NSA1 1979e). Many of these factory and farm occupations were broken up forcefully by authorities, often further radicalizing participants (USDS/NSA1 1979a, 1979b, 1979f; Véjar 1979, 516–518).

The intensity of the contentious activities of the popular organizations increased through the end of the 1970s, as did the repressive response of the state. But to most observers, the momentum was with the left. When Somoza fell in July in Nicaragua, the impact was dramatic on all factions – El Salvador looked like it would be next. Although many would not agree with the precise phrasing, few would disagree with the following characterization of this period by Edwin Corr, who was later to serve as the U.S. ambassador to El Salvador in the mid-1980s: "Mobs of the Popular Revolutionary Bloc (BPR) numbering 50,000 to 100,000 persons owned the streets. Ministries, factories, and large businesses were under siege; management was held hostage. Bombings began at dusk and continued through the night" (Prisk 1991, xvi).

On October 15, 1979, progressive junior military officers threw out the dictator. Reaching out to civilian counterparts, they hoped that with reform together they could stop the polarization and the violence. Instead of their hopes for civil peace, leaders of the new government found that the contention and violence of the 1970s was but a prelude to terrible tragedy. The right played a major role in sabotaging the new government's efforts. So, too, did the radical left. In addition to continuing their violent attacks, revolutionary leaders interviewed years later explained that they pursued a double-track policy during this period. First, they encouraged mass contentious activities to undermine the junta and bring about "more profound changes." Second, they played the contacts that they had within the new government. While trying to persuade their contacts of the necessity of a solution that included the left, they worked to split progressives in the government off from those to their right (Harnecker 1993, 212–213).

Conclusion

Individuals have interests and grievances. But to do something about them, they must draw together with others and organize. Organization usually begins around immediate interests. Teachers organize as teachers, students as students, labor as labor. In affluent, well-institutionalized democracies with their interest aggregating political parties, this level of organization often suffices. But in countries like El Salvador, activists have argued that existing socioeconomic structures are so biased against the vast popular majority that neither can specific group interests be secured nor can their shared interest in the institutionalization of a fair and free political system be accomplished without a higher order of organization.

This argument resonated well with the experience of many popular activists in El Salvador. National elections resulted in fraud. Strikes often were smashed and marches attacked by police. The university was subject to intervention and control taken away from its legitimately constituted authorities. Added on to a whole array of intense socioeconomic grievances, then, were additional sociopolitical grievances. Consequently, broad multisector popular organizations were developed that brought a level of sustained non-violent contentious activity to El Salvador during the late 1970s seldom matched elsewhere in the region.

The level of grievances in a population does not in itself explain the emergence of contentious movements. Instead, we must examine the dynamics highlighted by the resource mobilization literature – incorporated here into the configuration of political opportunities as the importance of allies and support groups to popular organization. The previously inactive are usually mobilized by activists advocating the individual's specific interests. The organization of individual groups themselves is often supported by others, such as the role of the Partido Comunista de El Salvador (PCS) in helping labor to organize in the 1960s, or the PCS and the new revolutionary organizations such as the Fuerzas Populares de Liberación (FPL) promoting secondary and university student organization in the 1970s.

The broad popular organizations that drove the Salvadoran protest cycle of the late 1970s and on into 1980 were not based on aggregating previously inactive individuals. Instead, they drew together already existing groups and their already active memberships into something new. The formation of the popular organizations themselves was facilitated by other allies and support groups. The birth of the first of these organizations, the Frente de Acción Popular Unificada (FAPU) was promoted by church workers active in the region where it emerged. Crucial to the formation of the second and most important, the Bloque Popular Revolucionario (BPR), was the revolutionary FPL, albeit acting in covert fashion.

The contention of the popular organizations was met by increasing repression, including murder in growing numbers. For a period of time, this violence only heightened the intensity of the nonviolent contention. But eventually, the state violence was so indiscriminate that it closed all space for nonviolent political activity. Large numbers of radicalized activists enlisted in the guerrilla cause. It is a tidy story – and theoretical model – but reality, however, is more complex than this.

At least in the Salvadoran case, the distinction between social movements and revolutionary movements and between nonviolent protesters and violent revolutionary militants is blurred. An indeterminate number of the activists in the nonviolent popular movements of El Salvador in 1979 were already clandestine members of the revolutionary organizations. Consequently, it is inaccurate to claim when they picked up arms and went to the countryside to fight in 1980 that this group became revolutionaries because of the ferocious repression of that time. They already were revolutionaries.

95

Nor can we necessarily say that repression turned them to violence. Instead, it might have been the case that their assignment within the revolutionary organization was to work with nonviolent groups but that they were already prepared to take up arms as, for example, urban commandos.

There was a second group of movement activists who were not themselves revolutionary militants but who knew something of the ties between the two sets of organizations, some of whom were perhaps sympathetic to the guerrillas and perhaps moving toward joining even prior to the onset of indiscriminate state terrorism. A third group (probably the majority), in contrast, were not members of the revolutionary organizations nor necessarily partial toward them prior to the rapid escalation of violence against protesters but instead were struggling primarily for the cause of their own organization (for example, many peasants). As an additional complication, even though not revolutionary in ideology or affiliation, tactically members of this third group could have been among the most contentious in behavior prior to 1980 and with the least normative constraints against the use of violence.

These distinctions are important to the protest-repression paradox. When state violence escalated in El Salvador in 1980, thousands of activists joined the guerrilla cause. But most (surviving) members of the popular organizations did not. Which were the ones most likely to take up arms? Which were the most likely to remain dedicated to the revolutionary cause when victory proved not to be imminent? A first hunch might be that the probabilities would be in the order of the three groups just discussed. But further complexities will be added in the chapters that follow.

4

The Emergence of Urban Contentious Movements

GUATEMALA

Contentious movements in Guatemala following the 1944 overthrow of dictator Jorge Ubico followed a path quite different from that in El Salvador. The mobilization of popular groups in El Salvador was slow and intermittent, but fairly steady across the decades until largely destroyed by heavy repression in 1980. In Guatemala, by contrast, there was an explosion of popular organizing during the reformist decade from 1944 to 1954, followed by several cycles of demobilization of protesters under the barrage of increasing repression and then reemergence of contentious movements when repression slackened. Through the years, the memories of the strong popular organizations that thrived during the reform period, especially during the early 1950s, sustained and inspired Guatemalan activists.

Memories of the reform period, the organizing experience gained during that time, and the strong emotions engendered from having had their just cause frustrated – and by the intervention of an overbearing powerful external force no less – all facilitated popular organizing in Guatemala compared to El Salvador. However, the United States, in alliance with domestic forces, overthrew Jacobo Arbenz largely because of their shared fears about the growing influence of communism in the country and its party, the Partido Guatemalteco del Trabajo (PGT). Ties to the Arbenz past were a mixed blessing for popular movements in post-"liberation" Guatemala, then, because the preeminent concern of the domestic right and the U.S. government in Guatemala during the Cold War was to prevent any return of communist influence.

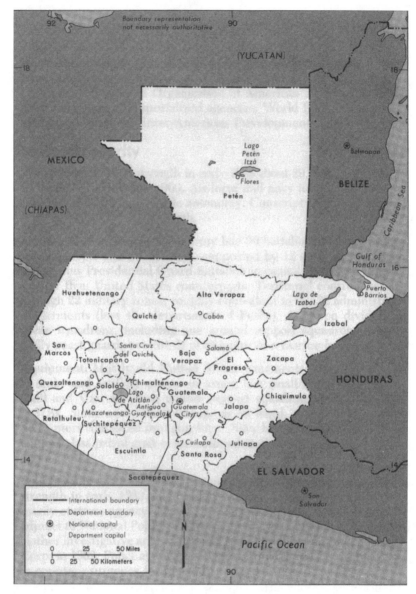

Map 4.1 Guatemala, Richard A. Haggerty, ed., *Guatemala: A Country Study*, Washington, DC: United States Government Printing Office, 1990.

Revolutionary Organizations I: The 1960s

Having eliminated the Arbenz regime on June 27, 1954, the aim of the United States was now to liberate Guatemala from communism: All communists needed to be found, tried if possible for criminal acts – possibly even on the charge "of having been [a] covert Moscow agent" (USDS 1954c) – and removed from Guatemala. Unfortunately, from the U.S. perspective, most of the leaders of the left immediately escaped from the country or gained refuge in foreign diplomatic missions. Altogether, about 770 Guatemalans (and some foreign supporters like Ché Guevara) took diplomatic asylum.

Before the 1950s were over, however, members of the left – including the radical left – were returning to Guatemala (see Chapter 7). The small remnant membership of the communist PGT had gone underground, taking refuge especially at the national university (San Carlos) and then in the labor movement as it reemerged. Frustrated by the domestic situation and inspired by the example of the Cuban Revolution, in 1960 the PGT accepted the legitimacy of armed struggle, though not then taking the lead itself. Instead, some party members journeyed to Cuba for military training in 1962, joined by members of its youth affiliate, the Juventud Patriótica del Trabajo (JPT), who were already in Cuba on educational scholarships.[1] The initiation of three and a half decades of intermittent armed guerrilla struggle, though, was to come from a very different institution.[2]

On November 13, 1960, some 30 percent of the Guatemalan army rose up in an effort to depose the duly elected president, General Miguel Ydígoras. Their grievances were varied, including dismay that their country was being used as the staging area preparing for the U.S.-led counterrevolutionary Bay of Pigs invasion of Cuba that would occur in April 1961. Although the uprising was put down, some of the instigators regrouped the following year. They took their first violent action at the beginning of 1962 as Guatemala's first (very small) guerrilla band, the Movimiento Revolucionario 13 de Noviembre (MR-13). In March 1962, they were very briefly

---

[1] The major source for this section is CEH (1999 1:122–147; 2:238–241; 6:89–98). Also see Aguilera Peralta and Romero Imery 1981; Gilly 1965; Gott 1972; Jonas (1991, 57–72); Kobrak 1999; REMHI (1999, 190–194, 201–203); and Wickham-Crowley 1992, as well as participant accounts by Macías 1998 and Ramírez 2001 and interviews in Harnecker 1984.

[2] The frequent characterization of three decades of "civil war" in Guatemala greatly distorts the reality of the 1960s and 1970s, especially with its implication of the existence of a strong armed challenge to the state throughout the period.

joined by a PGT-sponsored effort (the Movimiento 20 de Octubre), but it was quickly destroyed by the military in its first action.

In December 1962, the PGT proposed that the various groups prepared for armed struggle draw together. Out of this emerged the Fuerzas Armadas Rebeldes (FAR), which then carried on the insurgency of the 1960s. Essentially, this meant the PGT supplying political direction, resources, and recruits, and the MR-13 leaders implementing the military campaign. In 1963, FAR fronts were opened in the eastern departments of Zacapa and Izabal. Some successful military actions were taken, and some limited support was built among the peasants of the region. This led some militants and observers to believe that the FAR was a serious threat to the regime.[3] Instead, these gains had been permitted inadvertently by an ineffectual counterinsurgency effort. Once the rural insurgency was taken seriously by the Guatemalan military and its U.S. advisers, it was destroyed in little time. So, too, were the lives of countless thousands of innocent victims living in the counterinsurgency zones.

If they could, FAR militants slipped back to the capital (mainly those who came from urban areas to begin with). There, repression already had begun in seriousness, ironically simultaneously with a PGT decision to support the elections of 1966. Over the four months through March of 1966 and culminating early in that month, thirty-three leaders and activists from the radical left were kidnapped never to reappear (another twenty-one were arrested and later released). This was Latin America's first case of massive disappearances as an instrument of state terrorism. The dead included the leaders of the large peasant and labor confederations of the Arbenz period, one of whom was at this point the secretary-general of the PGT.[4]

---

[3] There is very little in the way of thorough firsthand accounts written of Guatemala's rural insurgency of the 1960s. The major one is Gilly 1965, a sympathetic account written near the peak of the guerrillas' strength. This is perhaps why even very good secondary accounts (e.g., Wickham-Crowley 1992) overstate the level of threat the guerrillas posed to the Guatemalan system. For a participant account, see Macías 1996, which is the story of "César Montes," one of the top guerrilla leaders of the period.

[4] They were Leonardo Castillo Flores of the Confederación Nacional Campesina de Guatemala (CNCG) and Victor Manuel Gutiérrez of the Confederación General de Trabajadores de Guatemala (CGTG). Evidence gathered by the Guatemalan truth commission shows that the victims were tortured and interrogated before their executions, all of which was known by the U.S. government at the time (CEH, 1999 6:97). The Guatemalan government, though, maintained its innocence before an assertive inquiry pushed by university students and the press, claiming it had no knowledge of the whereabouts of the missing. FAR's top two leaders were in the capital at the time of the March kidnappings and barely escaped through a firefight. One of them maintains that it was a disgruntled PGT

At the beginning of 1968 the PGT and FAR split (the MR-13 had earlier), with the PGT forming its own guerrilla arm, also using the FAR initials.[5] Both FARs pursued their urban insurgency, relying on selective assassinations, kidnappings, robberies, and bombings into the 1970s.[6] Incubating the revolution, these few PGT and FAR militants were instrumental in launching the much more significant revolutionary movements of the late 1970s/early 1980s, an account of which is better postponed until later in this chapter. Meanwhile, other members of the PGT focused instead on building a mass social movement, especially members of the party's central committee, that was also the element of the party most influential at the University of San Carlos (Kobrak 1999, 40). As with El Salvador, a crucial question then and now is the connections between these efforts and the social movements that were to emerge in Guatemala in the 1970s and then the relationships between these movements and the explosion of revolutionary activity in the early 1980s.

Guatemalan Students and Political Contention

Students have been critical actors in Guatemalan contentious politics going back decades. Indeed, Kobrak claims students at the University of San Carlos have "served as the 'democratic conscience' of the country" (Kobrak 1999, 5). Students catalyzed the popular movements in 1944 that led to the fall of dictator Jorge Ubico and then, within months, to the fall of his successor in the "October Revolution" that initiated ten years of progressive government. A quarter of a century later, those who followed the heroes

member who tipped off the U.S. embassy as to the left's safe houses (Macías 1998, 109–113).

[5] The PGT's new FAR was named the Fuerzas Armadas Revolucionarias.

[6] In addition to members of the Guatemalan economic elite, the assassinations included the ambassadors of the United States (August 1968) and Germany (spring 1970) and the head of the U.S. military mission (January 1968); kidnapped and later released was the U.S. labor attaché (March 1970). When the head of the U.S. military mission was questioned earlier by *Time magazine* about the use by the Guatemalan military of death squads that were killing peasants they considered guerrillas or "potential" guerrillas, Col. John Webber replied: "That's the way this country is. . . . The Communists are using everything they have, including terror. And it must be met" (*Time* 1968, 23). A few days before Webber's murder, "Miss Guatemala" of 1959 was kidnapped and killed. A U.S. embassy official observed that "many believe that the very brutal way the ex-beauty queen was killed, obviously tortured and mutilated, provoked the FAR to murder Colonel Webber in retaliation" (Wilkinson 2002, 324). It was also more personal. Rogelia Cruz Martínez was avenged by her boyfriend, Leonardo Castillo Johnson, whose father (Leonardo Castillo Flores) was one of the major victims of the 1966 disappearances (Macías 1998, 88–89, 122; Wilkinson 2002, 220–228).

of 1944 were in the forefront of similar efforts to bring down a military regime that they saw as equally illegitimate.

After the counterrevolution in 1954, students led demands for a restoration of constitutional liberties. They held marches and demonstrations asserting these liberties and were usually in the ranks of the victims of the repression that sometimes followed their protests. Even before the end of the first year of the new government of Colonel Carlos Castillo Armas, protesting students went on strike in June 1955 when police entered the Instituto de Señoritas Belén in Guatemala City to arrest a "communist" teacher. Their strike was soon joined by other schools in the capital and in Quetzaltenango, Guatemala's second largest city. The following year, the annual student Huelga de Dolores parade down the streets of the capital, traditionally used to satirize the pompous and the powerful, was defiantly used again just to that end in March 1956.[7]

The worst confrontation of the Castillo Armas period occurred a few months later, growing out of escalating conflicts between the government and students. The government banned demonstrations, but students marched anyway, with their demonstration of June 25, 1956 fired on by the police. Six were killed and dozens wounded. A state of siege was immediately declared, and the government reported 168 arrests, virtually all of them students.[8] Students went on strike and from this point on remained in opposition to the regime (ASIES 1995, 3:85). The victims were remembered in demonstrations on this date for years to come as martyrs to the cause for freedom.[9]

Castillo was assassinated in July 1957 and soon replaced through elections by General Manuel Ydígoras. A student-led movement almost brought Ydígoras down in 1962. Leadership of the 1962 movement, as in so many to come, was provided by the Asociación de Estudiantes Universitarios (AEU), which was formed back in an earlier contentious period in May 1920. However, as was seen in El Salvador, "public high school students filled the protest ranks and suffered much of the repression," then and as they would in the future (Kobrak 1999, 27). Especially important for mobilizing secondary school students was the Frente Unido Estudiantil Guatemalteco Organizado (FUEGO), which was formed in 1958.[10]

[7] ASIES (1995, 3:80–85); USDS 1956c.

[8] EIA (June 26, 1956); *NY Times* (June 29, 1956, 5); USDS 1956a; Kobrak (1999, 22).

[9] Establishing responsibility now for this key event is difficult; see the discussion in Chapter 7.

[10] FUEGO is a Spanish acronym for "fire." For a participant account, see Ramírez (2001, 69–103).

The contentious campaign of the winter and spring of 1962 was the most significant to unfold in Guatemala between 1954 and the late 1970s. It began with charges against the government of irregularities in the congressional elections of December 1961. After a series of protest demonstrations led largely by opposition political parties, contention died down, especially after the arrests of many participants. Then on March 1, the day when the new Congress was inaugurated, the AEU protested at the legislative building, holding a strike for the day. The protest expanded across the following days, exploding on March 13. Both university and secondary students went on strike for the day, taking to the streets and stopping much of the capital's traffic (especially activists from FUEGO). Contentious activities continued intensely for at least another week and intermittently through May 1. Ydígoras survived by bringing the military into the street fighting and then into his cabinet as well.[11]

Unsuccessful in bringing down Ydígoras directly, nonetheless the campaign was an important experience for the AEU. In particular, with the connections that it established with labor groups, the AEU "now constituted an institutional base for a social movement" (Kobrak 1999, 32). Some connections with the guerrilla organizations just now forming probably were also made. Certainly the revolutionaries played some role in heightening the intensity of the confrontation between challengers and the state (Ramírez 2001, 118), although it is impossible to determine to what extent. Secondary and university students also were important recruits into the new revolutionary movements. Second in command of the PGT's 20th of October Front, for example, was a past president of the AEU (1958–1959). When the Front was soon decimated in mid-March 1962, during a confrontation with the army in Baja Verapaz, among the dead were three FUEGO secondary students and two university students.[12]

However, the following years were not a propitious time for contentious movements. Their challenge to the regime was the major instigator of a coup on March 30, 1963 that initiated three years of direct military rule,

---

[11] IMP54 (Dec. 12, 1961; Dec. 14, 1961); IMP43 (Mar. 9, 1962; Mar. 13, 1962; Mar. 14, 1962); Kobrak (1999, 25–33); ASIES (1995 3:220).

[12] Also captured was Rodrigo Asturias, who was later released. A university student at the time, he later would become commander of the Organización del Pueblo in Armas (ORPA), one of the two main guerrilla movements of the 1980s, under the alias of Gaspar Ilom. Son of Guatemala's Nobel Prize–winning author Miguel Angel Asturias, he also was fortunate to have President Ydígoras as a godfather (Kobrak 1999, 30; also see CEH [1999, 1:125]; REMHI [1999, 192]).

with the country under state-of-siege restrictions almost continuously until the end of 1970. More than any other organization, it was the AEU that tried to maintain at least some visible presence during this period in what should have been the public arena. Chief among its public activities were marches on days of symbolic importance, such as the anniversary of the October 20 Revolution (e.g., in 1964, 1965, and 1967). These marches invariably occurred under heavy police vigilance, and sometimes they were called off because of significant threats of violence, such as a parade in 1970 to commemorate the dead of 1956 as part of a more general call for an end to repression. The AEU also joined with labor in February 1969 in sponsoring a rally protesting the high cost of living.[13]

Given the repressive climate after 1963, the AEU often turned to non-contentious political activities. In particular, it became one of the leading advocates in the country for human rights through institutional – but still bold – activities. Following the large mass disappearance in 1966, the AEU went to the Supreme Court, filing a legal request to have their whereabouts determined, the first time this measure ever had been attempted. The AEU also took the evidence it had gathered to a congressional commission that was supposed to investigate the case. In a remarkably brave effort, the following year the AEU not only investigated charges of torture, murder, and disappearances in the eastern region of the country but also issued a report listing the names of those its investigation held responsible for the crimes.[14]

The repression in Guatemala during the 1960s, especially as it hit the capital hard in the later part of the decade, radicalized political activists, especially at universities. Reinforcing this effect was the international trend, as noted earlier for El Salvador, such as the events in France and Mexico. A further important factor is what might be called the "ecological dimension."[15] The public university at San Carlos had been growing steadily across the years. In 1943, it had only 711 students; in 1954, 8,000; (Kobrak 1999, 13). In the early 1970s, most of its various divisions that had been

---

[13] IMP60 (Oct. 16, 1964; Oct. 21, 1965); IMP61 (Mar. 24, 1966); IMP46 (Oct. 21, 1967); IMP63 (June 24, 1970); ASIES (1995, 3:307).

[14] IMP65 (Mar. 23, 1966; Apr. 24, 1966; July 15, 1966).

[15] Zhao stresses what he terms the "ecological" dimension in his explanation of university student mobilization in China in 1989. For example, he highlights the importance of a walled-in campus where students could march inside their safe campus first before venturing out: "By marching and shouting, not only did they attract more and more students but they also created an atmosphere of excitement and heightened the pitch of their anger. Finally, they built up enough courage to march out. Although full of anger, students felt deadly afraid once on the street" (Zhao 1998, 1517). More generally, see Sewell, Jr. 2001.

scattered around downtown were moved and concentrated on a main campus further away from the city's center.[16] Concentration not only created a larger mass of students, faculty, and other staff, but also created a much larger campus area enjoying protection through the Latin American tradition of university autonomy. The importance of this ecological dimension to the contentious movements of the 1970s would be hard to exaggerate as San Carlos came to be known as the "liberated territory of Guatemala." As Kobrak adds, "It was the only space beyond the control and jurisdiction of state authorities: a place where social movements could collect funds and distribute literature; where unions and other progressive groups could meet in relative security; and where those persecuted by the State could go for temporary exile" (Kobrak 1999, 15).

As repression and radicalization increased, so did the leftist presence at San Carlos. Radical students dominated the AEU through PODER[17] (Participación Organizada de Estudiantes Revolucionarios), radical faculty won elections controlling their various schools, and in 1970 students and faculty elected a new rector who some later claimed was a member of the PGT at that time. Certainly, the PGT had a strong presence on campus as the 1970s progressed, especially among faculty, including some high level administrators.[18] Still, during the early 1970s there was a major Christian Democratic group on campus, with its hopes focused on the 1974 national presidential election. Denied victory because of fraud, the result was much like El Salvador two years before: a growing conviction that peaceful channels for change were closed. The AEU did call for a general strike in response to the fraud, but to no avail.[19]

By the mid-1970s, the dominant student party at San Carlos was FRENTE.[20] Winning student elections in 1976, FRENTE and its successors controlled the AEU through 1985. Much of its leadership belonged to the Juventud Patriótica del Trabajo (JPT), the youth movement of the PGT. In the late 1970s, along with their allies in the faculty, students also elected leftist deans and the rector of the university. Staff connected to FRENTE and the PGT also won control of the university's employees' union (the Sindicato de Trabajadores de la Universidad de San Carlos,

---

[16] Kobrak (1999, 38).

[17] PODER is a Spanish acronym for "power."

[18] CEH (1999, 4:116); Kobrak (1999, 40).

[19] Various demonstrations were held, many were arrested, and some were killed, often students. IPV (Mar. 8, 1974, 313); IMP48 (Mar. 7, 1974).

[20] FRENTE is a Spanish acronym for "front."

STUSC). As an indicator of the campus mood of the time, it should be noted that FRENTE's leaders tended to be less radical and confrontational than student leaders earlier in the decade and certainly less than their major opponent on campus, the Frente Estudiantil Robin García (FERG) (Kobrak 1999, 54).

Robin García Dávila had participated in an underground youth group while still in middle school. In 1976, he joined the Ejército Guerrillero de los Pobres (EGP), one of the country's new guerrilla organizations, working with its unit devoted to the organization of high school students. Continuing his EGP work with secondary students after entering San Carlos, García and a companion were killed in July 1977. FERG was named in his honor as an EGP front formed in 1978 that united radical secondary and university students for contentious but essentially nonviolent struggle (though not excluding Molotov cocktails) on behalf of revolution.[21]

Throughout the 1970s, the AEU continued its active human rights work. For example, in March 1975 it began an important campaign concerning the plague of disappearances and the plight of the affected families. It announced that it would undertake a national census of the number of disappeared to document the magnitude of the tragedy. The following month, the AEU initiated a series of events related to the issue, such as roundtables and rallies. It also took the bold step of a newspaper message demanding explanation from the national police about why it was acting against the security of the country's people.[22] Large demonstrations also were resumed at mid-decade with the opening of political space occurring under a new presidential administration (see Chapter 7). The AEU held the decade's first mass protest off campus on June 25, 1976 in the capital's center in recognition of the twentieth anniversary of the 1956 killings of student protesters. But all too quickly, violence returned. The October 20th commemoration of 1978 ended in tragedy when AEU President Oliverio Castañeda de León was murdered. Marches of 5,000 and then 40,000 over the next few days

---

[21] Kobrak (1999, 49, 54). Concerning Robin García, Stoll notes, "Whether or not he worked with the Guerrilla Army of the Poor, as many presume, the organization named after him did. By 1980 FERG activists were in rebellion against not just the dictatorship but a university administration controlled by the local communist party" that "viewed the radical left as immature and self-destructive" and that "was holding back from the insurrection into which the EGP was plunging" (Stoll 1999, 84). More generally, Stoll adds: "By January 1980, in reaction to the Lucas terror, San Carlos was boiling with newly organized and poorly disciplined guerrilla cells, particularly in the faculties of psychology, sociology, and law" (Stoll 1999, 84).

[22] IPV (Mar. 14, 1975, 66; Apr. 17, 1975, 261; Apr. 21, 1975, 234).

did not prevent the disappearance two weeks later of his successor, Antonio Estuardo Ciani García.[23] Many thought the deaths were a direct response by the new regime of General Romeo Lucas García to the historic urban uprising of early October, which is discussed in Chapter 9.

Perhaps the most important activity of students, though, and one of far-reaching importance to the development of a broad-based contentious movement, was their involvement in outreach programs to the country's disadvantaged populations. In one school after another, progressive changes in the curriculum sent students out into slums and the countryside, both to learn about the country's reality as well as to provide essential services to those with little or none. One after another, medical and dentistry students in rural areas and law students working with poor urban populations had their own consciousness raised. Perhaps the oldest of the internship programs, San Carlos's Bufete Popular played a crucial role in both urban and rural labor struggles, providing legal and organizational expertise badly needed in these movements. At the same time, often this assistance was not neutral in nature. Many of the advisers had an ideological agenda broader and more radical than the immediate concerns for economic security that usually are the meat and potatoes of labor movements.

Re-creating the Guatemalan Labor Movement

Following the overthrow of Jacobo Arbenz in June 1954, a frontal attack on organized labor was justified by the new regime as necessary to protect workers from communism.[24] However, the major effect of actions such as dissolving the four union confederations in August 1954 was to remove workers' protection. Antilabor actions by both private employers and the government were widespread, including wage reductions and mass firings without the required separation pay. Workers who complained, the U.S. embassy noted at the time, were "denounced as Communists and jailed." In fact, the firings were often motivated less by political reasons than by "the desire for 'spoils' or a wish to extend reprisals to all individuals who served the Arbenz regime," even all the way down "to the porters and scrubwomen" (USDS 1954a). More tragically, although the number of labor activists killed

---

[23] Kobrak (1999, 59–61); CEH (1999, 6:119–126); IPSET1 (Oct. 27, 1978); IMP63 (Oct. 24, 1978; Oct. 26, 1978; Nov. 10, 1978; Nov. 11, 1978).

[24] For the argument that communists dominated the labor movement during the Arbenz period, see Poblete and Burnett (1962, 114–118).

is unknown, a case brought before the International Labor Organization claimed forty-five dead just among United Fruit unionists, while a special Amnesty International report estimates altogether over two hundred killed from labor's ranks (CEH 1999, 1:180, n.70; 2:390).[25]

Given these repressive conditions, few workers participated in the International Laborer's Day events of May 1, 1955. Speakers were described by the local press as moderate and certainly stayed within the boundaries of the expected anticommunist rhetoric. Still, they also used the occasion to denounce the persecution of labor and peasants and to present the government with a petition of thirty-one demands calling for the preservation of the rights of labor won under the prior regime.[26] The following year, more-radical workers and students seized the stage from the scheduled May First speakers, giving what the press described as "incendiary" speeches emphasizing the gains of the October 1944 revolution and the need for workers to fight to restore rights and benefits. A few arrests did occur at the rally, but notably none of them were the unexpected speakers.[27] By the end of the 1950s, placards at the annual event routinely attacked Castillo Armas for betraying the country and moved from praising Juan José Arévalo, the more moderate of the prior progressive presidents, to honoring the more radical Arbenz – as well as Fidel Castro.[28]

These demands were not heeded. The right-wing government tightened the legal requirements that governed labor activities. Through a 1956 amendment to the 1947 Labor Code, the conditions for legal recognition of unions were made more difficult and those for a "legal and just" strike even more so. Unionization of public employees was prohibited, as were political activities by all unions. In the following decades, Guatemala was said to have the lowest unionized workforce in all of Latin America (Levenson-Estrada 1994, 8, 27–28).

FASGUA and the Reemergence of the Labor Movement

Despite this repressive climate, it is important not to lose sight of the labor activities that did occur. Within just a month of the regime change, social Christian forces friendly to the coup itself organized the Federación

[25] Also for this period, see ASIES (1995, 3:8–22); Brockett 2002.
[26] IMP28 (May 2, 1955); ASIES (1995, 3:53–56).
[27] IMP28 (May 2, 1956); Levenson-Estrada (1994, 38); USDS 1956d.
[28] IMP28 (May 2, 1959; May 2, 1960).

Autónoma Sindical (FAS – in July 1957, it added "de Guatemala" to its name, becoming FASGUA), intended as a labor federation independent of both the United States and of the PGT. Beginning with twenty-five unions representing some 50,000 workers (ASIES 1995, 3:27), FAS played an important role during the Castillo years in helping unions reorganize new leadership under the anticommunist constraints of the government so that they had a chance to assert the economic interests of labor. Indeed, it was even PGT policy by 1955 that the left support labor reactivation under the FAS umbrella. In mid-1956, bus drivers organized the first strike under the new regime. The first legal strike occurred two years later in 1958 and after a little over a month ended in victory for workers at Puerto San José. The 1960s began with a contentious strike at the Social Security Institute that drew on substantial support from other groups and featured such actions as a hunger strike, occupation of the institute's headquarters (followed by their forced eviction), and large demonstrations. In the end, they also won many of their demands. As the broad popular movement against Ydígoras expanded in early 1962, urban labor was deeply involved, not just at the many demonstrations but also through a number of strikes and work stoppages, with teachers and railroad workers especially militant in their actions.[29]

Although it was the vanguard of the contentious wing of the Guatemala labor movement into the late 1960s (there were other federations formed that allied internationally with the AFL-CIO), FASGUA was unsuccessful in terms of the key objective of a labor movement: organizing workers. In 1968 it had grown to only twenty-six unions, only fifteen of them of which were urban (ASIES 1995, 3:299). The repression of the 1950s and 1960s certainly was part of the problem faced. For example, a month before the military coup of March 1963, a number of FASGUA leaders were arrested and its headquarters was occupied for some months. After the military took over, strikes dropped and workers trying to organize were often fired, sometimes arrested, and more than once had their workplace occupied by the military.[30] The murder of activists that was initiated with the massive disappearances of 1966 continued from that point on. For example, founding members of FASGUA were killed in both 1967 and 1968. One also was a union secretary-general, as was an additional leader killed in 1967.[31] But another

[29] ASIES (1995, 3:26–113, 147–152, 192, 223–225); Levenson-Estrada (1994, 35–48); Aguilera Peralta and Romero Imery (1981, 188).
[30] Levenson-Estrada (1994, 39); ASIES (1995, 3:245–287); IMP34 (May 28, 1963).
[31] Aguilera Peralta and Romero Imery (1981, 188, 219); ASIES (1995, 3:315). A third founder of FASGUA was killed in 1972.

reason for the unions' lack of success in organizing workers, according to Levenson-Estrada, was the perspective of leaders themselves, which focused too much on questions of power at the state level and not enough on working with workers themselves (Levenson-Estrada 1994, 39). In this, they shared a problem generally with labor movements throughout Latin America.

The CNT and Increasing Labor Contentiousness

FASGUA was superceded as the most important labor organization by the Confederación Nacional de Trabajadores (CNT), which was formed in 1968. By the mid-1970s, it had become the most important labor organization since the Arbenz years, one now projecting "an imprecise yet fiery 'revolutionary' line"(Levenson-Estrada 1994, 90). Its origins also went back to progressive social Christian thought, both directly, as a number of its activists came out of the Catholic youth worker movement Juventud Obrera Catolica (JOC), and indirectly through the support it received from lawyers from the progressive wing of the Partido Democracia Cristiana Guatemalteca (DC). The emphasis within the JOC on personal and social transformation achieved within group solidarity undoubtedly was crucial to developing the personal resources necessary for years of sustained struggle against not only long odds but especially against continuing repression. Among those involved in the CNT's creation were two activists who would play critical roles in the Guatemalan labor movement for many years to come, Julio Celso de León and Miguel Angel Albizures.[32]

Conditions for labor organizing improved marginally in the latter part of the Carlos Arana Osorio government as he loosened up somewhat, believing that his draconian rule had eliminated the guerrilla threat from the country. The first important strike of this period, according to labor leader Albizures, was at a Guatemala City bus company in spring 1972, which ended with success. Shortly thereafter, though, a union leader was disappeared, and drivers responded with intermittent delays of service and street vandalism for up to a month (Albizures 1987, 28). Another significant strike occurred in the fall, this time by some three hundred workers at the CIDASA textile company. At first, it was allowed as legal by the labor court that later reversed and declared it illegal. After seventy-seven days, the strike ended unsuccessfully. CNT gave support to the strike, including a march from the central city, but authorities broke it up before it could reach the factory located outside

---

[32] Levenson-Estrada (1994, 80–104); ASIES (1995, 3:301–302).

of the capital. The following February, five of the union leaders were fired. In June 1973, the CIDASA secretary-general was disappeared. In between these two events (and others occurring as well), the CNT denounced what it portrayed as a terrorist campaign designed to destroy unionism.[33]

Greater success during this period was enjoyed by public employees. First were a series of strikes and work stoppages throughout the country by judicial workers in late 1972 and early 1973. Primary and secondary teachers then followed with the most important labor action of this period. Striking on two occasions and supported by a number of demonstrations, in the end they won what was seen as the biggest gain for labor since 1954. The CNT, though, was slow to offer its support, due to its mistrust of state employees and the "economism" of the teachers' demands.[34]

Other unions began to activate too, both encouraged by the favorable resolution of the teachers' strike and with the more permissive climate that often comes with presidential elections. They were also motivated by long-bottled-up grievances, now aggravated by worldwide inflation. Some 1,600 railroad workers – one of the most contentious labor groups since the late 1950s – went on strike for a week in January 1974. Later that month, their strike was followed by work stoppages by a number of public employees. Again in February, notably, 15,000 hospital employees struck for over a week. Workers then held back as the early March elections closed in but returned to contention right afterward: Bus drivers, hospital workers, utilities workers, bank employees, and others struck, some extending their actions into April.[35]

As the Arana administration closed, workers marched on May First for the first time during his tenure to celebrate International Workers' Day. The event ended in tragedy. On the one side was the readiness-to-use-repression long characteristic of Arana. On the other side was an ideological/strategic split in the broader popular movement that would plague the labor movement itself throughout the rest of the decade. Protesters led by CNT and FASGUA were given permission to march, but along an approved route that would by pass the centers of power. When the some ten to fifteen thousand marchers came to the critical turning point, a group of about two hundred

---

[33] ASIES (1995, 3:382); IMP5 (Oct. 6, 1972; Nov. 11, 1972; Dec. 5, 1972); IMP36 (Apr. 13, 1973); IPSET6 (CIDASA); IPSET8 (CTF); IPSET13 (CIDASA).

[34] IMP6 (Oct. 27, 1972); ASIES (1995, 3:387–391); Levenson-Estrada (1994, 138, 149).

[35] IPSET13 (Fegua); López Larrave (1976, 66); ASIES (1995, 3:390–401); Inforpress (Feb. 6, 1974, I; Feb. 27, 1974, II); IPV (Mar. 17, 1974, 288); El Imparcial (Feb. 25, 1974, 1; Mar. 1, 1974, 1; Mar. 11, 1974, 1).

insisted on a confrontation with authority, heading for the national palace. Other demonstrators such as Manuel Colom, the out going mayor of the capital and the leading progressive politician of the period, were unsuccessful in convincing the small minority otherwise. The confrontation occurred. The police threw tear gas, the rebels threw rocks, chaos ensued. The police started shooting, leaving seven dead, seventeen injured (including serious injuries to a DC congressional deputy), and over seventy arrested.[36]

Revolutionaries and the Labor Movement

The small revolutionary underground had survived the terror of the Arana period. As the social movements of the 1970s grew, their protest events were an opportunity for revolutionaries to push polarization.[37] They also sought to work within the student and labor movements, hoping to radicalize them ideologically and tactically. A long-established objective, by the early 1970s the PGT had an important presence in FASGUA. This inside work also became a FAR objective, and by 1974 both FAR and the PGT were gaining a presence in the CNT at the same time that the labor confederation was moving away from the Christian Democrats. Their efforts were facilitated by the disillusionment with the electoral path to change, given the fraud of March 1974, felt by some Christian Democrats within both the party and the labor movement, and their consequent covert enlistment into the guerrillas' ranks.[38]

This work to radicalize the labor movement also was joined by a new revolutionary organization, the Ejército Guerrillero de los Pobres (EGP). Generally, the PGT pushed a more cautious legal and political strategy, whereas the FAR and EGP sought to accelerate the radicalization and polarization they believed necessary for a successful mass-based revolution. Consequently, not only did the revolutionary groups have objectives other than those of most workers, but their competition for dominance within the labor movement ill served workers as well.[39]

---

[36] IMP49 (Apr. 30, 1974; May 2, 1974); ASIES (1995, 3:404).

[37] One of the crucial "causal processes" identified by McAdam, Tarrow, and Tilly 2001, it is important to note that polarization can be an objective as well as an outcome.

[38] CEH (1999 2:177; 6:184); Le Bot (1995, 159).

[39] Particularly good sources are ASIES (1995, 3:527–534, 540–543, 628–648) and Levenson-Estrada (1994, 132–5, 170–5). Both are based on extensive interviews, and both give prominent place to the views of labor leader Miguel Angel Albizures. In his own writings Albizures returns repeatedly to the damage done to the Guatemalan labor movement by the lack of unity caused by sectarianism and the drive for hegemony; see, e.g., Albizures 1980, 1987.

The Laugerud Political Opening

Conditions under the next administration of General Kjell Laugerud, who assumed the presidency in July 1974, were perfect for accelerating labor organizing and contentious political activities more generally. Most workers' grievances remained unmet but expectations were raised as more gains were registered than in any other period between 1954 and 1986. Selective violence against labor organizers by employers and death squads continued, but in Guatemala City itself government repression of peaceful protest ended.

Labor still faced the anachronistic employment practices of private employers, including hostile intransigence to its organizing efforts. For example, Guatemalan newspapers reported waves of large-scale firings in late 1974 and again in the months following the February 1976 earthquake. Often justified as business decisions, firings often coincided with organizing efforts. If workers then occupied their places of employment, as they often did, the police could be counted on to evict them promptly and often brutally.[40] But during the Laugerud period, labor did not have to contend with the government *always* backing management. Although the following examples are certainly not a full characterization of the Laugerud administration, neither are such examples found as frequently at any other time during the 1954–1986 period.[41]

- October 3, 1974: The national government successfully intervened in support of union demands to have banana companies rehire six hundred workers let go following the massive damages of Hurricane Fifi.[42]
- June 22, 1975: A labor judge ruled that the strike at INCATECU was just and legal, the first such ruling since 1954, one that emboldened workers elsewhere as well.[43]

A particularly tragic cost of this hegemonic drive was the unwise calling of meetings (and breakdown of security) that led to the mass disappearances of twenty-seven labor leaders on one occasion in June 1980 and then seventeen more in August 1980.

[40] As one example, hundreds were fired at the Fábrica Candelaria in the spring of 1976 in Antigua, just up the road from the capital. When workers held an authorized meeting at the factory, police came in, breaking it up, beating many trying to escape their blows (IPSET13 Fabrica Candelaria).

[41] For a different view, one minimizing the extent to which the Laugerud administration represented a meaningful change, see Albizures (1987, 33) and Levenson-Estrada (1994, 131–132).

[42] IPSET4 (bananeras).

[43] Levenson-Estrada (1994, 108).

- August 28, 1975: A satisfactory contract agreement was reached through government mediation between the union and management at the country's major brewery, as was repeated in February 1978 when another three-year contract was signed.[44]
- October 22, 1975: Through mediation of the Labor Ministry, an accord was signed between management and finca workers, regulating working conditions.[45]
- April 3, 1976: The Labor Ministry at Laugerud's request pressured the local Coca-Cola bottling company, site of one of the most contentious and lengthy labor conflicts of the 1970s and 1980s to recognize the union and to rehire workers with back wages. At the time, a solidarity strike of forty-eight unions was threatened. In the prior month, fourteen workers had been injured in conflicts at the plant and another seventeen arrested.[46]
- December 8, 1977: Through government mediation, the Pantaleón sugar mill settled a long-term conflict with labor. Located in the department of Escuintla, Pantaleón was one of the best-organized mills in the early 1950s, and as a result its labor-management relations were among the most tense in the following decades. A strike in May 1976 was declared illegal and thirty labor activists were fired–eventually about one hundred workers altogether. The 1977 accord did not restore the fired workers, but they were awarded severance pay and the company committed to no more firings. Just days before the accord was signed, some 5,000 supported the workers in a march in the department capital.[47]

CNUS and the Peak of Labor Mobilization

A big step for mass movements and especially labor was taken in July 1976 with the formation of the Comité Nacional de Unidad Sindical (CNUS). Conceived as a national front to advance progressive causes and as a strong stand against the violence continuing against the popular sector, CNUS

---

[44] IPSET6 (cerverceria).
[45] IPSET5 (campesinos).
[46] Levenson-Estrada (1994, 109–122); ASIES (1995, 3:430). Levenson-Estrada's book provides a thorough discussion of the overall conflict, one of the most important in Guatemalan labor history.
[47] IMP25 (Dec. 9, 1977); Levenson-Estrada (1994, 125); IPSET7 (CNUS); ASIES (1995, 3:440, 528); IPSET1 (Dec. 8, 1977).

united almost sixty unions (with the CNT at its core) with student and other mass organizations. It was CNUS that organized the threatened mass strike in solidarity with the Coke workers and the march in solidarity with the Pantaleón workers mentioned above.[48]

CNUS was active in supporting individual labor and peasant groups with their specific efforts. Some of its larger activities also remained focused on economic grievances, such as its "massive" demonstration along with the AEU in 1976 commemorating the October 20 revolution.[49] Other efforts, though, spoke to a broader position, such as its denunciation in May 1977 of a repressive plan by economic elites: "against the entire labor movement and its leaders, which has as its objective putting an end to the workers' struggles, silencing the trade-union movement, stopping its development, or destroying it.... This is being done to assure that the capitalist system continues to develop without obstacles and without the unified working class being able to protest the abuses and excesses that historically go along with capitalism" (quoted in Albizures 1980, 151).[50]

Someone did have a plan: The next month, Mario López Larrave was murdered. The most important of the legal advisers to the labor movement, López had been one of the driving forces behind the formation of CNUS. He also had played a crucial role in establishing the system of legal aid given by San Carlos students to worker and peasant organizations. The Escuela de Orientación Sindical (EOS), which was founded by law students in 1969, worked closely with FASGUA, offering needed legal advice to workers. When López became dean of the Law School in 1970, he made the EOS an official part of the school, working closely with it himself until his death.[51]

The mobilization peaks for the Guatemalan contentious movements came in the fall of 1978 and the beginning of 1980. But there is no doubt that the peak for confident enthusiasm came in November 1977. Repression generally and the murder of progressive activists specifically were much lower than they had been in the immediate past (or soon would be again). Unions were at their highest membership since 1954 and in 1977 undertook more strikes than at any time in the country's history up to this point

---

[48] IPV (July 5, 1976, 191); ASIES (1995, 3:432–445).
[49] This was unlike the smaller demonstration of the prior year, when a number of placards calling for armed struggle were visible (IPSET7 CNUS); Inforpress (Oct. 22, 1976, 14).
[50] Also see IPSET1 (Nov. 18, 1977, 19).
[51] El Imparcial (June 10, 1977, 1); IPV (June 16, 1977, 119); Albizures (1980, 151); Kobrak (1999, 48–49); Levenson-Estrada (1994, 128). López Larrave also authored a book on the Guatemalan labor movement (López Larrave 1976).

(Levenson-Estrada 1994, 127–128). Then in November, a small march by indigenous miners from the far northwest of the country captured the attention of popular forces throughout the country and catalyzed the largest demonstration witnessed in Guatemala since before 1954.

The CNT had established an office in Huehuetenango, and its young local representative, Mario Mujía, assisted with the organization of workers at Minas de Ixtahucán (and with several other unions as well). After months of labor disputes over dismal working conditions and pay, the company announced that it was shutting down. Mujía suggested a march by the miners to the capital to dramatize their grievances. They agreed, and the result was historic. The miners walked over three hundred kilometers largely of mountainous terrain in nine days. Common folk along the route urged them on. A parallel march left Escuintla from the Pantaleón site to arrive at the same time. Thousands joined them for the final day's march to the capital. Multitudes waited for them at the margins of the city to join the march to the center of national power. Somewhere between 100,000 and 150,000 people took control of the city's streets. No violence. Everything was possible. For at least a day.[52]

Mario Mujía – "the heart of the miners' march" – was assassinated in Huehuetenango the following July.[53]

Labor's momentum continued. Although unionization remained banned for them, public employees organized an alliance out of their individual associations, the Consejo de Entidades de Trabajadors del Estado (CETE).[54] Representing some 140,000 workers, CETE led a contentious set of (illegal) strikes in February and March of 1978, again using the window of opportunity of national elections, as had occurred four years earlier. And they did win salary increases from the Laugerud administration.[55]

But the regime soon changed, and so, too, did the rules under the new president, General Romeo Lucas García. The intensity of urban mass contentious activities continued to mount going into the fall of 1978. Conflict

[52] Some press reports at the time use the figure of 150,000, as Levenson-Estrada notes (1999, 128–130); ASIES uses 100,000+ (1995, 3:473). Also see IMP50 (Nov. 12, 1977); CEH (1999, 1:164).

[53] The quotation is from Albizures (quoted in ASIES 1995, 3:482); also see CEH (1999, 6:325–331). Mujía lived long enough to identify the author of his assassination (the killer had told him, presuming he would not live to tell), a local businessman. After the courts failed to hold him responsible, he was assassinated in turn by FAR in March 1979.

[54] The CETE emerged in 1976 as the Comité de Emergencia de los Trabajadores del Estado.

[55] IMP10 (Feb. 23, 1978); ASIES (1995, 3:493); IMP12 (Feb. 27, 1978); IPSET11 (empleados publicos); El Imparcial (Feb. 23, 1978, 1); IPV (Feb. 8, 1979, 204).

about bus driver wages and bus fares dominated the summer, and when bus fares increased, contention exploded. But it was met and contained by force. From this point on, selective assassinations by the state increased. The protest cycle was not yet over though. The highest peak for contention by labor came in early 1980, based now especially on rural organizations (see Chapter 5). Although economic gains were won, the true response of the government was an escalation of repression to new heights. These two peaks of contention in fall 1978 and early 1980 are among the most important periods for a close examination of the protest-repression relationship. As such, they will be at the heart of the analysis in Chapter 9.

By the spring of 1980, all momentum for organized labor and other popular movements had been lost. Repression eliminated all possibility for any nonviolent contentious activity. Guatemala was now dominated by those with the guns. But one side had far more than the other.

Revolutionary Organizations II: The 1970s and 1980s

The Arana administration (1970–1974) seemed to believe its public declarations that it had eliminated the guerrilla threat in Guatemala. But small cells survived that were essential to a resurgence of guerrilla activity, slowly increasing through the 1970s and then rapidly escalating in the early 1980s, for a short time even growing to be a serious threat to the survival of the military regime.[56] Most of the revolutionary organizations tried to work closely with the mass organizations that developed in the 1970s. When repression rapidly escalated in 1980, intensifying grievances and foreclosing peaceful protest, the guerrillas provided the vehicle by which thousands could take up arms against the murderous military regime.

Persistence of the PGT and FAR

Despite concerted efforts by the government since 1954 to destroy it, the Partido Guatemalteco del Trabajo (PGT) survived into and through the 1970s. The communist party had not for some time embraced armed struggle but rather emphasized nonviolent work with mass organizations, especially at the University of San Carlos, as discussed above. When militants disagreed, they usually moved into other existing armed groups. But in

---

[56] For overviews of the revolutionary movements of the 1970s and 1980s, see Black 1983a, 1983b; Handy 1984; Jonas 1991; Le Bot 1995; Stoll 1993.

117

1978, some members split off and formed a new PGT devoted to armed struggle.[57] As repression escalated in the following years, many others from the party followed them into revolutionary war, especially in 1980–1981.

The FAR, too, continued to operate, both through its new turn in the early 1970s to working with mass organizations as well as through continuing use of violence.[58] Perhaps the peak of FAR's urban terror campaign was 1970, especially its kidnappings of members of the economic elite and domestic and international political figures.[59] Under the resulting Arana repression, there was very little further overt FAR activity until later in the decade. When FAR did return to the news, it was usually as the result of police raids on, or surprise encounters with, small numbers of its purported guerrillas.[60] Still, occasional kidnappings of elite figures did continue, including one each in 1972 and 1976 and two in 1977 (CEH 1999, 3:484). Apparently, too, it was able to carry out some activities on the Pacific coastal plain. For example, in September 1972 a local landowner (and brother of former president Arévalo of the reform period) denounced the "terror and anxiety" FAR was spreading through the region (especially in San Marcos and Quetzaltenango) through attacks on local farms. He also charged that among their directors were professors at the university in Quetzaltenango and public employees of one of the municipalities in the region (*Inforpress* Oct. 3, 1972).

When guerrilla activity picked back up, FAR's presence was felt in Guatemala City once again with a series of kidnappings, assassinations, and bombings in 1980. However, its major zone of rural insurgency had shifted to the furthest corner of the country, the flat jungle, of El Petén. Most remaining FAR militants had retreated to this department in the far northeast of the country after the crushing blow received in 1970 in the

---

[57] For differing views of the split, contrast Harnecker's interviews with Mario Sánchez and Carlos González (Harnecker 1984, 258–293).

[58] CEH (1999, 2:244–256).

[59] This was the year of FAR's fatal kidnapping attempt of the German ambassador and the successful kidnappings of the U.S. labor attaché and the Guatemalan foreign minister, social democratic leader Alberto Fuentes Mohr (CEH 1999, 3:483).

[60] One example would be a surprise encounter in May 1975 in the Pacific coastal plain of Retalhuleu between police and a small group of purported FAR militants when their truck was stopped. One policeman was killed and one from the group, who was said to be a top FAR leader. Similar encounters returned the PGT to the news on occasion, most especially a police raid in December 1974 searching for the kidnappers of a leading industrialist that resulted in four deaths, including that of long-time PGT leader Humberto Alvarado (IPV Dec. 21, 1974, 63; Dec. 22, 1974, 56).

capital. Out in the jungle, it was again struck hard by the military in 1972. FAR then laid very low until the end of the decade when circumstances had changed. In one of its first notable actions, FAR blew up a small military headquarter in El Petén in 1980 and shot up the local police station (IPV Feb. 25, 1980, 237).

But, despite its years of being the revolutionary vanguard, FAR was now a minor actor in Guatemala's new revolutionary movement. Instead, armed struggle was driven by two new organizations, both of which had leadership that had broken years before from FAR and who were determined not to repeat the errors of the 1960s: the Ejército Guerrillero de los Pobres (EGP) and the Organizacíon del Pueblo in Armas (ORPA). To these new organizations, revolution would not be ignited by guerrillas confronting the military in the mountains through a Guevarista *foquista* strategy.[61] Instead, successful revolution would require years of preparation working directly with the country's poor, especially the vast majority in the countryside.

The Ejército Guerrillero de los Pobres

The most important of the new armed groups in strength was the Ejército Guerrillero de los Pobres (EGP).[62] Its origins were a small group of former FAR militants of the 1960s who regrouped outside of the country, along with others from the PGT's youth wing, the JPT, and a small contingent of Catholic students who had been working with peasants in Huehuetenango. Led by Ricardo Ramírez (alias "Rolando Morán"), in January 1972 the group of fifteen reentered the country from Mexico into the remote northern jungles of Guatemala to begin the slow work of building contacts and recruiting in the region.[63] Here in the Ixcán region and then as they moved a little further south into the Ixil Triangle, the population was almost totally Maya, as it was everywhere in the countryside that the EGP would later expand into. By necessity but also intention, the EGP was working to gain

---

[61] See, for example, Harnecker's (1984) interviews with Pablo Monsanto and Ricardo Ramírez, each a guerrilla leader in both periods. The classic articulation of the 1960s model is Debray's (1967) (misleading) interpretation of the Cuban experience. Jonas provides a good definition of *foquismo*: "a strategy of irregular warfare leading to popular insurrection, with the 'subjective conditions' being created by the exemplary actions of a revolutionary vanguard" (Jonas 1991, 67).

[62] In addition to the more general sources on the revolutionary organizations already identified, see CEH (1999, 1:173–175, 2:270–298, 6:199–203).

[63] The classic text is Payeras's (1983) account; he broke with the EGP over strategy in the early 1980s. Also see Macías 1998.

the support of the indigenous for the revolution and hopefully the active participation of many. But Marxist-Leninist in its ideology and Leninist in its organization, its approach to the Maya majority was based more on an orthodox class analysis and less on moving the issue of race itself to the forefront.[64] In this, it was distinguished from ORPA (see below). And it was distinguished from each of the other revolutionary groups by its belief that a revolutionary situation was closer at hand when the pace of mass mobilization escalated in the late 1970s. Consequently, the EGP differed with the others on strategic questions related to promoting rapid polarization in the country.

From the beginning, the EGP planned a division of the country into three different parts, each of which would play an important role in its strategy. The first was the western highlands. This is were the EGP began, protected by its remoteness and its difficult terrain and strategically important because it was home to the poorest and most numerous group in the country, the indigenous peasant. Second was the south coast, home of the vast agricultural estates central to the nation's agro-export economy and to its semiproletariat workforce. Third was the capital, not only the center of political power but also the location of the urban proletariat.

The EGP's first public actions came in 1975 with its execution in May of the first of some twenty military commissioners that it would kill in the far north. Then in June, in an event that received more national attention, they executed a particularly unpopular landlord in the same area – but a man who also had important political ties in the capital.[65] In response, the army initiated its counterinsurgency campaign in northern El Quiché. Similar EGP executions of important landlords followed in the next years, each provoking an increasingly indiscriminate military reaction of killing and torturing innocent peasants of the region. Nonetheless, by the end of the decade the EGP was operating more boldly in the northern zone. For example, on several occasions in early 1979 it occupied towns in the Nebaj area of the Ixil Triangle, disarming security forces in one and burning jails in others.[66] Furthermore, it now had expanded its presence throughout El Quiché and the southwestern highlands more broadly into other departments, especially Chimaltenango and Alta and Baja Verapaz.

---

[64] Le Bot in particular is strong on this critique (Le Bot 1995, 288–296). In contrast, see the relevant discussion in CEH (1999, 2:273).

[65] The unpopular landlord was José Luis Arenas Barrera (CEH 1999, 7:199–208).

[66] IPV (Jan. 23, 1979, 266; Feb. 17, 1979, 88). The first incident mentioned also was the occasion of one of the executions of a local landowner, in this case Enrique Brol.

By mid-1976, the EGP also was active on the south coast, especially in Escuintla, where a year later a band of about eighty was reported to be frightening local landowners. Generally, the guerrillas would briefly occupy large agricultural estates, hold a short meeting with the workers, take what money they found, and then burn as much as they could of such things as farm equipment and buildings. As the decade progressed, though, these actions more frequently included the murder of the *finca* (farm) administrator.[67]

The EGP's first urban action came at the end of 1975 with the murder of a former MR-13 combatant whom they charged with having defected back to the military, identifying revolutionaries for death by the repression of the 1960s (CEH 1999, 3:442). Similar applications of "popular justice" followed in April and August of 1976.[68] By the end of the year, the EGP also was attacking management as a way of supporting workers in their conflicts. In December, the EGP bombed at home the car of one of the owners of Aceros y Esmaltes, where twenty-three workers recently had been dismissed and then in March 1977 the same for the owner at Helenoplast, who was in the midst of smashing a strike effort at his factory.[69] Two EGP kidnapping attacks at the end of 1977 on the economic elite (with both victims purportedly tied to death squads) had differing results. One of the owners of the Pantaleón sugar mill, the largest in the country and the site of ongoing contention, was released a month after his kidnapping for a ransom of $2.5 million. The second victim, though, was injured in the kidnapping attempt and soon died. The action was defended by the EGP since he was an "enemy of the People and the Revolution," but it was condemned not only by the elite but also by labor.[70]

Despite the determination to avoid the *foquista* isolation of the 1960s revolutionary movement, coming into 1978 the EGP perceived itself as having given insufficient attention to working with mass organizations and redoubled its efforts in this direction.[71] This corresponded, of course, with the rapid growth of popular movements in the capital area, as already discussed in preceding sections, as well as with what was happening in the countryside, as will be examined in the next chapter. By the following year,

---

[67] IPV (Aug. 9, 1976, 345; Aug. 4, 1977, 330; Nov. 12, 1977, 139; Jan. 24, 1979, 257; Apr. 2, 1979, 379, 376).

[68] IPV (Apr. 23, 1976, 49; Aug. 9, 1976, 345); CEH (1999, 3:442).

[69] IPV (Dec. 19, 1976, 58); ASIES (1995, 3:528).

[70] CEH (1999 3:485, 6:263–267); IPV (Dec. 30, 1978, 6); ASIES (1995, 3:529).

[71] See Harnecker's (1984) interviews with both Monsanto and Ramírez.

the mass contentious movements had grown further and the EGP's links with them stronger. From the EGP's perspective, it and the country were entering a new phase: "the generalization of the war of the guerrillas" (CEH 1999, 2:279).

The Organización del Pueblo in Armas

Though not as strong as the EGP, the Organización del Pueblo in Armas (ORPA) in a historic sense was perhaps the most important of Guatemala's revolutionary organizations, manifesting a perspective and strategy more appropriate to the country's reality.[72] ORPA can also be traced back to the guerrilla movements of the 1960s, with its commander Rodrigo Asturias (alias "Gaspar Ilom") one of the survivors of the ill-fated band so quickly destroyed in March 1962. Several others of its organizers also were combatants in the 1960s. When they formed ORPA in 1972, they broke with FAR over both the *foquista* strategy but also more importantly over Guatemala's racial identity and what that meant for revolutionaries and revolution.

The indigenous Maya undoubtedly constitute the Guatemalan majority ethnically and in self-identification. Genetically, they also are part of much of the remaining population. The national question and issues of racism, though, were subordinated in other revolutionary organizations (especially in the 1960s) to the orthodox primacy of class conflict. ORPA accepted Marxism "as an instrument for analysis but not as dogma" (quoted in CEH 1999, 2:257). For Guatemala, the engine of revolution was not the proletariat but rather the "pueblo natural," the Maya majority. For the nonindigenous founders (*ladinos*) of ORPA, this meant locating in a heavily indigenous zone of the country and working patiently over many years to incorporate Mayas into what would be the vanguard of their revolution. Given the urban ladino backgrounds of the founders, ORPA is notable for its analysis, effort, and substantial successes. Nonetheless, Maya-ladino tensions existed within ORPA itself. In 1979, an indigenous group split off and formed a new organization, the Movimiento Revolucionario Popular-Ixim (MRP-Ixim), charging that although ORPA might "write about racism," there remained "a strong racism within" (quoted in CEH, 1999 2:259). MRP-Ixim would be joined by others who left the EGP for similar reasons.

ORPA established its initial zone of operations along the slopes of the volcanic chain that rises rapidly from the Pacific lowlands, extending south

---

[72] In addition to the general sources, see CEH (1999, 1:175–176, 2:256–270).

down from Mexico and on past the capital. This location provided not only protection but also access to sabotage operations in the agro-heartland below and to educational and recruitment work with the indigenous population throughout the area and into the highlands to the west. Its choice to work in these parts of the departments of San Marcos, Sololá, Quetzaltenango, and Chimaltenango, then, nicely complemented the decision of EGP to concentrate further into the interior.

ORPA also established a presence in the capital by 1974 and by 1979 was said to have some six hundred sympathizers in Guatemala City (CEH 1999, 2:259). As with the other revolutionary organizations, it did work with the nonviolent popular movement, but with an important difference. The others, and especially the EGP, were working to obtain a presence within the popular groups in order to influence their activities. ORPA instead believed a strict separation between the clandestine armed movement and the popular groups was necessary for the security of both. As one militant explained concerning efforts at San Carlos in 1975 when ORPA was said to have had much influence at the university, they were not interested in institutional politics to win top university administrative posts. Instead, their attention was focused on incorporating students and the professional staff into the "revolutionary political struggle at the national level" (quoted in CEH 1999, 2:260).

ORPA also was distinguished by its patience and therefore perhaps by a more realistic understanding of the immensity of the preparatory work that was necessary. Having initiated its effort in 1972, it remained clandestine for eight years. ORPA's first public action came in September 1979 when it attacked a finca in Quetzaltenango; such large agricultural estates would remain its major target. In November, it hit the news media for the first time with two actions in San Marcos, first at mid-month when several dozen of its personnel briefly occupied a town and eleven days later with what might have been its first armed encounter. According to official sources, three military were injured but seven guerrillas were killed.[73]

The Unidad Revolucionaria Nacional Guatemalteca

As in El Salvador, the guerrillas eventually realized the need to bring their organizations together into a united force. In February 1982, the formation of the Unidad Revolucionaria Nacional Guatemalteca (URNG) was

---

[73] IPV (Nov. 22, 1979, 55; Nov. 29, 1979, 34); CEH (1999, 2:265).

announced. The creation of the URNG occurred at the height of the guerrillas' strength and just as the indiscriminate violence of the military's counterinsurgency operations was to escalate again to horrific levels. Estimating the URNG's numbers and especially its levels of mass support is very difficult. Perera estimates the combined guerrilla forces might have numbered about 7,500 trained militants with support from about half a million peasants (Perera 1993, 10). Le Bot gives a lower estimate: 6,000 combatants and a base of support of a quarter of a million (Le Bot 1995, 195). The Guatemalan truth commission uses the figure of 270,000 organized by the guerrillas at the peak of their support.[74] Whatever the true number, they proved to be far too few in face of the capacity of the state for repression and its propensity to use it brutally.

The Central American Comparison

Individuals from just about every social group have played important roles in the contentious movements of Central America. However, as organized groups the role of students and of clandestine revolutionary organizations in urban-based movements stand out in their regional context. Teachers certainly were an important force in El Salvador but as an organized group were not as significant elsewhere in the region (although their 1973 strike was significant to the renewal of contentious activity in Guatemala). Organized labor was crucial to the contentious movements of both El Salvador and Guatemala but not as much in Nicaragua and even less in Honduras, corresponding to the different levels of industrialization in the four countries.

Students

Not only were secondary and university students a major source of recruits for contentious movements in Nicaragua[75] as in Guatemala and El Salvador, but their organizations played important roles as well, most especially in Guatemala. This has been true throughout the Third World.

---

[74] CEH (1995, 1:193). From original estimates of around 6,000 to 7,000 combatants, the military itself later revised its estimate up to 10,000 to 12,000 guerrillas, with another 100,000 as part of its infrastructure and 250,000 more in areas under control by the guerrillas (Schirmer 1998, 41). After-the-fact military estimates, though, might be inflated to make its "victory" look better.

[75] See Harnecker's (1990a) interviews with Sandinista leaders Bayardo Arce, Orlando Núñez, and Jaime Wheelock.

In his comparative examination of the revolutionary movements of Iran, Nicaragua, and the Philippines, Parsa (2000) provides a good summary of the many reasons why this has been so. Students are concentrated together at their schools and at the university level enjoy some level of autonomy, especially in Latin America. Many students are from higher status backgrounds, with all of the advantages and expectations that relative privilege brings. Compared to other groups, students often have greater interest in theoretical and ideological issues, first because many do not yet have the direct economic concerns that come with adult responsibilities but second "especially because they are immersed in the production and reproduction of knowledge and ideas" (Parsa 2000, 95).[76]

Herein perhaps lies the explanation for the persistent and courageous role of the Asociación de Estudiantes Universitarios (AEU) in Guatemala, unparalleled in the region and with few counterparts globally. From the mid-1950s on, the AEU was in the forefront of mass movements in Guatemala, often with other groups but in the darkest days of repression almost by itself. Guatemalan popular movements during this period were in part restoration movements. They were motivated to restore the movements, the gains, and the hopes of the 1944–1954 reform period that were seized from them by a conspiracy of domestic and international elites. Certainly, this was a powerful motivation for other leaders, such as in labor. But for most workers (and even more for peasants), immediate economic concerns would be more pressing, and as time passed, for younger workers the reform period was a past about which they knew little. For students, though, it was a progressive age that they studied and esteemed. They knew that students had been important to the success of the October Revolution of 1944. They knew students had marched against the counterrevolution in June 1956 and six had been slain. They were reminded each October 20 and June 26 that the banner was now in their hands.

Revolutionary Organizations

Clandestine revolutionary organizations also were significant to Central American contentious movements. Revolutionaries seek to create a revolutionary situation that will lead to the overthrow of the state both directly through their armed actions but also indirectly through their work with other organizations that operate aboveground. Since this work is done

---

[76] Also see Wickham-Crowley (1992, 33–37, 42–43).

covertly, we cannot establish with any accuracy how extensive it was in Central America during the 1970s. But enough is known to establish that it was important to the development of mass movements in Nicaragua, Guatemala, and El Salvador.

It would be a poor revolutionary organization that did not attempt to influence the direction of existing popular groups and to help to create such groups where they did not exist. Not only do nonviolent organizations and movements provide vehicles for legal pressures to weaken the regime, but they also are a source of recruits. This is commonplace to say – that aboveground organizations are useful to covert revolutionary organizations. What receives less attention is how important clandestine revolutionary organizations can be to the development of strong *nonviolent* popular movements. This was certainly the case in El Salvador, as described in the last chapter. It also was true in Guatemala, especially when rural movements are brought into the picture with the next chapter. In the mid-1970s, many progressive Salvadorans believed the electoral path to change was closed But for the same reasons, other forms of political activity also were difficult. Here the clandestine revolutionary leadership played an important role in not only the organization but probably also the energizing of the activities of the new popular organizations.

The focus of attention concerning Nicaragua is appropriately the armed struggle led by the Frente Sandinista de Liberación Nacional (FSLN). Here, too, though, covert ties between revolutionaries and nonviolent above ground organizations also were a crucial part of the effort that successfully overthrew the dictatorship in July 1979. The Sandinistas provided reassurance to those worried about possible Leninist vanguardist orientations within the FSLN should the revolution succeed by its inclusive approach. As FSLN leader Bayardo Arce explained a decade later, "We did not look for the masses to identify themselves as Sandinistas nor as revolutionaries, but simply that they organize themselves."[77] Reassurance also grew from FSLN willingness to work with other organizations. Notable were FSLN cooperation with the more moderate Group of Twelve and the more leftist Movimiento Popular Unido (MPU). After the revolution succeeded, however, the representative from each of these two groups on the new five-person governing junta, social democrat Sergio Ramírez of the Group of

---

[77] Quoted by Harnecker (1990a, 224); translated by present author. In contrast, as Jonas points out, Guatemalan "guerrillas did not develop an adequate strategy of alliances for gaining support from middle-class and moderate opposition groups" (Jonas 1991, 141).

126

Twelve and U.S.-educated Moisés Hassán of the MPU, turned out to have been covert FSLN members.[78]

It should be clear from prior chapters why a revolutionary movement did not develop in Costa Rica during these years.[79] An interesting theoretical question, though, is why a significant one did not appear in the final country, Honduras. After all, it was the poorest of the five countries. A second significant question is why revolutionaries in Nicaragua were able to build alliances far broader than did their counterparts in El Salvador and Guatemala, undoubtedly a major reason for revolutionary success in Nicaragua but not in the other two.

Honduras in the 1950s and 1960s was at a considerably lower level of development than the other Central American countries. The student sector was small and largely elite. Urban labor was at a minimal level of organization, reflecting the primitive level of industrialization. There were important unions in Honduras, and they did lead a historic strike in 1954. But these unions were at the multinational banana plantation enclaves on the north coast, remote from the country's capital. Grievances and popular organization in Honduras were rural-based. A powerful peasant movement did develop in the 1960s and 1970s, but the country still possessed enough public lands for distribution (and underused banana company lands vulnerable to expropriation due to scandal), that much of this discontent was mitigated by reform. When grievances did intensify, revolutionary organizations were heavily discouraged by the configuration of political opportunities, as Chapter 8 will explain.[80]

It is premature at this point to say much about the second question, that is, the broader alliances successfully built by the Sandinistas in Nicaragua in the 1970s compared to the failures to do the same in El Salvador and Guatemala. In part, the Sandinistas placed greater emphasis on constructing a broad antidictator front. But they also had a much greater opportunity to do so, as will be explained in Chapter 8. Given the differences in the resulting class alliances between the countries, the impact of repression when it escalated differed as well, as will be demonstrated in Chapter 10.

---

[78] Kinzer (1991, 73). For background on the Nicaraguan revolution, see Booth 1982.

[79] Costa Rica did have its "revolution," but it was back in 1948. There was an armed revolutionary movement that fought the government at that time, but it was social democratic in composition, with the communist party on the other side.

[80] For a more thorough exploration of this issue, see Goodwin 2001.

Conclusion

Contention requires organization. The last two chapters have detailed the primary urban organizations that formed the contentious movements in El Salvador and Guatemala and that kept the spirit of contention alive when repression prevented movements from forming. These two chapters also have highlighted the importance of allies and support groups to movement organization. Generally, the more disadvantaged the group and the more powerful its opposition, the more necessary the assistance of such allies and the brokerage that they provide.[81] Consequently, they were less critical to students and teachers and more important for the organization of labor. Even more significant was the assistance that they brought to peasants, as will be seen in the next chapter.

As important as these allies and support groups are to popular movements, we should not lose sight of the possible costs that they bring. As sincere and dedicated as organizers might be, their perspective will not be the same as that of the groups with which they work. And sometimes neither are their goals. Organizers often have broader ideological objectives than the usually more immediate and tangible concerns of those with whom they are working. Organizers can – and do – justify these differences in terms of their own greater ideological clarity. But those with whom they are working might have a greater practical wisdom – at least concerning their own circumstances.

This has been a problem especially for labor movements, with Guatemala in the 1970s a striking example. Recall that at least three of the revolutionary movements – the PGT, EGP, and FAR – were rivals for influence within the labor movement. In addition, labor was greatly assisted in its activities by legal advisers from San Carlos University, but not without those advisers coming into conflict with leaders who rose from within the ranks of labor itself. Finally, both the U.S. government and U.S. labor movement had been trying to determine the direction of the Guatemalan labor movement from the first days of the counterrevolution in 1954.

Long-time Guatemalan labor leader Miguel Angel Albizures has been eloquent and forceful on the consequent costs to labor of this competition by outside groups to influence the direction of the labor movement. For

---

[81] Brokerage seems to be one of the most important of the mechanisms identified by McAdam et al. 2001 (see pp. 120–121, 142–143). In the political opportunities model, the availability of allies and support groups is an important determinant of movement emergence and success. Brokerage is one of the key mechanisms by which that impact is created.

example, referring to the CNT (which he led) and the Coca-Cola union in the late 1970s as "party cakes that the various groups fought over to obtain the biggest slices, as if the working class were their private property" (Albizures 1987, 103), he adds, "The Guatemalan labor movement, in the most crucial moments of its history, weakened and destroyed itself, not only from the effects of the enemy's repression, but rather the national leadership entangled itself in its own contradictions and entered into an unchecked competition to win for itself the working class, which was not the property of any of them" (Albizures 1987, 107).[82]

McAdam, Tarrow, and Tilly (2001, 44) identify "social appropriation" as one of the causal mechanisms that they find operating across the different forms of contentious movements. The U.S. civil rights movement's appropriation of the black church is given as an instructive example of "challengers, rather than creating new organizations, appropriated existing ones and turned them into vehicles of mobilization." Given the lack of organizational resources, they suggest that this mechanism should be especially important in most of the rest of the world (p. 44).

Certainly, this has been borne out by this study of El Salvador and Guatemala. The effort at the social appropriation of the Guatemalan labor movement by the revolutionary organizations is precisely one of Albizures's key objections. Similarly in El Salvador, the creation of the popular organizations – most significantly, the Bloque Popular Revolucionario (BPR) – was at least as much of an effort by the revolutionary organizations to appropriate and direct the contentious energies of constituent groups like teachers and peasants as it was an effort by the memberships of those groups to forge a common alliance to advance their group interests. This process and its consequences for the peasantry is the subject of the following chapter.

---

[82] Translated by author.

5

Contentious Peasants and the Problem
of Consciousness Raising

Given the harsh economic conditions of everyday life, domination by local
elites, and memories of past repression (most terribly, the massacre of somewhere between eight and thirty thousand largely rural people in El Salvador
in 1932),[1] peasant mobilization in Central America has needed the assistance of outside allies and support groups. Coming first in small numbers,
over the years more and more religious workers, union organizers, urban
students, political party activists, international development workers, and
revolutionary guerrillas turned their attention to the peasantry and by the
last half of the 1970s had catalyzed substantial change in many rural areas.
From a once politically passive peasantry, throughout the region increasing
numbers were joining peasant organizations and then multisector contentious movements, asserting their demands to local elites and then to
national political leaders.

The importance of allies and support groups to the mobilization of people lacking political power is well established by case studies situated in
the United States, such as those of farm workers (Jenkins and Perrow
1977; Jenkins 1985), miners (Billings 1990), and the civil rights movement
(McAdam 1982).[2] The importance of such groups to peasant mobilization
also is one of the significant contributions of scholars writing from a political economy perspective.[3] Activists from outside of peasant communities

---

[1] A figure of 30,000 deaths in El Salvador's *La Matanza* (The Massacre) is often given, but
the most careful reconstruction estimates eight to ten thousand (Anderson 1971).

[2] For a dissenting view in the latter case, see Morris 1993.

[3] Much of the literature on peasant mobilization and collective action can be categorized
within three traditions. The political economy school views peasants as rational actors who
are mobilized through the efforts of outside agents appealing to the peasant's economic
self-interest; see Popkin 1979 especially, as well as Migdal 1974 and Singelmann 1981; for

130

provide organizational expertise, moral support, and counterhegemonic ideologies and identities that help to build and strengthen ties of solidarity among subordinate groups.[4] They also offer sources of economic assistance and protection that are alternatives to those provided by traditional – and dominating – patrons.[5] Without such assistance, or if it is too insubstantial, the politically weak are too vulnerable usually to risk overt protest and confrontation (Scott 1985). Support groups and allies, then, are "catalysts for change," as phrased by Pearce (1986, 108) following Cabarrús 1983b, because they favorably alter the configuration of political opportunities confronting challengers.

This chapter will discuss peasant mobilization and contentious movements in first Guatemala and then El Salvador, followed by a brief comparison to the rest of the region.[6] The last section of this chapter will focus on the problem of consciousness raising. Support group activists often view one of their principal missions to be changing the values and attitudes that discourage the political participation of the disadvantaged, especially peasants. Consequently, outside activists often see one of their important contributions to be raising the political consciousness of the disadvantaged groups with whom they work. However, the concept – and practice itself – is loaded with theoretical, empirical, and normative problems. Sorting through these issues will have important ramifications for the larger task of this study: unraveling the complexities of the protest-repression paradox.

an application to Latin American revolutionary movements, Wickham-Crowley 1991 and 1992; for a negative example, Hobsbawm's (1959, 90–92) analysis of the failure of Andalusian anarchists. The second approach – normally identified as moral economy – stresses the role of deprivation, particularly during times of subsistence crises, in generating moral outrage at the violation of prevailing notions of justice with Wolf 1969 and Scott 1976 as leading examples. Popkin has been criticized for misconstruing the moral economy position; see, for example, Moise 1982 and Tutino (1986, 19–20). A third approach follows a more explicit class analysis, with Paige 1975 as the preeminent example; also see his application of this model to Guatemala (Paige 1983). Regardless of which approach to peasant mobilization one takes, actions by the state, especially the mix it chooses between reform and repression, has important consequences for the scope, intensity, and success of mobilization, as stressed by McClintock 1984; Midlarsky and Roberts 1985; Skocpol 1982; Tilly 1978; and many others since, for example, Goodwin 2001.

[4] Schulz 1998 makes the point well for the Zapatista movement in contemporary Mexico, which has been more successful than one would otherwise predict because of its network ties, not only domestic but especially international.

[5] For a good conceptualization of "alliance systems" and their importance, see Klandermans 1990, which also includes a review of some of the relevant literature.

[6] The most in depth discussions of peasant movements in contemporary Central America are Brockett 1998 and Williams 1986.

Contentious Peasants in Guatemala

Contentious rural movements were at the heart of the controversies surrounding the government of Jacobo Arbenz in the early 1950s. Not only was the centerpiece of his administration an agrarian reform that struck hard at the domestic and foreign agro-elite, but it was accompanied by a concerted effort at organizing peasants. Formed in 1950, the Confederación Nacional Campesina de Guatemala (CNCG) quickly grew to a membership in the hundreds of thousands organized locally in unions and peasant leagues. Through these local organizations, peasants participated in numerous agrarian reform committees that had the purpose of initiating and monitoring land expropriations. When Arbenz was deposed, undoing this structure and demobilizing the peasantry was one of the primary motives behind the counterrevolution.[7]

Given the strength driving the rural counterrevolution, peasant organization returned to Guatemala only slowly. In the 1960s, attention focused on bringing peasant leagues back to life or organizing new ones, sometimes with the support of the U.S. Agency for International Development (USAID). Greatest success normally occurred in those areas that were at the highest level of organization under Arbenz, such as a number of communities in the department of Escuintla. These also often were areas where the Partido Guatemalteco del Trabajo (PGT) had been influential prior to 1954, and reestablishing these ties was part of the PGT's efforts to reestablish itself. By the mid-1960s, the majority of the peasant leagues in Escuintla were again guided by the communist PGT.[8] New national organizations also appeared, such as the Federación Campesina de Guatemala (FCG), established in 1966 under social Christian inspiration, and the Confederación Nacional Campesina (CNC), founded in 1973 (ASIES 1995, 3:254, 425).

Church workers were critical to the peasant mobilization effort in Guatemala, as they were throughout Central America.[9] Shared religious beliefs – and, for priests, their status – often gave church workers easier access to the peasantry and greater legitimacy to their efforts than was true for

[7] For general background on this section and sources beyond those mentioned below, see Brockett (1998, 102–108). This chapter goes considerably beyond that earlier effort.

[8] CEH (1999, 2:433). In turn, these were often areas where the guerrillas of the 1970s would focus their organizational efforts; see, for example, CEH (1999, 6:307–308).

[9] Kobrak, though, issues an important caution about generalizing this influence: "Guatemalans themselves speak of the radicalism of the Quiché diocese inspiring the radicalism of the Catholic masses, while in Huehuetenango people tell of priests there counseling caution with respect to the rebel movement" (Kobrak 1997, 130).

other actors.[10] The most important vehicle for this work in Guatemala was Catholic Action, which was initiated in 1946 by the church hierarchy as a conservative reaction to the changes catalyzed by the reforms following the October Revolution of 1944.

Life in Maya villages had been grounded in syncretic religious beliefs and practices combining Catholicism with pre–Columbian indigenous religion. A major purpose of Catholic Action was to further the Christian conversion of Mayas by attacking and undermining indigenous "superstitions." However, the message was taken into rural areas by missionaries who did not always share the perspective of the hierarchy. Furthermore, as Mayas cast off some of the traditional religious beliefs (more likely among the younger and the more educated), they also freed themselves from the conservative authority of traditional religious leaders and organizations.[11] One unintended consequence, though, was to create "fierce" divisions within indigenous communities. Indeed, by 1976 this was often the most important line of conflict in highland communities, even more than that with ladinos (non-Mayas) (Earle 2001, 292).[12]

If the catechists (as they were called) rejected some of the traditional customs, they did not reject their Maya identity.[13] Studies found that Catholic Action fostered among catechists a group consciousness that encouraged them to see "themselves as 'apostles' carrying the new 'social gospel' of the Catholic Church to their less fortunate Indian brothers and sisters" (Davis 1983a, 8). They organized literacy campaigns and created base communities for shared deliberation on the meaning of the social gospel for their

[10] A good introduction to the subject for all of Central America is Berryman 1984. More generally on "the force of faith in social movements," see Smith 1996b, especially the introduction as well as the chapter by Morris (1996) on the African American church in the U.S. civil rights movement.

[11] Le Bot's discussion of the way Catholic Action legitimated for catechists their struggle with both traditionalists and ladinos (Le Bot 1995, 138) is a good example of McAdam et al.'s causal mechanism of certification: "the validation of actors, their performances, and their claims by external authorities" (McAdam et al. 2001, 145).

[12] Also see Kobrak 1997. This could be dangerous for priests: In December 1976, a priest in Acatenango, Chimaltenango barely escaped a mob of two to three hundred people intent on lynching him over religious conflicts (IPV Dec. 21, 1976, 39–40). Kobrak 1997 is especially good on this and other lines of conflict within peasant communities that were then aggravated by community members affiliating with competing outside agents such as party activists, guerrillas, and the military. He explains, for example, "In many villages divided by a land fight or other issue, support for and opposition to the guerrillas often broke down along factional lines and created a hostile environment of mutual suspicion between collaborators and non-collaborators" (Kobrak 1997, 101).

[13] Brintnall 1979; Burgos-Debray 1984; Davis 1983a; Grandin 1997; Warren 1978.

own lives. Consequently, the conversion process promoted by Catholic Action attacked not only the traditional Maya hierarchy but also the system of social control benefiting ladinos. Where traditionalists worried about maintaining good ties with their ladino *patrones*, the catechists "tend to see such relationships as repressive and exploitive, blocking the progress of Indians and the leveling of the two ethnic groups" (Warren 1978, 135). This "liberation" through Catholic Action made the catechists more available for later mobilization by secular activists.[14] For example, the first fifty members of a peasant league in El Quiché discussed by Falla (himself a Jesuit priest involved in these efforts) all were Catholic Action catechists (Falla 1978, 485–489; 2001).

Reinforcing these efforts were the activities of the Partido Democracia Cristiana Guatemalteca (DC), which had close ties to Catholic Action. Party organizers established local affiliates in rural areas, encouraged supporters to run for local offices, and helped to organize cooperatives beginning in the 1950s and peasant leagues in the 1960s. Due to its Christian Democratic ties internationally, the DC also served as a broker for obtaining international funds for local development projects.[15] Furthermore, the party was critical to the achievement by the indigenous of some political power on the local level, especially in the election of 1974, one which was probably won at the national level by the Christian Democrats but denied to them by fraud. At the local level, though, DC candidates won in a number of towns.[16]

Historically, few indigenous communities had been served by priests. In order to promote Catholic Action and to meet the challenge of Protestant missionaries, foreign priests were welcomed to Guatemala. The concerns of many of these foreign priests, though, went beyond religious conversion. For example, U.S. Maryknolls began working in the northwestern department of Huehuetenango in the early 1960s. Their efforts expanded into rural development, including building schools, clinics, and credit cooperatives. As was occurring throughout the indigenous areas of the country, they gave prominent attention to the development of indigenous leaders,

---

[14] Among more general discussions of "cognitive liberation," especially influential have been McAdam 1982; Piven and Cloward 1977; Snow et al. 1986; and Snow and Benford 1988. For its application to the liberation theology movement, see Smith 1991.

[15] Le Bot mentions in particular DC national leader René de León Schlotter's ties to a West German foundation (Le Bot 1995, 139), a very good illustration of McAdam et al.'s causal mechanism of brokerage: "the linking of two or more currently unconnected social sites by a unit that mediates their relations with each other" (McAdam et al 2001, 142).

[16] See, for example, Brintnall (1979, 158–160); Stoll (1999, 90).

not only to carry out these projects but also to spread the reformist social message on to other villages. The Maryknolls also initiated their own colonization project in the late 1960s in the underpopulated Ixcán region of the far north of Huehuetenango.[17] Combined with its remoteness, these Ixcán communities were attractive for the initial revolutionary organizing efforts in the 1970s of the Ejército Guerrillero de los Pobres (EGP).

Rural development projects also were initiated by foreign governments and private organizations, including USAID. The administration of General Kjell Laugerud during the mid-1970s was more open to such efforts than were others in the past. This was especially true after the February 1976 earthquake. Hundreds of new organizations were welcomed into the country to work in the southwestern highlands that was the center of the earthquake's extensive damage.

All of these forces came together in the formation of the Comité de Unidad Campesina (CUC), Guatemala's most potent peasant organization since the CGTG of the 1944–1954 reform period. Although reconstruction of CUC's history is difficult because its formation and much of its operation occurred in secrecy and most of its activists had been killed by 1982, it clearly was aided by church, student, and union activists, as well as by development workers and guerrillas.[18] It also drew on self-consciously Mayan organizational efforts during the 1970s within indigenous communities that were more culturally oriented (Bastos and Camus 1996).

Most of CUC's early leadership came from southern El Quiché around the department capital of Santa Cruz, most drawn from the left wing of Catholic Action. Jesuit priests began consciousness-raising efforts in 1973 in the area, drawing in as well student helpers from San Carlos and other universities in Guatemala City. In a liberation theology context generally, and employing Paulo Freire's "pedagogy of the oppressed" specifically (Freire 1970b), they worked with a number of the indigenous community leaders, who soon were organizing by the end of 1975 what would become CUC. How critical their *direct* role in CUC's formation itself was is a matter of controversy, as is the relationship between these two and the guerrilla EGP.[19]

---

[17] Davis (1983b, 3–5). For a critical assessment of the leadership of the Ixcán project, see Morrissey 1978.

[18] This account is based largely on Fernández 1988 and Le Bot 1995. Also see Carmack 1988; CEH 1999; Grandin 1997; and Stoll 1999.

[19] Le Bot claims that the initiative for forming CUC came from non indigenous intellectuals (Le Bot 1995, 161). The best-known of the Jesuit team was Fernando Hoyos who, publicly left the Jesuits for the EGP in 1980. Hoyos told an interviewer (probably later in 1980) that

Priest-CUC ties were not unique to Quiché but also existed in other areas, such as Escuintla.[20]

Significant urban support also came from the national labor movement. The new umbrella mass organization centered on labor formed in 1976, the Comité Nacional de Unidad Sindical (CNUS), was to be a major force in contentious politics for the rest of the decade. Its leaders held visions of re-creating what workers and peasants enjoyed in the Arbenz period, that is, well-organized labor and peasant federations that worked closely together. The two major labor federations within CNUS, the Confederación Nacional de Trabajadores (CNT) and the Federación Autonóma Sindical de Guatemala (FASGUA), were already involved in rural organizing efforts, not only among workers on the large fincas (farms) of the Pacific coastal zone, but also advising peasant communities elsewhere that called on them for assistance. This was especially true of the CNT, which included as part of its membership the Federación Campesina de Guatemala (FCG).

CUC emerged publicly in April 1978 as a response to a complex organizational crisis within CNUS over international affiliations that provoked the FCG, its major peasant affiliate, to leave the organization.[21] CUC's historic ambition was to unite within one organization indigenous and ladino campesinos, be they Maya smallholders in highland villages, permanent workers on the large coastal estates, or the massive number of seasonal migrants moving between the two. Although it had little success with ladino peasants,[22] CUC did succeed in organizing on both the south coast and in the highlands.

he had been a covert EGP member since 1976 (Meléndez 1997, 194). Hoyos authored an article on Guatemalan peasant struggles for *Estudios Centroamericanos* under the pseudonym Carlos Felipe Castro Torres (1978) – C. (F. Castro) Torres suggests to me Camilo (Fidel Castro) Torres. Camilo Torres was a Colombian priest who joined the guerrillas of that country in the 1960s, later meeting his death in the struggle – as would Hoyos in 1982. Another member of the Jesuit team, Luis Pellecer, was kidnapped and tortured by the military in 1981 and claimed (in statements never since retracted) that the Jesuits were the founders of CUC (Le Bot 1995, 144–151; Stoll 1999, 98–9). The Jesuits denied the charges made by Pellecer in a September 1981 press conference, pointing out that he had been held incommunicado for 113 days beforehand by the police (ECA #396, 1073).

[20] A Belgium priest, Walter Voordeckers, began working in the Escuintla area in 1966. Inspired by liberation theology, he began working with peasant groups in the area. Apparently, this included CUC as well. He was murdered in May 1980, as was later that month another foreign priest working in Escuintla (CEH 1999, 6:303–306).

[21] For background, see ASIES (1999, 3:536–543).

[22] Le Bot offers a good analysis (Le Bot 1995, 168–171). For one illustration, see CEH (1999, 7:157).

Regardless of which type of peasant and location, organization generally proceeded along preexisting social networks. CUC organizing along the coast was facilitated first by the years of work in the region extending back to the Arbenz years by union, peasant league, and PGT activists. Additionally, it could follow the networks established by Catholic Action and other reformist Catholic groups working in the area.

In both lowlands and especially the highlands, village leaders often brought with them into CUC not only family members but many others allied with their leadership. Since for security reasons organizing occurred in secrecy, CUC activists could build "the organization behind traditional or seemingly innocuous masks such as *cofradías*, soccer teams, Catholic parishes, and evangelical churches" (Grandin 1997, 16). CUC's communication between highland villages could follow preexisting commercial and religious networks, especially Catholic Action networks. Following the earthquake of February 1976, religious and other activists traveled from less-affected indigenous villages to help those in the worst-hit areas (especially Chimaltenango), furthering links between activists from different zones. The earthquake also brought in large numbers of international development workers and resources, whose efforts often overlapped with those who were organizing what would become CUC. As important examples of these different networks, among the five CUC activists who died in the fire following the police attack on their occupation of the Spanish Embassy in January 1980, two were leaders in their home villages, as well as CUC highland organizers.[23] A third organizer was a plantation laborer, who enlisted recruits as he moved from one finca to the next.

In its origins, CUC was largely based among more prosperous families in the more prosperous communities of the indigenous heartland. It then spread to poorer and more remote communities, expanding its base among poorer peasants. Since this organizing effort was covert, it is impossible to know how much CUC was behind the increasing contention

---

[23] Which side ignited the embassy fire that killed thirty-seven people, leaving only one of the occupiers and one of their hostages alive, remains an issue of controversy. The police reacted quickly and ferociously, retaking the building by force against the wishes of the Spanish government and therefore against international norms. Writers normally blame the police for the deaths, but Stoll suggests that the student militants leading the occupation might have started the fire, preferring a quick martyrdom to the certain prolonged torture that they would face with arrest. The surviving hostage was the Spanish ambassador. The surviving occupier was seized from the hospital, tortured, and killed. Compare the accounts in CEH (1999, 6:163–182) and Stoll 1999. For a response to Stoll, see Arias 2001a, 2001b and then Stoll's response (Stoll 2001).

in the highlands in the later 1970s. Certainly, other groups were involved in organizing peasants, such as international NGOs. Escalating grievances played their role, especially the consequences of the earthquake, inflation (particularly in petroleum-based chemical fertilizer), and the military's repression – the same people attracted to CUC were the most likely victims of state violence. From November 1977 through December 1978, the regime murdered 143 Catholic Action leaders and catechists in northern El Quiché alone (CEH 1999, 2:384) and as many as 400 by the beginning of 1980 (Le Bot 1995, 145).

Whatever the configuration of causes, contentious political activities did increase. For example, an ongoing mass campaign against the mayor in Santa Cruz Balanyá, Chimaltenango, grew so intense in March 1979 that it was described in the press as an indigenous uprising. Later that year in October in the adjoining department of Sacatepequez, protesting peasants from a local finca decided to march to the capital, joining with a similar march leaving a Chimaltenango factory, for a total of some seven hundred protesters. Intercepted at the city of Chimaltenango by police throwing tear gas, many of the marchers then occupied the town cathedral. They were confronted by police again and evicted, with forty protesters detained, twelve of whom were arrested. One protester was killed. Similar contentious actions involving peasants were happening throughout the country. These included those already described in Chapters 1 and 2, as well as others such as reports of numerous land invasions by peasants in Suchitepequez in 1977 and in Jalapa in 1979.[24]

The peak of this nonviolent peasant contentious mobilization in Guatemala occurred just as the levels of state terrorism were about to escalate to unparalleled heights. Years of patient organizing paid off with the largest strike to have occurred in the country's history – and most certainly in its agricultural sector. Following short precursor strikes in the two previous months, on February 18, 1980 some seven hundred workers went on strike at the Tehuantepec sugar plantation in the Santa Lucia Cotzumalguapa municipality of the department of Escuintla. This area featured both

---

[24] IPV (Mar. 7, 1979, 154); ASIES (1995, 3:583–384); IPV (May 19, 1977, 183; Apr. 11, 1979, 334). For the workers at the Chimaltenango factory (Fábrica Hilados San Antonio), mediation by the government did not protect them. Firings were reported in November and then again in May 1980, when forty-two were fired, including union leaders (IPSET13 Fàbrica Hilados San Antonio). Unionizing efforts at the factory began in 1961 with the key organizer, Julio Celso de León, jailed and tortured more than once (ASIES 1995, 3:215). Celso de León was a key Christian Democratic labor leader for decades to come.

the largest sugar estates and mills in the country, as well as being the major CUC stronghold on the south coast.[25] Within two days, the strike had spread throughout the Pacific sugar and cotton estates of the coastal zone, with between 50,000 and 80,000 peasants striking at its peak.[26] During the course of the strike, peasants marched, maintained barricades across critical highways, barricaded entrances at several sugar mills and occupied others, and invaded numerous fincas, destroying substantial amounts of property in the process.

In early March, the government proposed a minimum wage increase that fell short of strikers' demands but that was substantially above what many landowners wanted to pay – a minimum wage increase of 186 percent. The next day, CNUS leaders met and decided to accept the offer and end the strike, although not without dissent. CUC in particular thought the offer should be rejected. Nevertheless, the strike and its settlement were historic.[27]

The Guatemalan peasant movement was to enjoy one more success before this mobilization campaign was eliminated by massive state violence. In September 1980, coffee harvesters went on strike for three days across the western piedmont of the departments of Quetzaltenango and Retalhuleu. Not harvested promptly, the coffee berries would lose value. The strike lasted only three days before peasants won a minimum wage increase (Fernández 1988, 48).

The most controversial question concerning external assistance to peasant organizing efforts in Guatemala is the extent of CUC's ties to the guerrillas, especially the EGP. Both organizations were expanding through largely the same areas at the same time. They shared a common commitment to the poor peasantry, especially the indigenous, and probably in many activists' views they were not far apart. Were their efforts parallel or connected? As repression escalated, CUC renounced struggle through legal channels and openly allied with the armed revolutionary cause, choosing the first anniversary of the deaths at the Spanish Embassy for its announcement, that is, on January 31, 1981 (ASIES 1995, 3:608). Was this a true change in orientation, or had CUC been functioning as a front group? In the foremost

---

[25] CEH (1999, 6:298).

[26] Sympathetic academic sources usually claim up to 80,000 participants, although press reports at the time usually were closer to 50,000 (see the next footnote).

[27] IMP11 (Feb. 23, 1980; Feb. 27, 1980; Feb. 28, 1980); IPSET5 (caneros); Fernández (1988, 43); Levenson-Estrada (1994, 167). On the CNUS-CUC conflict over settling the strike, see Albizures (1987, 103–107) and ASIES (1995, 3:602–610).

study of CUC available, Fernández is indefinite on this issue, but does allow that in the important Ixil area in the far north the EGP probably intended to dominate CUC from the beginning (Fernández 1988, 11). Le Bot concludes that if the leadership of the two organizations were not linked in the beginning, that tie was forged some time prior to 1980 (Le Bot 1995, 178).

When EGP leader Ricardo Ramírez was interviewed by journalist Marta Harnecker in 1982, he was quite open about the EGP relationship with the CUC, describing the latter as "a peasant organization related to the EGP," and adding that the "leadership of all our mass organizations is a secret leadership." How much this connection predated CUC's 1981 decision, though, is not clear. Nonetheless, he clearly understood CUC's covert method of organizing: "an initial group of CUC forms in a village, a secret committee which develops a propaganda effort until it wins over the majority of the village and incorporates it into CUC's mass work" (quoted in Stoll 1999, 99).

Regardless of when the CUC-EGP relationship was forged, as the regime's scorched earth counterinsurgency campaign spread across the highlands, CUC "served to channel radicalized peasants into the guerrillas' ranks" (Wickham-Crowley 1992, 132). By 1981, southern Quiché was "in a state of rebellion" (Stoll 1999, 101),[28] especially the Santa Cruz area where as many as a thousand Maya may have joined the guerrillas (Carmack 1988, 56). So, too, were communities in adjacent parts of other departments, especially Chimaltenango. How much this radicalized contention also reflected radicalized worldviews, and how this distinction is important for the protest-repression dynamic, will be analyzed below following the discussion of El Salvador.

Contentious Peasants in El Salvador

Peasant mobilization in El Salvador also received crucial assistance from outside support groups, with church workers again playing an especially significant role.[29] El Salvador's archbishop during the 1960s and much of the 1970s, Luis Chávez y González, took seriously the new reform currents

---

[28] Among others, see Davis 1983b.

[29] A leading scholar on the political role of the church in El Salvador, Montgomery describes it as "The principle catalyst" for the revolution in El Salvador (Montgomery 1982/1983, 209); also see Montgomery 1995, 81–99. Writing in explicit opposition to such standard progressive accounts of El Salvador, Grenier also gives the church prominent place in his analysis (1999, 129–156).

within the Catholic Church. Shortly after the 1968 Medellín conference of the Latin American bishops, well known for its call for a "preferential option for the poor," he began encouraging the development of Christian base communities in the country. Heading the effort was Bishop Arturo Rivera y Damas, the key progressive in the church hierarchy, then and since, with the short and notable exception of the archbishopric from 1977 to 1980 of the martyred Oscar Romero. Another of Archbishop Chávez's innovations came around the same time, when he created the Fundación para la Promoción de Cooperativos (FUNPROCOOP) to stimulate the development of rural cooperatives.[30]

Peasant organizing efforts in the 1970s are best documented in those areas where there was an active progressive church presence, and these also were where there was the most success. Especially important in this regard was the region around Aguilares and Suchitoto, both of which had active church teams working in their area. These teams included both resident workers and support staff who traveled from nearby San Salvador, as did a number of university students. Assistance also was provided by local school teachers – the majority of which in the Aguilares region belonged to ANDES, the leftist teachers' union. Recall, too, from Chapter 2 that this was the region hit by the Cerrón Grande hydroelectric project, especially Suchitoto, which not only displaced peasants from their lands but also tightened land markets. When combined with the decade's inflation, peasants in the area faced higher prices each year for the land they needed to rent for their crops.

In 1968, Father José Inocencio Alas was assigned as the parish priest for Suchitoto, which is about thirty miles to the north of the capital, and its twenty-five neighboring villages. The next year, he began training "delegates of the word" to go back to their villages and conduct weekly services, which is generally seen as the origin of the first Christian base communities in El Salvador. There were soon thirty-two functioning in the area. Perhaps emboldened by these small-group reflections on the social gospel, five peasant families in 1969 sought the assistance of the local justice of the peace in their conflict with a local landowner. Alas accompanied them while others organized a demonstration in their support. After threats were made against Alas, another demonstration was planned but then preempted when the Army and National Guard occupied the town. After presenting the church's position at a national conference on agrarian reform in 1970, Alas

---

[30] Montgomery 1982/1983, 1995; Hammond (1998, 26–29).

was kidnapped, tortured, and left naked in the mountains. Nonetheless, he continued his work in the area, joined by his brother in 1972, until forced by death threats to leave the country in 1977.[31]

In 1972, a Jesuit team initiated work in Aguilares, in what was the most important community pastoral effort undertaken in rural El Salvador during the 1970s. Located about twenty-five miles due north of the capital, the Aguilares parish of about thirty thousand people was dominated by large sugar haciendas.[32] Along with Suchitoto, Aguilares was a major site of organizational work and contentious activity in the years ahead, as discussed further below. The influence of these two projects extended over a broader area. Wood, for example, credits the influence of these organizational efforts as the major explanation for the higher level of mobilization and eventual peasant support for the FMLN found in the adjacent northern zones of the municipality of Tenancingo than in the zones further to the south (Wood 2003, 89–94).

Other areas of church activity that were to prove important were the northern departments of Morazán and Chalatenango. Both were marginal zones of poor subsistence peasants, many of whom migrated seasonally for harvesting work on commercial estates elsewhere. Father Miguel Ventura arrived in Morazán in 1973. He organized base communities throughout the region and encouraged the formation of peasant cooperatives and collectives. Ventura was beaten and forced to leave the area in 1977. The Ejército Revolucionario del Pueblo (ERP) entered Morazán in 1974 and stayed. A rugged mountainous area in the northeastern corner of the country and about as far as you can get from San Salvador, it was a perfect haven for a guerrilla stronghold. The ERP often worked through the existing base communities, cooperatives, and collectives in the area to strengthen its movement, sometimes working directly with Ventura (Raudales and Medrano 1994, 67). Among its accomplishments was the creation of peasant leagues that later became the base of LP-28, the ERP-affiliated popular organization.[33]

Similarly in Chalatenango, church workers were active throughout the 1970s, facilitating the development of a strong and militant peasant

---

[31] Hammond (1998, 26–27, 40–43); Pearce (1986, 102–105); Peterson (1997, 53); Montgomery (1995, 81–82, 98–99).

[32] For background on Aguilares and the pastoral effort in the area, see Cabarrús 1983b; Cardenal 1987; Carranza 1977; and Montes 1980.

[33] Binford 1996, 1997; Hammond (1998, 35); Peterson (1997, 54, 58); and Raudales and Medrano 1994.

movement. Here, too, in the northeastern corner, guerrillas established their stronghold, this time the Fuerzas Populares de Liberación (FPL), again working through these existing networks to expand its operations and to further mass mobilization. The focal point of these efforts was the Unión de Trabajadores del Campo (UTC), which was formed in late 1974 and characterized as "a combative and radical organization" from the start (Pearce 1986, 141).

A different type of region also enjoying significant peasant organization was on the south coast in the department of Usulután, which is dominated by large export estates. As described by Wood, church workers played an important role in this area, too, but more important were secular activists. Both the FPL and the ERP began working in the area in the mid-1970s.[34] They were followed by the popular organizations, which seem to have been the most important set of outside agents working in Usulután. The BPR was especially effective in promoting rural worker mobilization through strikes, blockades, and other contentious activities (Wood 2003, 99–103).

Other priests organized urban base communities, particularly in San Salvador. A Belgian team, for example, focused on poorer neighborhoods in the city's northern fringe, areas that supplied many activists to the contentious movements of the 1970s and 1980s, including the 1989 FMLN offensive that reached into the capital (Peterson 1997, 54). Others worked with high school students from affluent backgrounds who then became involved in community action work in urban slums or in rural areas. As FMLN leader Nidia Diaz noted about those days, "instead of taking off for the beach [during Holy Week vacation] we went to the countryside" (quoted in Hammond 1998, 36–37). Frequently "shocked by rural living conditions," the experience often was "transforming" for the urban participants (pp. 38–39).

Christian base community expansion, though, was limited in El Salvador because most of the country's bishops were opposed to them, for both institutional and theological reasons. More important in terms of numbers reached were the Centros de Formación Campesina, peasant training centers that were developed in the mid to late 1960s in the departments of Santa Ana, San Miguel, Usulután, Chalatenango, and San Salvador. Before they were shut down by repression around 1980, tens of thousands of peasants from throughout the country had attended the courses provided at these centers. In much compressed fashion, participants were exposed to much of

---

[34] For an account by an ERP leader, see Raudales and Medrano 1994.

the project of the base communities: shared critical reflection on everyday life through study of the Bible, along with attention to leadership training within a democratic structure. Or, as one staff member concisely expressed it, "the integral training of men [sic] for liberation" (quoted in Peterson 1997, 57).[35]

A crucial role in the organization of the Salvadoran peasantry also was played by the United States through the American Institute for Free Labor Development (AIFLD) (an affiliate of the AFL–CIO), which initiated training in 1962 of peasant leaders through an Alliance for Progress program. Assisted by USAID, the Partido Demócrata Cristiano (PDC), and the Salvadoran government, this project eventually led to the formation in 1968 of the Unión Comunal Salvadoraña (UCS). With an initial peasant membership of 4,000, by 1976 it had grown to claim 80,000 members. A very different regime effort at peasant organization also was initiated during the mid 1960s with the formation of the Organización Democrática Nacionalista (ORDEN). ORDEN functioned as an auxiliary to the National Guard for maintaining rural order and as an instrument of repression for which the regime could – hypocritically – deny complicity. Village ORDEN leaders also often were linked to the ruling party of the military, the Partido de Conciliación Nacional (PCN). Although its membership grew to about 100,000 rural people, it is usually claimed that all but about five to ten percent had joined only as a means of self-protection.[36]

The most important nonregime peasant organization in El Salvador during the 1970s was the Federación Cristiana de Campesinos Salvadoreños (FECCAS), which developed during the 1960s with the aid of church

---

[35] A parallel role was played in the U.S. civil rights movement by the Southern Christian Leadership Conference's "Citizenship Schools," as well as the "Freedom Schools" of the Student Nonviolent Coordinating Committee (Evans and Boyle 1986, 64–66). Both are examples of the "free spaces" identified by Evans and Boyle: "environments in which people are able to learn a new self-respect, a deeper and more assertive group identity, public skills, and values of cooperation and civic virtue. Put simply, free spaces are settings between private lives and large-scale institutions where ordinary citizens can act with dignity, independence, and vision" (Evans and Boyle 1986, 17). Wood's research among peasants living in revolutionary-controlled areas of El Salvador gives a similar sense: "This *exercise of agency in the realization of their interests* was experienced by participants as profoundly transformative: interviews demonstrate the emergence of a new insurgent political culture based on solidarity, citizenship, equality, and entitlement to contest the old-regime culture rooted in clientelism and coercion" (Wood 2001, 279).

[36] Montgomery (1995, 56); also see Cardenal (1987, 440) and McClintock (1985a, 204–209, 340–342). However, it should be noted that these estimates are by sources hostile to ORDEN.

Table 5.1 *Peasant Organizations and Their Links: El Salvador, 1960s through 1970s*

Political Orientation	Peasant Organization	Political Party	Popular Organization	Guerrilla Organization
Right				
	ORDEN (1965?)	PCN		
Middle				
	UCS (1968)	PDC		
	FECCAS (1964)	PDC		
Left				
	FECCAS		FAPU (1974)	ERP
			BPR (1975)	FPL
	UTC (1974)		BPR (1975)	FPL
	FTC (1978)		BPR	FPL

workers and the PDC.[37] Then falling largely dormant, it was revived in 1974 through the formation of the Frente de Acción Popular Unificada (FAPU), the first of the mass organizations linking urban and rural groups discussed in Chapter 3. FAPU originated in a May 1, 1974 march, with Suchitoto priest José Alas playing a critical role.[38] By linking peasants to urban leftist groups, such as students and teachers, FAPU brought new resources and support to organizing efforts in the countryside (see Table 5.1). By early 1975, though, FECCAS broke from its alliance with FAPU,[39] becoming part of the Bloque Popular Revolucionario (BPR) when it emerged later in the year. This brought FECCAS into a strategic alliance with the more radical peasant group, the Unión de Trabajadores del Campo (UTC), also a BPR affiliate. Before long, the two peasant groups merged in 1978 into the Federación de Trabajadores del Campo (FTC).

Membership in the BPR also strengthened peasant links to the FPL, the largest of the covert revolutionary organizations, as also discussed in

---

[37] Cabarrús 1983b is probably the most in-depth source on FECCAS. One of the Jesuits working closely with FECCAS in Aguilares during 1974–1977, he sees the larger Salvadoran revolutionary movement as having been born out of the peasant movement (Cabarrús 1983a, 83).

[38] A similar march the same day in La Paz had a different denouement. Marchers assaulted the municipal building in San Francisco Chinameca and cut phone lines while police arrested about a dozen, one of whom died a few days later – but cause and effect is hard to establish (LPG 5/4/1974, 4). Similarly, another FECCAS-UTC La Paz march, this time in Zacatecoluca in May 1978, was broken up by police, with two marchers killed (LPG 5/18/1978, 60).

[39] FPL leaders interviewed years later claimed the FPL fostered FECCAS's break with FAPU (Harnecker 1993, 126).

145

Chapter 3. Indeed, FECCAS "contributed substantial membership to the guerrilla movements" (Harnecker 1993, 132), while its secretary-general (and continuing in that capacity with the FTC), Apolinario Serrano, joined the FPL some time during this period (Pearce 1986, 153). Similarly, one of the UTC's founding leaders, Facundo Guardado, went on to lead the BPR and through the FPL became the only top FMLN leader from a peasant background (Harnecker 1993, 132).

As peasants became more assertive, new grievances were created. Many participants in a successful May 1973 strike by 1,600 laborers supported by church workers at the La Cabaña sugar mill near Aguilares were later fired and had trouble finding work elsewhere or even fields to rent. The same was also true for peasants thought to be allied with FECCAS or other projects supported by the progressive clergy and seminarians. Instead, employees at the sugar mills were under pressure to join ORDEN.[40] All of these pressures undoubtedly prevented some peasants from affiliating with FECCAS. Still, Aguilares was the area of its greatest organizing success. By the end of 1976, it had 639 members in the area, another 260 sympathizers, and already had mounted ten demonstrations (Cardenal 1987, 440–443). On other occasions during this period, the reaction to contentious peasants went beyond intimidation to violence. Most notably, in November 1974, peasants who were occupying private land further to the southeast near La Cayetana (San Vicente), were evicted, with seven killed, thirteen disappeared, and over a dozen arrested.[41]

At the national level, the pace and boldness of FECCAS-UTC activities mounted. They presented several proposals in late 1976 to officials concerning rural wages and land rental prices. When these overtures were rejected, simultaneous demonstrations were held in mid-November in the departments of Cabañas, Chalatenango, La Paz, and La Libertad, with the latter in the town of Quezaltepeque (located a little to the north of the capital) of some 2,500 marchers repressed by authorities. The peasant organizations then switched to more aggressive tactics in the following months, occupying lands throughout the center of the country in the departments of San Salvador, La Paz, San Vicente, and Cuscatlán. These invaded lands then became major sites of confrontation between the peasant organizations and the government across the next year or so. For example, when the military invaded and occupied Aguilares and neighboring El Paisnal in March 1977,

---

[40] Cardenal (1987, 276); IDHUCA (1988, 29); Pearce (1986, 116).
[41] Cardenal (1987, 448); ECA (#313, 804–806); IDHUCA (1988, 26).

defiling its church and murdering the region's leading activist priest, Father Rutilio Grande, among its objectives was the eviction of peasants from lands previously occupied in the area.[42] At the end of 1978, other peasants were forcefully evicted in La Paz and San Vicente.[43]

As in Guatemala, organized progressive Salvadoran peasants faced not only opposition from state authorities but also from the more traditionally oriented within their own communities. Indeed, in El Salvador this opposition was particularly well organized through ORDEN. As the country polarized in the latter part of the 1970s, so, too, did many rural communities and even neighbors and extended families through these rival sets of organizations (e.g., Cabarrús 1983b, 218). Protest activities by FECCAS-UTC often were met with violence by ORDEN. A particularly notable example was the sequence of events that occurred at the end of March 1978 during Holy Week in the San Pedro Perulapán region of Cuscatlán, about twenty-five miles east of the capital.

As FECCAS grew more assertive in the San Pedro Perulapán area, especially with demonstrations and land occupations, disappearances of its members began, reaching fourteen by March 1978. FECCAS denounced the role of ORDEN in these disappearances, charging that ORDEN identified progressive activists to the National Guard, which then kidnapped them. ORDEN responded with counter demonstrations and death threats. In late March, night attacks on the homes of FECCAS activists began, with one killed on March 21 and the list of injuries on both sides mounting. Two days later, an ORDEN mob of two hundred attacked the store/house of a FECCAS activist, robbing and destroying it. Later in the day, the mob of now about one hundred attacked another house where it was repelled by FECCAS supporters. The next day, another FECCAS member was killed and a number were captured. On March 27, security forces occupied the region, supposedly to restore peace. Land occupiers were evicted, and large numbers were arrested. ORDEN continued to burn homes and fields.

---

[42] The 1977 murder of Father Rutilio Grande probably had the biggest impact of any single attack on church workers in El Salvador until the slayings of Archbishop Oscar Romero in March 1980 and then the four U.S. churchwomen in December 1980. Eleven priests and a seminarian were assassinated in the country from 1972 through 1982, not counting the four U.S. churchwomen. At least sixty priests were expelled or forced into exile during the same period (Montgomery 1982/1983, 218). According to former FPL leader Napoleón Romero García, many of the seminarians working with FECCAS incorporated into the FPL following Grande's murder (Prisk 1991, 17).

[43] Cardenal 1987; ECA 1978.

Thousands of peasants fled the area. Finally, on March 31 the authorities returned fifty-seven of their prisoners to their villages (ECA 1978).

FECCAS-UTC/FTC were active not just in their home areas. Member activists frequently traveled for actions elsewhere, especially to the capital. Indeed, revolutionary leaders were later to praise peasants as the most important participants in the BPR's numerous contentious activities of the late 1970s (e.g., Harnecker 1993, 191). As state violence skyrocketed in 1980, thousands of peasants in El Salvador, as in Guatemala at the same time, flocked to the guerrilla organizations, expanding them into largely peasant armies. A much larger number of peasants gave the guerrillas their support, often at considerable personal risk. But as with Guatemala, what remains to be examined is the extent to which radicalized activity reflected radicalized worldviews.

Consciousness Raising and the Ideology of the Oppressed

Are outside agents such as the church workers, party activists, and revolutionaries discussed above needed in order to raise the consciousness of the oppressed, liberating them for political action from a false consciousness that perpetuates passivity? If domination and exploitation are in part maintained by hegemonic ideologies that reinforce mass subservience and quiescence, then the consciousness raising role of outside agents is critical to mass mobilization. But do the oppressed really internalize the masks and roles forced on them by their oppression, accepting their suffering as inevitable and maybe even legitimate? Some contemporary scholars have argued for this point, notably the influential Barrington Moore (1978).[44] This position is sufficiently characteristic of the literature on popular movements in Central America that it can be regarded as the conventional wisdom. Typical is the following observation from a nun who worked with Salvadoran peasants for seven years: "When I first arrived in Tamanique, every time a child died the family would say, 'It's the will of God.' But after the people became involved in the Christian communities, that attitude began to change. And after a year or so I no longer heard people in

---

[44] There is, of course, an extensive literature on the subject, especially among scholars influenced by Karl Marx and/or Antonio Gramsci. Among the works read for this section that are not explicitly commented on below are Eyerman 1981; Femia 1975; Gaventa 1980; Jessop 1982; Lears 1985; Porpora 1985; Rudé 1980; Sassoon 1982; and Williams 1977. Closer attention will be given to the work of Nicholas Abercrombie, Paulo Freire, James Scott, and Byron Turner.

the communities saying that. After a while they began to say, 'The system caused this'" (quoted in Montgomery 1982, 104).

This explanation highlights attitude change catalyzed by the conscious-ness-raising activities of agents from outside of the peasant community. To sympathetic outsiders, the poor residents of the peasant community were objectively oppressed, yet their plight had been fatalistically accepted. Indeed, because it was the "will of God," it would be hard for the oppressed to question the legitimacy of their situation. However, with a change of attitudes, suffering turned into grievances against the system, thus making popular mobilization and contentious politics possible.

When scholars look for the sources of the hegemonic ideologies internalized by the disadvantaged, they often turn to traditional reli-gion and its message of fatalistic acceptance of one's lot in this vale of tears. But in recent decades, religious activists often have played a transformative social role, drawing on themes of liberation from within the same religious traditions. Where orthodox Marxism empha-sized religion as "the opiate of the masses,"[45] more recent scholar-ship highlights the dual role of popular religion, that is, as a source of themes and symbols for both acceptance and activism.[46] Perhaps

---

[45] The famous phrase comes from his "Critique of Hegel's Philosphy of Right." Marx then explains:

The abolition of religion as the illusory happiness of the people is required for their real happiness. The demand to give up the illusions about its conditions is the demand to give up a condition which needs illusions. The criticism of religion is therefore in embryo the criticism of the vale of woe, the halo of which is religion.

Criticism has plucked the imaginary flowers from the chain not so that man will wear the chain without any fantasy or consolation, but so that he will shake off the chain and cull the living flower. The criticism of religion disillusions man, to make him think and act and shape his reality like a man who has been disillusioned and has come to reason, so that he will revolve round himself and therefore round his true sun. Religion is only the illusory sun, which revolves round man as long as he does not revolve round himself. [Marx 1959, 263]

[46] A good beginning is Kselman, who points out that popular religiosity "is a complex, his-torically conditioned set of beliefs that claims to provide remedies for problems in the here-below as well as the hereafter" (Kselman 1986, 31). Similarly, Billings portrays re-ligion "as a relatively autonomous sphere of social life that acts as a mediating variable between oppression and opposition or submission" (Billings 1990, 2). Scholarship in part has been responding to changes in the Catholic Church beginning with Vatican II and with the role of Catholic church workers in liberation movements in Poland and Latin America, as well as to the roles of the African American church in the U.S. civil rights movement (e.g., Evans and Boyle 1986; Morris 1996) and Islam in the Iranian revolution (e.g., Moaddel 1992). At the same time, scholars are finding an important mobilizing role of religion in earlier social movements, such as rural Brazil (Diacon 1991) and Appalachian U.S. (Billing 1990). Still, Hannigan 1991 faults social movement scholars for purposely

nowhere has this been more important than in contemporary Central America.[47]

One especially clear example of this perspective is provided by Foroohar's analysis of the role of religious leaders in the transformation of the attitudes of the Nicaraguan peasantry, a precondition for their involvement in the revolutionary movement that deposed the Somoza dictatorship. Foroohar writes of the traditional role: "the dominant view among the Nicaraguan peasantry regarding their economic and social misery was that it was inevitable and ordained by God. To explain the situation, the campesinos usually used familiar phrases such as, 'God has made us poor and we don't have to change,' or 'Christ was poor. He came to teach us to suffer.'.... the Catholic Church in Latin America had played a major role in creating passivity and fatalism among the population, and for centuries had provided an ideological justification for the sociopolitical system" (Foroohar 1989, 153).[48] However, a strong progressive movement developed in the Central American Catholic Church, one that has chosen to exercise its "preferential option for the poor." Within this context, Foroohar quotes a Nicaraguan church activist's explanation of consciousness-raising as "a process by which a person comes to discover his identity as a human being, his rights as a citizen, his possibilities to shape his proper destiny" (Foroohar 1989, 153).[49]

---

ignoring religious movements. Ten years later, Aminzade and Perry find, "scholars have often emphasized ways in which churches serve as mobilizing networks, and have sometimes also noted the importance of religious beliefs and symbols as a source of collective action framing. Less frequently, however, have they ventured beyond a purely instrumentalist perspective to explore the expressive dimensions of religious conviction in processes of contention" (Aminzade and Perry 2001, 155).

[47] For an excellent overview of liberation theology written from a social movement perspective, see Smith 1991. The most thorough discussion of the catalyzing role of the Catholic Church in Central America is Berryman 1984. Also see Levine 1990b and Lernoux 1980. More generally on "the disruptive potential of sacred transcendence," see Smith 1996b, especially the introductory essay to the edited volume, as well as the essays by Nepstad and Morris.

[48] An even stronger statement of this aspect of religious belief is offered by Serra, an Argentine sociologist who moved to Nicaragua in 1979. He claims that there was a coherent dominant ideology during the Somoza period, one that was reproduced especially through religious institutions. Serra states that among the major values of this ideology was fatalism, which he characterizes as the following: "The social order, like the natural order, is not an historical product of human activity, but an eternal system, unchangeable – a product of Destiny, God, or Nature" (Serra 1986, 57–58).

[49] For a parallel account of attitudinal transformation in post-revolutionary Nicaragua, see Barndt 1985. Other works on the importance of religion to the Nicaraguan revolution include Dodson and O'Shaughnessy 1990; Lancaster 1988; and Williams 1989. One of the leading scholars on religion in Latin America, though, issues a caution about "much

The essential assumptions of such accounts are sufficiently standard that they are usually asserted rather than examined.[50] After all, the hegemonic power of ideas is intuitively attractive to intellectuals, especially to those of us whose own intellectual journeys are marked by a struggle to develop a critical consciousness at odds with the dominant beliefs transmitted through our own socialization. However, the assumption that subordinate classes and groups actually internalize a hegemonic ideology that rationalizes the social order as legitimate and inevitable has been insightfully critiqued by Scott (1977, 1985, 1990), in part through his able use of the powerful analysis of this perspective by Abercrombie, Hill, and Turner 1980.[51]

The existence of a dominant ideology is not contested by Abercrombie et al., but rather the assumption that it is clear and coherent. More importantly, their historical analysis of the European experience argues that although *dominant* classes might be incorporated by a dominant ideology, *subordinate* classes have not, and especially not during the feudal and early capitalist stages of development.[52] That peasants and proletarians were generally quiescent cannot be contested. What Abercrombie et al. stress is that this "factual acceptance" of the system "need not involve any signs of normative acceptance or indoctrination" (Abercrombie et al. 1980, 122). Instead, mass political passivity is explained by other factors, foremost among them state

recent writing on liberation theology and Nicaragua, where misstatement, exaggeration, thin description, and open distortion abound. Matters get worse when the subjects are combined" (Levine 1990a, 230).

[50] It is, as well, the preferred explanation by elites for the cause of discontent among the masses – that is, grievances are the consequence of subversion by "outside agitators."

[51] Abercrombie et al. 1980 explicitly critique both Marxian theories of a hegemonic ideology (especially Gramsci), as well as the parallel perspective of Parsonian value integration theories. The argument is summarized on pp. 156–159. Also see Abercrombie 1980 and Turner 1983. For a response, see Thompson 1986, who, claiming they have overstated the case, adds, "It is more fruitful to think of the ideological terrain as a complex of discourses which have ideological effects, and the balances of forces in that field as being always in flux and the site of contestation over meanings. The complex of discourses recruits people as subjects and constructs ideological communities" (Thompson 1986, 48).

[52] Grenier argues that "the evidence strongly suggests" that for El Salvador the impact of the church "on the lower strata, especially in the countryside, has probably been exaggerated by most observers, whereas its influence on urban, middle-class youths, mostly through education institutions, has certainly been underestimated – if estimated at all – by the same observers" (Grenier 1999, 156). Montgomery notes that the Jesuit Universidad Centroamericana in San Salvador had "a clear commitment to implant in the children of the oligarchy a socio-political perspective markedly different from that of their parents – to instill in them a sense of social justice" (Montgomery 1982/1983, 216). Hammond points out that for many affluent young people, "working in Christian base communities was a transforming experience" (Hammond 1998, 39).

repression (p. 122) and economic compulsion, the latter of which "oblige[s] people to behave in ways which support the status quo and to defer to the decisions of the powerful if they are to continue to work and to live" (pp. 154–155).[53] Scott then goes beyond this demonstration that oppressed subordinates do not necessarily accept their social order as legitimate to also show that neither do they accept its inevitability (Scott 1985, 330–335; 1990, 80–82).

In an observation concerning slave/master relationships more supportive of his opponents' position than his own, Moore notes: "With this mixture of anger and dependence – very likely also anger at dependence – the relationship could often be a highly ambivalent one, changing from rage to dependence and even affection quite rapidly, according to momentary circumstances and expectations" (Moore 1978, 464). Scott and Abercrombie et al. argue that it is these "circumstances" and "expectations" that are most important for understanding the behavior of oppressed subordinates. Peasants often do manifest attitudes of powerlessness and fatalism, not because they internalize their suffering as inevitable and legitimate, but because the configuration of political opportunities that they face usually precludes individual or collective confrontations with authority. The disadvantaged are usually politically passive because of their realistic estimates of the odds against them rather than because of the fatalistic attitudes that are the consequence of these assessments. Wood makes the point well for Salavadoran peasants, "Whatever their feeling of moral outrage and willingness to act on defiance, *campesinos* with no proximity to insurgent forces rarely acted in support; even the defiant were not suicidal in the Salvadoran context" (Wood 2003, 237).

The appearance of new sources of assistance and protection, though, can change these strategic calculations of risks/opportunities and therefore can alter the balance between conflicting attitudes/feelings and, consequently, perhaps behavior as well. Support groups and allies from outside of peasant communities can be "catalysts for change" because they change the configuration of political opportunities. Because they alter the configuration of power relationships in the countryside, these catalysts facilitate the

---

[53] Abercrombie et al. also discuss internal divisions among subordinate classes and the effects of reformism (Abercrombie et al. 1980, 123). In contrast, advocates of the importance of hegemonic ideologies point out that "the construction of hegemony . . . invests common sense with a meaning consistent with both lived experience and class exploitation. An acceptable notion of exploitation is thus constructed, in the sense that surplus extractions do not invite immediate and sustained retaliation" (Akram-Lodhi 1992, 198).

transformation of peasant attitudes from the powerlessness manifested by the isolated individual to attitudes of solidarity and strength that grow from collective action (1977, 244, 500–506).[54]

In a Central American context, probably the best argument for this perspective on the role of outside agents is White's participant-observer study (1977) of the involvement of Catholic Church actors in the development of the Honduran peasant movement in the 1960s and 1970s.[55] What began as an attempt to evangelize soon transformed into a program to assist the mobilization and organization of peasants and even to support them in their confrontation with elite interests – until elite opposition in the 1970s pushed the church back into a less confrontational posture. Some of these activities were based on a consciousness-raising model, and results were interpreted in that light. White, however, stresses changes in power relationships. Church activists (and others, such as labor union organizers) were tied to urban political forces and resources and sometimes to international supporters. Their programs and organizations "established a development communication system which bypasses the rural elites and the central place towns and reaches directly into the outlying rural communities" (White 1977, 401). Although "conscientization and leadership training clearly appears to have been one factor in an increasing challenge of rural elites," White stresses that "the more important factor is the structural fluidity or 'loosening' of community structures so that lower-status campesinos felt free to engage in aggressive conflict tactics" (p. 403).[56]

---

[54] Similarly, Billings 1990 finds that "the plausibility of oppositional beliefs" was able to take hold in pre-WWII U.S. Appalachian coal fields because the larger context was more supportive than in North Carolina textile mills where they did not take hold. Miners were supported by a national labor movement (United Mine Workers of America, UMWA), which had no counterpart in textile organizing. Among the most effective of the UMWA organizers were its miner-preachers whose mass organizing meetings included "powerful prounion sermons" (Corbin 1981, 159, as quoted by Billings 1990, 21). In contrast, the few outside textile organizers were hostile to southern religious traditions.

[55] Gould's 1990 account of the mobilization of Nicaraguan peasants also gives substantial and sophisticated attention to the role of outside organizers. See Brett and Brett 1988 for a more recent and more general discussion of the Catholic Church in Honduras than White 1977.

[56] Similarly, the penetration of the Guatemalan countryside by outside organizers during the reform period of 1944–1954 facilitated unprecedented organizing by peasants. The significance of their role is well captured in the following comment by Adams: "Indians and Ladinos found that it was possible to seek out other authorities and sources of power than those familiar in the unitary patronal system. Whereas before, the *patron* or the elders had the last word, it was increasingly assumed that not only were they no longer the final authority, but they also could be ignored almost at will. The operation of these new organizations

However, as compelling as this political opportunities argument might be, it appears to me to be overstated. Although authors such as Abercrombie et al., Scott, and White clearly establish the central importance of power relationships, we have too many testimonies of "changed consciousness" by the disadvantaged themselves to discount the importance of consciousness-raising activities to the mobilization of the oppressed.[57] As Smith points out, at the heart of liberation theology as a social movement has been "the deliberate development, diffusion, and institutionalization of a change in consciousness" (Smith 1991, 57). Especially telling is the empirical work of Salvadoran priest-sociologist Martín-Baró (1990), which shows Christian base community participants claiming almost without exception a progressive change in their political attitudes in comparison to a group of evangelical Pentecostals, the majority of whom profess conservative attitudinal change.[58] The issue here is complex because the cognitive and emotional life of the individual is complex,[59] as is the relationship of that interior life to one's experience of the surrounding social reality.

One set of objections to taking seriously the phenomena associated with consciousness raising is the contention that the concepts of *higher* and *false*

---

demonstrated that *campesinos* could expect some satisfaction without retribution from the local landowner or the local council of elders" (Adams 1970, 191; also see 205).

[57] Stokes 1991 explicitly critiques Scott on this point, based on her eighteen months of research with urban movements in Peru while Akram-Lodhi does so in terms of Scott's own Malaysian village case study, arguing that "hegemony negotiates the unification of multiple social realities in a manner consistent with class domination. Everyday forms of resistance are a vent for inconsistent individual experience which do not threaten such domination" (Akram-Lodhi 1992, 180). Beyond the examples discussed in this chapter of internalized oppression and/or the experience of gaining freedom from such constraints, see, among many: Diacon 1991 on Brazilian peasant millenarian movements; Dobyns et al. (1971, 104) on Peruvian peasants; Foley 1990 on Mexican peasant women; Levine (1990b, 744–747) on Venezuelan base community participants; Shin 1994 on Korean protest movements; and Wood 2001 and 2003 on Salvadoran revolutionary peasants. Finally, of course, there is the voluminous literature on womens' liberation in the United States, notably Friedan's 1963 discussion of the "click" when one realizes that the "problem with no name" is socially constructed and not one's individual failing.

[58] Fully 97.4 percent of the seventy-eight base community members surveyed claimed progressive attitudinal change, while 54.9 percent of the fifty-one Pentecostals moved in a conservative direction, with statistical significance at p < .0001. Martín-Baró was one of the six Jesuit priests at the Universidad Centroamericana murdered by the Salvadoran military in 1989. Also see his analysis of Salvadoran peasant attitudes on what turned out to be the eve of their political mobilization, especially his discussion of the pervasive fatalism (Martín-Baró 1973).

[59] For example, altering one's thinking can change one's feelings (cognitive therapy), while releasing repressed feelings can change one's thoughts (cathartic therapy).

forms of consciousness invariably lead to a sense of superiority on the part of those who presume they have the higher consciousness over those they characterize as having the false consciousness.[60] This elitism can lead to the dangers of Leninist vanguardism – "trust me, I know what is best for you."[61] Vanguardists often believe they are justified in creating front organizations without informing "less conscious" participants of the full connections and purposes of their organizations until they, too, develop sufficient revolutionary awareness.[62] Yet, while these dangers are real enough, as seen in both the Guatemalan and Salvadoran cases, they are not evidence that negates the existence of qualitatively different stages of consciousness. If nothing else, there is the qualitative growth involved in understanding consciousness itself: "consciousness as consciousness *of* consciousness" (Freire 1970b, 67).

To make this discussion a little more neutral than the loaded terms of "lower" or "false" consciousness and "higher" or "revolutionary" consciousness, I suggest instead the terms "dominated consciousness" and "critical consciousness."[63] A critical consciousness is similar to what Warren means

---

[60] See, especially, Berger 1975 and Wickham-Crowley (1991, 20–22, 104–115) for application of this argument to Latin America.

[61] Freire gives a strong warning against this tendency: "those who work for liberation must not take advantage of the emotional dependence of the oppressed – dependence that is the fruit of the concrete situation of domination which surrounds them and which engendered their unauthentic view of the world. Using their dependence to create still greater dependence is an oppressor tactic" (Freire 1970b, 53). Still, others claim that in his work Freire is also guilty of this tendency; see, for example, Schipani (1984, 22–23).

[62] Stoll quotes a student who accompanied the peasant delegation that would die on January 31, 1980 in its occupation of the Spanish Embassy during its earlier visit at San Carlos University, "I suppose that the campesinos didn't understand where it would all go. Vicente Menchú wasn't the leader; he was led. . . . When you're desperate, in a crisis, you look for support from the first people you find, and it was the [San Carlos] students who took advantage of them" (Stoll 1999, 87). As an example, Stoll suggests that the statement the peasant group presented at the national congress in September 1979 was written by urban activists, reflecting their national perspective rather than the specific grievances of the peasant delegation (p. 68).

[63] Both terms can be found in Freire's work, but he generally uses other – more obtuse – terms for these distinctions. For his discussion of "critical consciousness," see Freire (1973, 18–20). He defines "dominated consciousness" as when one "does not have sufficient distance from reality to objectify it in order to know it in a critical way" (Freire 1970a, 36). In a third work, he insightfully discusses a dominated consciousness as including both the "internalization of the opinion the oppressors hold of them" (Freire 1970b, 49), as well as the belief that the characteristics of the oppressor are the ideal of what it is to be fully human (Freire 1970b, 30–55).

by "rational autonomy": "the ability to reflect on and direct one's desires in such a way that one can develop a life-plan" (Warren 1990, 601).[64] Others can assist us in this process, but how could they truly know what is best for us in any given situation? As Freire points out, "while no one liberates himself by his own efforts alone, neither is he liberated by others" (Freire 1970b, 53).

Gramsci's notion of a "contradictory consciousness" helps to further advance this discussion. Gramsci claims that the beliefs of subordinate classes are influenced not only by hegemonic ideologies but also by their "life-experiences and interests."[65] The latter, because they are class-specific, also are "implicitly oppositional" (Abercrombie 1980, 117–118), which makes possible the development of "counter-hegemonic cultural forms" (Sider 1980, 26).[66] Sometimes the opposition is more than implicit, such as when there is a popular political culture of resistance.[67] Gramsci's concept of a "contradictory consciousness" is meant to capture the coexistence of these two belief systems within the mind of each individual.[68]

---

[64] In his excellent discussion of "what should a critical theory of ideology do," Warren adds: "Although one's desires are inevitably constructed by social and cultural forces, the capacity to reflect on these forces is also socially and culturally constructed, not only as a set of cognitive competencies, but also by situations that enable or frustrate the balance between desires and self-reflection necessary for constructing a unified self. Autonomy, as every student of child psychology knows, is a social achievement. That is, I do not mean 'autonomy' to refer to an absence of social formations of individual capacities for choice, but rather to distinguish between social processes that develop these capacities and those that do not" (Warren 1990, 601).

[65] Gramsci, of course, has been extraordinarily important to the discussion of hegemony and dominated consciousness. However, his writings on hegemony are well characterized as "elliptical and scattered" (Sider 1980, 23) throughout his *Prison Notebooks* (1971), thereby instigating a large literature that attempts to explicate his not always clear meaning. Take for example these two definitions of hegemony itself: first, "hegemony refers to the dominance of one particular class within the domain of culture" (Sider 1980, 23); second, "hegemony is used in the sense of influence, leadership, consent rather than the alternative and opposite meaning of domination. It has to do with the way one social group influences other groups, making certain compromises with them in order to gain their consent for its leadership in society as a whole" (Sassoon 1982, 13).

[66] Three good case studies that give close attention to the development of counterhegemonic cultural forms among Nicaraguan peasants, Newfoundland fishermen, and eighteenth-century English workers are, respectively, Gould 1990, Sider 1980, and Thompson 1978. Also see Lears 1985.

[67] See "an impulse of resistance" that Martin finds in a Mexican village and its "process of 'remembering history'" (Martin 1992, 178), as well as Selbin 1997b, and Wickham-Crowley on Cuba (1992, 131–132).

[68] The central – and always cited – passage is Gramsci (1971, 333). Garson 1973 makes a similar point for the "multiple consciousness" of U.S. automobile workers, "one finds them to be

It is contradictory because of the inherent tension between the two parts.[69]

However, the normative grounds for the collective action of subordinates are found not only in the counter hegemonic values growing out of their class-specific experiences; dominant ideologies also have been used by subordinates to justify their struggles against dominant elites. Accordingly, dominant belief systems can be drawn upon by oppressed subordinates to either rationalize their passivity or to justify their resistance. This is especially true of religious beliefs, as discussed above.

Thus far, this discussion is still incomplete because like almost all scholarship it overstates the role of cognition and minimizes or ignores the importance of emotion. The acceptance or rejection of ideologies is not a cognitive activity alone but also based on emotional responses.[70] Furthermore, contentious action is driven not by ideological thoughts alone but also by emotions, especially when under conditions of acute grievances and high risks.

We are now working at two levels. The first is that of the contradictory belief systems (or frames) that are socially created and available to each person. The second level is the interior life of the individual, each with one's own idiosyncratic set of contradictions.[71] Whether peasant or professor,

full of ambiguity and overlays of consciousness. Different and seemingly contradictory orientations will be evoked depending upon the context" (Garson 1973, 164).

[69] Drawing on Gramsci, Jenkins (1985, 6) begins a brief argument along the lines of this paragraph.

[70] As much as anyone, making this point most clearly are Calhoun 1982; Smith 1991; and Scheff 1990. In his analysis of class consciousness, Calhoun adds the astute observation that the usual "assumption that greater rational clarity of perception of interests is inexorably connected to greater commitment to collective action" is wrong. Instead, at least in England, "diminished emotional commitment accompanied increased analytic clarity" (Calhoun 1982, 136). Smith points out that insurgent consciousness "is not simply a rational, self-interested calculation, but an experience that involves the human mind, will and emotion" (Smith 1991, 62). Scheff argues that "class domination has a basis in the emotions of the subordinate classes, as well as in the control of force by the elite class" (Scheff 1990, 131). To make his case, he draws little on social science but turns instead to literature, giving close examination to Goethe's *Werther*, whose humiliated fury, rather than being consciously connected to "the personal, social, political, and economic forces which are oppressing him" is instead turned against himself, leading ultimately to suicide (Scheff 1990, 131). Also see Moaddell's 1992 discussion of the role of ideology in the Iranian revolution.

[71] As one leading explicator of Gramsci's notion of "contradictory consciousness" points out, "The thinking of the common [person] is neither coherent nor consistent over time; it is instead 'disjointed and episodic'; elements of intellectual and moral approbation coexist in unsteady equilibrium with elements of apathy, resignation, and even hostility" (Femia 1975,

our consciousness is a composite of ambivalent responses to imperfect situations. On the one hand, we often accept the boundaries of imperfect situations in order to obtain the maximum of benefits (material and emotional) from within the situation itself. On the other hand, we might experience feelings ranging from mild resentment through rage if we believe those boundaries themselves to be unjust.[72] These perceptions of injustice and feelings of anger might be hidden from powerholders and other observers; at times, they might also be submerged for the individual as well.[73]

It is clear that oppressed subordinates can imagine alternative social relations, as Scott maintains, and that sometimes they contentiously act inspired by these visions. Even so, the seeming inevitability of one's subordinate situation still usually plays a critical role, as seen in the importance of religious fatalism in Central America. Whether peasants might imagine hypothetical social orders or not, they still confront the inevitability of the everyday forms of social relations. Except under the most unusual of circumstances, today will be like yesterday, tomorrow like today, next week like last week, etc. Under normal circumstances, the peasant's lot is one of acceptance – the acceptance of a fate that is full of hardship and indignities. At the same time, it is the only life that one has, and finding meaning in it for oneself is important. In such situations, religiously based justifications can be a helpful support.[74] Comfort can be gained from socially available belief systems, such as claims about "God's will."[75] However, fatalistic statements

---

45). Femia adds, "Clearly, the states of mind associated with different types of compliance – fear, habit, indifference, acquiescence, positive attachment – are interwoven in different ways in the social personalities of individuals" (Femia 1975, 45). A good illustration is Gould's discussion of "lesbian and gay ambivalence" (Gould 2001, 136–142).

[72] For a very good parallel discussion, see Beissinger's discussion of "the mobilization of identity as a political process" (Beissinger 2002, 150–159).

[73] Scott's (1990) distinction between "public" and "hidden transcripts" insightfully captures the first point, as does Kuran's (1989, 1995) between "private truths and public lies." However, neither deals with a "contradictory consciousness" that might include fatalistic attitudes that are deeply felt rather than being just part of the individual's public performance. Either way, these distinctions mean, of course, that the conclusions of any social science work about the attitudes of oppressed subordinates – no matter how carefully done – must be taken as tentative.

[74] For an application of attribution theory to the psychology of religion to explain how people use religion to make sense of their world, see Spilka et al. 1985.

[75] Freire quotes a Chilean priest who on a visit to Brazil in 1966 asked families living "in indescribable poverty" how "they could bear to live like that," and he says they always answered the same: "'What can I do? It is the will of god and I must accept it'" (Freire 1970, 163 n.40). What the vignette leaves out is the point that no matter how miserable the conditions, some way must be found to make it bearable.

that might be taken by the outside observer as manifestations of resignation reinforced by a "dominated consciousness" are more likely to be part of a complex array of conflicting feelings and beliefs that are unlikely to be shared, except perhaps with intimates, and of which one is perhaps not fully conscious oneself. When external circumstances change sufficiently, there can be an explosion of activism by oppressed subordinates like peasants that catches just about everyone by surprise.[76] Conversely, should the situation turn excessively dangerous, then that activism might quickly disappear as fast as masks of fatalistic passivity can reemerge.

In a fuller sense, then, our "contradictory consciousness" should be understood not in cognitive terms alone but as combining thoughts and feelings.[77] These are often organized in narratives that we tell ourselves to make sense of our lives. As the imperfect situations we live in give rise to conflicting feelings and thoughts, so, too, do we have conflicting narratives, ones that we might switch back and forth between during the course of just one day.[78] Conflicting narratives are probably especially prominent in situations that are important to us but not fully under our control (e.g., close personal relationships), especially if they involve subordination (e.g., peasant-landlord, patriarchal marriage).[79]

---

[76] This is what gives rise to the "moments of madness" identified by Zolberg: "Liberated from the constraints of time, place, and circumstance, from history.... Dreams become possibilities" (Zolberg 1972, 197). It is within this context that we also can best make sense of "the explosions of consciousness" identified by Mann when previously quiescent groups "suddenly" activate, voicing radical sentiments that are sometimes taken to be the sign of the rapid emergence of a "revolutionary consciousness" (Mann 1973, 44–49). However, Mann's overly cognitive approach misses the deeper dynamics at work. Also see Kuran's (1989, 1995) discussion of "preference falsification," his distinction between private truths and public lies and how truth telling can have a bandwagon effect as widespread regime opposition grows rapidly when before there *appeared* to be little (e.g., Eastern Europe in 1989).

[77] Collins points out: "The rhetoric of 'consciousness raising' is analytically misleading in implying that the process is primarily one of cognition; the dynamic is centrally emotional, and therefore strongly time-bound" (Collins 2001, 32).

[78] Drawing on Stryker's notion of identity salience, McAdam and Paulsen offers a parallel approach to explain movement recruitment. They quote Stryker (1981, 23–24) as follows, "identities are conceptualized as being organized into a hierarchy of salience defined by the probability of the various identities being invoked in a given situation or over many situations" (McAdam and Paulsen 1993, 646–7).

[79] Smelser notes that a relationship of dependence features a restricted freedom to leave and therefore "entails a certain entrapment." Therefore, his "general proposition is that dependent situations breed ambivalence, and correspondingly, models of behavior based on the postulate of ambivalence are the most applicable" in such situations as opposed to

Consciousness raising might be approached as a largely ideological project by the organizer, but for the participant it will involve the contradictory array of thoughts, feelings, and narratives identified above. Whether the participant's consciousness will change from fatalistic acceptance to a sense of agency based on social attribution for one's suffering might in part be the result of what is learned about how society works. A growing presence of sympathetic activists bringing resources with them lowers the risks of changing from passivity to activism. So, too, this transformation is also facilitated by the process itself, that is, the experience of participating with peers in a democratic structure.[80] Finally, the process of developing a critical consciousness will be influenced by how much trust participants have in organizers themselves and the narratives that they tell, a trust to be won on the basis of many intangible and largely non cognitive factors.[81]

Indeed, one of the most crucial tasks facing activists is the articulation of narratives that both resonate with the experience of the target population as well as providing a legitimate motivational basis for contentious action.[82] This task is captured well by the concept of "collective action frames," that is, a set of beliefs and meanings that "perform this mobilizing function by identifying a problematic condition and defining it as unjust, intolerable, and deserving of corrective action" (Snow and Oliver 1995, 587).[83] Given the existence of competing change-oriented frames as well as others that reinforce passivity, to become the dominant frame for the targeted population a movement's framing must be empirically credible, commensurate

models based on postulates of freedom of choice, such as rational actor models (Smelser 1998, 8).

[80] Concerning El Salvador, see Peterson (1997, 50–60).

[81] I am indebted to Heather Tosteson for this point, as well as for much assistance in thinking through the following two paragraphs.

[82] Tarrow points out: "The major symbolic dilemma of social movements is to mediate between inherited symbols that are familiar, but lead to passivity, and new ones that are electrifying, but may be too unfamiliar to lead to action" (Tarrow 1998a, 107). He then gives the example of Solidarity's symbolic innovations in Poland, quoting Laba's observation concerning *"the extent to which the dominant symbols were invented during the strikes,"* and the degree to which dominant symbols and rituals were lifted from nationalist and socialist tradition and transformed" (p. 122; emphasis added by Tarrow). Javeline 2003 also nicely illustrates the key role of political entrepreneurs in facilitating mobilization through helping people solve the blame attribution problem.

[83] Snow and Oliver define collective action frames "as emergent action-oriented sets of beliefs and meaning that inspire and legitimate social movement activities and campaigns" (Snow and Oliver 1995, 587). Also see Snow et al. 1986 and Snow and Benford 1988, as well as Berejikian 1992; Klandermans 1992, 1997; Tarrow 1992, 1998a.

with their experience, and resonate with existing cultural narratives (Snow and Benford 1988).[84]

Passivity in the face of suffering and indignities comes at high psychic cost.[85] However, what discussions of consciousness raising often miss are the possible psychic costs of framing human suffering in terms of social attribution as opposed to religious fatalism. Belief that suffering is "God's will" mitigates against social change; it also relieves personal responsibility for suffering, such as the premature death of one's children. If suffering is socially created, however, then one is either part of the solution or, finally, complicit with the consequences.[86] If the system caused the death of Salvadoran babies in Tamanique, as in the example at the start of this section, then parents need to change the system. But what a huge burden to carry for people whose realistic assessments of their own situation would indicate that change is impossible and activism potentially suicidal. Yet what guilt does one carry if one does not act? Alongside anger against "the system" or perhaps against a particular landlord (and the problems of how to manage these dangerous feelings), how much anger is there turned against oneself? And how is this anger managed? To not act might be wise, but it is a choice. Among the deepest narratives by which we order our experience, make sense of our lives, and manage our conflicted feelings are those by which we deal with what is our own responsibility. How much of the failings in our lives are, finally, our own responsibility as opposed to our fate?[87]

Consciousness raising with the disadvantaged in Central America, then, involved much more than bringing peasants from some "naive consciousness" to "ideological awareness." It also involved more than changing power relationships. In ways that were unique for each individual participant and their own interactions with fellow participants and organizers, the transformation of consciousness involved altering a complex array of feelings as well as thoughts. With this transformation, large numbers of

---

[84] This is a good context for understanding the importance of the mechanism of "category formation," that is, the creation "of collective identities through invention, borrowing, or encounter" (McAdam, Tarrow, and Tilly 2001, 143; also see pp. 55–58 and 319–321).

[85] This is captured effectively by Scott 1990. As Eyerman notes, "being part of the oppressed means feeling oppression and being forced to deal with it" (Eyerman 1981, 132).

[86] Scheper-Hughes 1992 is eloquent on this subject concerning impoverished mothers in Brazil.

[87] Sennett and Cobb 1972 insightfully explore such "hidden injuries of class" among the U.S. working class.

participants became community activists, many of whom also became committed political activists, and some even revolutionaries. Many others, it should not be forgotten, did not. Even in Aguilares, the site of the most concerted peasant mobilization effort in El Salvador and one explicitly based on Freirean methodology, organizers estimated that these efforts had some effect on about one-sixth of the zone's 30,000 residents, with a significant effect on about 1,500, with maybe 300 residents becoming committed activists (Cardenal 1987, 350–351). Perhaps some residents rejected activism because they remained attached to religious fatalism. Others even with Progressive consciousness change perhaps found the configuration of political opportunities still too dangerous for activism. And perhaps others were not offered frames and vehicles for activism with which they could be comfortable, ideologically and/or tactically.

For many Central American peasants who did become politically active, religious beliefs and symbols continued to be important to them as a support for activism through liberationist biblical interpretations. As repression increased, many survivors ended their activism, seeking safety in passivity – or in migration. Undoubtedly, many switched their dominant interior narrative from religious liberation to fatalism. However, others continued with the struggle, even in the face of escalating risks. Additional elements of their religious tradition often supported this dangerous activism, especially the powerful frame of martyrdom, as will be discussed in Chapter 10.

The Central American Comparison

A peasant movement developed in Nicaragua in the late 1970s in time to play an important role in the struggle against the Somoza dictatorship, but the extent of its ties to the Frente Sandinista de Liberación Nacional (FSLN) raises similar questions about its autonomy to those discussed above for peasant movements in El Salvador and Guatemala. In the years following the success of the revolution, two peasant organizations did succeed at times in gaining modifications in agrarian policy, but their continuing ties to the governing FSLN again raise the issue of the extent of their independence.[88]

---

[88] The Asociación de los Trabajadores del Campo (ATC) split in 1981, with the ATC representing rural wage earners and the new Unión Nacional de Agricultores y Ganaderos (UNAG) representing small and medium-size producers. Significant changes were made in Sandinista agrarian policy in the mid-1980s, in no small part due to pressures from the UNAG. See Luciak 1995 and, more generally, Brockett (1998, 156–184). UNAG was more autonomous but less peasant in composition; ATC was more peasant but less autonomous.

Autonomous peasant movements in Costa Rica at times have been assertive. However, given the lower level of rural grievances in this more prosperous and democratic country with its more equitable distribution of resources, along with the smaller percentage of the peasantry in its overall population (see Table 2.3), Costa Rican peasant movements have not been important national political actors in recent decades.[89] Accordingly, the most important autonomous peasant movements in the region outside of El Salvador and Guatemala are to be found in Honduras.

Honduran peasants were among the best organized in all of Latin America in the latter 1960s (Astorga 1975, 17). Their favored tactic was the occupation ("recovery") of land whose ownership was disputed with large landowners. Their political pressure led to the appointment in 1967 of a sympathetic director of the agrarian reform agency and to subsequent favorable adjudications of land conflicts. A hunger march on the capital in 1972 was partially responsible for a beneficial military coup, followed by an important agrarian reform measure. A campaign of massive and simultaneous land occupations in 1975 provoked a further round of land redistributions. However, by early 1977 the configuration of political opportunities changed to their detriment. Government responsiveness disappeared as opponents of reform triumphed within the military leadership. Although civilian government returned in 1982, the role of Honduras as a staging area for the U.S. war against Nicaragua both increased the repressive capacity of the Honduran state and legitimated for elites their opposition to contentious popular action.

The Honduran case clearly demonstrates the importance of allies and support groups to peasant mobilization discussed earlier in this chapter. Honduras also demonstrates the importance for peasants of the objectives of their allies, that is, whether outside activists are working more to help develop autonomous peasant organizations or more to harness peasant organizations to advance their own political objectives. It is my conclusion that for the peasantry itself – the majority of the population during these years in these countries – the outcome would have been better if agrarian policy in Sandinista Nicaragua had been dictated more by peasant wishes and less by urban revolutionary planners and if progressive peasant movements in El Salvador and Guatemala had remained more progressive and

---

[89] The UPANacional was especially assertive in the mid-1980s, but its membership was only about 16,000, although this was double that of any other Costa Rican peasant organization. See Anderson 1994 and, more generally, Brockett (1998, 201–214).

peasant directed and less subordinated to the objectives and strategies of revolutionary urban activists.[90]

Conclusion

Grievances and the contentious movements they fuel are not a direct product of socioeconomic circumstances but instead are mediated by power relationships on the one hand and individual psychological coping mechanisms on the other. When the configuration of political opportunities dooms contentious action by the disadvantaged, strong grievances are unlikely to be manifested. Indeed, discontent might be pushed to the edges of consciousness, where it is only dimly perceived and felt, a denial perhaps reinforced by prevailing frames and ideologies. If the external constraints are taken as givens, as not changeable in the foreseeable future, then the normal response is to adopt strategies for survival (including psychic survival) based on an acceptance of those constraints.[91]

The penetration of the countryside by activists from the outside alters the existing power configuration and, therefore, the possibilities and calculations of the disadvantaged. The involvement of support groups and allies from outside of peasant communities was a factor of supreme importance throughout Central America in the 1960s and especially in the 1970s. These catalysts for change usually were critical to the mobilization of peasants into assertive peasant organizations, in part because of their organizational skills and activist values systems, but also because their presence and activities altered the configuration of power in the countryside. Activists and their organizations offered alternative sources of economic assistance and protection to peasants directly and through their links to urban and international groups.

As the possibilities for collective action increase and their risks decline, so, too, does the psychological calculus. Feelings and thoughts that previously were too dangerous and dysfunctional are now encouraged, not

---

[90] One of the members of the religious team that worked with FECCAS confessed later: "In the interest of short term effectiveness and efficiency we fell into elitism and detached from the base. We did not walk WITH the people" (Carranza 1977, 851). Also see ECA 1987 and, more generally, Scott 1979 and Colburn 1994. For an alternative view, see White 1986.

[91] Scott 1985 demonstrates, though, that those strategies need not be completely submissive; they can and do include the covert "weapons of the weak" found in "everyday forms of resistance" to domination.

only by the "consciousness raisers," but by the changing configuration of political opportunities itself. But the relevant political opportunities and constraints include much more than allies and support groups. The critical roles of economic and political elites in facilitating and restricting popular contentious movements will be brought into focus in the remaining chapters.

PART TWO

Opportunity, Contention, and Repression

6

Cycles of Contention

Popular movements achieved historic successes in 1944 in both El Salvador and Guatemala. Long-term dictatorships were brought down in both countries by nonviolent campaigns involving thousands of people that continued day after day. Jorge Ubico fled Guatemala on July 1, ending thirteen years of tyranny. In El Salvador, General Maximiliano Hernández Martínez left power on May 9 in the face of "the most impressive" civic strike in Latin American history (Ackerman and DuVall 2000, 260). His tight-fisted rule also began in 1931, but in his case it was consolidated with a massacre in January 1932 of ten to thirty thousand peasants and suspected leftists following their aborted uprising. After this 1944 peak of popular success and jubilation in both El Salvador and Guatemala, however, the trajectories of popular movements in the two countries differed sharply for the next decade and a half.[1]

In Guatemala, Ubico's successor soon was forced to flee as well during the "October Revolution" of 1944, which ushered in ten years of progressive government. First under the reformist Juan José Arévalo and then under the more radical Jacobo Arbenz, government responded to popular aspirations and facilitated labor and peasant organizing. But this experiment in popular rule was doomed by the Cold War. There was communist influence in Arbenz's administration, provoking the overthrow of his popularly elected government in 1954 by the combined forces of the Guatemalan right and the U.S. government. Under the new military regime, popular mobilization was crushed – for a time.

---

[1] For further information on the 1944 campaigns and their aftermath, see Blasier 1976 on Guatemala and for El Salvador: Ackerman and DuVall 2000; Parkham 1988; and Williams and Walter 1997.

Events in El Salvador flowed in the opposite direction. Following the demise of the dictator, it looked like a democratic opening was possible. Within six months, though, the military had imposed its control. El Salvador would continue to have military presidents until 1979. There were different factions within the military, and at times the regime manifested a reformist orientation, at least in urban policy. But there was little room in which a democratic civilian opposition could organize during the first half of this period.

By 1960, popular forces were mobilizing again in both countries. In the following decades, cycles of contention would develop, that is, periods of contentious activity at higher than normal levels and with peaks at much higher levels. The intensity of these cycles would depend on changing configurations of grievances and especially of political opportunities. Labor organizing occurred in public ministries and at factories, leading to occasional strikes and demonstrations. Other urban groups held marches and rallies during the 1960s, joined by peasants in the 1970s. More combative tactics became frequent in the latter part of the 1970s – for instance, land and factory occupations, as well as occupations of churches and public buildings. The first armed revolutionary groups appeared in both El Salvador and Guatemala shortly after the Cuban revolution's success at the very end of 1958. Their successor movements of the 1970s were strong enough by the early 1980s to represent serious threats to the governments of both countries. What is most notable across these decades is that no matter how fully popular movements were repressed, the collapse of their contentious activities was only temporary. Even following periods of widespread indiscriminate state violence, as soon as it slackened, protest reemerged.

This is the general picture of contentious movements in El Salvador and Guatemala that emerges from the political histories that have been written on the two countries. The purpose of this chapter is to establish more precisely the trajectories of contentious movements in both countries using events data collected from multiple, and largely domestic, sources. This chapter will introduce the cycles of contention that are analyzed in subsequent chapters, as well as introduce the contention data that are the basis of this work, clarifying their strengths and limitations. The contention data for Guatemala are more complete than for El Salvador, which is also true of the political violence data used for both countries. The violence data are explained in the appendixes to Chapters 7 and 8.

The concept of cycles of contention (or protest cycles) is in itself a matter of contention. The concept is most closely associated with the

170

work of Sidney Tarrow 1989, 1998a, 1998b). Protest cycles, according to Tarrow, begin when the configuration of political opportunities turns more favorable to challengers, encouraging groups to act on both new and long-standing grievances. The contention of these early mobilizers then encourages other groups and movements to activate as well. This activity builds, peaks, and then declines back to more normal levels. For example, in his detailed study of the Italian protest cycle, Tarrow records protest events averaging more than three times higher for the six-year period beginning in late 1968 compared to those of the three years before (Tarrow 1989a, 62).

Critics have conflated the descriptive and analytic uses of cycles that are associated with different levels of analysis.[2] Used descriptively, it is true that cycles are no more than a summary of the aggregate activity of contentious movements and therefore cannot be regarded as an independent variable. However, this overlooks that when analyzing any individual group or movement, the protest cycle is an important part of the context in which it acts.[3] When location at different stages of the cycle has different consequences for challengers, it is then a meaningful explanatory variable. This argument will be developed further in Chapters 9 and 10 as fundamental to resolving the paradoxical relationship between protest and repression.

Cycles of Contention in Guatemala

Very complete contentious events data were compiled for Guatemala for the years 1973 through 1980, which corresponds with the rise and fall of arguably the country's most important cycle of contention.[4] Data also were collected forward through 1984 and back all the way to 1955, although not at a level of thoroughness that approaches the 1973–1980 period. These data on contentious political activities are divided into three categories: nonviolent, illegal, and violent. Each will be discussed separately, along with the presentation of appropriate data, following a discussion of the overall database and its sources.

---

[2] Among others, see Jasper and Goodwin (1999, 118–119). As examples of the analytic utility of the concept of protest cycles, see Hipsher 1998; Koopman 1993; and Minkoff 1997. More generally, see McAdam and Sewell Jr. 2001 and their discussion of temporality in the study of contentious movements.

[3] As Tarrow notes, "the very movement of a cycle from an expansive to a contracting phase alters the strategic situations of all participants" (Tarrow 1998b, 55).

[4] For a good discussion of the advantages and disadvantages of the four major ways in which scholars use events in "historically based collective action research," see Tarrow 1998b.

Data and Sources

The data on Guatemalan contentious political activities were compiled by the author primarily from three different Guatemalan newspaper archives maintained at the Centro de Investigaciones Regionales de Mesoamérica (CIRMA) in Antigua, Guatemala.[5] First is the vast clipping archive of *Inforpress Centroamericana* (a weekly newsletter published in Guatemala City), which is drawn from all major Guatemalan newspapers.[6] This source provides extensive coverage of events during the 1973–1980 period and was one of the sources for 55 percent of the records in the database. Second is the clipping archive of the major Guatemala City newspaper *El Imparcial*. These clippings come from multiple Guatemalan newspapers organized by many different themes, starting with the mid-1950s and continuing to the end of the 1970s. I searched through all of the numerous themes that had any possibility of relevance. This was a source for 14 percent of the records. Third is the bound daily editions of *El Imparcial*. Numerous monthly volumes were reviewed, especially as a double-check for periods that emerged as critical from the prior sources or when information from other sources was incomplete. The daily edition was used in this manner for the period 1955–1984 and is a source for 13 percent of the records. Information for this same overall period also was gathered from a number of other sources, largely published in Central America, such as a four-volume history of the Guatemalan labor movement published in Guatemala City (ASIES 1995) that was a source for 10 percent of the records and the report of the

---

[5] Studies of newspaper coverage of protest events in the industrialized democracies do find selection bias and often assume description bias as well (McPhail and Schweingruber 1998; also see Koopmans 1998; Koopmans and Rucht 1999; Rucht and Neidhardt 1998; Rucht and Ohlemacher 1992). Nonetheless, at least for First World countries, Koopmans's conclusion is reasonable: "Newspapers . . . are an extremely biased source and are absolutely unsuitable for answering questions" such as "the 'true' number of protest events or the 'true' distribution of protests." However, "it is not so much the precise levels that are interesting, but trends and differences, and these can also be inferred from biased sources, provided that the bias is more or less constant, and as long as the number of protest events reported is large enough to allow the detection of significant trends and differences" (Koopmans 1998, 96). For Third World countries, one can only assume even greater problems with both types of bias, and consequently the researcher needs to pay even greater attention to these issues.

[6] The *Inforpress* archive is organized by topic. I reviewed all thirty-two volumes in the "Violencia" series for 1973 through 1980 (typically up to four hundred clippings each); half of the twenty-six volumes in the "Socio-económico – trabajo" series (which is organized by specific subjects alphabetically, so I sampled half across the same period); and ten volumes in the "Eventos Políticos" series (around the elections of 1974 and 1978).

Guatemalan truth commission (CEH 1999), the source for another 4 percent, and memoirs of activists themselves. Finally, the *New York Times* also was used, both its index and full news stories; it was the sole source for only 1.4 percent of the records.

Altogether, there are 3,100 separate records included in the database on Guatemala.[7] Most are records of contentious political activities, but also included are responses by the government, including its most important acts of repression directed against contentious movements across these decades into 1980, when the armed conflict intensified. The database is constructed so that each record could potentially have up to three separate contentious activities occurring on the same day, as well as up to three separate government responses. The total number of contentious events in the database is 2,407.[8]

This research corroborates Aguilera et al.'s (1981, 160) earlier finding for Guatemala (and Beissinger 2002 for the Soviet Union) on the importance of using multiple sources because events found in one source are often not found in others and since critical information on the same event is scattered across sources. So many sources were consulted for the central focus of this study, the 1973–1980 period, that it is reasonable to assume a high degree of accuracy for the database, especially for the capital and its surrounding area. Once the civil war and state terror intensified in 1980, coverage by the Guatemala press became spottier. Indeed, the pages of *El Imparcial* diminished markedly each year until its publication ceased in 1984. Similar problems with coverage also existed during prior years of intense repression, especially 1966–1972.

In their influential cross-national quantitative study, Gurr and Duvall (1975, 142) attempted to measure "manifest political conflict" by "multiplying the reported number of non-governmental participants by the event's duration in days." This is exactly how it should be done. However, even using sources far superior to those of Gurr and Duvall, it proved impossible to do so in any meaningful way with this study's

---

[7] Intercoder reliability is not an issue; all were recorded by the author into the FileMaker Pro database.

[8] The basic unit of analysis of the empirical study, then, is the contentious event, with an operational definition similar to that used by Rucht and Neidhardt for the "protest event," "a collective, public action by a non-governmental actor who expresses criticism or dissent and articulates a societal or political demand" (Rucht and Neidhardt, 1998, 68). However, unlike many studies, no threshold is set here for "collective" since this information is often not available.

data.[9] Even using multiple domestic sources, for many of the contentious activities included in this study, such as demonstrations and strikes, no information was discovered on the number of participants. Or, at best, a rough estimate is provided, such as "thousands" of marchers. Similarly, the duration of strikes and work stoppages is often not given. Accordingly, the only meaningful indicator possible for these types of contentious activities is just the number of occurrences of each, with no measurement of duration or number of participants. An alternative approach would be to focus on a subset of a particular activity for which approximations of its qualitative dimensions is possible. This will be done, for example, with a subset of demonstrations in Chapter 7. Despite these limitations, the data compiled for this study are probably the most complete for contentious political activities for any Latin American cases and among the best for any outside of the industrialized democracies.

Measuring Nonviolent Contentious Activities

In the presentation of data that follows in this chapter, usually two trends are given, both the national and the "central area." In countries like Guatemala and El Salvador most contentious activities occurred in the capital (with the exception of rural insurgency). To analyze the relationship between contention and repression, then, it makes sense to focus analysis on the general area where most contention occurred. Restricting attention just to the capital city, however, seems too narrow. In Guatemala, important sites of labor organizing and contentious political activities were factories in other cities located in the surrounding department of Guatemala. These factories continued down the highway into the adjacent department of Escuintla, long an important site of labor conflict, in part because it was one of the two locations for United Fruit Company operations in the country. Escuintla's large commercial agricultural estates and processing mills also were sites of much labor organizing from the 1940s through the 1970s, as well as the prime location of the most important worker movement to occur in Guatemala, the agricultural strike of February 1980. Consequently, for Guatemala the

---

[9] Gurr and Duvall do note: "Of course many of these figures are very rough estimates" (Gurr and Duvall 1973, 142). Their source is the very limited *New York Times Index* (see Brockett 1992).

"central area" is identified as the combined departments of Guatemala and Escuintla.[10]

Demonstrations   Demonstrations have been the most important nonviolent means by which Guatemalan popular forces have registered their discontent and brought pressure to bear on public officials.[11] As used here, the category *demonstrations* includes marches, rallies, and similar protest gatherings. Marches often conclude with rallies, and some rallies kick off marches. Such cases are counted as one event.

Although the entire 1955 through 1984 period could not be examined as fully as 1973–1980, the week before and after the three dates on which political demonstrations are most likely to occur in Guatemala were checked in the *El Imparcial* daily edition for every year across the full three decades. These dates are May 1 (International Workers' Day), June 25, and October 20. The latter two commemorate key events in the struggle against the dictatorship that fell in 1944, with the June date additionally important because of lethal violence turned against the 1956 demonstration. Since this search turned up only a few minor demonstrations not already identified through the other sources, the data for demonstrations can be regarded as having an adequate degree of accuracy for the entire thirty-year period.

Figure 6.1 summarizes the data collected on demonstrations for the 1955–1984 period with both national and central area trends. The first peak of demonstrations, occurring in March and April of 1962, climaxed a longer process of increasing contention that began in 1959. This cycle accelerated when widespread perceptions of a fraudulent congressional election in late 1961 reinforced growing concerns over government corruption. From this arose a contentious movement that grew in the assertiveness of its tactics and demands, eventually becoming a movement calling for the president's resignation. Instead, they were met with intransigence and violence. Repression eventually overcame the movement, and contentious activities dropped dramatically.

A minor upswing in demonstrations occurred briefly in 1966 during a period of presidential elections and the restoration of civilian government.

---

[10] An additional reason for focusing on the central area is the greater data accuracy for this area compared to the rest of the country, especially its rural regions. This issue is addressed in Chapter 7's discussion of the political violence data in its Appendix.

[11] For a good historical discussion of the demonstration as a form of protest, see Tilly (2003, 200–213).

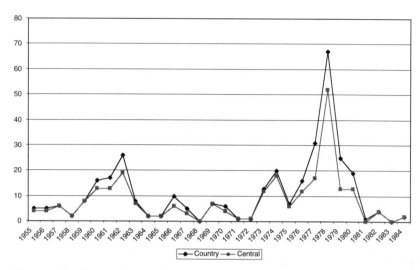

Figure 6.1 Guatemala: Total Demonstrations in Country and Central Area by Year, 1955–1984

Rather than a democratic opening, though, the following seven years were a time of intense repression. Judging from the data on demonstrations, political opportunities must have opened in 1973. From then through 1980, this form of contentious activities was maintained at a level unmatched in the past except for the early 1960s, with an especially prominent peak in 1978. But then demonstrations virtually disappeared from 1981 through 1984.

Labor Strikes   Labor's gains during the democratic years of 1944–1954 were among the major accomplishments of that period and their curtailment among the leading reversals of the counterrevolution that followed. Struggling for recognition of effective rights to organize, bargain, and strike in the post-1954 era, workers faced the intransigence of employers too often backed by violence from the state and, beginning in the mid-1960s, allied death squads. Furthermore, strikes when they did occur had to be declared just and legal by the government in order to lead to collective bargaining. Accordingly, contentious labor activities during the period of this study qualify as deeply political in nature. As can be seen from Figure 6.2, the national trends for strikes and work stoppages largely mirror those for demonstrations, with the importance of the years 1962, 1978, and 1980 especially vivid.

176

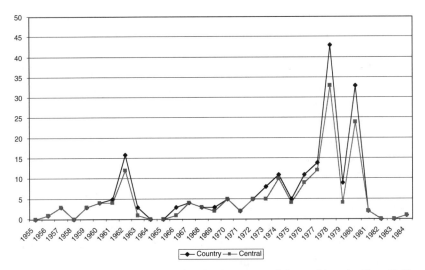

Figure 6.2 Guatemala: Total Strikes for Country and Central Area by Year, 1955–1984

Unfortunately, strikes and work stoppages cannot be identified as accurately as demonstrations. Conceptually, the distinction between the two is often not apparent in sources. What is called a strike in one news report might be called a work stoppage in a second source or in a second event by the same source. For uniformity of expression, from this point on they will be grouped together as *strikes*. Even more problematic, many strikes do not make it into the newspapers. When they do, and if they occur during a wave of strikes (which is often the case as a cycle of contention unfolds), they are often lumped together in a general story rather than identified individually.

Comparing the data collected here to official statistics for industrial strikes and work stoppages occurring between 1966 and 1978 published by Figueroa (1991, 131), only 38 percent of the full number are included in this database.[12] However, the trends portrayed by Figure 6.2 for the database are consistent with the official totals. Figueroa breaks the official data down by the three presidential administrations of this twelve-year period: 21 percent occur during 1966–1970 (a total of 51), 30 percent during 1970–1974 (74), and 49 percent during 1974–1978 (119).[13] The Guatemalan presidential

---

[12] Almost all of the disparity is accounted for by three of the four peak strike years (1970, 1974, and 1978).

[13] The same proportion holds true for the official data on total days of no work due to strikes and stoppages.

term begins July 1. When this study's data are broken down by presidential administration, the corresponding percentages of 17, 28, and 57 capture the same trend. Figueroa's coverage stopped at the point that labor activity exploded. The official total for the year 1978 was an incredible 229 strikes/work stoppages, compared to 157 for the combined prior eleven years (UN 1985, 911). The database only captures 19 percent of the 1978 peak. However, for 1979–1981 the database contains 72 percent of the official total. In summary, as shown by Figure 6.2, the database portrays with reasonable accuracy, at least for 1966–1981, the annual variations in strike levels, with the main exception of overstating 1980.[14]

It is likely that the most politically significant labor actions are covered by the press and therefore included in this study. These are, first, contentious activities by public employees. Some support for this confidence is also supplied by Figueroa (1991, 134–135). His annual totals (also using domestic sources) for eight categories of contentious activities for 1973–1980 are almost always below those for the data compiled for this study, including for strikes and work stoppages by public employees. Second, we can assume that the domestic press covers the largest and most dramatic actions by private-sector unions. Among the most significant examples are the 300 kilometer march to the capital by striking miners from the mountains of Huehuetenango in November 1977 and the hunger strike in front of the national palace in March 1978 by forty workers from the Esmaltes y Aceros factory, a demonstration that continued for fourteen days with much publicity until the country's president himself mediated a solution.

Student Strikes Guatemalan students played a critical role in the contentious activities examined in this study. Students from the national University of San Carlos organized some of the most important of the first protest demonstrations of the post-1954 period. Notably, they defied a government ban when they marched on June 25, 1956 to commemorate the anniversary of the death of a teacher in the 1944 struggle against dictator Ubico. Four new martyrs were created that day when police fired at the peaceful 1956 marchers. Students were again in the forefront of the mass

---

[14] A few other years also are overestimated, although not as seriously. Indeed, for a few years with low totals the database actually reports a higher total than the official figures (one more in 1969, 1971, and 1972; two more in 1979). However, the database's events for these years are well documented.

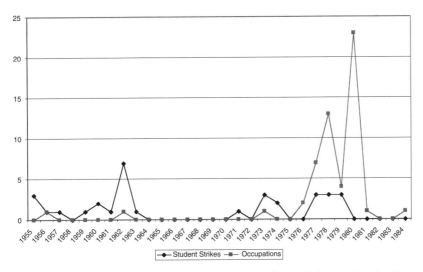

Figure 6.3 Guatemala: Total National Student Strikes and Occupations by Year, 1955–1984

movement of 1962, both in activists and in victims killed in the resulting repression.

In addition to their participation in demonstrations, a favorite student tactic was to strike from attending their classes. Many student strikes found in the newspaper archives have objectives addressed just to directors of their own educational institutions; these are not included in this study. The total number of student strikes in the database is small (32), so Figure 6.3 reports only the country total. Still, on notable occasions these strikes were important components of broad popular movements, such as the 1962 campaign, the historic teachers' strike of 1973, and the mass movement of the late 1970s.

Occupations   The final category of nonviolent contentious political activity analyzed here is sit-ins and occupations. These do not seem to have entered into the protest repertoire until the 1970s, as can be seen in Figure 6.3, but they were an important movement tactic in the cycle of contention that ended in 1980. As dramatic activities, occupations (as they are commonly referred to in Central America) are probably well covered by the press. However, if a number occur at the same time, they are not necessarily differentiated in press reports. Most of the occupations reported here are by workers, both urban and rural, occupying their sites of employment.

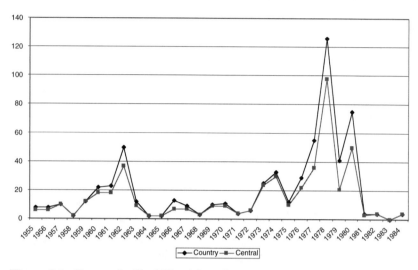

Figure 6.4 Guatemala: Total Nonviolent Contentious Activities for Country and Central Area by Year, 1955–1984

In September 1978, though, striking workers at a Swiss-owned company occupied the Swiss embassy to bring heightened attention to their cause. For parallel reasons, another set of workers occupied the Mexican embassy in June 1979. The tactic was then adopted by other organizations, most notably students and the Comité de Unidad Campesina (CUC). Their thwarted occupation on January 24, 1980 of the offices of the Organization of American States (OAS) was a prelude to their joint seizure of the Spanish embassy on January 31 and the tragic events that followed when the building exploded in flames under attack by the police, killing thirty-seven people.

Total Nonviolent Contentious Activities   Figure 6.4 brings these four dimensions of nonviolent contentious activities together. Both the national and central area trends clearly portray the rise and then collapse of two cycles of contention in Guatemala. The first begins in 1959, peaks in 1962, and is clearly over by 1963. The second extends over a longer period and reaches a much higher peak of contention, corresponding with events unfolding in El Salvador and Nicaragua. This cycle begins some time in 1973, dips at mid-decade, climbs to the highest peak for this thirty-year period in 1978, looks like it is fading in 1979, but recovers in 1980, and then collapses by 1981.

180

Measuring Illegal and Violent Contentious Activities

Challengers have other, more contentious tactics available to them. These are grouped together in this study as either illegal or violent activities, with the distinction largely based on the extent of threat of physical harm to others. Typically, challengers utilize higher levels of illegal and violent activities later in cycles of contention as frustration sets in and especially when regimes respond to peaceful protest with violence.[15] Violent revolutionary organizations certainly are active in periods outside of cycles of contention but their best window of opportunity for developing a revolutionary situation – and perhaps even a successful mass insurrection – normally occurs when regime violence radicalizes a highly mobilized protest movement.

Illegal Urban Contentious Activities   Data were collected on street vandalism and on burnings. Street vandalism covers activities from rock throwing at police, window breaking of stores and other buildings (and the robbery that might follow), building barricades across streets, and covering streets with tacks. Burnings are primarily of vehicles (often public buses) but include some buildings. Information also was compiled on burnings in rural areas, typically of sugar cane fields. However, they are not included in Figure 6.5 because so many of these rural burnings occurred in 1977 that they overwhelm the rest of the burnings data. Therefore, Figure 6.5 is restricted to urban illegal activities. Occupations are normally an illegal act, but in their nature they seem less in character with street vandalism and burnings and more with the other nonviolent activities with which they are classified in the prior section.

The trends shown by Figure 6.5 largely track those of the nonviolent contentious activities. To the extent there are differences, they are in keeping with the generalizations above. That is, illegal activities group around the peaks late in the cycles of contention even more than do the nonviolent activities. This difference is actually much greater than that portrayed by these data. If only one barricade is mounted during a period of low activity, it probably appears in news stories. However, during the most intense days of contention in early October 1978, for example, which was one of the main mobilization peaks for the entire thirty years, news stories refer to the existence of numerous barricades, but these reports give no guidance to

---

[15] For evidence from the nationalist movements bringing an end to the Soviet Union, see Beissinger (2002, 284–293).

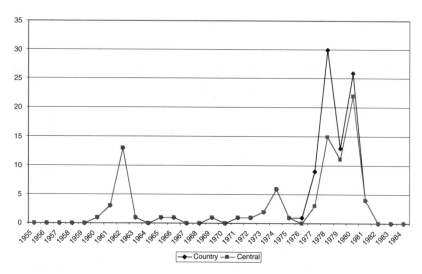

Figure 6.5 Guatemala: Total Illegal Urban Contentious Activities for Country and Central Area by Year, 1955–1984

the researcher as to how many that might be. Accordingly, the convention followed in this study is to report no more than one occurrence per day for each type of street vandalism or for burnings. This means, then, that the torching of one bus in March 1977 and of seven buses on one day in October 1978 are recorded the same. Multiple barricades on that same October day are also scored as just one separate activity, as are the many disparate cases of window breaking.

No direct effort is made here to determine the extent to which the trends portrayed by Figure 6.5 accurately represent the Guatemalan reality. However, since these illegal activities are a tactical radicalization largely associated with the latter phase of cycles of contention, they are not expected to occur with much frequency during other periods. Since this is what Figure 6.5 demonstrates, it seems reasonable to assume that its trends do mirror reality.

Violent Contentious Activities In contrast, it is much more difficult to collect data on violent contentious activities and to assess their representativeness for at least three reasons. First, violent activities are primarily associated with the tactics of revolutionary movements. Their urban activities might be reported by the press, as might their early limited rural actions. But once a serious rural insurgency develops, any meaningful track of their

182

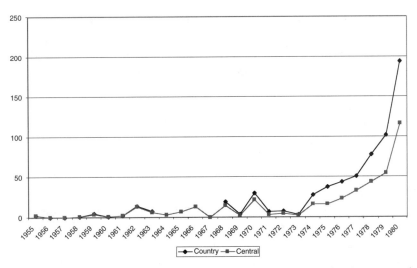

Figure 6.6 Guatemala: Total Violent Contentious Activities for Country and Central Area by Year, 1955–1980

actions becomes impossible for the press. Second, even if the press had the capacity for complete rural reporting, there were periods in Guatemala when little reporting was allowed by the repressive state on either insurgent or counterinsurgent actions.[16] Third, although peaceful and illegal protest activities largely disappear during periods of severe repression, the same is not true for violent contentious activities. Instead, clandestine violent actions are the only tactics that are left to challengers during periods of extreme repression. But whether censorship kept them out of the press is difficult to establish twenty – or thirty-five – years later. Accordingly, the data reported in Figure 6.6 must be regarded as very tentative. No attempt is even made to report country scores for the rural insurgency years of 1964–1967 nor for either the country or the central area during the revolutionary situation in 1981–1984.

Violent contentious activities combine armed attacks, kidnappings, and bombings. In many news reports, the agents of armed attacks are reported as unknown, but usually their victims are given. Counted within this category are armed attacks against the person or property (only a few cases) of security forces, public officials, owners of large businesses and landholdings,

---

[16] For example, concerning the guerrilla insurgency during 1963–1966, Adams notes that the "government kept almost all information of their activities out of the newspapers" (Adams 1970, 268).

and family members of leading figures in any of these categories. In an armed confrontation between police and unknown others, it is counted if the unknown others initiated the attack but not if the police did (in which case, they might have been apolitical criminals). Kidnappings are treated in the same manner as armed attacks. Bombings are another variable like street vandalism, where actual occurrences can be counted when there are few of them but not when, for example, hundreds throughout the country are reported to have occurred during the several days leading up to May 1, 1980. This indicator, then, counts no more than one bombing per day per department, which means that when violent activities expand the extent of their peak is understated.

Despite the limitations of the data on violent contentious activities, several interesting findings emerge from Figure 6.6. First, the data do represent the peaking of urban terrorism described in the literature for 1968 and 1970, which were years when repression kept peaceful and illegal activities low. Second, violent activities do peak with cycles of contention, notably in 1962, and in the late 1970s going into 1980. In 1962, repression smashed contention, but the dynamic of the latter period was very different. Although repression eliminated peaceful and illegal activities, violent contention exploded. This, then, will be a critical period for an in-depth examination of the repression-contention relationship, the central topic of Chapters 9 and 10.

Cycles of Contention in El Salvador

Data on contentious political activities in El Salvador were collected for a three-decade period beginning with 1960. However, source limitations raise serious doubts about the representativeness for the first half of this period, so the figures that follow use a shorter period, covering 1975 through 1991. Good sources still allow the tracking of two Salvadoran cycles of contention, as with Guatemala, but occurring over a shorter period of time. The reemergence of sustained nonviolent protest in the capital of San Salvador in the mid-1980s following the violent repression of the prior cycle of the late 1970s/1980 is of particular theoretical importance.

Data and Sources

The data on contentious political activities in El Salvador were compiled by the author primarily from *Estudios Centroamericanos* (ECA), an almost-monthly publication of perhaps Central America's most distinguished university, the Universidad Centroamérica José Simeón Cañas (UCA), a Jesuit institution located in San Salvador. The leading journal published in Central America, ECA began publishing a monthly chronicle of political events in El Salvador as popular contention intensified during September 1979 and continued publishing past the end of the civil war at the close of 1991. ECA is a source for 58 percent of the Salvadoran records. Extensive use also was made of the *New York Times* for the Salvadoran data (unlike for Guatemala). Through the *Times Index*, potentially relevant stories were identified and then the full stories were read and coded.[17] The *NY Times* stories are a source for 27 percent of the records but the sole source for only 16 percent. Another 6 percent have U.S. declassified documents as their sole source. Five percent of the records have a Guatemala City source, either the *El Imparcial* daily edition or the weekly regional report published by *Inforpress*. The Salvadoran newspaper *La Prensa Grafica* is a source for two percent of the records. Many other sources also were used, especially books published in El Salvador, often by UCA's press. Altogether, the El Salvador database contains 1,760 records, which include 1,442 separate contentious events.

It is important to keep in mind a point made in the Guatemala section: during periods of intense activity sources seldom attempt to give full counts of individual forms of contentious activities.[18] Accordingly, the peaks reported in the data do not represent the full disparity between them and the periods before and after. This is especially true for the period between October 1979 and May 1980 when the best source, ECA, merely reported that "many" or "numerous" demonstrations, occupations, and bombings occurred throughout that month. Unless specific events are cited, the best

---

[17] The *NY Times* stories were read and summarized by three undergraduate research assistants (Maggie Giel, Scott Maule, and Jaret Pfluger), who then wrote concise summaries of the relevant information on a score sheet prepared by the author. This information was then entered into the database, Maggie Giel. All of these records were double-checked by the author against the *NY Times Index* and in a number of cases against the full texts of the stories.

[18] Consider this tantalizing but impossible-to-use report from the U.S. embassy in San Salvador: "On unprecedented scale, radical groups in past few weeks have been occupying or otherwise harassing agricultural operations, raising possibility of serious losses in major harvest now underway. Exact information on number of farms involved is not available.... One agricultural group claimed that ... fifty coffee plantations, twenty-five cotton farms, and fifteen cattle ranches had been 'attacked' by 'mobs of extremist fanatics'" (USDS/NSA1 1979c).

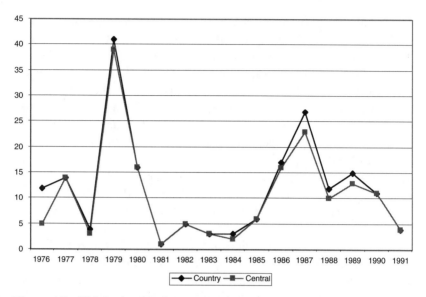

Figure 6.7 El Salvador: Total Demonstrations for Country and Central Area by Year, 1976–1991

that could be done in the database was to score one per month for each type of activity mentioned.

Measuring Nonviolent Contentious Activities

The measurement of Salvadoran contentious activities follows the guidelines explained in the prior section on Guatemala and will not be repeated here. The one major difference for Salvadoran nonviolent activities is that the student strike does not seem to have entered the contentious repertoire in the way it did in Guatemala. Only two were indicated in the sources consulted for the entire period; they are included in the total for nonviolent activities but not presented separately.

For most years during the 1975–1991 period, the most important form of peaceful contention was the demonstration. As shown by Figure 6.7, the peak both for the country total and the central area of the capital city and the surrounding department of San Salvador is in 1979.[19] There is then a

---

[19] Metropolitan San Salvador extends on the west into the department of La Libertad, and accordingly an unknown number of events in that department are included when sources identified them just as occurring in the metropolitan area. Events located by sources as

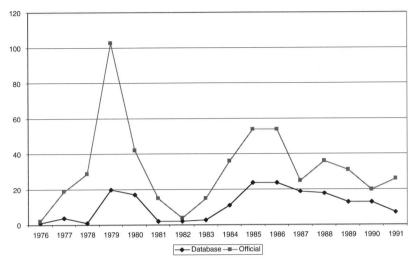

Figure 6.8 El Salvador: Total National Strikes from Database and Official Figures by Year, 1976–1991

sharp drop into 1980 (with most of those occurring in just the first quarter of the year) and the virtual disappearance of demonstrations for the next few years. Remarkably, though, given that El Salvador was still in the midst of civil war, this form of protest returned in a sustained way for the rest of the decade.

Figure 6.8 shows the relevant trends for strikes, comparing this study's national totals to official data. Unlike Guatemala, the comparison is not as smooth. Roughly, the trends track across the period, but the crucial contentious years of 1978 and 1979 are woefully underrepresented in the database while the last half of the 1980s are overrepresented. More precisely, for the first six years of Figure 6.8 the database contains an annual median of 21 percent of the official total while for the last ten years it jumps to 44 percent (and 65 percent for the last five). This means that it needs to be kept in mind that the extent of the contention peak of the late 1970s compared to other years is understated in the figures presented in this study. Still, the trends for strikes are clearly the same as with demonstrations: a sharp drop for 1981–1983 and then a noticeable recovery for the rest of the 1980s, especially in 1985–1986.

occurring in Santa Tecla, which is at the metropolitan fringe in La Libertad, are included as part of the central area.

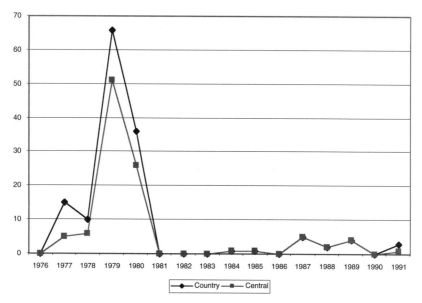

Figure 6.9 El Salvador: Total Occupations for Country and Central Area by Year, 1976–1991

An especially important part of the contentious repertoire of the first Salvadoran cycle was occupations, as indicated by Figure 6.9. Prominent sites for these occupations were churches and public buildings in the cities and large estates in the countryside. The overwhelming majority of these occurred in 1979–1980. As the most combative of the peaceful tactics, it is notable that they were much less important to the protests of the last half of the 1980s.

Pulling all of these forms of nonviolent contentious activities together in Figure 6.10, what is portrayed is an intense cycle of contention peaking in 1979/1980 and then the virtual elimination of protest during 1981–1983, which was a period of extreme state violence directed against challengers. The extent of the contention peak and then its collapse was actually more dramatic than Figure 6.10 indicates. The worst underrepresentation in the database of strikes is for 1978–1979 (and therefore might be for the other forms of nonviolent contention as well).

Yet even with the period of extreme state terrorism and with the civil war still continuing, in 1984 nonviolent contention reemerges in Figure 6.10, led by labor conflicts. The following year, demonstrations increase as well and a new cycle of contention is underway for the remainder of the decade,

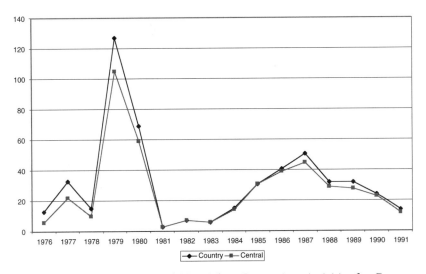

Figure 6.10 El Salvador: Total Nonviolent Contentious Activities for Country and Central Area by Year, 1976–1991

at least in the capital. Explaining these trends, and especially the appearance and strength of the second cycle, will be, major concern of the chapters that follow, especially Chapters 8 and 10.

Measuring Illegal and Violent Activities

Portraying trends for illegal and violent activities is more difficult for El Salvador than for Guatemala. The Salvadoran database is limited concerning these types of activities prior to 1978, which is used in Figure 6.11 as the beginning year. The sources consulted seldom mentioned these forms of contention when they occurred outside of the capital until the civil war began in 1980. Given the significant scale of the insurgency that did develop in El Salvador, it would be impossible to represent with any confidence national trends for illegal and violent activities. However, since the civil war seldom actively entered the capital, looking at trends for these two forms of contentious activities within metropolitan San Salvador should be meaningful. But there are two further caveats. Figure 6.11 excludes any activities associated with the major guerrilla offensives of January 1981 and November 1989, which is especially important for 1989 since it did feature substantial fighting within the metropolitan area. Second, inferring from the ambiguous descriptions in the source material, I conclude that undercounting over the entire period for Figure 6.11 is probably worst for illegal activities

189

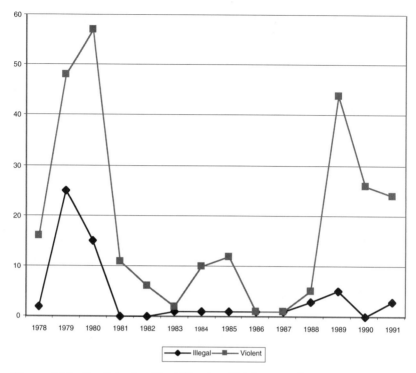

Figure 6.11 San Salvador: Total Illegal and Violent Acts by Year, 1978–1991

during the 1979–1980 period, followed by violent activities for the same period. It would be more accurate to regard these scores – especially for illegal activities – as summarizing the number of months during the year for which each of the associated types of activities occurred, rather than the number of individual occurrences.

The differences in the two trends in Figure 6.11 are striking. Illegal activities peak at the same point as do nonviolent contentious activities, that is, 1979–1980, and then largely disappear. Unlike nonviolent activities, which recover and increase from the mid-1980s on, few illegal activities are associated with this second cycle of contention. In contrast, violent actions in the metropolitan area not only peak with the overall first cycle, they also reappear late in the second cycle, almost reaching the level of the first cycle. Understanding what drives the different trends in these three distinct forms of contentious action, especially their relationship to repression and other aspects of the configuration of political opportunities, is a central purpose of the chapters that follow.

Concerning Analytic Techniques

This is an empirical study. It is based on what might be the most complete set of data for contentious political activities in Latin America and among the most ambitious for any Third World cases. Nonetheless, it should be apparent from the prior discussion that this set of data is still only a loose approximation of the reality that it attempts to represent. While the fit is good enough for some purposes, it is my position that it is too loose an approximation to warrant statistical analysis. Statistical techniques are powerful because they allow the aggregation of so much data into so few numbers. The precision of the results unavoidably suggest an accuracy to the data that was processed to reach that result. The more sophisticated the statistical technique, the more powerful the suggestion. To me, this is a serious defect in the literature on cross-national quantitative studies using events data from Third World countries. The results of such studies are of uncertain value because there is so little reason to have faith that the collection of data that is the basis of the analysis bears any meaningful relationship to the social reality it purports to represent.[20]

The contentious events data used in this study are far better than those used in most quantitative studies in this field. But in interpreting results, both the author and the reader need always to remember that these indicators are still rough measures. The same is also true for the data on political violence that are used in this work, even though they are much better than the corresponding data that normally have been used by past studies. Accordingly, no statistical analyses are undertaken concerning the relationship that is the theoretical heart of this study, that is, between repression and contentious movements. The analytic techniques employed in this study are no more sophisticated than the comparison of trends across time already presented in this chapter.

Two general theoretical approaches have been pursued in the quantitative literature seeking to understand "why [people] rebel." One approach, framed well by Muller and his many associates, stresses political variables. The second, especially associated with Gurr, gives greater attention to

---

[20] McAdam and Sewell Jr. highlight an additional problem for statistical analysis when events data are utilized: "event research has erred in weighting all protests, demonstrations, and speeches as equally important.... we would argue for a more nuanced form of event analysis that would focus...the degree of public attention and significance that came to attach to *particular* events nested in the broader stream of protest" (McAdam and Sewell Jr. 2001, 124).

grievances, which are often conceptualized in terms of relative deprivation. Efforts to link quantitatively contentious behavior directly to socioeconomic variables face additional problems beyond data accuracy. Two are mentioned here, and others (such as ecological inference problems) were discussed in Chapter 2.[21]

Central American countries are dominated by their capital cities. This is *the* site of protest activity. Next in importance will be other major cities (e.g., Quetzaltenango in Guatemala), especially those located close to the capital (Escuintla in Guatemala, Santa Ana in El Salvador). Needless to say, these are also the locations most likely to receive coverage in domestic newspapers. All things being equal, smaller towns that are closer to the capital also will be more important sites of protest because they can draw on assistance from support groups based in the capital, such as university students and religious workers. For example, the small towns of Aguilares and Suchitoto were crucial to the development of contentious movements in El Salvador in the 1970s, as was the southern region of the department of El Quiché in Guatemala. The presence of unique religious projects in these areas of both countries and their proximity to the capital (as well as Quetzaltenango for El Quiché) are undoubtedly better explanatory variables for the higher levels of contentious mobilization in these areas compared to towns further away from the capital than would be any set of socioeconomic characteristics of their inhabitants.[22]

Furthermore, using department level data is problematic because in both countries some departments extend from the Pacific coast up into the

---

[21] Given the difficulties discussed here and in the next chapter, it should not be surprising that the quantitative literature testing the relationship between inequality and protest has had such contradictory conclusions. In an excellent review of these studies, Lichbach 1989 finds support for all possible relationships: positive, negative, concave, convex, as well as no impact. His conclusion is still warranted: "The evidence thus supports the view that, in general, economic inequality is neither necessary, sufficient, nor clearly probabilistically related to dissent" (Lichbach 1989, 464). Cross-national quantitative work on the subject has continued, generally arguing for a relationship between income inequality and political violence (e.g., Boswell and Dixon 1993; Muller and Seligson 1987; Muller, Seligson, and Fu 1989; Robinson and London 1991; and Schock 1996). Others, though, dissent (e.g., Wang 1995 and Weede 1981, 1986). Despite their theoretical and methodological sophistication, the meaningfulness of these studies is problematic because of the shortcomings in the data generally used (Brockett 1992; but see the defense by Dixon, Muller, and Seligson 1993).

[22] In turn, Wood highlights the proximity of northern Tenancingo to Suchitoto and Aguilares as more important for understanding peasant support for the Salvadoran revolutionaries compared to the southern part of the *municipio* than any socioeconomic differences between the two zones (Wood 2003, 89–94).

highlands, thereby including three major and distinct zones: the mountains, dominated by poor peasants with minimal land; the piedmont, dominated by coffee estates with residential workforces and seasonal migrants; and the coastal lowlands, dominated by huge commercial estates based on migratory and day labor with some resident workers. Socioeconomic data are available at the smaller and often more homogeneous *municipio* level. However, reports on contentious events outside of the metropolitan region often do not give sufficient information to identify the department; even less possible is the identification of municipalities. Finally, contentious activities are concentrated in the capital and its surrounding department while whatever contention that does occur in other regions is less likely to be reported by the press.

The practical problems faced by any effort to test quantitatively the relationship between socioeconomic variables and this study's data on contentious political activities for El Salvador and Guatemala strike me as insurmountable. Accordingly, as with the relationship to repression, a statistical analysis of the relationship of contention to socioeconomic variables will not be attempted in this study.

Conclusion

This preliminary look at the events data collected on contentious political activities in El Salvador and Guatemala establishes two full cycles of contention for each country. Prior chapters discussed the contentious movements and their grievances that drove these cycles. The following two chapters examine whether and how these cycles were related to changes in the configuration of political opportunities. After this analysis, we will then be well positioned to use these four full cycles of contention to examine closely the paradoxical relationship between repression and contentious political activity, the larger theoretical question of this study.

7

Changing Political Opportunities and Contentious Challengers

GUATEMALA

As grievances intensify, potential challengers have new incentives to act. With support from allies, they gain encouragement and resources. But whether movements will emerge and persist and whether they will succeed in achieving any of their objectives will be substantially determined by factors outside of their control. These central dimensions of the configuration of political opportunities are the subject of this chapter, which examines Guatemala, and the next chapter, which analyzes El Salvador and then concludes with a comparison of both with the other three countries of Central America.

Critics claim that the distinction between mobilization and political opportunities is often muddled in case studies using the political process approach. Poletta and Amenta note that critics particularly object to "a posthoc quality" to such accounts, which identify as "'opportunity' any political development that preceded mobilization" (Poletta and Amenta 2001, 307). This and the next chapter accept this challenge, first identifying key changes in political opportunities and then predicting the expected direction of popular mobilization. These predictions are tested with data for key indicators of contentious politics: demonstrations for Guatemala and strikes for El Salvador.

The Configuration of Political Opportunities

The relative openness or closure of the institutionalized political system, the stability or instability of elite alignments, and the capacity and propensity of the state to rely on repression are key aspects of the configuration of political opportunities facing contentious challengers. These have important consequences for their mobilization as well as their possibilities for

194

success. Following brief conceptual discussions of each, they will be utilized jointly to analyze this study's two cases. Since repression is the central theoretical concern of this study, it is also treated individually and in further depth in Chapters 9 and 10.

In their recent work, McAdam, Tarrow, and Tilly 2001 have stressed as the appropriate focus for our analysis the *attribution* by social actors of opportunities/threats[1] as opposed to the "objective *conditions* confronting acting individuals" (Merton 1996, 154). In my view, both approaches are important. In earlier chapters, attribution received considerable attention, as it will in Chapters 9 and 10. The emphasis of this chapter and the next, though, is the political context external to contentious actors, the political variables that exist independent of their perceptions and strategies, that so much determine the outcomes of their actions.

Political Access

Outside of rare revolutionary transformations, the claims of challengers are handled, if at all, within existing political structures. Political opportunities for challengers, then, vary with the availability of meaningful access points within the political system itself.[2] The relevant access points are well known: from interest aggregating institutions such as political parties to legislatures to bureaucracies and to top-level executive decision makers.

---

[1] Goldstone and Tilly 2001 correctly point out that it is a mistake to treat threats as "merely the flip side of opportunity" (p. 181). They distinguish between current and anticipated "harm," that is, "costs of repression" (pp. 184–185). Repression is but one dimension of the configuration of political opportunity and does have its own dynamics (p. 181) that differ from those of the other dimensions. As will be discussed thoroughly in this and subsequent chapters, both current and anticipated repression (threats) create new grievances, providing perhaps enough motivation to override constricting opportunity in order to sustain existing mobilization or to spur new activities.

[2] Amenta et al. 2002 point out that the "institutionalized political system" is a concept so inclusive that it "might conceivably incorporate any and every aspect of the state or polity" (p. 52). They give considerable attention to disaggregating this dimension of the configuration of political opportunities, but notably their discussion is almost entirely in terms of First World examples. Variations in the vertical and horizontal distributions of power and in electoral procedures (pp. 56–69) are theoretically important where they are politically meaningful, i.e., in well-institutionalized democracies. They have far less analytic value in nondemocratic systems. For example, in Mexico's seven decades of domination by a one-party state, the fact that it was formally a federalist system with a separation of powers at each level was of little relevance for contentious movements. However, with the opposition's victory in the presidential elections of 2000, both the states and the national legislature quickly assumed importance for challengers.

By meaningful is meant both institutionalized and power–wielding. Access to political parties has little meaning if elections are fraudulent or if responsive administrations are overthrown; access to legislators, if legislatures have little power; access to bureaucrats, if their decisions are usually overturned. Meaningful popular access to the political system was not institutionalized in Central America during the period under study except in Costa Rica. Accordingly, fluctuations in the opening and closing of meaningful access to the political system was a crucial dimension of the configuration of political opportunities for all contentious movements in the region. More specifically, the crucial aspects of political access in such countries are regular fair and free elections and respect for basic political freedoms, such as the right of assembly.

Although the major thrust of the political opportunities literature is that *expanding* opportunities facilitate popular mobilization, it also is the case that *contracting* political access can promote mobilization – but only under certain conditions.[3] For example, fraudulent elections and declining government responsiveness (as well as repressive acts) become new grievances, adding to already existing grievances. Together, these new and old grievances could fuel a level of contentious activity that might not have been reached through the preexisting grievances alone. Generally, contracting political opportunities are more likely to have this catalyzing effect the higher the level of preexisting mass mobilization. Examining this relationship more specifically is an important purpose of the chapters that follow.

Elite Alignments

Movements asserting the claims of the disadvantaged invariably confront a formidable array of elite interests. When political, military, and economic elites are cohesive, the political opportunities for challengers are usually minimal; as elites fragment and especially as they come into conflict, opportunities open.[4] In rare cases, elite fragmentation and conflict contribute

---

[3] Goodwin and Jasper 1999 use this contradictory relationship to close their case against the political opportunities model but in a way that I would not. Their argument will be addressed in the conclusion of the next chapter.

[4] Elite fragmentation and conflict is a crucial variable for many scholars. For example, Joseph's 1986 study of the War of the Caste in Yucatán, perhaps the most successful peasant rebellion in Latin American history, finds agrarian transformation as the source of grievances with elite fragmentation as the source of opportunity. As a different example, Lachmann points

to a regime crisis so severe as to allow for a revolutionary outcome.[5] The relationship also can work the other way: Contentious politics can contribute to elite fragmentation.[6]

This component of the configuration of political opportunities is as complex as it is critical. First, the salient elites might be not only domestic but also include those of a hegemonic power, such as the United States when the subject is Central America.[7] Second, elite fragmentation and conflict are dimensions that can and do vary independently with differential implications for collective action.[8] A third aspect of elite alignments is the existing pattern of elite-state relations.[9] A cohesive elite dominating the state presents potential challengers with a discouraging situation, usually more so than a state with some measure of autonomy from dominant economic elites, especially when the state is dominated by a personalistic dictator.[10] Fourth and confounding any easy direct relationship, Javeline points out that with a

out from his examination of cases from over six centuries of European history: "Non-elites mobilize when heightened elite conflict creates the opportunities and alliances which can justify the risks of collective action" (Lachmann 1997, 74). He concludes that "the degree of conflict among elites determines the efficacy of mass action" (p. 73).

[5] Among many, see, of course, Skocpol 1979.

[6] Piven and Cloward note, "Indeed, we think the role of disruptive protest in helping to create political crises...is the main source of political influence by lower stratum groups" (Piven and Cloward 1995, 160).

[7] Scholars of contentious movements, it is said, have underestimated the importance of international variables. For example, McAdam observes that "social movement scholars, unlike their brethren who study revolutions, have truncated our understanding of the rise of social movements by ignoring the *international* forces that frequently shape the structure of *domestic* political opportunities available to challenging groups" (McAdam 1998, 265). McClintock, though, says the same for revolutions as well: "Scholars of revolution tend to underestimate the importance of the international context to the outcome of a revolutionary effort" (McClintock 1998, 201). For good attention to bringing the international context into their analysis of contentious movements, see Jenkins and Schock 1992; McClintock 1998; and Schock 1999a.

[8] Sidney Tarrow originally pointed out to me the importance of this distinction. For example, a situation of medium to high elite fragmentation would probably facilitate the mobilization of the disadvantaged, but if combined with low elite conflict there would be a low probability for significant changes in the distribution of power and resources.

[9] See, for example, Evans, Rueschemeyer, and Skocpol 1985. Barkey's 1991 comparison of sustained peasant rebellions in France, but not the Ottoman Empire, for example, highlights whether state penetration of the countryside divided rural classes or promoted cross-class alliances. Similarly, see Jenkins 1983b.

[10] This is a crucial distinction for many analysts, as it will be in this and the next chapter and especially for the Central American comparison that concludes Chapter 8. Among others, see Goodwin 2001; Goodwin and Skocpol 1989; Midlarsky and Roberts 1985; Parsa 2000; and Wickham-Crowley 1992.

197

coherent elite at least challengers know where blame lies. As elites fragment, though, and as "lines of authority are confused . . . aggrieved individuals are less likely to make specific attributions of blame and less likely to mobilize" (Javeline 2003, 119–120).

For now, the central point is this: As elite and elite-state alignments vary, so, too, do the opportunities for challengers to assert their claims and to gain favorable outcomes. Fundamental differences in these alignments between the five Central American countries go a long way toward explaining the different courses and consequences of contentious political activities between them, as will be explained at the end of the next chapter.

Repression

Used in a broad sense, repression would not be analytically much different from the closure of the institutionalized political system.[11] Therefore, a narrower understanding will be employed here: *Repression* is the illegitimate use of force against citizens by the state.[12] As defined here, a government ban on demonstrations and then the enforcement of that ban with beatings, torture, and murder are analytically distinct dimensions of the configuration of political opportunities. However, these analytic distinctions are not always easy when applied to case material – social reality is a whole that we carve with our concepts to suit our theoretical purposes. Some events are less amenable to our carving than others, and some concepts cut less cleanly than others.

The intensity of repression directed at popular forces is not directly related to the level of threat perceived by elites. Neither is it a straight function of coercive capacity. Instead, regimes and leaders vary both in their willingness to tolerate popular mobilization and in their willingness to respond with violence when they don't. The state's capacity for violence is obviously a necessary precondition for repression; but when it comes to having the trigger pulled, propensity becomes the more crucial factor. Repression,

---

[11] Tilly 2003 identifies the same causal mechanisms and processes at work across all forms of collective violence, including state terrorism.

[12] Johnston and Mueller 2001 claim that "Of all the concepts in the tool kit of political process theorists, none can compare with state repression in the lack of consensus on its meaning, theoretical status, operationalization, or empirical relationships with other variables." Also see Amenta et al. (2002, 53, 66–67).

then, has two dimensions: both the state's capacity and its propensity for repression.[13]

The important distinction between these two dimensions is well illustrated by the different responses of Salvadoran General Maximiliano Hernández Martínez to threats he faced in 1932 and 1944. Referring to the civic strike that brought his dictatorship to an end in 1944, Ackerman and DuVall 2000 quote Martínez as explaining in an interview afterwards, "Then I no longer wanted to fight. At whom was I going to fire? At children and youths who did not completely realize what they were doing?" Ackerman and DuVall then note, "The general who had not blanched at the killing of thousands of peasants a decade before could not use his weapons when his moment of greatest peril arrived" (p. 261).

The configuration of political opportunities facing Central American popular movements in the decades of this study varied widely to a significant extent because of great differences in regime reliance on repression, both within and between countries. It also had differed in the decades prior to 1960. The individual and collective memory of past repression is part of the calculation of the risks involved in contentious action contemplated in the present. The historical memory in repressive societies can both legitimate coercion to elites and discourage collective action by popular forces, thereby serving to uphold the "culture of repression."[14] Conversely, the last days of the Soviet Union demonstrate what happens when a previously repressive regime is widely perceived as having lost the will to repress as necessary to survive (Beissinger 2002).

Political Opportunities and Guatemalan Contentious Movements

The events data on cycles of contention in Guatemala examined in Chapter 6 portray substantial fluctuations in the level of contentious

---

[13] The capacity and propensity of the state for repression became part of the standard iteration of the configuration (structure) of political opportunities with Brockett 1991b. Goodwin and Jasper 1999 criticize this conceptualization (referring to McAdam 1996b), arguing that it "collapses the actual use of repression, which is a strategic choice, into structural capacities for repression, which are more a matter of physical and human resources" (p. 34). Although their distinction seems correct from one perspective, from the perspective of regime challengers (which is the reference point for the configuration of political opportunities), the propensity for repression is no less part of a challenger's external political context than is the capacity for repression.

[14] The phrase "culture of repression" comes from Huizer 1972, who developed it based on experience working in rural El Salvador.

activity. This chapter tests the predictive value of changes in the configuration of political opportunities for social movement activity. First, key changes in political opportunities are identified for the years 1954 through 1986. Based on the direction of these changes, this overall time span is divided into twelve periods. Second, predictions are made from these changes in opportunities for the expected direction of social movement activity for each period. Third, these predictions are tested with one indicator of contention: protest demonstrations.

It is true that Guatemala was ruled throughout almost all of this period by military leaders. If they had all been hard-line tyrants, there probably would have been little fluctuation in either political opportunities or social movement activity, making Guatemala an especially inappropriate case for testing the utility of the political opportunities approach. Fortunately for both challengers and this study, they were not all the same. General Miguel Ydígoras allowed considerable space for popular movements for much of his tenure in the late 1950s/early 1960s. Most importantly, the administration of General Kjell Laugerud during the mid-1970s was significantly less repressive than the ones that preceded and followed.

Each of the four dimensions of the configuration of political opportunities refers to a complex social reality. Given the need to be concise, what follows are brief sketches of the major shifts in opportunity that occurred, with primary attention given to access to the institutionalized political system and to state repression. The remaining two dimensions of elite alignments and elite allies are explicitly discussed only in those periods where such changes played a particularly important role. Each period is labeled with both the direction of change in the configuration of political opportunities and the relevant prediction for the direction of social movement activity.

Five different categories for changes in opportunities are utilized: closed, opening, relatively open, restricting, and closing. A "relatively open" situation for noninstitutionalized democracies such as Guatemala during the period of this study is not expected to reach the level of openness that characterize institutionalized democracies. Although elections are held regularly in a "relatively open" situation, they are not necessarily open to all. Challengers might face some harassment and regime intimidation, but outright repression is relatively low. "Restricting" and "closing" opportunities are distinguished as increasing degrees of movement by the regime away from openness and toward closed opportunities. Typically, a "restricting" period features elite conflict between those wanting to maintain a more open system and those wanting to reduce opportunities for challengers. Often central to this conflict is the issue of repression. As the hard-line groups triumph, elite conflict lessens and the situation deteriorates for challengers to "closing" opportunities and perhaps further to a "closed" situation.

1. Closed opportunities; social movements demobilized, 1954

The single most important political event in twentieth-century Guatemala was the overthrow of the government of Jacobo Arbenz.[15] His forced departure from the presidency and the country in June 1954 ended ten years of elected progressive government and increasing popular mobilization throughout the country. Not only had urban and rural unions proliferated, but so, too, had radicalized agrarian reform committees that drove the most polarizing reform of the period. By the end of 1953, there were some 1,500 agrarian committees throughout the countryside, often influenced by the communist party, the Partido Guatemalteco del Trabajo (PGT) (CEH 1999, 1:102).

To Guatemalan elites and the rest of the right, the elimination of what they perceived as the communist threat of the Arbenz years was crucial to the purposes of their counterrevolution. Independent U.S. observers at the time reported some two hundred to two hundred fifty summary executions in the months following the overthrow.[16] This was not enough, though, for the hard right, who "openly claim they would like to see a blood bath to purge Guatemala of its alleged Communist population" (USDS 1955). In some rural areas, they had their way, with the numbers killed impossible to estimate accurately.[17] Meanwhile, the jails were filled "to overflowing;" according to U.S. embassy figures, over 5,000 were jailed in the coup's aftermath (USDS 1954b). However, before year's end all but a handful had been released.

The counterrevolution also meant for elites a return to their privileged position, a dominance justified by a level of socioeconomic

---

[15] The best discussion of issues related to the Arbenz government, including its overthrow, is Gleijesis 1991.

[16] Given what has happened in other counterrevolutions, such as in Chile in 1973, it is notable that no members of the Arbenz government were killed. However, assassination of Arbenz-period leaders had been the subject of CIA discussion for some time (Haines 1995, 8). This section on the 1954–1960 period is based on Brockett 2002, which should be consulted for further documentation.

[17] An independent effort of its own to estimate the death toll for this period was beyond the scope of the Guatemalan truth commission. Instead, it cites estimates from other sources of two to three thousand deaths for the Castillo Armas years (CEH 1999, 1:108).

underdevelopment that still required elite "guidance." Any mass politics or reformist policies in the "post-liberation" period for elites and the rest of the right were too reminiscent of the prior "communist" years, and, accordingly, they used the club of anticommunism to attack left-of-center political parties, labor organizing, and any reforms that might threaten their vested interests.

2. Slow opening of opportunities; slow return of movement activity, 1955 through 1958

However, the right faced two big problems. First, their ally in the overthrow of Arbenz, the U.S. government, had different objectives for what was supposed to follow. Second, popular forces did not intend to remain demobilized.

The Eisenhower administration fully shared with Guatemalan elites and other rightists the desire to rid the country of any further communist threat. At the same time, the United States wished to turn postliberation Guatemala into an anticommunist "showcase for democracy."[18] Repression of the left by the new government of Colonel Carlos Castillo Armas had the full backing of the United States, which stood aside as he consolidated his position with sham legislative elections and presidential plebiscite. However, early plans by Castillo Armas and his circle to govern by decree for several years to stabilize the country in an apolitical environment were opposed by U.S. officials who after the first few months exerted considerable effort to move Castillo in a more democratic direction. As he responded, already existing tensions with the Guatemalan hard right grew, especially as popular mobilization soon reemerged.

Castillo's rule after the first repressive months was less draconian than often portrayed in accounts of this period. More importantly, Guatemalans from across the political spectrum were less passive and soon began to assert their interests. Popular leaders who had experienced the recent "free space" of democratic politics were dedicated to winning it back. Crucial also was the overthrow's impact on attitudes, especially those of young progressives, as well captured by Stoll: "The trauma was all the greater because these were young men and women who had grown up in an era of free expression, reform, and boundless possibility that suddenly ended as

---

[18] While this intention was naïve and lacking in commitment, it was not a façade, as a reading of the State Department documents of the period demonstrates.

they reached adulthood. What remained was a powerful sense of patriotic mission" (Stoll 1999, 46).[19]

Leading civil society were urban labor and university students, as described in Chapter 4. For example, there were the unscheduled workers and student speakers who seized the stage at the May 1, 1956 commemoration, giving "incendiary" speeches emphasizing the gains of the October 1944 revolution and the need for workers to fight to restore rights and benefits. And there was the prohibited march led by university students on June 25, 1956, when protestors were fired on by the police, with 6 killed, dozens wounded, and at least 168 arrests.[20]

Establishing responsibility for this, the worst confrontation of the Castillo period, is difficult. The press at the time reported that Castillo had given orders that the march be broken up but without violence, and he was said to be upset over what occurred.[21] Certainly, it was well known at the time that the right was unhappy that he had not carried out a more thorough purge of Guatemalan society, and perhaps they were reassured by Castillo's acquiescence to cracking down on popular mobilization. In contrast, the U.S. ambassador warned Castillo that "violent response plays into [the] hands of [the] communists" (USDS 1956b).

Castillo Armas was assassinated in July 1957, sending into motion a process that would lead to a greater opening of opportunities for challengers. The first elections held to replace him were widely seen as fraudulent, and as disorder spread the army stepped in, vitiated the results, and called new elections for January 1958. Because the government's candidate (and presumed U.S. favorite) lost, the fairness of the results can be assumed. The winner was General Miguel Ydígoras. Supported by "the extreme right-wing element of the country, including big landowners" (NY Times Mar. 2, 1958, 30), many of the top leaders of his movement had been prominent in the Jorge Ubico dictatorship of 1931–1944 – as had Ydígoras himself – and hoped through Ydígoras for a return to the "good old days" of the Ubico period. However, in office Ydígoras generally moved in a more moderate

---

[19] Stoll claims, "If there is a single reason for the guerrilla movement and its premise that Guatemala required armed liberation, it was the CIA's overthrow of an elected government in 1954" (Stoll 1999, 46–47). He gives the example of two key EGP leaders: Ricardo Ramírez, who was a student leader at the time of the coup and was forced to take refuge in an embassy (where he met Ché Guevara, who had taken refuge in the same embassy), and Mario Payeras, fourteen at the time, who also described it as the key event for himself.

[20] *El Imparcial* (June 26, 1956); NY Times (June 29, 1956, 5); USDS 1956a.

[21] *El Imparcial* (June 26, 1956; July 20, 1956).

direction, attempting to construct and maintain a broad populist coalition. For his first two years, repression declined considerably. Most important for what would come, he extended the approach of the junta that preceded him of opening political space, knowingly allowing a return of the left as part of his policy of national reconciliation.[22]

Developing mainstream political parties was the primary focus of challengers. One nonregime political party already had formed in 1955, the moderate Partido Democracia Cristiana Guatemalteca (DC). Now taking advantage of this more hospitable climate, the moderate left formed a new political party in August 1957, the Partido Revolucionario (PR), in order to advance once again the ideals of the October Revolution of 1944.[23] Although aware that banning the party would backfire, U.S. officials were concerned that the PR provided a vehicle for the participation of the more radical left. They worried that the PR might bring back to power the Juan José Arévalo forces that preceded Arbenz in office and then, they feared, the far left once again. This concern, shared with the Guatemalan right, deepened as growing numbers of political exiles, including communist leaders from the prior period, were allowed by the Ydígoras government to return, many against the specific counsel of U.S. officials (USDS 1957). Indeed, the PR was in the forefront of contentious activities for the next half decade, along with the Federación Autonóma Sindical de Guatemala (FASGUA) leading labor and the Asociación de Estudiantes Universitarios (AEU) leading students. Their movement was to peak in spring 1962 with the most significant contentious campaign to occur between 1944 and the late 1970s.

3. Relatively open; increasing activity, 1959 to Oct. 1961

The PR scored its first big electoral victory in July 1959, winning the mayoralty of Guatemala City. Ydígoras considered annulling the election but backed down under the prospect of significant popular opposition. As a consequence, the right-wing went "into a panic," according to the U.S.

---

[22] CEH (1999, 1:113); Kennedy (1971, 148); NY Times (Mar. 2, 1958, 30). More generally on the Ydígoras period, see CEH (1999, 1:112–130 and Ebel 1998). Handy gives a good, concise characterization of the Ydígoras administration: "a farce of incompetence, corruption and patronage" (Handy 1984, 152).

[23] The dilemma for the PR would be that it "tries to identify itself with the revolution, but at the same time looks to the right for permission to survive" (Adams 1970, 198). For background on the Guatemalan party system of the 1950s and 1960s, see IIPS 1978.

embassy, deciding "this was the ultimate proof that Ydígoras was 'soft' on communism and that a return to Arévalo-Arbenz was just around the corner."[24] Fidel Castro had triumphed only six months earlier and such fears heightened as Castro radicalized the direction of the Cuban revolution. Intensifying rightist concerns further were chants and placards praising Arbenz and Castro in a June 1959 demonstration, praising Castro and attacking Ydígoras the following May First, burning effigies of Ydígoras and John Kennedy in front of the U.S. embassy in April 1961, and a few days later attacking the same targets, with Eisenhower now added, while shouting pro-Castro slogans.[25]

Street protests by forces to Ydígoras's right as well as left grew through 1960 and 1961, generally without too much harassment. There were exceptions for sure, such as a demonstration in July 1960 attacked by peasants brought in for that purpose with hundreds of protestors detained. These disorders were followed by a short-term state of siege, and then another was issued in November. The worst confrontation occurred in April 1961 when a pro-Castro demonstration was challenged by anti-Castro marchers. A man dressed in plainclothes at the front of the rightist march opened fire on the protestors and when the shooting was over three were dead and fifteen were injured. None of the guilty were arrested.[26]

4. Restricting opportunity; rapid movement escalation, Nov. 1961 to May 1962

With the opposition already at a high level of mobilization, ample evidence of regime corruption and incompetence, along with worsening economic conditions, intensified grievances against Ydígoras while the continuing relative absence of repression provided a permissive context for further mass mobilization. However, fraudulent legislative elections in December 1961 indicated a turn by the regime toward more restricted popular access to governing institutions. Adding to the pressures on the regime in March 1962

---

[24] USDS 1959. The State Department analyst then added two observations, in retrospect now so chilling in their tragic accuracy: "The fact that the Army is now examining the political picture and thinking of taking an active part is perhaps the most explosive new element in the Guatemalan scene." And then he added, "The Right seems to have learned nothing and to think only in terms of crushing the Left."

[25] IMP64 (June 26, 1959); IMP27 (May 2, 1960; Apr. 19, 1961); IMP46 (Apr. 19, 1961); IMP56 (Apr. 25, 1961).

[26] ASIES (1995, 3:151, 161, 210); IMP46 (Apr. 20, 1961); IMP56 (Apr. 20, 1961).

were the first actions undertaken by Guatemala's new armed revolutionary movement.

5. Closing access; decreasing activity, June 1962 to March 1963

As the anti-Ydígoras campaign grew through the spring of 1962, the regime responded with increasing harshness, especially after it declared on April 25 that no more demonstrations would be allowed. Furthermore, the president was forced to lean more and more on the military for support as the year progressed. With the 1963 presidential election approaching, the PR proposed as its candidate Juan José Arévalo, the social democratic president of 1945–1951. These various challenges were too much for the military and for the right, many of whom had been disappointed with the inability of the government from the first days of the counterrevolution to rid the country of the left. Arévalo made his first return to the country on March 29, 1963; two days later, Ydígoras was deposed and Colonel Enrique Peralta Azurdía assumed power.[27]

6. Closed opportunities; demobilized, April 1963 through 1973

Shortly thereafter, all political parties were banned and a state of siege was promulgated; it was to last eleven months. Another was issued in February 1965, lasting this time over sixteen months. Both during and after, the right to assemble was seriously abridged. The traditional May First labor parade was banned in 1963, the government justifying the prohibition as necessary to avoid the usual harmful agitation by "unscrupulous leaders that act as obedient instruments of international communism."[28] Neither was a parade allowed the next year, although hundreds led by FASGUA marched anyway without incident, with speakers bravely comparing the current repression of labor to that under dictators of the past. Not until the fall of 1964 was a major march authorized, this one for the AEU to commemorate the October 20, 1944 revolution. A May 1, 1965 march was also permitted, but police still found cause to arrest around forty protesters on a number of charges, especially for possessing "subversive literature." They also tried to arrest the AEU president because of his "incendiary"

---

[27] Concurrence from the United States was sought at least two weeks in advance (CEH 1999, 6:90 n. 259).

[28] Translation by author from IMP27 (May 2, 1963); also see CEH (1999, 1:249); ASIES (1995, 3:240–241).

speech, but he escaped. When hospital workers tried to strike for higher wages, the government simply militarized the hospital.[29]

While the military junta kept the nonviolent opposition contained, the armed threat from the guerrilla movement located in the mountains of the east continued to grow. The military's response was effective – but extraordinarily brutal. Elections were held in March 1966 to return the country to constitutional government, thereby meeting a key demand of moderate democratic forces, but counterinsurgency operations were sharpened and expanded, with ample input from U.S. officials who shared concerns with the right about the growing strength of the left and the lackadaisical approach of the military up to this point in fighting an insurgency largely consisting of their former colleagues. It is widely acknowledged that the price paid by the winning PR candidate, Julio Méndez Montenegro, in assuming office in 1966 was to concede to the military a free hand to conduct counterinsurgency operations. Indeed, another state of siege was imposed the month after the election. The military and allied paramilitary death squads soon eliminated not only the guerrillas but also thousands of innocent peasants in the eastern zone during 1966–1968, apparently believing in the deterrent effect of widespread, systematic terror.[30]

It was early in this period that the first widespread disappearances of urban leftist leaders occurred. Just days before the 1966 election, some thirty-three leaders of several radical organizations disappeared, never to reappear.[31] Later, when the surviving guerrillas retreated from the countryside to Guatemala City, undertaking a number of well-publicized kidnappings, assassinations, and bombings, their provocation was met by another broad wave of state terrorism, this time in the capital itself. Finally, after the right kidnapped even the archbishop of Guatemala City, both Colonel Carlos Arana Osorio, the head of the counterinsurgency campaign in the eastern zone, and the defense minister were sent to diplomatic posts overseas and levels of violence dropped.

Trends for this regime violence are given by Figure 7.1 for the 1960 through 1979 period. As the Appendix at the end of this chapter explains, these data are least accurate for the rural counterinsurgency of the late 1960s, grossly undercounting the extent of the violence that occurred at that

[29] IMP27 (May 2, 1964; May 2, 1965); IMP60 (Oct. 16, 1964); CEH (1999, 4:89).
[30] For discussions of this period, see Amnesty International 1981; Booth 1980; Bowen 1985; Johnson 1973; Jonas 1991; and McClintock 1985b.
[31] CEH (1999, 1:135–136; 6:89–98).

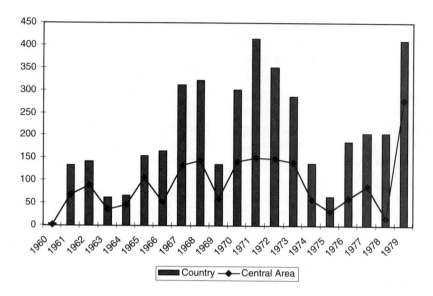

Note: *For explanation of the calculation of total deaths and definition of "central area,"
   see the Appendix to Chapter 7.
Source: Ball, Patrick. (1999). AAAS/CIIDH database of human rights violations in
   Guatemala (ATV20.1). http://hrdata.aaas.org/ciidh/data.html (downloaded May
   2000).

Figure 7.1 Guatemala: Total Deaths by Repression: Country and Central Area
by Year, 1960–1979*

time. Nonetheless, it does indicate the escalation in deaths by state violence
during this period. More accurate across the entire period is the trend
within the Central Area – the capital and the departments of Guatemala
and Escuintla (see the Appendix for further explanation). Discounting a few
lulls, the general trend in just this central region is an increase in state killing
from 1960 to a plateau across the late 1960s into the early 1970s at about
150 political murders annually by the state and its associated death squads.

   Although there was a civilian government, there was little room for popular movements through the rest of the 1960s given the constraints imposed
by the military and its violence. Nonetheless, intermittent and courageous
efforts continued to keep popular aspirations in the open, especially on
symbolic days such as May 1 and October 20 and through occasional labor strikes.[32] Although some 5,000 marched on May 1, 1967, for example,

---

[32] At some point, the symbol of June 26 – the date of the slaying of a protesting teacher in
   1944 and the six protesters in 1956 – had been appropriated by the regime, which used it
   to celebrate "Teachers' Day" with much official ceremony.

they did so with the promise that they would be "absolutely apolitical" and would not let anyone participate who would distort their objectives (IMP26 5/2/1967). Instead, it was economic grievances that motivated the few contentious events during this period, such as a successful strike at Cantel in May 1969, one of the most important strikes in Central America up to this point.[33]

The March 1970 elections were mixed for popular forces. Winning the mayor's race in the capital, the country's second most important elected position, was the leading progressive politician of the 1970s, Manuel Colom Argueta of the Frente Unido de la Revolución (FUR). Winning the presidency, however, was the military's candidate. Arana Osorio, the head of the vicious counterinsurgency campaign recently completed in the eastern region, was back from his "diplomatic exile" and now ready to bring his strong-arm rule to the entire country.

Labor agitation had grown through the election period, usually a window of opportunity for contentious activities. In the face of the threat of new labor actions, a state of siege was declared in April and repression increased once again. A planned AEU march in July supporting human rights and an end to the violence was called off because of reports that extremists planned to massacre the protesters. The Arana government would brook no opposition. After a series of small student demonstrations in the fall, a state of siege was promulgated that was to last for a full year, until November 1971.[34] As an observer stated at the time, a "regime of terror and violence may be said to have been institutionalized" (Johnson 1972, 17). During the course of the Arana administration, at least fourteen journalists were murdered.[35] Even when the state of siege ended, open political space returned only slowly. For example, any May First parade was banned in both 1972 and 1973; FAS-GUA felt free to commemorate the event only at its own headquarters.[36]

Even in the face of this repression, including the targeting of labor leaders for murder, there still were occasional strikes by workers during the Arana administration, especially in his last year. Most significant were actions taken by public employees, led by judicial workers and then most importantly by primary and secondary teachers. A first strike was settled in May 1973 only after the president's intervention. Then teachers went back

---

[33] ASIES (1995, 3:307, 335–336, 343).
[34] IMP63 (June 24, 1970; Sept. 26, 1970; Sept. 28, 1970; Oct. 1, 1970); CEH (1999, 1:253).
[35] CEH (1999, 3:157).
[36] IMP27 (May 2, 1972; May 2, 1973).

out on strike in July, turning to the streets not just with demonstrations but also intentionally disrupting traffic and even occupying churches to put pressure on the government. Although protesters at times were harassed and a July 27 march attacked, with injuries and arrests resulting, there was little state violence – though certainly protestors had no reason to assume their safety. Teachers won a big victory. Although their 25 percent salary increase was only half of what they were seeking, it was the biggest labor gain since 1954. Clearly, something was changing – certainly, at least in part, because the guerrilla threat appeared thoroughly vanquished.[37]

7. Opening of opportunities; slow return of activity, 1974 to Feb. 1976

With the possibility of victory in the March 1974 elections the ultimate target, other groups soon mobilized as the opposition gathered behind the Partido Democracia Cristiana Guatemalteca's (DC) candidate General Efraín Ríos Montt and his vice presidential choice, one of the top social democratic leaders of the period, Alberto Fuentes Mohr. Less than a week after the settlement of the teachers' strike, the AEU and other groups marched, nominally to protest the high cost of living, but more to demonstrate against the government. Calls for "revolution" were frequent in songs and chants. The same groups were emboldened enough to march again the following month on the occasion of Independence Day in September 1973 even though denied a permit. Predictably, they were broken up by police with tear gas. The march in honor of the October Revolution, though, occurred without incident.[38]

However, the 1974 elections had the same mixed results as those of four years before. The opposition was allowed to keep the capital's mayor office, but the military kept the presidency, this time requiring fraud to do so (the results were held up for nine days). Yet a significant change still occurred. The new president, General Kjell Laugerud of the military's party, the Partido Institucional Democrático (PID), pursued a more enlightened socioeconomic policy than did his predecessors and certainly met with the civic opposition more.[39] His administration also opened a much wider

---

[37] IPSET2 (Apr. 28, 1973; July 15, 1973; July 25, 1973; July 27, 1973); ASIES (1995, 3:387); CEH (1999 1:160).

[38] IMP47 (Aug. 8, 1973; Oct. 22, 1973); IPV (Sept. 17, 1973, 120); ASIES (1995, 3:389).

[39] In his inaugural address, Laugerud declared: "Poverty, discrimination, and injustice can not wait. . . . I call [on the most powerful sectors] to participate in an ordered and peaceful process that will eliminate excessive inequality and I ask these sectors that they help to

political space for popular organizing. Significantly, no violence was used against demonstrations in the capital during his time in office.[40]

But there were contradictory forces within the regime, too, as symbolized by the vice president and coalition partner, Mario Sandoval Alarcón. The long-time head of the political party of the far right (the Movimiento de Liberación Nacional – MLN), the head of the national congress during the Arana administration and hoping to be president of the country some day, Sandoval was the reputed godfather of Guatemala's notorious death squads. While political space opened in other senses, targeted murders of popular leaders continued. Serious splits between the president and vice president and the factions they represented were apparent just months into the new administration. In December 1974, one of the top MLN leaders tagged Laugerud's press secretary as a communist.[41] More directly, following a 1976 Laugerud meeting with labor leaders from the Comité Nacional de Unidad Sindical (CNUS), Sandoval declared that the president had fallen into a communist trap and denounced as subversive the government's reformist program. Indeed, he claimed that communists had infiltrated the government (CEH 1999, 1:163).

These dark forces took particular advantage of the period following the 1974 election and prior to Laugerud's July inauguration. Protests over the electoral fraud were met firmly. Christian Democratic (DC) activists were harassed throughout the country, especially in the departments of Huehuetenango, Alta Verapaz, and Zacapa. At least one DC activist was murdered in Huehuetenango, the home region of DC presidential candidate Ríos Montt, as were three in Alta Verapaz. As with the latter department, Zacapa was an area with well-organized rightist paramilitary groups carried over from the counterinsurgency campaigns of the 1960s. Right after the election, three medical student election observers were killed, as was a PR activist; the life of the winning DC candidate for mayor in the department capital was so threatened he had to move to Guatemala City. During this period in the capital, a number of activists also were killed, as was a journalist. Mayor Colom himself was injured in an assassination

---

satisfy the legitimate aspirations of the disadvantaged" (quoted in ASIES 1995, 3:484). Translated by author.

[40] There was, though, the horrible massacre at Panzós that was discussed at the beginning of Chapter 1. It occurred during the lame-duck period after the election of 1978 and prior to the inauguration of Lucas García.

[41] And, it was said, the campaign slogan of "Kjell and Mario" already had become "Kjell or Mario" (Inforpress Dec. 5, 1974, 1).

attempt in April that left the AEU president critically wounded.[42] Finally, there was May First, the only Labor Day demonstration held during the Arana tenure. The police killed seven, injured seventeen, and arrested seventy more. A newspaper ad published a few days later by the MLN blamed it all on armed rebels of the communist party and condemned "the criminal act committed by the communists and their christian-democratic allies."[43]

Terrible human rights abuses did continue throughout the Laugerud administration. To what extent the president was either complicit or ever attempted to bring under law the security forces operating under his "leadership" is unknown.[44] Nonetheless, conditions for popular mobilization were clearly improved during this period. The decline in deaths tied to the state and its agents can be seen in rough form by referring back to Figure 7.1. It can be seen more clearly by breaking down the trend monthly, as Figure 7.2 does for the Central Area. Disaggregated at this level, state deaths from mid-1973 through the Laugerud administration (July 1974 to July 1978) fluctuate between zero and thirteen a month in the Central Area. A dozen state killings in a month, while incredibly high, was in fact a big drop from the Arana period, when forty-nine were recorded in just January 1973 alone and thirty-seven in April 1973. The Laugerud administration averaged three state killings a month in the Central Area, in contrast with an average of 8.8 under Arana and a ghastly 24 under the administration that would follow in mid-1978.

8. Relatively open; rapid escalation, March 1976 to June 1978

The massive earthquake that hit rural western Guatemala in February 1976 killed some 27,000 and left around one million people homeless.

---

[42] IPEE (Mar. 6, 1974, 68); IMP48 (Mar. 7, 1974); IPV (Mar. 5, 1974, 329; Mar. 6, 1974, 324; Mar. 7, 1974, 318, 319; Mar. 8, 1974, 310; Mar. 15, 1974, 298; Mar. 16, 1974, 264, 294; Mar. 18, 1974, 286, 287; Mar. 20, 1974, 282; Apr. 6, 1974, 247; May 16, 1974, 159; June 4, 1974, 126).

[43] IMP49 (May 4, 1974). Translation by author.

[44] This is one of the important topics in recent Guatemalan history still apparently unresearched. In August 1977, Laugerud did announce a reorganization of the top command of the national police to get rid of "bad elements" (IPV Aug. 11, 1977, 246) and denounced some of the most notorious murders of the time, claiming that such crimes brought shame to Guatemala before the eyes of the world – "not even in the stone age did they commit monstrosities so big" (IPV Aug. 11, 1977, 238; author's translation). Two years later, violence would touch Laugerud more personally: his son was shot dead in a bar under mysterious circumstances (IPV Aug. 21, 1979, 281; Oct. 6, 1979, 138; Mar. 15, 1980, 113).

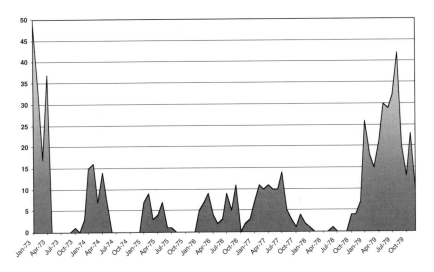

Note: *For explanation of the calculation of total deaths and definition of "central area", see the
Appendix to Chapter 7.
Source: Ball, Patrick. (1999). AAAS/CIIDH database of human rights violations in Guatemala
(ATV20.1). http://hrdata.aaas.org/ciidh/data.html (downloaded May 2000).

Figure 7.2 Guatemala: Total Deaths by Repression: Central Area by Month,
1973–1979*

The earthquake greatly intensified grievances and then pressures on the
government. It was also followed by a large number of relief workers and
development-oriented organizations, both domestic and especially international, entering into the damaged areas, that is, by numerous new allies. Many stayed to initiate development projects beyond their immediate
relief work. The Laugerud administration's attitude toward their development efforts, including cooperatives, was one of cautious encouragement
in contrast to the skepticism (or hostility) of earlier administrations.

The same contrast was true of its socioeconomic policy more generally.
Although limited in its conception and by the class alliances of the government, Laugerud's socioeconomic policy was less conservative than any
administration since 1954 and has been matched in this regard by few,
if any, of the civilian administrations that followed beginning in 1986.
Labor still faced the anachronistic employment practices of private employers, hostile intransigence to its organizing efforts, and intermittent
murders of its leaders. But as discussed in Chapter 4, at least during this

213

period labor did not have to contend with the government always backing management.[45]

As an important example of the difference, a key point in contentious activity in Guatemala occurred in November 1977 with the march of the miners from the far northwest of the country in Huehuetenango to the capital that was discussed in Chapter 5.[46] The government did issue warnings, categorizing recent marches and demonstrations as part of a subversive plan that took advantage of the good faith of the workers and declared that public order would be upheld. Yet there was no government repression on November 18, as somewhere between 100,000 and 150,000 people accompanied the miners on their triumphant march into the center of the capital for a huge rally. To the contrary, hoping to take some of the fire out of the protest, President Laugerud prevailed on the company to reopen the mine and recognize the union.[47]

9. Restricting opportunities; continuing escalation, July 1978 to Dec. 1978

Given the fraud of 1974 and the "legal" exclusion of Colom Argueta and his party from the March 1978 presidential election, the abstention rate hit 65 percent. The winning candidate, Gen. Romeo Lucas, García (Laugerud's defense minister), was almost defeated by the even further to the right candidate of the MLN, the head of the 1963 junta, General Peralta Azurdía. The third and more moderate candidate was also a general – and a nephew of Peralta Azurdía. As a candidate for his party's nomination, Lucas García had portrayed himself as "the center-left soldier" picking up the fallen banner of the Revolution of 1944.[48]

---

[45] For a different view of Laugerud, see Albizures (1987, 33) as well as McClintock (1985b, 136–140), and of this period, Albizures 1980. A concise and balanced account is provided by Handy (1984, 172–174).

[46] As the miners set off on their march, a solidarity demonstration was planned for the same day in Guatemala City. Almost at the last minute, the government said it would not permit the solidarity march and at one point loud speakers ominously warned that the unauthorized march must disband. Even more ominously, Vice President Sandoval was the acting president in the temporary absence of Laugerud. Understandably nervous, the 5,000 protesters led by the AEU and CNUS continued. Fortunately, there was no further government response (beyond cutting the electricity off to the lights at that evening's rally) IMP50 (Nov. 12, 1977); IPSET1 (Nov. 18, 1977, 195).

[47] IMP50 (Nov. 12, 1977); IMP73 (Nov. 18, 1977); ASIES (1995, 3:473–482); CEH (1999, 1:164).

[48] IPEE (1978 F–K, 224). His vice president actually did come from that tradition. A former leader of the Partido Revolucionario (PR), Francisco Villagrán Kramer eventually left the

214

It was soon apparent that Lucas would be the enemy of that spirit as the configuration of political opportunities immediately began restricting after his election. On May 29, 1978, some fifty-three unarmed Q'eqchi' Maya were shot down by the military during the protest in Panzós discussed in Chapter 1 and another forty-seven were injured. On August 4, 1978, one month after Lucas's inauguration, an unauthorized march against violence by some 10,000 protesters was broken up by police. Whereas teargas had not been used in the capital during the Laugerud period,[49] just on this one occasion the force of 1,500 police threw about 750 tear gas canisters, leaving over 250 gas injuries, 31 serious enough to require hospitalization. Tear gas was thrown directly at journalists covering the attack. Afterwards, the new administration declared that under no circumstances would it permit illegal acts.[50] However, political space disappeared gradually, not all at once. For example, an even larger march on September 13 was left alone by authorities.

10. Closing opportunities; decreasing activity, 1979–1980

Following a regime crackdown in October 1978, the killing of political activists continued to increase throughout 1979 at levels that would have been far more than enough to prevent the emergence of oppositional movements under other circumstances. But at this point, Guatemala was well into a cycle of contention marked by high levels of mobilization. A relationship to be explored in depth in Chapters 9 and 10, there is reason to posit that under such circumstances increasing state violence spurs continuing contentious activity, at least for a time, rather than depressing it immediately. Furthermore, Guatemalan contention occurred in a larger regional context. In neighboring El Salvador, popular movements grew in strength and assertiveness throughout 1979 (traveling by bus, one can have lunch in the capital of one country and dinner in the other). Meanwhile, from the fall of 1978 Nicaragua was in a state of mass insurrection, with dictator Somoza's power coming to an end in July 1979. As Guatemalan

administration to go into exile as the Lucas-directed state terrorism escalated. The 1978 election results were also tainted by charges of fraud from the opposition.

[49] Police did use tear gas on March 4, 1977, against protestors in Quetzaltenango, Guatemala's major city in the western highlands, claiming that they were first attacked by demonstrators throwing rocks and sticks when they attempted to break up an unauthorized march (*El Imparcial* Mar. 5, 1977, 1; Mar. 7, 1977, 1).

[50] IPSET1 (Aug. 5, 1978); IMP63 (Aug. 5, 1978); ASIES (1995, 3:546).

demonstrators chanted on September 13, 1978, "Today Nicaragua, tomorrow Guatemala."[51]

However, political opportunities under Gen. Lucas were soon squeezed until none were left through a repression that reached unimaginable levels, even in light of what had happened a decade earlier. For urban social movements, the repression escalated rapidly from the beginning of 1980 from selective but frequent assassinations to widespread murder, as indicated by three key events:

- May 1: Shots are fired at participants in the annual International Workers' Day demonstration; thirty-two people disappear on this day alone.
- June 21: Twenty-seven labor leaders who gathered for an emergency meeting are seized, never to reemerge alive.
- August 24: Seventeen more labor leaders disappear from a "secret" meeting.

This escalation of urban state terror can be seen by referring back to Figure 7.2. It shows a monthly median of 22 deaths for 1979 in the Central Area, then an enormous jump to 195 in January 1980 alone, and then peaking again for July and August combined at 198 deaths. And then this massive assault against the civilian population of the Central Area fell, its objectives having been accomplished.

11. Closed; demobilized, 1981 through 1984

For rural movements, the escalation from selective assassinations was far worse, growing into a scorched-earth counter insurgency campaign that across three administrations between 1978 and 1985 committed 601 massacres, destroyed over 400 villages, and murdered tens of thousands of largely indigenous peasants innocent of any illegal activity (CEH, 1999,

---

[51] The situation in Central America at this time was similar to what Oberschall (1996, 121) describes for Eastern Europe: "The success of the popular movement in East Germany convinced Czechs and Slovaks that they too were capable of a successful, peaceful revolution against communism." The same argument can be made for the protest cycle against Ydígoras in 1962 as many on the left in the Caribbean basin believed Cuba was but the first of many victories soon to come against military presidents and dictators. Of course, the same climate reinforced the intransigence of those on the right in Central America in both periods.

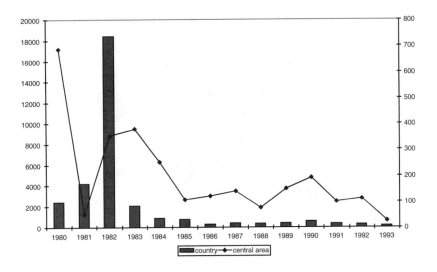

Note: *For explanation of the calculation of total deaths and definition of "central area,"
see the Appendix to Chapter 7.
Source: Ball, Patrick. (1999). AAAS/CIIDH database of human rights violations in
Guatemala (ATV20.1). http://hrdata.aaas.org/ciidh/data.html (downloaded May
2000).

Figure 7.3   Guatemala: Total Deaths by Repression: Country and Central Area
by Year, 1980–1993*

3: 257). The results are starkly portrayed by Figure 7.3. The disparity in
state violence against civilians in rural areas compared to that in urban areas was so great that different vertical axes for the 1980–1984 period are
required for the country total than that used for the Central Area. Lucas's indiscriminate violence succeeded in smashing nonviolent opposition movements but contributed mightily to the rapid expansion of the armed revolutionary movements and of mass support for the insurgency. In 1979,
most state killings were in the Central Area, but from that point on they
were overwhelmingly in the countryside as the regime's counterinsurgency
campaign grew increasingly indiscriminate in its murder of noncombatant
citizens.

By the March 1982 elections, the war against the guerrillas was going
poorly, the economy was collapsing, corruption was rampant among the
circles around the president, and the urban violence was too excessive even
for most Guatemalan opponents of the left. The United States under the
new Reagan administration wanted to assist the Guatemalan regime in its

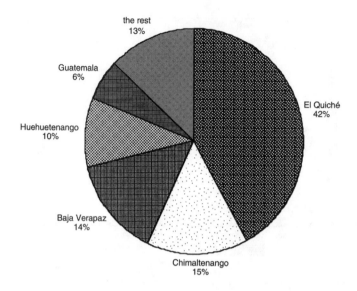

Note: *For explanation of the calculation of total deaths, see the Appendix to Chapter 7.
Source: Ball, Patrick. (1999). AAAS/CIIDH database of human rights violations in
    Guatemala (ATV20.1). http://hrdata.aaas.org/ciidh/data.html (downloaded May
    2000).

Figure 7.4 Guatemala: Total Deaths by Repression by Department, 1980–1984

"fight against communism" but was constrained by U.S. congressional restrictions against aiding a notorious human rights violator like Guatemala.
The U.S. pressured Lucas to hold fair elections in 1982, hoping that
the results would bring a legitimate and moderate government that the
nation could then assist. The Lucas administration responded to all of
this in characteristic fashion: Its candidate was given victory through
fraud.

The following month, junior military officers successfully revolted,
putting in place a junta headed by Gen. Ríos Montt, the DC candidate denied victory in 1974. Immediately, rural violence escalated even more, while
a more effective counterinsurgency strategy was put into place (Schirmer
1998). Overwhelmingly, the rural dead continued to be the indigenous of
the western highlands, most innocent of any revolutionary involvement.
But not in the eyes of the Ríos Montt administration, which damned the
indigenous as subversives to be killed (CEH 1999, 3:182). Figure 7.4 gives
some documentation of this point, breaking down the death total at the

hands of the state for the 1980–1984 period by the departments with the highest number of victims. Close to one-half of all of the deaths by state violence in Guatemala during this period came from just one department, the indigenous western highland rural department of El Quiché. The next three ranked departments shared the same characteristics: Each was rural, located in the western highlands, and with a largely Mayan population. Eighty-one percent of all of the violations recorded by the Guatemalan truth commission across the thirty-three years of its investigation occurred during just the three years of 1981–1983 (CEH 1999, 2:320).

Ríos Montt soon overstepped, concentrating too much power in his own hands and alienating too many with his sanctimonious evangelical fervor. After eighteen months, he was deposed and replaced by General Oscar Mejía Víctores. The overall counterinsurgency program, though, was similar with both administrations. By 1984, the guerrillas were essentially defeated, although their greatly reduced forces held out for another twelve years.

12. Slow opening of opportunities; slow return of activity, 1985 on

As the primary justification for military rule disappeared with the defeat of the insurgency, its failures on other fronts loomed more apparent. The economy continued to decline. Sorely needed international assistance was conditioned on improved human rights practices and democratization. Consequently, domestic economic elites joined middle-class groups in pressuring for a democratic transition. Fair elections were finally held in 1985, with the winner a civilian. Taking office in January 1986 was Vincio Cerezo, a Christian Democratic leader with a long record of fighting for human rights in the face of great personal risks.[52] In office, though, he was more cautious than many expected, even considering how constrained he was by the military as an institution generally and by hard-line factions that threatened coups repeatedly through his tenure, trying more than once. Cerezo did make it to the end of his term, though, and since then only civilians have followed him in the presidency.

Popular forces began cautiously reorganizing even before the end of the military regime. Perhaps the first important action occurred at the Coca-Cola plant in Guatemala City. After the owner closed the facility, claiming

---

[52] For an example, see IPV (Mar. 10, 1976, 210; Mar. 11, 1976, 206).

bankruptcy, some five hundred workers occupied the plant in February 1984. Holding it for a year until the business reopened under new owners, the site became a symbol of resistance and an important gathering center for other workers, along with supportive San Carlos students. On May First, 1984, it provided a safe space for the first public commemoration of International Worker's Day since 1980, with some eight hundred in attendance.[53]

Among the first popular organizations to appear was the Grupo de Apoyo Mutuo (GAM), which was formed by twenty-five brave souls in June 1984. Among those playing a leading role was Nineth Montenegro, whose husband, a labor activist, had been disappeared two and a half months earlier.[54] In part intended to provide mutual support to families of the disappeared, GAM also pressured the government for release of the detained and information on the disappeared, going beyond meetings with officials to soon holding vigils and demonstrations. For example, it organized in October 1984 the first mass public protest since May 1, 1980, with a twenty-four-mile march to the front of the national palace. More generally, it became the organization to which people turned to denounce human rights violations. Tragically, two of GAM's founding members joined the ranks of the murdered before its first year was completed.[55]

Predicting Social Movement Activity

Among the many possible indicators of social movement activity, this study utilizes just one: mass demonstrations in the capital, Guatemala City. Demonstrations have been the most important nonviolent means by which Guatemalan popular forces have registered their discontent and brought pressure to bear on public officials, with the capital by far the most important site for this form of social movement activity.[56] Two scores are

---

[53] Levenson-Estrada (1994, 210–211, 224) and Reed (1996, 5).

[54] Montenegro's husband, Edgar Fernando García, was another of the activists at the San Carlos Labor Orientation School. Becoming one of the foremost voices for popular forces up to this writing, Montenegro was elected to Congress in 1985 on the ticket of the leftist Frente Democrático Nueva Guatemala (FDNG) and later the Alianza Nueva Nación (ANN).

[55] Héctor Gomez and Rosario Godoy were kidnapped two weeks apart in spring 1985. Some 1,000 marched on April 13, 1985, after the death of Godoy, about two-thirds of them indigenous women. For background on GAM, see Bastos and Camus (1996, 69–74) and Blacklock and Madonald 1998.

[56] See Chapter 6 for an explanation of the data.

Opportunities and Challengers in Guatemala

Table 7.1 *Levels of Monthly Social Movement Activity by Periods of Changes in Political Opportunities: Guatemala, 1954–1986*

Period	Change in Opportunities	Predicted Change in Social Mov. Activity	Participation Score	Contention Score
1. 1954	closed	movements demobilized	0	0
2. 1955–1958	opening	return of activity	23	40
3. 1959–10/61	relatively open	increasing activity	53	88
4. 11/61–5/62	restricting	rapid escalation	157	300
5. 6/62–3/63	closing	decreasing activity	20	40
6. 4/63–1973	closed	demobilized	10	12
7. 1974–2/76	opening	slow return of activity	20	24
8. 3/76–6/78	relatively open	rapid escalation	141	159
9. 7/78–12/78	restricting	continuing escalation	312	400
10. 1979–1980	closing	decreasing activity	126	165
11. 1981–1984	closed	demobilized	5	5
12. 1985 on	opening	slow return of activity	–	–

Source and explanation: See text.

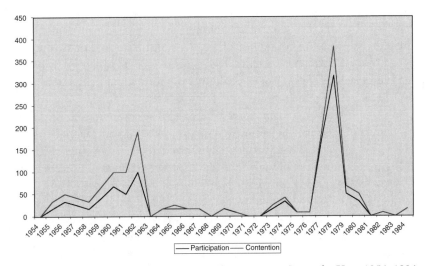

Figure 7.5 Guatemala: Participation and Contention Scores by Year, 1954–1984

provided in Figure 7.5 on an annual basis and in Table 7.1 for each of the twelve periods identified above. The first score measures levels of participation, while the second attempts to assess levels of contentiousness. Although a participation score based on the actual number of participants

221

Table 7.2 *Mean Social Movement Activity Scores by Configurations of Political Opportunities: Guatemala, 1954–1986*

Configuration of Pol. Opportunities	Number of Periods	Mean Score	
		Participation	Contention
Closed	3	5.3	6
Opening	2	21.5	32
Relatively Open	2	97	123.5
Restricting	2	234.5	350
Closing	2	31	49

Source: Calculated from Table I.

would be preferable, given the imprecision of the archival sources, instead an ordinal score is created as follows: Under 5,000 participants is scored 1; up to 10,000 is scored 2; up to 20,000, 3; up to 40,000, 4; up to 80,000, 5; over 80,000, 6. Demonstrations also vary in their contentiousness, that is, how antiregime the tenor of participants (e.g., revolutionary slogans) and how assertive their behavior (e.g., marching in defiance of a prohibition or throwing rocks at windows). Because archival information here is especially limited, the scoring is even more imprecise. Those demonstrations that were more contentious than the norm have one or two points added to their participation score.[57] Both scores are standardized by dividing their totals by the appropriate number of months and then multiplying by 100 to create whole numbers.

Although there are many years when a closed configuration of political opportunities virtually eliminated mass popular protests in Guatemala, these data still demonstrate substantial variation in social movement activity, as Figure 7.5 shows for annual scores. Interestingly, though not surprisingly (Tarrow, 1998, 24–25), the difference between the participation and contention scores peaks when the scores themselves do–that is, demonstrations are more contentious than normal at the point when participation peaks.

The critical issue, though, is whether these trends in social movement activity are related to changes in the configuration of political opportunities. Tables 7.1 and 7.2 provide impressive confirmation of a strong relationship between the two. Table 7.1 summarizes the configuration of political opportunities facing challengers for each of the twelve periods, along with

[57] With both scores, the author is making a judgment based on all primary and secondary sources utilized and a comparison to knowledge of other demonstrations during the period under study.

the corresponding change predicted for the direction of social movement activity. Participation and contention are standardized with monthly scores for each period. The change in social movement activity is almost always in the predicted direction. Furthermore, the differences between period scores are often substantial. That is, there are periods of closed political opportunities that correlate with very low social movement activity scores, others with relatively open opportunities and skyrocketing social movement scores, and other periods that fall in between. However, there is also the theoretically interesting apparent anomaly that the highest scores are registered when opportunities are "restricting." This finding will receive substantial attention throughout the remainder of this study.

More concretely, the most important opening of political opportunities came with the Laugerud administration of July 1974, but after so many years of repression remobilization was slow. The first large demonstration did not come until June 9, 1977, when some 15,000 to 20,000 marched in grief, anger, and resolve over the assassination of Mario López Larrave, ex-dean of the law school at the national university and one of the key advisers to a reviving labor movement. From this point on, large and contentious demonstrations occurred almost monthly, maintained especially by labor and students. The steady assassination of movement leaders by clandestine death squads placed ending regime violence at the forefront of protestors' demands, along with their social justice objectives. The high level of contentious mobilization is captured when participation and contention scores are calculated for the first half of 1978: 312 and 367, respectively. When this period is expanded back to June 1977, the best point to identify the beginning of a full cycle of contention, the corresponding scores are still almost as high: 300 and 339.

With Lucas García's inauguration in July 1978, political opportunities were soon to close down once again. In the first months, the response of the new administration to mass demonstrations was mixed, alternating repressiveness and permissiveness. It was during this period that participation and contention scores peaked at 312 and 400, respectively, for the last half of 1978.

Table 7.2 aggregates the different time periods according to the relevant configurations of political opportunities. Mean scores then are calculated for the five different configurations for both participation and contention. The results are dramatic. When opportunities are closed, the mean monthly participation score is 5, but when opportunities are relatively open the corresponding score is 97 and then explodes to 234.5 during the short periods of restricting opportunities before falling to 40 as opportunities are closing further and then back to the miniscule score of 5 during the closed periods. The same results hold for the contention scores but even more so.

That both scores peak when opportunities are restricting means that a direct relationship between opportunities and level of movement *activities* is too simplistic – other variables intervene. Many of these variables are well captured by the concept of "the cycle of contention." In addition, affective motivation and cognitive attribution of threat must also be taken into account. A thorough exploration of these relationships is the central task of Chapters 9 and 10. It is important, though, not to lose sight of the critical fact that this peak in *activities* is brief and then falls drastically as repression smothers nonviolent contention. The relationship between political opportunities and movement *persistence*, then, is a strong one. Although other variables are also involved when it comes to public policy *outcomes*, certainly the prospects for activists' policy goals are far better when political opportunities are opening rather than restricting or closing.

The prediction for the final period in Table 7.1 could not be assessed quantitatively here because the sources used for this study were among the victims of the repression. However, ample support is given in the descriptive literature. Understandably, urban contentious activities from organizations such as the Grupo de Apoyo Mutuo (GAM) resumed prior to any in rural areas. Peasants not only suffered the military's scorched-earth strategy but also continuing military occupation, including through the Civil Defense Patrol, a civilian adjunct manned by almost one million Mayas largely through military coercion.[58] Still, in rural areas, too, it was not long after the regime change before mass organizations began reappearing. The first was a newcomer. Soon after Cerezo came into the presidency, Father Andrés Giron led some 15,000 peasants from the south coast of Escuintla up to the capital in April 1986, calling for land for the landless. By the end of

---

[58] Kobrak provides a more complex analysis of the civil patrols, especially for communities that were in less conflictual areas, such as his study area, the Aguacatán region of Huehuetenango. For example, he points out that "Numerous patrollers I spoke with praised the Ríos Montt army for 'organizing the people,' for giving them an active way out of the conflict through the civil patrols, and for providing a way of distancing themselves from a guerrilla army that many were weakly committed to, if at all.... This allowed survivors to clearly choose a side to be on and opened the door to making peace with the same army that had devastated hundreds of communities in the name of fighting a small rebel army" (Kobrak 1997, 205–206). He adds, "the civil patrol systems, besides being a technique of domination, also represents a negotiation between the state and its citizens, one that produces practical and selective benefits for its participants" (p. 253).

1988, he claimed a membership of 115,000 for his Asociación Nacional Campesino (ANC). Committed to nonviolence and the market economy, nonetheless its tactics were contentious: marches, rallies, and hunger strikes.[59]

Even more notable was the return of the Comité de Unidad Campesina (CUC). Outside of the guerrilla organizations themselves, few groups had been more targeted by the military's violence than CUC. Survivors regrouped, deciding at a meeting in March 1986 to begin rebuilding its base, drawing especially on hostility in the highlands toward the civil patrols, as well as resuming work with peasants on the south coast fincas. CUC then reemerged publicly in 1988, joining a labor march in the capital in January protesting the high cost of living and then turning out a large contingent for the May First march. Organizing by CUC and other groups on the south coast was sufficient to bring 60,000 workers out on a one-week strike in January 1989, another strike at the end of the year, as well as another at the end of 1991.[60]

One of the most distinctive characteristics of this new wave of mass mobilization in Guatemala is the extent of its indigenous complexion.[61] As GAM grew, much of its expanded membership was indigenous. CUC always has been overwhelmingly indigenous in composition. The same was true of a number of other popular organizations appearing in the 1980s as political space opened, such as one formed in September 1988 for war widows – the Coordinadora Nacional de Viudas de Guatemala (CONAVIGUA) – and another for the displaced – the Consejo Nacional de Desplazados de Guatemala (CONDEG) – formed in September 1989. It was fully true of the Consejo de Comunidades Etnicas 'Runujel Junam' (CERJ), as well as a series of other less directly political Mayan groups organized during this period.

CERJ grew out of a meeting concerning how to gain freedom from the civil patrols held in June 1988 by representatives from towns throughout the highland department of El Quiché. It emerged publicly that August with a march all the way from the department capital to the nation's capital, a distance of about one hundred miles. Marchers sought the removal of the patrols specifically while also stressing larger themes of overcoming oppression and discrimination and the necessity of indigenous organization

---

[59] CEH (1999, 1:217–218); NY Times (Dec. 27, 1988, 3); Trudeau (1993, 96–100).

[60] Bastos and Camus (1996, 62–69).

[61] Bastos and Camus 1996. Also see Warren 1998.

to accomplish these goals. The struggle remained a dangerous one: By mid-1992, twenty-six members had been killed.[62]

Conclusion

The resurgence of popular movements in Guatemala in the mid-1980s contradicts any assumption that grievances are such a constant among the disadvantaged that they are not useful for explaining movement emergence. Certainly, movement participants in the 1980s had long-standing and intense grievances. At the same time, a number of the new organizations were formed around specific and more recent grievances that were a consequence of the military's war against its citizenry, especially the indigenous. GAM organized to give voice to the families of the disappeared, CONAVIGUA to war widows, CONDEG to the displaced, and CERJ to the indigenous more generally.

These new grievances by themselves, though, are not sufficient to explain the return of social movement activity in Guatemala in the mid-1980s. There also had to be a relaxation of repression and a more general opening of other political opportunities. Domestic and international elite pressures reinforced cleavages within the military regime. With the containment of the guerrilla threat in 1984, political opportunities already were opening before the elections in late 1985 that returned civilians to power in early 1986.

In order to understand the processes by which these new groups emerged and developed in the mid-1980s, the lead provided by McAdam, Tarrow, and Tilly 2001 is helpful with many of the causal mechanisms they specify at work in this period. In addition to the all-critical "attribution of opportunity," the mechanism of "social appropriation" can be seen with the Grupo de Apoyo Mutuo (GAM) as it became increasingly a voice for the indigenous. However, much of the indigenous mobilization of the 1980s was through specifically Maya-identified organizations. Here, "category formation," that is, the creation of new collective identities, seems especially relevant. Divided into twenty-two linguistic groups and, within each, further by more local loyalties, the emergence of a pan-Maya identity and movement in the 1980s is undoubtedly one of the developments of this decade of the greatest significance for the future of Guatemala.

It is astonishing how quickly popular movements reemerged in Guatemala when violence lessened and political access began to reopen

---

[62] Bastos and Camus (1996, 83–86).

in the mid-1980s. Given the continuation of killings targeted against activists through the remainder of that decade and even up to this writing, their resurgence is impressive testimony to the courage and perseverance of committed popular leaders. The reemergence of popular organizations and contentious activities in Guatemala is also testimony to the importance of expanding political opportunities as a variable for explaining the rise of contentious movements.

Appendix: Guatemalan Political Violence Data

One of the most accurate databases on deaths from political violence for any country is now publicly available for Guatemala. The International Center for Human Rights Investigations (CIIDH) began working with human rights groups in Guatemala in the mid-1990s collecting and processing evidence on human rights violations. A project of the American Association for the Advancement of Science (AAAS), CIIDH also provided important technical assistance to the Guatemalan truth commission (as it has to those of other countries as well). Its database, available over the Internet (Ball 1999), is based on a review of Guatemalan newspapers for the entire 1960 through 1996 period, the archives of human rights groups, and thousands of interviews (Ball, Kobrak, and Spirer 1999). CIIDH's Guatemalan database provides information on 17,423 documented human rights violations, including 13,626 cases of deaths and disappearances (many involving more than one individual, sometimes many more).

Although much of this killing through the 1970s was done by death squads, their ties to the state security forces is well established (CEH 1999, 2:111–120). The indicator used here from the CIIDH database combines killings, disappearances, and disappeared later found dead, minus deaths attributed to the revolutionary opposition – the Unidad Revolucionaria Nacional Guatemalteca (URNG) and its predecessor organizations.

The importance of using data compiled from domestic sources for studies of political violence rather than the more common use of nondomestic sources is apparent when CIIDH's figures are compared to the Guatemalan data offered by the *World Handbook of Political and Social Indicators* (Taylor and Jodice 1985). The *World Handbook* is the conventional source for quantitative studies of political violence, yet its data for Latin America are drawn from the *New York Times Index*. The *World Handbook's* total deaths from political violence in Guatemala for 1960 through its last year of data, which is 1977 (including the additional *Handbook* variables of political executions and assassinations), is only 295 deaths, including only 6 deaths for the last four years of this period. CIIDH documents 3,479 political deaths for 1960–1977, including 603 for the last four years.[63]

Even with CIIDH's superior data, accuracy problems remain. Having looked at many thousands of Guatemalan newspaper articles, it is clear to me that the Guatemalan press gave thorough coverage to deaths and disappearances in the Central Area, at least for 1973 into the early 1980s. Although some reports also identify deaths in other departments, including small villages far from the capital, it would be impossible to provide anywhere near the same level of coverage for remote rural regions as for the Central Area.[64] Documentation of the point is provided by Aguilera and Romero et al. (1981, 160). In its study of Guatemala, undertaken as part of an international project analyzing political violence throughout Latin America, this research team interviewed one hundred people living in rural areas in seven departments of high political violence. They found that 60 percent of the deaths discovered through their interviews were not to be found in contemporaneous press coverage. Tragically, one of the lead authors of this study, as well as other members of the research team, were themselves victims of the state violence they were analyzing.

Neither can we assume that the magnitude of these inaccuracies in the death totals for the overall country are relatively consistent across the years. Instead, data limitations are the biggest problem for estimating totals for the late 1960s and 1970. During this period, there were several waves of large-scale indiscriminate killings in the eastern part of the country, especially in the countryside, as part of the military's counterinsurgency operations. Consequently, the country totals for 1967 and 1968 especially, but also 1969 and 1970, were in reality far higher than represented by Figure 7.1 and, therefore, the central area's percentage of the total far less. This problem recurs when trying to assess the scope of state violence during the scorched-earth counterinsurgency campaigns that began in 1980 in the western highlands. Although data for this 1980–1984 period are much better than for the earlier period of massive repression, and although deaths that are documented reach extraordinarily high levels (necessitating the

[63] Moving to another region for the same indicator, the *World Handbook*'s median annual error for Argentina, Chile, and Uruguay is 344 percent for a total of forty-two years between them (Brockett 2003; also see 1992). Since these three are among the most socioeconomically advanced countries outside of the industrial democracies, it is probable that press coverage is worse and data errors greater for less-developed countries.

[64] Corroborating this point, see Ball et al. (1999, 52–55).

change of value axes for Figure 7.3 from Figure 7.1), their accuracy still falls far short of the tragic truth.

The Guatemalan truth commission's estimate for the thirty-six-year period of its study is that the total number of deaths might have been as much as four times greater than the number documented, which would be a total around 200,000 deaths (CEH 1999, 1:73).

8

Changing Political Opportunities and Contentious Challengers

EL SALVADOR AND CENTRAL AMERICA

Contentious movements reached high levels of activity in El Salvador in a democratic opening in the early 1930s and again in 1944, when popular forces brought down a long-governing dictator.[1] Otherwise, political space was too limited for any effective organizing into the 1960s, with only brief exceptions. Consequently, activists in El Salvador in the 1960s and 1970s were attempting to mobilize a population with limited experience in contentious politics, certainly compared to their Guatemalan counterparts, who instead were struggling to energize remobilization following the 1954 overthrow of Arbenz and the repression that it brought.

Progressive activists succeeded in mounting three different contentious campaigns in El Salvador during the three decades after 1960. The first led up to the election of February 1972. The second, and far more intense protest cycle, led into the civil war that began in 1980. The third is as astonishing as its counterpart in Guatemala: the resumption in the mid-1980s of a nonviolent protest movement in the capital once state violence directed at movement activists declined sufficiently, yet occurring in the midst of a continuing civil war. Heightened grievances were important to each of these campaigns as was the mobilization of organizational resources, as detailed in prior chapters. Critical, too, was the opening of greater political opportunities. Although each dimension of the configuration of political opportunities usually played a role in facilitating movement emergence, their rise and fall were often tied to corresponding fluctuations in the use of violence by the state against social movement activists.

---

[1] For background on Salvadoran politics after 1930, see Baloyra 1982, as well as Dunkerley 1982 and Montgomery 1995.

The First Campaign: Late 1960s/Early 1970s

In the decades following the overthrow of the dictator in 1944, El Salvador had presidential elections, but the winners were always soldiers.[2] The military's electoral vehicle was the Partido de Conciliación Nacional (PCN), formed in 1961 with the intention to create a broad umbrella hegemonic party like the ruling Partido Revolucionario Institucional (PRI) in Mexico. There were different tendencies within the Salvadoran military, mirroring those among politically attentive civilians, most notably between those tied to the traditional agro-export economy and others who sought a more rapid economic development through industrialization and a better-educated population. Generally, the latter were more moderate politically and often younger. This split within the military grew more prominent in the 1970s as better-educated younger officers began to believe that such development might require structural reform, a perception reinforced by some progressive civilians who were seeking alliances with them (Williams and Walter 1997, 93–97).

With the small elite tightly in control of the economy and the military in control of the national political system, democratic reformists focused first on local elections, especially the key office, the mayor of the capital San Salvador. The centrist Partido Demócrata Cristiano (PDC) scored success in 1964 with the election of José Napoleón Duarte, who was then reelected twice.[3] This was also the period during which labor-organizing efforts were beginning to pay off, as discussed in Chapter 3. The opening of the political system continued with the election of Colonel Fidel Sánchez Hernández in 1967 for a five-year presidential term marked by a more tolerant attitude toward mass organizing and open discussions of reform. Indeed, the change was already apparent in the lame-duck period prior to his assuming office. Valle explains the success of the historic Acero strike of that April in part due to the fact that the outgoing president did not wish to leave a legacy of bloodshed from his final days, nor does it seem that the incoming president pressured for such repression (Valle 1993, 9).

As the Sánchez term progressed, the most important protest cycle in Salvadoran history up to this point developed. As indicated in earlier chapters, this was the most contentious period for Salvadoran labor until

---

[2] For a good treatment of the Salvadoran military within the context of Salvadoran political history, see Williams and Walter 1997.

[3] For background on Duarte, the PDC, and this period in general, see Webre 1979.

the late 1970s, as well as its most successful. The same was true for students and for teachers. Much of the hopes of popular forces at this time focused on securing entry as full participants in the institutionalized political system. Reformers came close to taking control of the national congress in the election of 1968, only to fare more poorly in the elections of 1970, most likely the result of renewed tensions with Honduras, coming just a short time after the recent brief "Soccer War" between the two countries. Reformers regrouped, focusing on the 1972 elections, especially for the presidency. Their candidate was the PDC's Duarte, running with Guillermo Ungo of the social democratic Movimiento Nacional Revolucionario (MNR), as well as enjoying support from other political forces, such as the small Partido Comunista de El Salvador (PCS) participating through the Unión Democrática Nacionalista (UDN).

How different subsequent Salvadoran history would have been had the right played fair. But the ruling military and economic elites were in a state of alarm at the growing mass mobilization. To many, it appeared "that leftist agitation was rampant in the country" (Webre 1979, 152) and that without preemptive action El Salvador would follow the frightening road of Chile – a Christian Democratic government (like Chile's Eduardo Frei, elected in 1964) preparing the way for a Marxist government (like Salvador Allende, elected in 1970).

It is hard to overstate the importance of the 1972 electoral fraud for subsequent Salvadoran events.[4] Reformist forces were at a high level of mobilization and expecting victory. They tried to overcome the fraud first through a general strike in February and then by throwing their support behind a coup attempt in March. The coup was smashed, with over one hundred killed, over two hundred injured, and widespread arrests.[5] A state of siege followed. University students, in particular, were highly energized at the time and very active in the campaign. Enraged by the fraud, "students protested massively." The military responded by closing the university in July for two years, arresting hundreds, "exacerbating the students' anger and causing many to despair of an electoral road to political reform" (McClintock 1998, 252, also see 105). As one example, Ana Guadalupe Martínez Menéndez, who was to become the Ejército Revolucionario del Pueblo's (ERP) second in command, said the election was the turning point for her: "elections didn't work. So we

---

[4] For background on the critical events of this year, see Hernández et al. 1973.
[5] Hernández et al. (1973, 94); IDHUCA (1988, 23–24); NY Times (Mar. 27, 1972, 1).

sought another way to change the politics of the country" (McClintock 1998, 255).[6]

The Second Campaign: Late 1970s/1980

Due to the repression that followed the 1972 elections, there was only sporadic nonviolent contentious activity until later in the decade.[7] But there was substantial organizational work conducted during these years by both violent revolutionary and nonviolent popular groups, as described in Chapters 3 and 5. The approach of presidential elections in February 1977 once again afforded a window of opportunity for mobilization, although on a more limited scale than in 1972. Once again, however, fraud was used and protesters attacked viciously. With announcement of the fraudulent results, protesters occupied the central plaza in San Salvador; their numbers grew to around 15,000 after a week. On February 28, police issued a warning to disperse and then assaulted the 1,500 to 2,000 protesters remaining in the plaza. By government admission eight were killed and fifty wounded; other sources claim as many as one hundred dead, two hundred wounded, and five hundred arrested.[8]

Under General Carlos Romero, the regime moved even further to the right than it had been under Colonel Arturo Molina, growing more rigid and repressive. One estimate places the total number of political assassinations by security forces during Molina's five years to be about thirty-seven, with another sixty-nine disappearances. The death toll jumped dramatically under Romero, with 461 estimated political assassinations and another 131 disappearances in his little over two years in office (López Vallecillos 1979, 871).[9] Popular movements, though, were stronger than in 1972 and refused to be cowed. Furthermore, they were encouraged by parallel developments in Nicaragua and Guatemala, by growing distance between the dictatorship and the Carter administration in the United States over human rights

[6] Also see the similar statement by ERP commander Joaquín Villalobos (McClintock 1998, 253). Both Martínez and Villalobos were university students at the time.

[7] Reasonably accurate data on the number of deaths due to repression do not begin until 1978.

[8] ECA (#342, 329); IDHUCA (1988, 39); NY Times (Mar. 1, 1977, 9). The highest figure given here comes from Berryman (1984, 121–122); Dunkerley suggests total deaths reaching two hundred (Dunkerley 1988, 375).

[9] Later, IDHUCA would estimate 500 killed and 180 disappeared for just 1978, with 72 new political prisoners, and many others exiled (IDHUCA 1988, 44). Both López-Vallecillos and IDHUCA were affiliated with the Universidad Centroamericana.

issues,[10] and by support for movements of the disadvantaged by higher-status allies, such as peasants received from church workers.

With revolutionary terrorism growing, Romero tightened the lid further in November 1977 with the promulgation of a draconian Law for Defense and Guarantee of Public Order, characterized as both the "most repressive law in [Salvadoran] history" (Morales et. al. 1988, 50) and as "practically a license to kill" (Baloyra 1982, 66). In the next half year, six strikes were violently broken up, as were at least eight demonstrations (Véjar 1979, 519). Contentious activities then exploded when the Public Order law was removed at the end of February 1979. Some of the top military wanted to continue the crackdown against the still growing threat from the left, but, according to the U.S. embassy, Romero explained to them that "he is unable to take the necessary action to combat local terrorism and crime because he is hampered by pressures from international human rights organizations, the Catholic Church, and the human rights policy of the United States government" (USDS/NSA2 1979b).

Instead, he succeeded in alienating the hard right within the country. When Somoza was overthrown in July by a vast popular movement in Nicaragua, Romero's days were clearly numbered. Reform-minded Salvadoran military officers were reinforced in their belief that structural reform was needed to preempt revolution. Conservative officers came to a different conclusion: Somoza's fall resulted "from his lack of resolve in dealing with mass organizations linked to the armed Left" (Williams and Walter 1997, 96). As Figure 8.1 indicates, civilian deaths by the state and its allied death squads would escalate tremendously, both for the country as a whole and for a rough measure of urban victims (see the Appendix to the chapter for explanation).

The reformist faction of junior officers organized a coup first, deposing Romero on October 15, 1979. They quickly established a progressive government that included many of the civilians who had been prominent in the coalitions opposing the military's candidates in the 1972 and 1977 elections.[11] In addition to its progressive reform program, the new government

---

[10] For example, in July 1977 the U.S. State Department announced that the United States would hold up the sale of police weapons to El Salvador because they could be used to suppress human rights (NY Times July 18, 1977, 4).

[11] The events of the next few months are crucial to understanding all that follows in El Salvador for years to come, but they are far too complex to be able do them much justice here. Because interpretations of this period vary widely, multiple sources should be consulted, such as Baloyra 1982; Berryman 1984; Dunkerley 1982; LeoGrande 1998; Montgomery

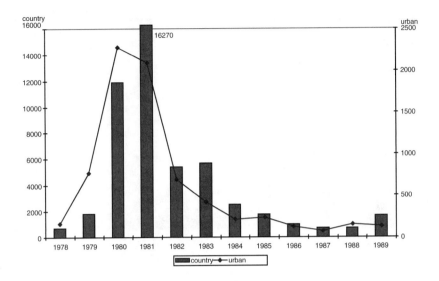

Source: 1978-1981, 1983-1984: Socorro Jurídico as reported in Morales (1988, 189-201). "Identified urban civilians" is obtained by removing both unidentified victims and peasants.

1982: Socorro Jurídico's country totals for this year are suspect, and UCA's are used instead (ECA #441, 78). ECA's annual total in turn is adjusted by higher Tutela Legal figures for September and October (ECA reports its own figures as too low for these months) (ECA #407, 949-950; # 409, 1036). Data for the last quarter of 1982 are missing for urban civilians. A score for these months was created by using an average of three months of actual scores (e.g., October is the average of the prior three months; December is the average of September along with January and February).

1985-1989: Tutela Legal as reported by Americas Watch (1987, 7-8, for 1985 and 1986; 1990, 199-200, for 1988 and 1989) and McClintock (1998, 117, for 1987). Urban victims are Tutela Legal's category "targeted killings by the military and death squads." Because the categories used by Americas Watch and McClintock differ, the average ratio between their data for 1986 and 1988 was used to calculate a comparable 1987 score from McClintock's score for assassinations for that year.

Figure 8.1 El Salvador: Total Annual Civilian Deaths by Repression for Country and Identified Urban Victims, 1978–1989

also promised to end the repression and preside over a democratic transition. Consequently, political space for contentious activities widened substantially. The mass popular organizations were caught off guard by the coup but within a few days had denounced it as motivated by the intent to debilitate the left. Persuaded that the junta was only a temporary stage prior to victory by the masses, the left fully utilized the political opening provided by the junta with constant contentious activities, ranging from

1995; Prosterman and Riedinger 1987; Stanley 1996; Williams and Walter 1997. Especially good is the reporting in *Estudios Centroamericanos* (ECA).

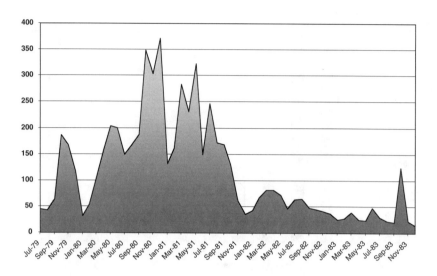

Source: Socorro Jurídico as reported in Morales (1988, 189-201). "Identified urban civilians" is obtained by removing both unidentified victims and peasants. Data for the last quarter of 1982 is missing for urban civilians. A score for these months was created by using an average of three months of actual scores (i.e., October is average of the prior three months; December the average of September along with January and February).

Figure 8.2 El Salvador: Identified Urban Civilian Deaths by Repression by Month, July 1979–1983

marches and demonstrations to occupations of public buildings, embassies, and private businesses.

The reformist military group was not in control of the military as an institution – it was just the faction that got its plans for a coup in motion first. More powerful within the military were the moderate-conservative and the hard-right factions. Their own coup plans frustrated, in the months that followed they further solidified their domination of the military, unleashing violence as necessary. The new government's inability to control military violence further alienated the left, such as on October 29, when the military attacked a demonstration, killing anywhere from twenty-four to seventy protesters and injuring as many.[12] At the same time, the government's inability to control contentious actions from the left, be they nonviolent or violent, further alienated the military and civilian right. A

[12] NY Times (Oct. 30, 1979, 1) reports twenty-four; ECA (#372, 1007) reports up to seventy.

truce brokered by Archbishop Oscar Romero in November brought a temporary respite of challenger activities but then broke down as state violence continued against urban activists, as indicated by Figure 8.2. As the mass movement returned to the streets, state violence actually did drop in December and into January. However, when the defiant challengers mounted a massive demonstration on January 22, 1980 of over 100,000 protestors, security forces attacked the marchers, killing anywhere from twenty-two to forty that day and injuring between one and two hundred protesters.[13] From this point polarization and violence on both sides – but most especially by the state – escalated rapidly. Figure 8.2 shows over one hundred urban activists killed each month for the twenty consecutive months from March 1980 through October 1981. During this period, the monthly average was 210 urban activists killed and on four occasions the monthly total was over 300. The same horrific pattern is found for the country as a whole, as shown by Figure 8.3, with the worst period extending two months longer. For this twenty-two-month period extending through the end of 1981, the average monthly number of civilians killed by the state and its associated death squads was 1,253. The right also changed the legal order in a more repressive direction. Notably, Decree 507 issued in December 1980 permitted detentions without charges or recourse to legal counsel, allowed confessions as admissible trial evidence, and so broadened the definition of subversion as to virtually eliminate rights of association and dissent (Americas Watch 1982, 6, 15).[14]

Complete polarization and full civil war, however, were avoided. In no small part this was due to the intervention of the United States.[15] Some scholars deny that the U.S. intervention was the decisive factor in preventing a revolutionary victory in El Salvador since, after all, the left was also defeated in Guatemala without any significant U.S. involvement.[16] Others, though, emphasize how critical U.S. assistance was to defeating the FMLN's

---

[13] The lower figures come from NY Times (Jan. 23, 1980, 5); the higher from ECA (#375, 106).

[14] As Americas Watch points out, these two measures "encourag(e) the use of force to extract self-incriminating statements from detainees held incommunicado" (Americas Watch 1982, 6).

[15] Another topic far too vast to do justice to here; see, among others, Aronson 1993; Baloyra 1982; LeoGrande 1998; and McClintock 1998.

[16] Wickham-Crowley (1992, 282–292, 316–318) makes the most effective case for this position.

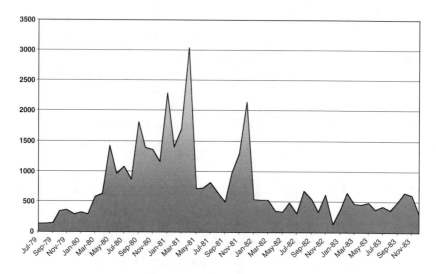

Source: 1979-1981, 1983: Socorro Jurídico as reported in Morales (1988, 189-201).
 1982: Socorro Jurídico's country totals for this year are suspect and UCA's are used instead (ECA #441, 78). ECA's annual total in turn is adjusted by higher Tutela Legal figures for September and October (ECA reports its own figures as too low for these months) (ECA #407, 949-950; #409, 1036).

Figure 8.3 El Salvador: Total National Civilian Deaths by Repression by Month, July 1979–1983

revolutionary objective.[17] Certainly, U.S. involvement in El Salvador was massive. U.S. aid during the 1980s totaled about $3.6 billion, making it the fifth largest recipient of U.S. aid during the decade. This works out to more than $200,000 per guerrilla. As late as 1986 and 1988 the amount of the Salvadoran government's budget covered by U.S. assistance varied between 20 and 43 percent (McClintock 1998, 221–223).

However, going back to the beginning of this period, the United States was unprepared for the October 1979 coup and the events that followed. Many of the progressive civilians who joined the new government in October left it in frustration in early January 1980 the remainder in March, both times replaced by civilians to their right. During early 1980, the U.S. intervened heavily in Salvadoran domestic politics, attempting

[17] McClintock notes: "Scholars and political leaders agree virtually unanimously that U.S. aid to the Salvadoran government prevented a takeover by the FMLN" (McClintock 1998, 9). She also points out that "Scholars of revolution tend to underestimate the importance of the international context to the outcome of a revolutionary effort" (p. 201).

238

to shore up a centrist government that had a real reform program but doing little to rein in the military and its violence. When Ronald Reagan came into office at the start of 1981, the importance of socioeconomic reform diminished and even less concern was paid to the massive human rights abuses committed by the state. In contrast, the military component greatly expanded following a strong but failed "final offensive" by the guerrillas in January 1981 that they had hoped would present Reagan with a *fait accompli* on entering the White House.

The Third Campaign: Mid-1980s/Early 1990s

For a mix of motives, however, the Reagan administration soon attached growing importance to "democratization" as part of its Salvadoran policy, as it gradually did elsewhere in the Third World.[18] The incremental implementation of this democratization project in El Salvador had major consequences for popular mobilization. Democratization by the Reagan administration was largely understood as the institutionalization of fair and free elections as the means by which governing authorities are selected.[19] The first election occurred in March 1982 for a constituent assembly to draft a new constitution. Won by the right, the assembly also served as a provisional legislature and selected a provisional president.

Two other sets of actions by the United States during this period reinforced this important opening of political space for mass movements. First, the Reagan administration – finally and very late – made explicit and strong statements to Salvadoran authorities in late 1983 that human rights abuses had to stop for U.S. support to continue.[20] As Figure 8.1 indicates, civilian

---

[18] Note, for example, the change of Reagan policy toward countries such as Chile, Haiti, and the Philippines in the mid-1980s.

[19] How fair and free these elections were in reality is a matter of controversy. Good and differing analyses are provided by Baloyra (1982, 167–184), McClintock (1998, 108–129), and Montgomery (1995, 155–164). Certainly, politicians of the left did not feel safe to participate in elections until the late 1980s. By many important criteria, the elections fell far short of good democratic standards. On the other hand, they were a big improvement over the elections of the past.

[20] The statements were made by Ambassador Thomas Pickering in November 1983 (US House 1984, 248–257) and Vice President George Bush in December (US House 1984, 246–247). Of the various ways in which the Reagan administration influenced events in El Salvador, among the most important was a nonaction: the lack of any strong pressures against state murder of noncombatants for almost three years, certainly a green light to state terrorists in El Salvador. Administration efforts to win appropriations for El Salvador from the U.S. Congress were consistently constrained during the same period by growing

deaths had fallen sharply after 1981 but still were at horrendous levels, averaging 46 per month for urban activists for 1982 and 1983 combined and 462 for the country as a whole. The high country totals reflected civilians caught in the civil war and the inability/unwillingness of the military to differentiate between civilians and combatants in conflicted zones.[21] Although this annual total was cut in half in 1984 and continued to decline gradually until 1989, the number of noncombatants killed by the military remained extraordinarily high throughout the civil war. Most relevant for protest activities, though, is what happened in the cities. Here, as shown by Figure 8.4, the drop in the number of urban activists murdered by the state proved to be more encouraging (see Chapter 10). When aggregated on a quarterly basis, the average death toll for identified urban civilians fell from 524 in 1981, to 173 in 1982, 106 in 1983, and then down to 55 in 1984.

Second, the U.S. blocked the ascension to power on at least two occasions of Roberto D'Aubuisson, the most notorious leader of Salvadoran death squads, the author of the assassination of Archbishop Romero, and the most charismatic political figure in Alianza Republicana Nacionalista (ARENA), the political party organized by the right to compete in the new electoral process.[22] As a consequence, more-moderate factions within ARENA were reinforced in their argument that for the party to come to power it would need to assume a less reactionary position.

Political activity soon focused on the renewal of presidential elections, set for March 1984. This election period opened further space for mass politics, building on the strong U.S. human rights warnings of late 1983. And it then opened much further, at least in the capital, when Duarte was inaugurated president on July 1, but with much of his reform coalition of twelve years

congressional – and public – concern over the massive abuses of the Salvadoran military. See Arnson 1993; LeoGrande 1998; U.S. House 1982 and 1984.

[21] See the Appendix to this chapter for further discussion.

[22] The report of the UN-created Salvadoran truth commission is clear: "There is full evidence that . . . former Major Roberto D'Aubuisson gave the order to assassinate the Archbishop and gave precise instructions to members of his security service, acting as a 'death squad,' to organize and supervise the assassination" (Betancur et al. 1993, 131). Without the U.S. pressure, D'Aubuisson would have been selected provisional president in 1982; he was forced to settle for leadership of the legislature. In 1984, he was Duarte's runoff opponent for the presidency. Not only did the U.S. make it very clear that a D'Aubuisson victory would be a disaster for further U.S. support, it gave considerable financial support to the Duarte campaign, much to the consternation of Senator Jesse Helms (R-NC), who maintained contact with D'Aubuisson (NY Times May 11, 1984, 8).

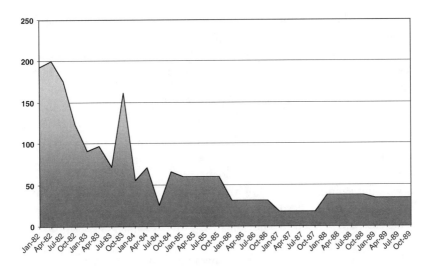

Source: 1982-1984: Socorro Jurídico as reported in Morales (1988, 189-201). "Identified urban civilians" is obtained by removing both unidentified victims and peasants. Data for the last quarter of 1982 are missing for urban civilians. A score for these months was created by using an average of three months of actual scores (e.g., October is the average of the prior three months; December the average of September along with January and February).

1985-1989: Tutela Legal as reported by Americas Watch (1987, 7-8 for 1985 and 1986; 1990: 199-200, for 1988 and 1989) and McClintock (1998, 117, for 1987). Urban victims are Tutela Legal's category "targeted killings by the military and death squads." Because the categories used by Americas Watch and McClintock differ, the average ratio between their data for 1986 and 1988 was used to calculate a comparable 1987 score from McClintock's score for assassinations for that year.

Figure 8.4 El Salvador: Identified Urban Civilian Deaths by Repression by Quarter, 1982–1989

earlier now part of the opposition. Open challenges to the government were further facilitated when the PDC also gained control of the congress the following year. As detailed in Chapter 10, during this period a new cycle of contention developed in the central area, allowed by this significant change in political opportunities. But the relationship worked both ways. As the new mass movement grew, became more contentious in its activities, and as suspicions of its ties to the FMLN mounted as well, counterresponses developed within the government.

On June 2, 1987, General Adolfo Blandón, the head of the armed forces, held a press conference charging guerrilla influence in recent protests, and the next day another military spokesman warned that street protests had reached the limits of what would be tolerated. Similarly, on March 9, 1988 Defense Minister Vides Casanova claimed captured guerrilla documents

241

proved that the urban mass movement was a FMLN front group and its actions were part of an orchestrated plan against the government.[23] These warnings were not idle, especially not after the FMLN increased its violent attacks in 1989 on ARENA officials and on military headquarters in San Salvador.[24]

With the failure of Duarte to deliver on his promises of peace and reform and the continuing decline of the economy, along with severe splits in the PDC and credible reports of rampant corruption in the government, the right was able to retake the government. ARENA gained control of the congress in 1988 and then the presidency in the elections of March 1989. Its winning candidate, Alfredo Cristiani, represented the more moderate faction of the party. Despite strong opposition from the new mass movement, Cristiani seemed to enjoy majority popular support at least through his first year. An Instituto Universitario de Opinión Pública (IUDOP) national survey at that point found his overall positive evaluation to be at 55 percent with negatives at 29 percent and with all social sectors giving majority support except the marginal, which still gave 48 percent approval. This positive evaluation came despite a negative view of the economic situation, which 57 percent saw as having worsened (by majorities in all social sectors except the upper/upper-middle). All social sectors also viewed respect for human rights to have deteriorated more under the

---

[23] ECA (#463, 363). This was not the first time the government cited captured FMLN documents as evidence of a strong connection (as another example, see NY Times 1985, iv, 5). The government bolstered its case with testimonies such as those of human rights workers arrested in May 1986 who, on release, claimed that many human rights and church organizations were funneling international funds to the FMLN (ECA #451, 480; NY Times Aug. 3, 1986, 12). Certainly, it would have been a wise strategy for the FMLN to seek to infiltrate and manipulate mass organizations and, if successful, for both them and the groups to deny any connection. Conversely, even if there were no connection, it would not be surprising that the government would charge (and believe) that there were. In 1985, a top leader with FENASTRAS denied any FMLN connection, explaining instead: "What exists is a convergence of objectives" (NY Times June 16, 1985, iv, 5). James LeMoyne, the primary *New York Times* reporter in El Salvador in the late 1980s, was shown purported captured documents laying out plans for using popular organizations "to mount more frequent and more violent demonstrations," and his stories were written as if an FMLN-UNTS connection had been demonstrated; see, for example, NY Times (July 17, 1987, 3).

[24] As the *New York Times* reported following FMLN assassinations of both a presidential adviser and the attorney general in April 1989, these FMLN attacks were widely interpreted "to be part of a growing campaign intended to prompt a military and right-wing crackdown. They say the rebels seem to hope that will drive the center to embrace their cause and provoke the United States Congress to cut aid to the almost-bankrupt government" (NY Times Apr. 20, 1989, 8).

ARENA government than to have improved (again with the exception of the upper/upper-middle).[25]

Although Cristiani had no known connection to the death squads, the violent right was emboldened by the ARENA victories. Given the continuing viability of the FMLN and its alleged ties to the urban contentious movements, repression was the response, especially in 1989. Estimated total assassinations and disappearances committed by the right grew from 155 in 1986 to 191 in 1988 and to 261 in 1989. Even more notable was the targeting of popular sector leaders, increasing from only one in 1986 to eight in 1988 and up to forty-one in 1989.[26]

In November 1989, the FMLN unleashed its largest and most successful offensive since January 1981, bringing the war into the streets of the capital after almost a decade of failed efforts by the regime to defeat the revolutionaries. At the same time, the military did defeat the FMLN offensive. With no end of the fighting in sight and deepening polarization a too real possibility, the conflict in El Salvador finally came to an end, in large part because of shifts in external alliances. The FMLN received moral and fluctuating material support from the Frente Sandinista de Liberación Nacional (FSLN), which had governed Nicaragua throughout the course of the Salvadoran civil war. However, in February 1990 the FSLN was voted out of office, to be replaced by a conservative pro-U.S. government. Concurrently, the Soviet Union and the Communist bloc was collapsing, ending those sources of support as well.

Meanwhile, in the United States Reagan was replaced in the presidency by George Bush at the start of 1989. Bush placed greater priority on the prompt settlement of Central American conflicts so he could avoid continual costly battles with Congress and focus instead on his more central concerns. The U.S. Congress reinforced the point in October 1990, suspending half of El Salvador's military funding, conditioned on progress in solving the murders of six Jesuit priests that occurred in the midst of the November 1989 offensive (see Chapter 10). Germany followed a few days later, suspending all aid.[27] Leading the international changes, though, was a regional peace process initiated in 1987 by Costa Rican president Oscar Arias and committed to by the region's presidents

[25] IUDOP 1990; also see IUDOP 1989 for a similar survey on Cristiani's first one hundred days in office.

[26] The number of deaths of leaders is McClintock's (1998, 114) estimate; the more general figures are from Tutela Legal, as reported by McClintock (1998, 117–118).

[27] ECA (#504, 923–4); LeoGrande (1998, 553–579) NY Times (Oct. 20, 1990, 1).

at Esquipulas, Guatemala in August 1987 and at a series of meetings held thereafter.

Peace negotiations between the Salvadoran government and the FMLN were conducted under the auspices of United Nation's Secretary-General Javier Pérez de Cuéllar. With his term expiring at the end of 1991, pressures for a settlement intensified, especially from the UN and the U.S.[28] As the year ended (literally), the two sides came to an agreement, which was then signed on January 16, 1992 at Chapúltepec, Mexico.[29]

Predicting Social Movement Activity

Political opportunities for contentious movements in El Salvador fluctuated significantly during the years covered by this study. As with Guatemala, then, the opening and closing of political opportunities permit predictions concerning the rise and fall of contentious political activities. The most complete set of data available over the longest period of time for any of the Salvadoran contentious political activities is for strikes. This is a valid indicator of Salvadoran political contention for at least two reasons. First, potential strikers always faced the possibility of not just employer intransigence but also state repression. Second, much of organized labor was tied to political groups. Consequently, labor's contentious activities, including strikes, often had a direct political purpose in addition to specific economic goals.

Figure 8.5 uses official data to track strikes from 1972 through 1991. From this chapter's portrayal of fluctuating Salvadoran political opportunities, we should expect strikes to fall after 1972, probably dramatically. Strikes should then slowly build to 1979, which would probably be the highest peak for the entire period covered. Strikes would be expected to continue at a high level into the first part of 1980 and then fall off dramatically as repression escalated. With the decline of urban repression in 1984 and the election of Duarte to the presidency, strikes would be expected to resume and continue to build in frequency. For the remaining years, political opportunities do not vary as widely as in prior years (except for the violent year of 1989). Accordingly, any annual fluctuations in the frequency of strikes after 1985 probably were driven more by changes in the level of grievances and in challenger political tactics. Looking at

---

[28] ECA (#517, 1056); NY Times (Dec. 28, 1991, 4).
[29] ECA (#517, 1057); NY Times (Jan. 1, 1992, 1; Jan. 17, 1992, 1).

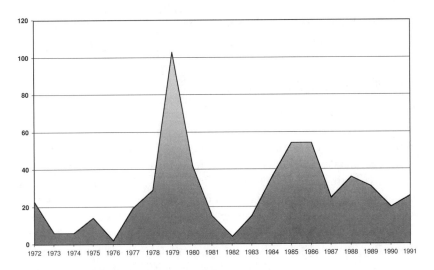

Source: ILO 1975, 1985, 1995.

Figure 8.5 El Salvador: Total Annual Number of Strikes and Lockouts, 1972–1991

the trend portrayed in Figure 8.5, these predictions appear to be well supported.

The Central American Comparison

During the late 1970s, strong and sustained contentious movements developed in both El Salvador and Guatemala. When repression foreclosed peaceful protest, already existing revolutionary organizations rapidly grew in numbers and in their threat to the existing regimes. In part, they drew their inspiration from the revolutionary movement in Nicaragua that succeeded in assuming state power in July 1979. However, in neither El Salvador nor Guatemala were the guerrillas able to overthrow the government and bring about a revolutionary transformation. In even greater contrast, no meaningful revolutionary movement developed in Honduras and none at all in Costa Rica. Some of the reasons for these differences were presented in prior chapters, such as different levels of grievances and of organization. An important part of the explanation, though, was different configurations of political opportunities between the five countries. These differences are highlighted below, first in a comparison of elite alignments

245

and political access and then in terms of the capacity and the propensity of the state for repression.

Elite Alignments and Political Access

There have been important differences between the countries of Central America in elite cohesion, as well as in the relationship of dominant classes, such as the agrarian bourgeoisie, to the state. A good beginning point is Midlarsky and Roberts's insightful comparison of El Salvador and Nicaragua in this context. They identify the pre-1979 military regime of El Salvador as an "instrumentalist state" – that is, one where "the state is essentially... [though] never entirely – an instrument of class domination" (Midlarsky and Roberts 1985, 181).[30] Salvadoran elites viewed the land issue as zero sum in nature, given both the extreme inequality in land ownership and the scarcity of land availability. Government inflexibility on the issue was required and ensured by the military regime's willingness to serve the agrarian bourgeoisie's fundamental interests.[31]

The Somoza dynasty in Nicaragua, though, was an "autonomous personalist state" – a clear example of where the "interests served by the state are those of the personal ruler and his cohorts, rather than those of a unified dominant class, that state as an institution, or national development."[32] The

[30] This relationship between the economic elite and the state began to alter with the regime change of October 1979 and with the subsequent strengthening of the military. As Williams and Walter note, "During the course of the 1980s, the military became much less dependent upon the oligarchy and much more autonomous as an institution with its own set of interests" (Williams and Walter 1997, 124). To some extent, then, El Salvador became more like the description of Guatemala below. But only to some extent, because as the state gained autonomy from the domestic elite, it grew more dependent on its international sponsor, the United States (unlike Guatemala). For a discussion of "the price of U.S. assistance" for the Salvadoran military, see Williams and Walter (1997, 141–150).

[31] Wickham-Crowley classifies pre-1979 El Salvador as a "collective military regime" (Wickham-Crowley 1992, 282), but his analysis is compatible with this paragraph and the analysis that follows.

[32] Drawing on others, Wickham-Crowley uses the phrase "patrimonial police state" to characterize the Somoza dynasty (Wickham-Crowley 1992, 270), an analysis which he also effectively applies to the Fulgencio Batista regime in Cuba that was overthrown by the Castro-led revolutionaries. Other examples of this type of rule would be Rafael Trujillo of the Dominican Republic, Alfredo Stroessner of Paraguay, and Ferdinand Marcos of the Philippines. Similarly, Goodwin highlights the role of "personalistic, neopatrimonial dictatorships" (Goodwin 2001, 183) and stresses "that revolutionary movements became strong only where militarized yet infrastructurally weak states were consistently exclusionary,

agrarian bourgeoisie of Nicaragua never had developed the coherence or the political power of its counterparts in El Salvador and Guatemala. In part, this was because of significant armed interventions by Great Britain and the United States, with the latter continuing up to 1932, and then because elites were preempted by the Somoza dynasty that began in 1938.[33] Although the policies of the dynasty often benefited the economic elite, interests could also diverge. Increasingly, they did during the 1970s as the growing greed of the last of the dynasty's presidents, Anastasio Somoza Debayle, created conflict with and resentment among the economic elite. Under the right circumstances, then, an antidictator coalition including both peasants and landlords, workers and industrialists, could, and did, form.[34]

Somoza had another vulnerability that set him apart from the other regimes of the region: His was the one most dependent on the United States. Relatively autonomous from and superior to economic elites domestically, the Somoza dynasty was a client of the regional hegemonic power (and clearly the two points are related). A relatively inconsequential and unsuccessful force during the 1960s, the then rural-based insurgency of the Frente Sandinista de Liberación Nacional (FSLN) represented a greater threat to the dictatorship by the early 1970s. Consequently, Somoza declared martial law in December 1974, which lasted thirty-three months. The vicious rural repression of 1974–1976 carried out by the National Guard was relatively unnoticed in the United States, but Somoza faced (and responded to) a far different situation in the years that followed.

antireformist, and more or less indiscriminately repressive of their political opponents (moderates and reformists as well as revolutionaries)" (Goodwin 2001, 143). Goodwin goes beyond prior analyses in his "state constructionism" approach with his emphases that "there is a sense in which certain state structures and practices actively form or 'construct' revolutionary movements as effectively as the best professional revolutionaries, by channeling and organizing political dissent along radical lines. . . . people do not make revolutions under circumstances chosen by themselves, but within specific political contexts directly encountered, given, and transmitted from the past. State structures and practices invariably matter, in other words, for the very *formation* of revolutionary movements" (p. 25).

[33] Paige 1985 provides a particularly good account of these dynamics. Also see Wickham-Crowley (1992, 264–269).

[34] In their analysis of the Nicaraguan revolution, McAdam, Tarrow, and Tilly highlight the role of three causal mechanisms. One of them fits here, which is what they term the "infringement of elite interests" (McAdam, Tarrow, and Tilly 2001, 199–201). As they point out, the defection by elites from the old regime is a crucial explanatory factor in the comparison of successful revolutionary outcomes to the unsuccessful, certainly including in the literature on Nicaragua itself (pp. 197–198).

By early 1977, the Sandinista threat appeared largely quashed. Many in the U.S. Congress and the new Carter administration now viewed the Nicaraguan situation in terms of human rights violations (Schoultz 1981). In response to U.S. pressures, Somoza ended martial law and political space was opened for oppositional activities. Open mass opposition grew dramatically, and the resurgent Sandinistas were better able to organize in urban areas (benefiting as well from Somoza's second heart attack, in July 1977). his second). Following popular revulsion at the slaying of leading opposition figure Pedro Joaquín Chamorro in January 1978,[35] the FSLN unleashed mass insurrections in major cities in February and September of 1978 and May 1979. These constraints from its hegemonic ally help to explain why, although Somoza's repression of the mass insurrections themselves and the subsequent "mop–up" operations were horrendous, in between these events nonviolent oppositional leaders and activists did not disappear in Nicaragua with anything like the frequency occurring in nearby El Salvador and Guatemala. Furthermore, this international "decertification" of the regime reduced its domestic legitimacy, moving new people into opposition, and emboldening those already challenging the government.[36]

With the fall of Somoza imminent, by 1979 the United States altered its policy toward the region with the primary objective of avoiding any further revolutionary situations and, certainly, outcomes. Pressures were applied on the governments of El Salvador and Guatemala to improve their human rights practices and to undertake reforms in order to forestall a victory by the left. Since El Salvador was already on the verge of a revolutionary situation, it was both the object of greater concern and was more vulnerable to external pressure. These pressures from the United States reinforced splits already deepening in the Salvadoran military. The regime change of October 1979 and the political and economic changes heavily pushed

---

[35] McAdam, Tarrow, and Tilly make good use of the concept of "suddenly imposed grievances" to capture the electrifying effect of the Chamorro assassination on popular mobilization (McAdam, Tarrow, and Tilly 2001, 201–204). Not only did this (the second of their causal mechanisms in this case) affect groups across the social spectrum, its impact was especially strong on the economic elite of whom Chamorro was a prominent member. As they point out, the assassination of Benigno Aquino in the Philippines in 1983 had a similar effect. Indeed, each of their three causal mechanisms operated with similar results in the demise of the Marcos regime in the Philippines.

[36] This is the third of the causal mechanisms used by McAdam, Tarrow, and Tilly to explain the success of the Nicaraguan revolution. As they note, parallel actions by other countries reinforced this decertification effect, especially steps taken by Costa Rica, Mexico, Panama, and Venezuela (McAdam, Tarrow, and Tilly 2001, 204–207).

by the U.S. in early 1980, especially the agrarian reform, broke the subservience of the state to landed elites, attacking some (though certainly not all) of that elite's fundamental interests. This fragmentation and conflict between elites opened political opportunities for popular forces during late 1979 through the first half of 1980, and their mass mobilization gained not only policy results but brought the country close to a revolutionary transformation.

However, the revolutionaries in El Salvador did not cloak their ideology with pragmatic rhetoric as had the Sandinistas in Nicaragua, and neither did they follow the FSLN lead and seek to forge an alliance with upper-class elements.[37] Instead, the Salvadoran economic elite continued its support of the military, even as the latter broke the terms of their long-time alliance. As an additional contrast, the Nicaraguan revolutionary movement began to take off during a time when the Carter administration disclaimed any U.S. security concerns in Central America. However, the United States certainly was not prepared to allow "another Nicaragua" to occur, especially once Reagan entered the presidency. In face of the significant radical threat in El Salvador, the military eliminated the split within its ranks as 1980 progressed by eliminating the reformist faction from its ranks, with no effective restraint from the United States. Symbolic was the fate of the leader of the reformist faction, Colonel Adolfo Majano: He was forced out of the ruling junta in December 1980 and then out of the country in March 1981.[38] The newly reunified Salvadoran military was restrained, then, by neither domestic elites nor international allies during the murderous years through 1983. The democratization process instigated by the United States, though, brought new lines of fragmentation among domestic elites and their international allies, as discussed earlier in this chapter. This again provided an opening for popular forces, at first only barely, then boldly in the mid 1980s, and eventually to the point where following the end of the civil war, the FMLN candidate was elected mayor of San Salvador in 1997.

---

[37] The consequences of the approach in Nicaragua (and Cuba) are explained well by Wickham-Crowley: "Those three features, moderate allies, moderated messages, and mass media access, fed and fueled one another, consistently increasing the strength of the opposition and furthermore weakening the willingness of the United States' administrations (of Eisenhower and Carter, respectively) to continue supporting dictatorships under American domestic pressure to support democratic movements abroad" (Wickham-Crowley 1992, 271–272).

[38] The story is told well in Williams and Walter (1997, 100–111).

Midlarsky and Roberts classify Guatemala, in a brief remark, as an instrumentalist state along with El Salvador. Certainly, the resemblance is substantial. However, the Guatemalan military's control of the state by the early 1970s was more total and secure than in El Salvador with greater state autonomy from economic elites. A more appropriate classification for Guatemala, then, would be as an "autonomous military state."[39] This autonomy and firm control placed the Guatemalan military in a better position to resist pressures from the Carter administration, pressures that were much less than those applied to El Salvador anyway.[40] Furthermore, as Jonas notes, the Guatemalan economic elite of the time "has remained staunchly more oligarchic, less modernizing, less reformist than any other in Central America" (Jonas 1991, 147).

A very different pattern is provided by Honduras. As late as 1960, both its agrarian bourgeoisie and its state were quite weak in comparison to its neighbors, largely because of the lack of a significant domestically controlled exportable crop to provide the capital necessary for either elites or the state to expand. Although that expansion followed rapidly in the subsequent decades, Honduras through the mid-1970s presented the best possibility in the region for the redirection of public policy toward the interests of the disadvantaged – especially the country's peasant majority – without prior changes in class-state relations.

After a reformist government was overthrown by the military in 1963, access to the national political system for popular forces began to open in the late 1960s, largely due to popular opposition to fraudulent municipal elections in March 1968 and the repercussions of the loss of the war

---

[39] This would be a cousin to the "bureaucratic authoritarian state" of the military regimes of the more developed countries of the Southern Cone, as conceptualized by O'Donnell 1973. Wickham-Crowley classifies Guatemala, as he does El Salvador, as a "collective military regime," but his analysis is compatible with this paragraph and the analysis that follows. He adds, though, that under Lucas García (1978–1982) Guatemala was moving in a personalistic direction (Wickham-Crowley 1992, 290). Even more so was this personalistic tendency under the next military ruler, Gen. Efraín Ríos Montt, which is a major reason why the military removed him after a year and a half.

[40] However, economic assistance to Guatemala continued during this period, as did the delivery of military aid already in the pipeline (Schoultz 1983, 188–189). Guatemalan officials rejoiced when Reagan defeated Carter in 1980 because it was widely expected that the new president would sharply alter policy toward their country. Although the record is clear that the Reagan administration would have liked to do more than it did, it was constrained by the U.S. Congress and the U.S. human rights lobby.

with El Salvador in July 1969. Government responsiveness, though, virtually ceased with the election of a conservative president in June 1971. In response, a peasant hunger march on December 4, 1972 on the capital was partially responsible for a coup that brought General Oswaldo López Arellano to power, along with a group of progressive junior officers. Having explicitly aligned himself with popular classes prior to the coup, López soon issued an emergency land reform measure, which was followed in January 1975 by an agrarian reform law.[41]

However, a new military government pushed López aside in April, refused to implement the law, and began to respond with violence to peasant mobilization. As peasant grievances escalated, so did their contentious action, including marches and demonstrations and a record number of land occupations. In response to this unprecedented level of popular pressure, the government finally acted with a program for the redistribution of public and idle private lands. A significant agrarian reform, it was facilitated by the availability of an amount of public lands unparalleled in the region and by the vulnerability (due to scandal) of United Brands (successor to United Fruit) to expropriation. Consequently, rural discontent dropped. By early 1977, though, opponents of further reform within the government and among economic elites had clearly won; the last of the progressive military were sent into "diplomatic exile," and government responsiveness disappeared.[42]

Conditions for popular political activity improved with the return of civilian government in 1982. However, the role of Honduras as a staging area for the U.S.-led war against Nicaragua both increased the repressive capacity of the Honduran state and legitimated for elites their opposition to contentious mass action. It was during this period that Honduras had its experience with state terrorism. Tragic as they were, the 179 documented disappearances by the state are also symbolic of the Honduran difference compared to El Salvador, Guatemala, and Nicaragua (Human Rights Watch 1994, 119).

In great contrast to the rest of Central America, the coffee bourgeoisie of Costa Rica was larger, less wealthy, and less parasitic from the first years of

---

[41] It should be noted, though, that López also led the coup that overthrew the elected progressive civilian government of Ramón Villeda Morales in 1963.

[42] For further discussion, see Brockett 1998. Goodwin provides a good discussion of "why [there was] no revolutionary movement in Honduras" (Goodwin 2001, 169–176).

the coffee boom of the nineteenth century, for reasons that go back, in part, to its distinctive colonization pattern. The coffee bourgeoisie's share of political power declined as society became more urban, industrial, and democratic (but not without conflict). With the regime changes following from its civil war of 1948, Costa Rica for decades has provided Latin America's closest approximation of the "polyarchical state" – an institutionalized polyarchical political system with an important measure of autonomy from economic elites. Contentious movements in contemporary Costa Rica have lacked the intensity of those elsewhere in the region. In part, this is because socioeconomic grievances are less intense. But it is also because murder by the contemporary state is unknown.

The Relative Capacity and Propensity for Repression[43]

Capacity of the State Security Apparatus El Salvador and Guatemala traditionally had larger and more competent security forces than did the other Central American countries. Table 8.1 demonstrates this difference. The first column gives the number of personnel in the armed forces in each country during the late 1970s with two exceptions, which is why the table refers to "security forces." Costa Rica disbanded its military after its 1948 "revolution;" the figure here is for its Civil Guard. Second, El Salvador had a large and important National Guard with responsibilities for maintaining rural order; accordingly, it is included here. The five countries vary widely in area, which should be taken into account to determine their relative coercive capability, especially since much of the challenge to the state has been armed rural insurgencies, usually located in remote areas difficult to reach.[44] This rough measure – the number of security force personnel per square mile – indicates a much stronger coercive capacity in El Salvador, followed by Guatemala.[45] This more highly developed capacity facilitated state terrorism and counterinsurgency in these two countries

---

[43] This section is a substantially revised version of Brockett 1991b. Additional references may be found there and in the relevant country chapters in Brockett 1998.

[44] A more complete analysis might also consider differences in terrain and transportation infrastructure. On other, but less salient, indicators, the country rankings shift, such as for military expenditure as a percentage of gross national product and for military manpower per thousand working-age persons (see Taylor and Jodice 1983).

[45] Salvadoran guerrilla leader Joaquín Villalobos has been cited as seeing this as a key characteristic of El Salvador affecting revolutionary strategy (Lungo 1996, 83).

Table 8.1 *Security Forces of Central America in Late 1970s*

Country	Number[*]	Area[**]	Number Per Square Mile[+]
Costa Rica	3,000	20,000	.15
El Salvador	8,930	8,200	1.09
Guatemala	17,960	42,000	.43
Honduras	11,300	43,000	.27
Nicaragua	7,500	57,000	.13

Note: * Total number in armed forces in late 1970s, except the following: Costa Rica, with no armed forces, data are for Civil Guard; El Salvador, includes the 2000-man National Guard.
** Total area in square miles.
+ Number of security force personnel per square mile.

Source: Armed Forces (except Nicaragua): Kurian (1982, 451, 572, 693, 770).
Nicaragua: Black (1981, 52).
El Salvador National Guard: McClintock (1985a, 215).
Reprinted from Brockett (1991a, 68).

while the lesser capacity acted as a constraint in the others. The contrast with Nicaragua is especially notable.

When other security forces are taken into consideration, the magnitude of the difference becomes even greater. In addition to the personnel already listed, El Salvador at the end of the 1970s also had a National Police notable for its size (2,000), as well as the over 1,000 members of the Treasury Police, notorious for their brutality (McClintock 1985a, 215–216). Finally, there was the Organización Democrática Nacionalista (ORDEN), a 100,000-member rural paramilitary organization tied to the National Guard. This was the contemporary manifestation of a system of rural reserves tied to the military going back to the late nineteenth century. Indeed, by 1930 "the Salvadoran countryside, especially coffee-growing areas, had come largely under military control or surveillance" (Williams and Walter 1997, 17). This meant that when peasants began organizing in the 1970s, the Salvadoran armed forces had "the advantage of nearly half a century of pervasive paramilitary organization in the countryside" (Williams and Walter 1997, 17).

Similarly, numerous well-organized paramilitary death squads tied to the military operated in Guatemala following their initial appearance in 1966. These death squads were especially important to the rural repression in the east during the rest of the 1960s, as they have been in the capital ever since.[46] The National Police also became agents of the military during the 1960s, a dominance tightened under Lucas García and his notorious police director, General Germán Chupina. The same also was true for the Treasury Police.[47]

Completing the repressive forces in Guatemala were the military commissioners found throughout rural areas after their establishment in 1938. Following the 1954 coup, their services to the military were increased, serving not only administrative functions such as rounding up recruits but also as an on-the-ground intelligence network. Usually former soldiers, many were members of the party of the counterrevolution, the Movimiento de Liberación Nacional (MLN), and many were also tied to local landed elites. When the counterinsurgency effort began in seriousness in 1966, their numbers increased, averaging about 4,000 throughout the country with higher peaks in the late 1960s and in 1973. When the armed confrontation intensified in the early 1980s, their numbers doubled again, averaging 8,000 to 12,000 throughout that decade. When the Patrullos de Autodefensa Civil (PAC) were initiated in 1981, the local military commissioner often served as the head.[48]

The greater coercive capacity of El Salvador and Guatemala also is clear when the competence of the various security forces is examined.[49] The Salvadoran National Guard, for example, was described in 1960 by a U.S. security specialist as providing "the most complete and beneficial [!] civil police services ever observed by us in Latin America" (quoted in McClintock 1985a, 197). Similarly, the professional competence of its National Police was praised in comparison to the rest of the region, including Guatemala (p. 198). The development of a modern army in Guatemala began in 1871, simultaneous with the spread of coffee cultivation for export. By 1922, the military had garrisons in the smallest towns throughout the country, and during the following decade they penetrated into remote rural areas (McClintock 1985b, 8–18). The military continued to modernize in the

---

[46] CEH (1999, 2:111–120); McClintock (1985b, 85–90).

[47] CEH (1999, 2:147–157).

[48] CEH (1999, 2:158–181); also see Adams (1970, 199, 271–272); and McClintock (1985b, 65–69).

[49] Viewed individually, the military of any one country could be seen as weak. For example, Williams and Walter portray "the effective strength of the Salvadoran armed forces" during the 1960s as "quite limited" (Williams and Walter 1997, 75, 92–93). In a comparative context as in this study, the view is different.

following years, and by the mid-1960s it had become "a coherent political institution capable of dominating the country's political life" like its counterpart in El Salvador had for decades (p. 69).[50]

In contrast, it was not until the early 1950s that the military of Honduras "began to achieve a certain primitive level of institutionalization" (Morris and Ropp 1977, 43). Further development was promoted by the country's humiliating loss in the "Soccer War" of 1969 with El Salvador. By the mid-1970s, the military had consolidated a central position within the national political system (pp. 44–45). However, it still did not penetrate rural society like in the other two countries, although gains had been made in this regard since 1963.[51] A substantial enhancement of the Honduran military's capacity instead occurred in the 1980s as a consequence of the immense buildup of forces undertaken by the United States in order to conduct its war against the Sandinista government in Nicaragua.

An important reason for the success of the Sandinista armed insurgency in Nicaragua was that the National Guard of Nicaragua was small by comparison with its neighbors. Indeed, as indicated by Table 8.1, it was the smallest in the region in the late 1970s in relationship to the size of the country.[52] Furthermore, the Guard was a personal instrument of Somoza family rule from its early days to its end in 1979, undermining its effectiveness as a military force. Continual intervention by the three Somoza dictators (especially the first and the last) into Guard personnel and policy decisions secured for the family a compliant force not threatening its power. But this interference corroded the Guard's effectiveness as a coercive institution capable of maintaining the status quo once a significant armed challenge developed. The Guard did fight ferociously for Somoza, but its institutional interests would have been better served by defecting from the dictator in a preemptive move to neutralize the revolutionary mobilization.[53]

There is a further significant difference between the Nicaraguan National Guard and the military of El Salvador. Due to human rights

---

[50] For thorough and well-documented discussions of the role of the United States in the development of the security forces of these two countries, see McClintock (1985a, 1985b).

[51] Ropp (1974, 521).

[52] As the revolutionary movement expanded through 1978, Somoza did rapidly double the size of the National Guard (Goodwin 2001, 191).

[53] For background on the Nicaraguan National Guard, see Millett 1977, as well as Black 1981 and Booth 1982. Wickham-Crowley provides a similar analysis for both Nicaragua and Cuba. Concerning the latter, he notes that under Batista the Cuban military "was institutionally weak and personally controlled" in an "utterly unprofessional" manner (Wickham-Crowley 1992, 158, 173).

considerations, the U.S. reduced its military assistance to Nicaragua, cutting it back 43 percent from 1977 to 1978 and then completely for 1979 (Booth 1982, 128–129). Due especially to the Nicaraguan Revolution, the United States poured money into the Salvadoran military as its size exploded from 7,250 armed personnel in 1980 to 42,640 in 1986 (Williams and Walter 1997, 140).

Propensity for Repression As popular groups mobilized throughout Central America in the 1960s and 1970s to press their grievances, they encountered different government responses also because of the reinforcing effect of differences in political cultures and elite subcultures. As Gurr has pointed out, "historical traditions of state terror . . . probably encourage elites to use terror irrespective of . . . structural factors" (Gurr 1986, 66).

The point here is two-fold. First, the agrarian class structures of Guatemala and El Salvador historically had been more rigid and exploitive than in the other countries, thereby requiring – and receiving – protection by more elaborate and extensive repressive systems. Consequently, mass mobilization in these two countries probably would be perceived by elites as more of a fundamental threat than would similar levels of mobilization elsewhere. Second and to the point of elite subcultures, given the scope of the violence that had been used in the past, elites would be more likely to believe violence an acceptable and effective response to any perceived threats in the present.

Elites in El Salvador could and did look back to the massacre of 1932 when some 8,000 to 30,000 were murdered by the state during a time of social unrest as "a model response to the threat of rebellion," as well as to the four decades of "social peace" that it brought (McClintock 1985a, 99–100). Guatemalans contemplating the employment of state violence in the late 1970s needed to refer back only to 1966–1970, when probably over 10,000 were murdered, or back to the counterrevolution of 1954, or they could go back to the twenty-two-year "reign of terror" (Munro, 1918, 53–54) of Manuel Estrada Cabrera early in the century. Going progressively further back in time, the patterns of elite violence employed in the conversion of subsistence peasant farmland to elite coffee estate cultivation or earlier in maintaining colonial society distinguished Guatemala and El Salvador from the other three countries of Central America (Brockett 1998).

If we assume that the "massive slaughter of members of one's own species is repugnant" to humans (Kuper 1981, 84), then the existence of such economic "reasons" as the above is an incomplete explanation for state terrorism; attention must also be given to variables that facilitate the dehumanization of potential victims.[54] Two of the most important have been political ideologies and social cleavages.

Ideologies can portray "foreign" ideas as threats to society, thereby turning (suspected) advocates of these ideas into mortal enemies, regardless of whether these advocates intend to employ violence themselves. Most salient in Latin America during the Cold War, of course, was a national security ideology promoted by the United States that imbued in the militaries of Latin America and among economic elites an identification of radical thought with communism and communism with the Soviet threat to the hemisphere.[55] This national security ideology helps to explain the prevalence of state terrorism generally in Latin America during the Cold War but does not explain differences between individual countries. Instead, social cleavages are more useful for understanding country differences in the propensity for repression.

Gurr points out that "the greater the heterogeneity and stratification in a society, the greater the likelihood that a regime will use violence as a principle means of social control" (Gurr 1986, 58).[56] He states the argument strongly: "it seems almost universally true that the ruling classes in highly stratified societies are ruthless in their use of violence to suppress threats to their domination. Underlying the frequent resort of elites to violence in heterogeneous and stratified societies is probably a lack of empathic identification between elites and non-elites. Social distance, whether based on ethnic difference or on class barriers, makes it psychologically easier to dehumanize and murder opponents" (Gurr 1986, 58).

On a class basis, this social distance in Central America has been the greatest in El Salvador and Guatemala. As one indicator, Table 2.1 demonstrated that in these two countries there has been a much smaller intermediate category of farms separating the small landed elite from the large and impoverished peasant majority.

A social cleavage of perhaps even greater importance has been ethnicity. The indigenous population of Guatemala in the 1970s was estimated

---

[54] Good discussions can be found in Duvall and Stohl (1983, 209–210) and Kuper (1981, 84–100).

[55] Lopez 1986, 1988; McClintock 1985a; and Pion-Berlin 1989 provide good discussions.

[56] Duvall and Stohl emphasize the importance to dehumanization of "the perceptual social distance between the government and the victim population" (Duvall and Stohl 1983, 209). Also see Kuper (1981, 84–85).

(conservatively) at around 44 percent, with the comparable figure for Costa Rica less than 1 percent and for the other three countries ranging between 5 and 7 percent (Kurian 1982). Among these latter three countries, there have been important differences. The remaining indigenous populations of Honduras and Nicaragua generally have been isolated in the remote and underpopulated Caribbean lowlands, but such physical segregation is not true of El Salvador. Furthermore, the 1932 massacre in El Salvador was particularly aimed at the indigenous, promoting many of the survivors to relinquish their cultural identity.

The noncombatant group most likely to supply the innocent victims of state terrorism in Central America during the decades of this study were the Mayas of Guatemala's western highlands. The reign of terror directed at the Maya during 1980–1984 was the contemporary manifestation of the racism that stretches back to the liberal reforms of the nineteenth century, which violently expropriated land and labor from the indigenous, and back further to the Conquest itself. The reinforcing effect of this racism and of the national security ideology in promoting the dehumanization necessary for this brutality is clearly shown in Richards's interviews with military personnel involved in the subjugation of the remote Ixil region of northern Guatemala in the early 1980s. Both officers and soldiers perceived the Ixil "as backward and culturally, and even mentally, less developed" (Richards 1985, 101). As a consequence of such attitudes, "the Ixiles are not afforded real human status" (p. 102). When combined with the national security doctrine, this racism produced the following cold-hearted attitude: "the death, destruction, and displacement of the human population were simply unfortunate consequences of a strategy couched in the clinical design of counterinsurgency" (p. 99).

The Guatemalan truth commission documents about 7,000 Ixil killed – almost 15 percent of the entire population of this group. Seventy percent of their communities were destroyed; 60 percent of the people were left displaced (CEH 1999, 3:359). The Ixil are one of four ethnic groups for whom the commission charges the Guatemalan government with practicing genocide (p. 358).[57] Many Mayas were murdered as part of the military's scorched-earth counterinsurgency campaign in areas where revolutionaries had established some presence – such as the EGP in the Ixil Triangle. But many other victims were not living in conflicted areas, as Earle 2001 reminds us. Doubly innocent – neither revolutionaries themselves nor even living

[57] Also see Sanford (2003, 76–120).

in areas where some revolutionary threat might be located – they were the ultimate victims of the Guatemalan state's racism.

Conclusion

Some of the political opportunities literature claims that opening political opportunities are a *prerequisite* for the emergence and success of contentious movements. That position is not defended here, as there are too many contradictory examples and too many different types of movements (e.g., the difference between marginal groups in noninstitutionalized democracies compared to mainstream groups in well-institutionalized democracies). Nonetheless, a strong opportunities thesis is still amply supported by the evidence on Central America provided by the last two chapters. That is, changes in the configuration of political opportunities are *often critical* for explaining the emergence of contentious movements, as well as their trajectories and outcomes.

In a provocative essay, Goodwin and Jasper go beyond challenging the necessity of change in political opportunities to diminishing the significance of political opportunities for "many, if not most," movements (Goodwin and Jasper 1999, 39).[58] They do not restrict their position to institutionalized democracies but instead portray mobilization even for Third World movements as "often a defensive response to contracting political opportunities" (p. 39).

---

[58] Here they have been encouraged by comments concerning the U.S. gay rights movement made by McAdam 1996, who distinguishes the dynamics for "late-comer" movements compared to "early risers" during a "cycle of contention," that is, a period marked by higher than normal levels and intensity of mobilization (Tarrow 1998, 24–25). McAdam notes that "it would appear as if the [gay] movement arose in a context of *contracting* political opportunities" (p. 32) and concludes that because of a theoretical focus on early risers, "we may have exaggerated the role of political opportunities in the *emergence* of collective action" (p. 33). Exaggeration, perhaps, but McAdam concedes too much. Some aspects of the configuration of political opportunities might be more discouraging for latecomers, including a less responsive state and probably a conflict-weary general public. Some short-term political trends might be to their disadvantage as well, such as Richard Nixon's presidential victory in 1968 that McAdam cites. However, the defiant Stonewall bar riot in New York City in June 1969, which marks the critical point for the emergence of the gay movement, occurred within the context both of increasing militancy across movements on the left (Adam 1995, 79–89; Duberman 1993, 170–172) and of *lessening* police harassment of gays in cities such as New York and San Francisco – indeed, the Stonewall police raid itself was apparently aimed at the bar's mob owners' tax avoidance rather than the bar's clientele (Duberman 1993, 110, 194).

Goodwin and Jasper's example is the successful revolutionary mobilization against Somoza in Nicaragua. They are correct that at this stage in the Nicaraguan cycle of contention challengers indeed were provoked to heightened levels of activity by contracting political opportunities, especially increasing repression. However, Goodwin and Jasper's analysis leaves out three important points.[59] First, the *emergence* and *growth* of the strong popular challenge that was targeted by this repression is explained in large part by *expanding* political opportunities, as discussed in the prior section. Especially important were the new opportunities for challengers created by elite fragmentation when Nicaragua became one of the key targets of the emerging human rights policy of first the U.S. Congress and then the Carter administration, both reinforcing the growing opposition to Somoza by Nicaraguan economic elites and encouraging the dictator to loosen restrictions on oppositional political activities.

Second, the folding of Nicaraguan social movements into a successful revolutionary movement is the exception; successful revolutions are rare. Normally, regimes that are willing to use whatever amount of repression that is necessary to hold on to power succeed, even as they are creating new grievances. Far more representative than the Nicaraguan case, then, was the violent elimination of social movements in contemporaneous El Salvador and Guatemala and then the successful containment of the resulting threat from revolutionary movements. Third, and most important, had there been no contracting political opportunities in these three cases – or even better, opportunities expanding rather than contracting – popular social movements undoubtedly would have *persisted* and *gained* more of their objectives at a much lower cost in human lives and suffering.

It is correct that contracting political opportunities are likely to be the source of new grievances, especially when there is a severe change, such as increased repression or an unpopular military coup. However, the extent to which these new grievances actually will fuel additional contentious activity will be dependent on the complex relationship between grievances, the level of existing mobilization, and each of the various dimensions of the configuration of political opportunities. It is this dynamic, and especially the protest-repression paradox, that is the subject of the next two chapters.

---

[59] For an elaboration of their position, see Goodwin 2001 (especially pp. 176–179, 237–240).

Appendix: Salvador Repression Data

There is no authoritative source for estimating deaths from repression in El Salvador corresponding to the truth commission report for Guatemala utilized in prior chapters.[60] Indeed, controversies over government responsibility for the escalating death toll in El Salvador in the late 1970s/early 1980s were intense, as human rights monitors were attacked for their reporting not just by the Salvadoran government but by the U.S. government as well. Even once it was well established that the overwhelming majority of civilian deaths were attributable to the state either directly or indirectly through its allied death squads, controversies continued throughout the civil war as the two governments attempted to minimize estimates of the numbers of civilians killed in the course of military operations.

A truth commission was mandated by the Salvadoran peace agreements to investigate "serious acts of violence that have occurred since 1980 and whose impact on society urgently demands that the public should know the truth" (Betancur et al. 1993, 11).[61] A panel of three distinguished commissioners[62] was assembled along with an international team of investigators, and the report it issued has fulfilled an important purpose. The commission investigated thousands of individual complaints as well as other sources of information. But it only had six months to complete its work, so its report necessarily lacks the scope and thoroughness of the Guatemalan report. The major focus of the Salvadoran report is individual cases of violence that were especially significant, and its conclusions for these cases played a critical role in establishing responsibility, such as for the murders of Archbishop Romero and the six Jesuit priests. More generally, the report indicates that 85 percent of those giving testimony identified the agent of the violence as the state/death squads (p. 43).[63]

As the violence escalated in the late 1970s in El Salvador, two groups undertook efforts to compile data on the mounting toll, one at the Universidad Centroamericana (UCA) and the other under the auspices of the Roman

---

[60] Perhaps the best effort using annual data is Seligson and McElhinny 1996.

[61] For both background on the commission and an analysis of the report and its impact, see Americas Watch 1993.

[62] The three are Belisario Betancur, chairman and former president of Colombia; Reinaldo Figueredo Planchart, former foreign minister of Venezuela; and Thomas Buergenthal, former president of the Inter-American Court of Human Rights.

[63] The results of the testimonies were compiled in an annex to the report but not released. Instead, they are on file at the United Nations.

Catholic Archdiocese of San Salvador. Of the two, the latter is generally recognized as the more thorough. In 1975, a small group of Catholic lawyers and law students started Socorro Jurídico to offer free legal aid to victims of human rights violations. In late 1977, they moved to the archdiocese and by the beginning of 1978 released weekly compilations of human rights violations. Receiving strong support from Archbishop Romero on the one hand, Socorro Jurídico was sharply criticized on the other by the government and harassed intensely. Their reports also were repeatedly questioned by the U.S. embassy as biased and unreliable. In contrast, Americas Watch found Socorro Jurídico's methodology to be "meticulous" (Americas Watch 1982, 3), "conservative" (p. 16), and its data "a valid guideline to official repression, within limitations due to the political situation" (p. 7).[64]

Nonetheless (and perhaps in response to this pressure), in May 1982 the archdiocese set up its own human rights office, Tutela Legal (Brown 1985, 122–135). Socorro Jurídico continued to operate for several more years under other auspices, but most observers continued to rely for their data on the office of the archdiocese, meaning now Tutela Legal. Comparing the monthly totals of Tutela Legal (TL) and Socorro Jurídico (SJ): Sometimes they are very close, sometimes one is higher, sometimes the other. This study relies on SJ data as much as it can because it is the only source that published human rights data prior to the initiation of the cycle of contention of the late 1970s/early 1980s.

In a few tables, countrywide data are reported for civilian deaths from repression. However, as with Guatemala, what is theoretically most important is fluctuations in repression in the capital and its surrounding area.

---

[64] The U.S. relied for its data on the Salvadoran press, resulting in lower death estimates than the more thorough efforts of the human rights groups, which also included information provided by victims' families. For the U.S. perspective, see U.S. House (1984, 202–208, 289–290) and for a thorough critique, Americas Watch 1984, which is republished in U.S. House (1984, 291–342). Also see U.S. State 1982, which in addition to comparing its reports to those of Socorro Jurídico and UCA, greatly downplays rightist violence (especially pp. 79–80). After its running battle with the U.S. government across the 1980s, Americas Watch came to this strong conclusion: "Of all the attempts to discredit critics of the government, perhaps none was so pernicious as the [U.S.] embassy's denunciation of human rights monitors. In a country where thousands have been murdered or have disappeared for far less offense than speaking out against government abuses, the embassy's campaign to protect the Salvadoran government by defaming its critics was unconscionable. This is especially true given the number of Salvadorans who have lost their lives carrying out human rights or humanitarian work" (Americas Watch 1991, 130). The FMLN also released casualty figures throughout the conflict, but these often seem very inaccurate. See, for example, NY Times (Jan. 12, 1986, 7).

This can be and is done for the data on contentious activities. Unfortunately, this data cannot be derived as easily for victims of repression, so instead rough estimates were made. The SJ provided data broken down by whether the victim could be identified, as well as by the victim's occupation, if known. The assumption made here is that murdered activists and their closest supporters are likely to be identified and their occupations are likely to be known. From this category, peasants were removed, leaving "identified urban civilians." The biggest defect of this approach is that many of the participants in the urban contentious activities of the late 1970s–early 1980 were peasants and presumably so, too, were the victims. However, increasingly through 1980 and then very much afterward, most of the victims of Salvadoran repression were peasants in the countryside, victims of the military's counterinsurgency campaign.[65] If a consistent rule is to be used across the dataset to estimate urban victims, the error of underreporting in the early years by removing peasant victims is less than the error would be of including peasants across the entire period. An additional problem is that these "identified urban civilians" were not necessarily residents of the metropolitan San Salvador area but could have resided in other cities. Yet this problem is mitigated by the fact that SJ was located in the capital, and therefore probability of the inclusion of any abuses in its data is probably inversely related to the distance where it occurred from the capital.

Although the SJ data are the only systematic data for the late 1970s, unfortunately it is not complete across the entire period of this study.[66] First, its monthly data for 1982 clearly underreports the national total when compared to other sources and to the trends SJ reports for the years before and after. Consequently, for 1982 the national totals compiled by Universidad Centroamericana (UCA) (and reported in ECA) are utilized. The SJ data for identified urban civilians seem to be consistent for 1982, except for the last quarter, when no relevant data are reported for the last two months and

---

[65] Perhaps the biggest controversy through the 1980s between the Salvadoran and U.S. governments and human rights monitors was establishing the extent to which those killed in military actions were civilians or guerrilla support groups; see, for example, Americas Watch 1986. Given the difficulties of reporting from rural – and especially remote – areas, the usual assumption is that civilian casualties are underreported. For example, Tutela Legal lists 1,045 unidentified deaths in army operations in 1995, where the majority were thought to be civilians but could not be verified (Americas Watch 1986, 2).

[66] The source used here for the Socorro Juridico data is Morales and González (1988, 189–201).

the prior month appears unreliably low. The procedure used to estimate data for these three months is explained on the relevant tables.

Second, the SJ data stops with 1984. For the rest of the decade, Tutela Legal (TL) data are used, primarily drawn from various Americas Watch publications. Unfortunately, these are annual data. In the relevant tables in this study deaths from repression are reported by quarters, which is actually averaged from the annual TL data. This is defensible because by this point fluctuations in repression are small enough that they do not appear to be theoretically relevant, with the exception of late 1989/early 1990. To estimate urban victims, the TL category used is targeted killings by the military and death squads (thereby excluding civilians killed in counterinsurgency operations). These TL data were not obtained for 1987; the procedure used for creating an estimate for this year from other TL data reported by McClintock 1998 is explained in the relevant tables. Similarly, McClintock 1998 is the source for the TL national totals for 1986–1988.

These various estimates in the Salvadoran dataset on deaths from repression would be a serious weakness if they were utilized for statistical analysis. However, for the identification of trends relied upon in this work they do not appear troublesome to me. Indeed, even with these imprecisions, the accuracy of the dataset on deaths from repression created and utilized in this study for El Salvador far exceeds the accuracy of data used in most quantitative studies of political violence.

9

Contention and Repression

GUATEMALA

It should be well established by the prior chapters that the relationship between popular contention and government repression is crucial for understanding both El Salvador and Guatemala in recent decades. More generally, this relationship is an especially intriguing one theoretically for social scientists because after decades of good work by many scholars the fundamental puzzle remains. Following his thorough review of the existing literature more than two decades ago, Zimmerman identified "theoretical arguments for all conceivable basic relations between governmental coercion and group protest and rebellion except for no relationship" (Zimmerman 1980, 181).[1] Seven years later, the dilemma remained, well captured in the title of Lichbach's (1987) oft-cited theoretical analysis: "Deterrence or Escalation? The Puzzle of Aggregate Studies of Repression and Dissent." Judging by the most recent reviews of the literature, such as Davenport 2000; Goldstone 2001; and Goldstone and Tilly 2001, the puzzle persists.

Clearly, repression often succeeds for the state, deterring popular protest, for reasons thoroughly elaborated in the scholarly literature. At other times, repression provokes heightened popular mobilization, including sometimes increased support for, and participation in, revolutionary movements. Again, probable reasons for this opposite effect are amply explored in the literature. Accordingly, the real task before us has been, as Opp and Roehl (1990, 523) point out, to determine "which effect is to be expected under what conditions."

---

[1] Zimmerman also provided excellent direction for future scholarship: "In general, we can suggest that an adequate account of protest (and rebellion) requires specification of motivational factors such as discontent and ideology as well as of mobilization factors of resource organization and power contention. The goal for future research should not be to supplant either approach but to combine them in a more fruitful way" (Zimmerman 1980, 223).

Bringing some resolution to the puzzle of the paradoxical relationship between repression and protest is the principal task of this and the next chapter. A major deficiency in much of the prior scholarship has been the lack of appropriate data to examine this relationship. The innovation of this study is that, first, it utilizes political violence data drawn from domestic sources that are far more accurate than those commonly used. Second, it utilizes protest events data collected from domestic sources for two countries whose characteristics provide the basis for a meaningful and generalizable evaluation of its hypotheses. These data have already isolated key periods for examining the protest-repression paradox. Chapter 7's analysis found Guatemalan contentious activities peaking in both periods when political opportunities were restricting in the face of growing challenges to the regime in power: late 1961/early 1962 and again in late 1978. Chapter 8 demonstrated a parallel period for El Salvador in late 1979/early 1980.

The Protest-Repression Paradox

One of the strongest theoretical expectations concerning repression is for a curvilinear relationship, both between regime type and for any regime, by the amount of repression employed. For regime type, Muller and Seligson 1987 claim that aggressive political participation is to be expected more in semirepressive regimes than in either extremely repressive or democratic ones.[2] Concerning the use of repression with any regime, DeNardo notes that "middling repression is less effective than either no repression at all or harshly draconian reprisals against demonstrators" (DeNardo 1984, 216). He explains that at first "the political backlash caused by the regime's repression exceeds the deterrent effect, and the movement actually mobilizes more people than it would have if there had been no repression at all." However, as repression increases, "deterrence exceeds moral backlash, and the regime finds that each extra measure of repression reduces the movement's support even further" (p. 216).[3]

Empirical tests of the repression-protest relationship, however, have had contradictory results.[4] To some extent, this has been due to "inadequate

[2] Also see Muller and Weede 1990, 1994, among others. For a similar approach, but using two variables (democracy and capacity), see Tilly 2003.

[3] For further discussion in the earlier literature, see Gurr 1970 and Hibbs 1973.

[4] As a sample of studies that will not be discussed below, see Bwy 1968; Davis and Ward 1990; Gupta, Singh, and Sprague 1993; Lichbach and Gurr 1981; and McCammant and Duff 1976.

theory and inappropriate methods" (Hoover and Kowaleswski 1992, 150). At least as important, however, have been data deficiencies as the data used are usually drawn from the *New York Times Index* or similar nondomestic sources.[5] Among contemporary scholars making the best efforts to work through the contradictory findings in the quantitative literature, Moore (and varying associates) has attempted to replicate the findings of other scholars, using alternative data sources and sophisticated analytic methodologies.[6] Some of these findings contradict the theoretical thrust developed in this study. However, because their data are still largely drawn from the *New York Times Index*, the validity of these results is open to question. There is also the problem, as with many statistical studies in this area, that what is primarily individual behavior is tested with aggregate data.[7]

In what seems to me the most promising development in the study of popular contention and repression, a few scholars have turned to domestic and appropriate regional news sources to build their datasets. The few resulting studies do not support a curvilinear hypothesis; however, their cases probably are not the most representative ones from which to generalize.

Rasler uses events data collected from multiple domestic and foreign sources to analyze Iran in the late 1970s. As she hypothesizes, her results show that "repression decreased Iranian protest in the short term, but in the long run repression helped launch micromobilization processes that rapidly brought large numbers of people in the streets" (Rasler 1996, 143). In this case of the Iranian revolution, of course, there is no curvilinear relationship: Mass mobilization overthrew the Shah's repressive monarchy.[8]

Neither does Francisco 1995 find support for a curvilinear hypothesis in his analysis of the collapse of the communist regimes of the German Democratic Republic and Czechoslovakia, along with the case of Palestine.

---

[5] See the discussion in the Appendix to Chapter 7.

[6] See Lee, Maline and Moore 2000; Moore 1998, 2000. For more theoretical discussions, also see Moore 1995a, as well as Lichbach 1995.

[7] For example, Moore 1998 finds support for Lichbach's (1987) hypothesis "that nonviolent protest and violent protest are substitutes." That is, "if the state represses nonviolent protest behavior, then the dissidents will respond with violent protest behavior" and vice versa (p. 854). Even if this is a valid finding at the aggregate data level, it might not be at the level of individual behavior. Although substitution of tactics often would be accurate for revolutionaries for whom nonviolence is a tactical choice, it is not normally true for nonviolent protestors, who are normally far more numerous than the revolutionaries.

[8] Moore 1998 replicates Rasler 1996, as well as others, with *New York Times Index*–based data for Peru and Sri Lanka.

Also using multiple news sources, he does find evidence for two other hypotheses: the backlash (high repression provokes heightened mobilization) and the adaptive (protestors learn from state actions, adapting their behavior accordingly).[9]

Although the cases examined by Rasler and Francisco are important ones and their results help us to specify the conditions that affect the relationship between repression and contentious political activities, these are not the best cases for understanding the repression-protest paradox. Eastern Europe in 1989 and Iran are examples of successful revolutions, that is to say, examples of the fullest failure of repression. Successful revolutions, though, are rare. Furthermore, the Eastern European countries had been totalitarian systems maintained in place by a hegemonic external power (the U.S.S.R.) that successfully restricted political participation using little violence. Finally, Palestine is not an independent country; Palestinians do not see themselves as repressed by *their* government but rather by an occupying power (Israel) that denies them self-determination.

Following the reasoning of Muller and Seligson it should be most fruitful to examine the paradox in countries with semirepressive regimes. In an extremely repressive regime (such as in pre-revolutionary Eastern Europe), "opportunities to engage in collective action of any kind will be quite limited" (Muller and Seligson 1987, 429).[10] Democratic regimes, in contrast, "afford a variety of opportunities for dissident groups to participate legally and peacefully in the political process" (p. 429). However, in semirepressive regimes, since "opportunities for genuine participation are restricted, many politically activated citizens may come to perceive civil disobedience and violence as being more efficacious than legal means of pseudoparticipation.... rational actors may well attach a relatively high utility to aggressive political behavior" (p. 430). Furthermore, to provide a good test of the repression-protest paradox there should be a wide variation in the regime's repressive behavior, from periods of relatively low repression to selective targeting of opponents to indiscriminate violence against dissenters.[11] In addition, challengers respond not just to repression but also

---

[9] Lee, Maline, and Moore 2000 replicate Francisco 1995 with data for Peru, Sri Lanka, and Zimbabwe.

[10] For a good theoretical discussion and empirical study of the repression-protest relationship in Leninist regimes, see Johnston and Mueller 2001 and Opp 1994.

[11] On regime-targeting strategy, see Goldstone 1998b; Mason 1989; and Mason and Krane 1989. Also see della Porta 1995 on the "complex relations between repression and social movement activities" (p. 79), comparing policing strategies in Germany and Italy. She

to accommodation.[12] The relative mix and consistency of protest and accommodation, then, should also vary across time. The cases of Guatemala and El Salvador meet all of these conditions.[13]

This relationship between protest and repression, though, is a function of more than grievances and organization on one side and regime behavior on the other.[14] The core argument that follows is that this relationship is strongly conditioned by the overall level of popular mobilization preexisting at the point that repression either is initiated or increased. That is, the key to resolving the protest-repression paradox is the intervening temporal variable of location in the cycle of contention. Cycles are more than the aggregate of social movement activity itself. Whether challengers are acting within a strong cycle or outside of one in a period of negligible contentious activity is an important part of their political context. Their efforts will most likely receive different responses from both those they hope to mobilize and from the state depending on their cycle location. The argument is demonstrated effectively by Beissinger's analysis of the "tide of nationalism" that swept through the former Soviet Union, a concept inspired by Tarrow's protest cycle (Beissinger 2002, 27–34). Especially to the point is Beissinger's concept of "thickened" history, which he describes as "a period in which the pace of challenging events quickens to the point . . . they come to constitute an increasingly significant part of their own causal structure" (p. 27).

Repression creates new grievances; state terrorism at the levels reached in Guatemala and El Salvador does so in immense numbers. When family, friends, and comrades are tortured, and killed such grievances are intense. But even so, new grievances will not always lead to new or greater political action. When repression overwhelms challengers, flight or withdrawal is often the response. Expectancy of some chance of success does make a difference – as certainly does expectancy of survival itself.[15] The level of repression that is necessary to overwhelm challengers is less at the lower levels of overall popular mobilization that define the absence of a protest cycle than is the level of repression that is required during the higher mobilization

points out that "repressive, diffuse, and hard techniques of policing tend to, at the same time, discourage mass and peaceful protest while fueling the most radical fringes" (p. 80).

[12] Tilly 1978; also see Krain 2000; Rasler 1996.

[13] So did Mississippi in the 1960s. See Andrews's (1997) provocative study of the impact of repression both on black mobilization and on outcomes.

[14] To distinguish repression from other dimensions of the configuration of political opportunities, as explained in Chapter 7, it is defined here in a narrow sense, that is, *repression* is the illegitimate use of force against citizens by the state.

[15] Muller 1979; Muller, Dietz, and Finkel 1991.

that marks a protest cycle itself. Similarly, less repression is required by the state to smother protest during a weaker cycle than during a broader cycle of contention, and less repression is required at the early stages than when the cycle is at its peak of strength.

However, the relationship between protest and repression is a function of more than numbers. The strength of a cycle of contention is determined by more than the sums of people mobilized and of groups involved. Strength is also indicated by the intensity of protesters' commitment and the assertiveness of their actions. As their commitment intensifies, the level of repression that will be required to contain and reduce their contention will be greater than what would be predicted by their numbers alone. Ample examples will be found in this chapter and the next while systematic attention to this critical aspect of the cycle of contention as the key to resolving the protest-repression paradox will be provided by the final section of Chapter 10.

When challengers have developed a broad and strong cycle of contention against a repressive regime that is widely perceived as illegitimate, the regime usually turns to even greater repression in order to preserve itself. Sometimes its efforts are unsuccessful (perhaps sometimes in part because of self-restraint in the employment of state violence) and it is removed from power by the opposition, as seen in Nicaragua and Iran, whose successful revolutions validate the backlash hypothesis. This study is concerned with the far more frequent occurrence: when a regime escalates repression as necessary to maintain itself successfully in power.

In an earlier work (Brockett 1995), I proposed a (less well elaborated) protest-cycle resolution to the repression-protest paradox, using the cases of Guatemala, El Salvador, and Nicaragua. However, the evidence provided was descriptive rather than systematic (and more than one commentator was not convinced). The present study expands the earlier explanation and, more importantly, evaluates it with events data systematically collected from largely domestic sources for both Guatemala in this chapter and El Salvador in the next. The explanation offered here is restricted to "semirepressive" regimes but which will be labeled here "authoritarian" since repression itself is the independent variable under examination. The basic propositions for a protest-cycle resolution of the repression-protest paradox in authoritarian regimes (under usual circumstances) are the following:

1. *Repression by authoritarian regimes – along with other means of limiting access to the political system – normally keeps nonviolent protest at a minimal level.*

2. *For social movements to emerge in authoritarian regimes, not only must other political opportunities open but repression must be held at a sufficiently low level to provide potential protesters hope that they will not be immediately repressed.*

3. *When authoritarian regimes increase repression against nonviolent activities that occur outside of a protest cycle, the lower the level of overall mobilization the more quickly and fully protest will be reduced (given similar levels of repressive capacity and propensity).*

4. *Once a protest cycle is underway in authoritarian regimes, gradually escalating repression will not deter contention. Instead, gradually escalating repression usually will ignite a more radicalized and perhaps an even higher level of contentious activities, often creating a crisis for the regime. The stronger the protest cycle is prior to the intensification of repression and the more gradual and inconsistent the escalation of repression, the greater the probability that repression will have this counterproductive impact.*

5. *As repression increases during a protest cycle in authoritarian regimes, the frequency of illegal and violent acts by challengers increases.*

6. *Massive repression by authoritarian regimes, including the indiscriminate murder of protesters and nonprotesters alike, will normally end the protest cycle, reducing nonviolent contentious activities to a minimal level or even eliminating them altogether.*

7. *Violent revolutionary organizations challenging authoritarian regimes experience rapid growth in both new participants and supporters during and immediately following the period when indiscriminate mass murder by the state kills the protest cycle.*

8. *When authoritarian regimes have the capacity and propensity for massive repression in areas where violent revolutionary organizations operate, including the indiscriminate murder of noncombatants, the regime will normally defeat its revolutionary challenge.*

9. *When repression lightens and other political opportunities open in authoritarian societies, popular movements will reemerge. The pace and intensity of movement emergence will be related to the prior level of contention achieved in the past, on the one hand, and the ferocity and length of the repression recently experienced, on the other.*

Evidence from Guatemala

In the prior chapters, information was presented that allows the identification of the most appropriate periods in Guatemala since 1954 for evaluating each of the propositions just advanced concerning the protest-repression paradox. In addition, in this section the contention events data will be brought together with the data on state violence to provide a quantitative test of these propositions. This combined data is best for the crucial 1973–1980 period, which accordingly will receive the most attention below.

> *1. Repression by authoritarian regimes – along with other means of limiting access to the political system – normally keeps nonviolent protest at a minimal level.*

When early 1963 brought renewed popular demonstrations, the possibility of a victory by progressives in the upcoming presidential elections, and a radical insurgency, the Guatemalan military reacted more fully than in the past, now taking over the government. First, a curfew was put into effect, followed by a state of siege that eliminated political space for nonviolent protest. In effect for eleven months, it was followed by numerous other rounds of similar restrictions on constitutional "guarantees" whenever the military believed "disorder" threatened, such as restrictions implemented for sixteen months beginning in both February 1965 and again in November 1966, for a year beginning in November 1970 and for a number of briefer occasions in between.[16] These measures were backed by state violence as necessary, including the murderous counterinsurgency in the rural east during this period as well as the assassination and disappearance of leftist leaders throughout. Consequently, the incidence of any protests remained very low (and were minor when they did occur) during the period when the hard line within the military dominated the country, that is, until the opening that came with the elections of 1974. These years in Guatemala are but one of numerous examples from many authoritarian regimes of the validity of Proposition One on the everyday deterrence effect of repression.

> *2. For social movements to emerge in authoritarian regimes, not only must other political opportunities open but repression must be held at a sufficiently low level to provide potential protesters hope that they will not be immediately repressed.*

The easing of repression in Guatemala in the late 1950s allowed the growth of the strong contentious movement that was then quashed in 1962–1963. Given the length and ferocity of the repression that followed across the next decade, certainly there would have to be a change in regime

---

[16] CEH (1995, 1:249–253).

behavior for popular mobilization to reappear, as Proposition Two asserts. Feeling secure that it had eliminated the guerrilla threat, the Arana administration let the last state of siege expire at the end of 1971. This change in circumstances was first noticeable in July 1973, when the two-week nationwide teachers' strike for higher salaries in the face of escalating inflation brought popular protest back to the streets in a meaningful way for the first time in over a decade. Although the regime eventually lost patience with protesting teachers and students, breaking up several demonstrations with tear gas and arrests, there were no murders. And on August 3, the government granted teachers a 25 percent raise. Although only half of what they wanted, it was the biggest increase won by any union since 1954. Observers correctly predicted that the settlement would encourage a new round of public employee mobilization, as it indeed did.

3. *When authoritarian regimes increase repression against nonviolent activities that occur outside of a protest cycle, the lower the level of overall mobilization the more quickly and fully protest will be reduced (given similar levels of repressive capacity and propensity).*

When a new elected civilian administration entered office in mid-1966, popular forces perceived an opening window of opportunity for their remobilization. Bravely testing the new political context, some six hundred students and unionists marched that fall in commemoration of the October 20 Revolution of 1944. But the small guerrilla remnant, having been defeated in its rural insurgency, initiated a campaign of urban terrorism at the same time. The regime clamped down in early November with a lengthy and well-enforced state of siege, and nonviolent protest activities quickly stopped.

During this period, the regime by all appearances had little internal dissent over the use of repression as necessary to contain any leftist opposition. Consequently, popular contention was contained, and its nonviolent manifestations easily so. In contrast, a mixed opening of political opportunities began in 1973, the last year of the Arana administration. This partial opening seems to have been based largely on the regime's confidence that the left had been defeated, including the guerrillas. As popular contention grew through the end of 1973 and then the election period of early 1974, the regime returned to violence, notably its attack on the May First demonstrators that killed at least seven protesters. But then Arana's tenure was over.

The hard-line approach represented by Arana continued with a prominent position in the next administration, notably with the forces around

Vice President Mario Sandoval Alarcón, the reputed godfather of Guatemala's vicious death squads. However, President Kjell Laugerud and his supporters were more tolerant of mass movements and their demands (if not too contentious and if not too radical) than any administration since 1954 and perhaps even up to the present. Given these different factions, popular movements had sufficient space to mobilize during the Laugerud administration. At the same time, repression continued, but never at the levels that would be needed to demobilize challengers.

> 4. *Once a protest cycle is underway in authoritarian regimes, gradually escalating repression will not deter contention. Instead, gradually escalating repression usually will ignite a more radicalized and perhaps an even higher level of contentious activities, often creating a crisis for the regime. The stronger the protest cycle is prior to the intensification of repression and the more gradual and inconsistent the escalation of repression, the greater the probability that repression will have this counterproductive impact.*

Contentious political activity can range from peaceful protest rallies to illegal but still nonviolent actions, such as road blockades and building occupations, to such violent activities as bombings and armed attacks. In this section, the focus is on nonviolent protest. Figure 9.1 brings the two subjects of this study together, portraying the relationship between nonviolent

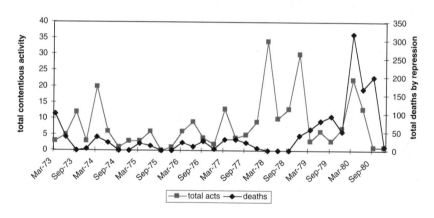

Source for deaths: Ball, Patrick. (1999). AAAS/CIIDH database of human rights violations in
Guatemala (ATV20.1). http://hrdata.aaas.org/ciidh/data.html (downloaded May 2000).

Figure 9.1 Guatemala: Nonviolent Contentious Political Activities and Deaths by Repression: Central Area by Quarters, 1973–1980

protest activities and deaths from repression for 1973 through 1980, broken down by quarters. There are four notable peaks in nonviolent contentious activities, the first quarters of 1974, 1978, and 1980 and the last of 1978. The first two periods are quite similar, both dominated by public employee strikes before and after general elections contested by opponents as fraudulent. The last two peaks presented even sharper challenges to the regime and will be discussed further below. Generally, the overall trend in Figure 9.1 is a gradual increase in nonviolent contentious political activities from the beginning of 1973 through the end of 1978, with the level of contention high enough by June 1977 to specify this as the beginning point of the protest cycle. As repression increases at the end of 1978, protest drops through 1979 but then rises sharply to its final peak in early 1980. But so does repression – rapidly to levels never before experienced in Guatemala's central area.

Clearly, the peak of nonviolent political activities for post-1954 Guatemala occurred in the final quarter of 1978. This peak is even greater as strikes are underrepresented in the database for this year (see Figure 6.2). October 1978 was a key turning point for both regime behavior and mass mobilization. As preludes to this period, there was first the massive tear gas attack by the new administration of General Romeo Lucas García on the unauthorized march against violence by about 10,000 people on August 4 led by the labor movement. Another march by even more demonstrators on September 13 was peaceful, even though many protesters were chanting "Today Nicaragua, tomorrow Guatemala." The next day, the Nicaraguan ambassador to Guatemala was assassinated by guerrillas. That night at the annual Independence Day celebration, a gang of youths began throwing rocks at speakers and a riot ensued. Windows were broken, stores set on fire, and in return, tear gas thrown indiscriminately, with forty hospitalized and many more arrested. No one was killed in either of these confrontations – but such restraint was soon to change.[17]

Controversies concerning bus service and fares had plagued Guatemala City throughout the summer – fare increases were always a key issue for students and poor people. When fares went up at the end of September, contention was inevitable. Poorer neighborhoods threw up barricades. Secondary and university students went on strike. Confrontation with authorities grew day by day, with streets blocked, buses burned, and store windows broken. Overlapping this mobilization was the most significant wave of strikes yet. Some private sector unions were already on strike,

---

[17] *El Imparcial* (Sept. 16–20, 1978, 1).

notably at the Swiss-owned Duralita plant, whose workers occupied the Swiss embassy on September 29. The first general strike in many years was called for October 3. Highly successful for that day among public workers, it drew disappointing support in the private sector and then even that faded. However, public employees intensified their efforts and mounted an impressive strike for close to two weeks, one that spread throughout the country. Tactics radicalized as striking workers occupied numerous public buildings.

Mass attitudes had radicalized as well in the face of continuing economic hardship and repression. Revolution was in the air in Central America, led by the Sandinista uprising against the Somoza dictatorship in Nicaragua. Their revolutionary counterparts in Guatemala City were actively involved in the fall mobilization, as certainly authorities knew. The regime cracked down. When the strikes and confrontations ended at mid-month, thirty people were dead, over three hundred wounded (many by gunfire), and hundreds arrested, and damages reached millions of dollars.[18] Among the dead were several labor leaders, clearly assassinated. Selective killings of popular sector leaders, especially student and labor leaders, then escalated dramatically from this point. The regime was in crisis, and its response was to use repression as necessary.

The data collected for this study show no student leaders killed during the four years beginning with 1972, then one in 1976, five in each of the following three years, and then doubling to ten murdered student leaders in just the first four months of 1980. As activists were killed, many others understandably retreated from any further activity in hopes of preserving their lives or went into exile. But repression also creates new grievances and for some activists intensifies the mix of outrage, defiance, and desire for revenge and/or justice. As a result, many activists redoubled their commitment to public protest and others went underground into the violent revolutionary opposition.

On October 19, 1978, the name of AEU Secretary-General Oliverio Castañeda de León appeared on a widely circulated death list issued by a death squad. He still gave the lead speech at the next day's demonstration commemorating the October Revolution of 1944, concluding with these words: "They can kill our leaders, but as long as there is a people, there will be revolution." Castañeda was murdered after leaving the rally just

---

[18] IPV (Nov. 5, 1978, 293). More generally, see ASIES (1995, 3:560–565); and Levenson-Estrada (1994, 147–160).

one block from the National Palace by some fifteen men appearing in five cars, most likely military intelligence.[19] Six days later, some 40,000 people marched in mourning, protest, and outrage. Their numbers and statement could not protect Antonio Estuardo Ciani García, who had stepped forward into Castañeda's position. Ciania was detained on November 6, never to reemerge alive. The following year, AEU leader Julio César Cortez Mejía was to give the organization's speech at the 1979 October commemoration. Instead, he was disappeared earlier in the day by an armed group (probably police) from the San Carlos main campus itself.[20]

This continuing commitment by student activists to their causes in the face of increasing risk to their lives is poignant evidence that gradually escalating repression does not deter contentious activity once a protest cycle is underway. Instead, it creates intense new grievances, igniting a more radicalized and perhaps an even higher level of popular mobilization.

Testimony to the same commitment in the face of great risks is also provided by the Guatemalan labor movement. The data collected here show an average of about five labor leaders killed annually between 1973 and 1977, with the exception of eleven in 1976. Rather than deterring labor protest, its largest mobilizations were still ahead. The death toll then jumps: Fifteen leaders were killed in 1978 and fourteen in 1979. Despite even these deaths, the most sustained assertion by labor was still to come in early 1980.[21]

These trends can be seen more closely with Figures 9.2 and 9.3, which disaggregate the data down to the monthly level. As state killings fall, indeed largely disappear during the first nine months of 1978 (see Figure 9.2), contentious activities hold at a median of around five per month through the same period, but with two peaks at much higher levels – the election period early in the year and then in October. Following the October 1978 mobilization, repression escalates, averaging about twenty-five murders per month in the Central Area. Looking at just Figure 9.2 for just 1979, it could appear that repression had succeeded in deterring further protest. Indeed, recorded protest marches are becoming less frequent by this point; and

---

[19] CEH (1999, 6:119–126); *El Imparcial* (Oct. 21, 1978, 1).

[20] Kobrak (1999, 127).

[21] Political party activists were targeted as well by the violence. The two leading progressive politicians of the 1970s were both murdered in early 1979, Manuel Colom Argueta and Alberto Fuentes Mohr (CEH 1999, 6:133–144). Between 1978 and 1981, nineteen other leaders of Colom's party were killed, as were fifteen others from that of Fuentes Mohr (CEH 1999, 1:189).

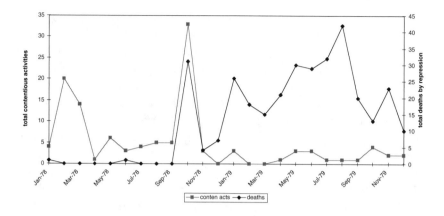

Source for deaths: Ball, Patrick. (1999). AAAS/CIIDH database of human rights violations in
Guatemala (ATV20.1). http://hrdata.aaas.org/ciidh/data.html (downloaded May 2000).

Figure 9.2 Guatemala: Nonviolent Contentious Political Activities and Deaths
by Repression in Central Area by Months, 1978–1979

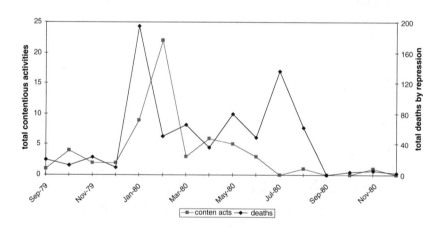

Source for deaths: Ball, Patrick. (1999). AAAS/CIIDH database of human rights violations in
Guatemala (ATV20.1). http://hrdata.aaas.org/ciidh/data.html (downloaded May 2000).

Figure 9.3 Guatemala: Nonviolent Contentious Political Activities and Deaths
by Repression in Central Area by Months, Sept. 1979–Dec. 1980

when they do occur, they do so with fewer participants (recall Figure 6.1). That challengers turned away from marches as a protest tactic is understandable since regime repression and intransigence increased apprehension about their safety and dubiousness about their efficacy.

Although contentious activities do drop during 1979, it was in fact a time of intense organizational effort. As a result, mass mobilization recovers, as Figure 9.3 demonstrates, climbing in January and especially February 1980 with the most important wave of strikes in the post-1954 period. Following short precursor strikes in the two previous months, on February 18, 1980 some seven hundred workers went on strike at the Tehuantepec sugar plantation in the department of Escuintla. Within two days, the strike spread to about sixty plantations across the south coast departments, with tens of thousands of peasants participating. On February 22, one to two thousand workers gathered to decide with their leaders from the Comité de Unidad Campesino (CUC) and the Comité Nacional de Unidad Sindical (CNUS) how to proceed, while the government bolstered its forces in the area following meetings with worried owners, both blaming the troubles on outside leftist agitators.[22]

Given the record of the military regime, the threat of a severe repressive response was omnipresent. Nonetheless, not only was contention widespread during the strike period, but demonstrators were aggressive in their actions. Three thousand peasants maintained barricades across critical highways on February 22, coming into conflict with police tossing tear gas. Rural workers then barricaded entrances at several sugar mills and occupied the Pantaleón mill – the largest in the country and long a site of labor-management conflicts. An occupation attempt at the Santa Ana mill was repulsed, but over one thousand workers remained at the mill's gates. The strike spread to fifteen cotton plantations, and a loaded cotton truck was stopped on the highway and incinerated. The same day – February 27 – two thousand peasants invaded eight fincas, destroying substantial amounts of property; the last sugar mills operating in the region were shut down by strikers; over four hundred workers at Industria Papelera Centroamericana, located adjacent to one of the plantations, joined the strike; and another three thousand marched in the funeral of a striker killed earlier by security guards in the occupation at Pantaleón. The next day, dozens more fincas were occupied, again with damages. Meanwhile, some industrial workers

[22] The sugar growers had long been considered among the hardest of the hard right among the country's elite; see, for example, Schirmer (1998, 208–209).

were also on strike, with one union briefly occupying its workplace before being forcefully evicted by police. Although the strike was settled on the cotton fincas on February 29, the next day CNUS threatened to broaden industrial strikes unless a successful resolution was brought to the remaining agricultural strikes.

The government intervened on March 2 – not militarily but with a minimum wage increase. It fell short of strikers' demands but was substantially above what many landowners wanted to pay – a minimum wage increase of 186 percent. The next day, leaders in the labor central CNUS met and decided to accept the offer and end the strike. Altogether, the strike lasted fifteen days. Sympathetic academic sources usually claim up to 80,000 participants although press reports at the time usually were closer to 50,000. Regardless of the number, this contentious campaign was historic in its scope and results.[23]

5. *As repression increases during a protest cycle in authoritarian regimes, the frequency of illegal and violent acts by challengers increases.*

It is characteristic of protest cycles that in their later stages challenger tactics become more assertive, with illegal and violent contentious activities becoming more frequent and a larger proportion of all activities.[24] The more repressive the response by the state, the more true this should be for challengers. Certainly, it was true for Guatemala during the years of this study. Figure 9.4 portrays trends by quarters across the 1973–1980 period for the urban Central Area.[25] There was very little recorded illegal contentious political activity prior to the escalation of the protest cycle and then not until its later stages, with quarter totals never going beyond five until late in the decade. This type of activity then explodes with the October 1978 mobilization and reaches its peak with the movement of the first quarter of 1980. The disparity between most of the period and these two quarters (and to a lesser extent the next highest quarters that hover between counts of four and six activities) is actually much greater because

---

[23] See Fernández (1988, 43); Levenson-Estrada (1994, 167); and daily coverage during this period in *El Imparcial* and IPSE (Trabajo: caneros), as well as CEH (1999, 6:319–324) for the tragic aftermath for Panteleón workers in the years following.

[24] della Porta 1995; Tarrow (1998, 147–157).

[25] Recall from Chapter 6 that burnings are largely of vehicles but also include some buildings. Street vandalism includes window breaking, rock throwing, barricades, and laying tacks across highways. Unlike in Chapter 6, occupations also are included in Figure 9.4 as an illegal activity. In the latter phase of the Guatemala cycle, they became an important tactic, and it is useful to have that portrayed.

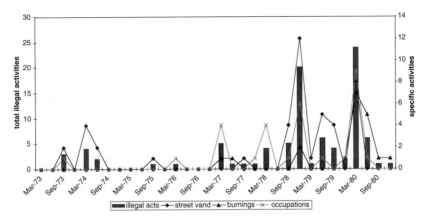

Figure 9.4 Guatemala: Illegal Contentious Political Activities in Urban Central Area by Quarter, 1973–1980

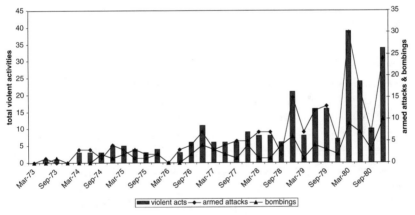

Figure 9.5 Guatemala: Violent Contentious Political Activities in Central Area, 1973–1980

it is impossible to count the number of actual occurrences during a mobilization peak.[26]

Violent activities escalate even more so during the last stages of a protest cycle. This is clearly shown by Figure 9.5, which is for the full Central Area (rural and urban). *Armed attacks* counts shootings at the person or

---

[26] As explained in Chapter 6, the convention followed in this study is to report the number of days for which any activity summarized under street vandalism or burnings occurred. For occupations, though, an attempt was made to record the actual number of occurrences, although again this undercounts what actually occurred during periods of peak activity.

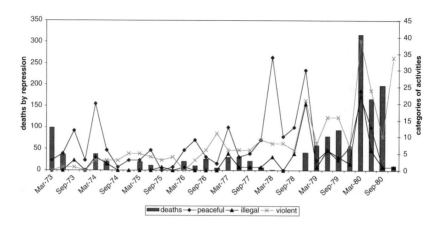

Source for deaths: Ball, Patrick. (1999). AAAS/CIIDH database of human rights violations in Guatemala (ATV20.1). http://hrdata.aaas.org/ciidh/data.html (downloaded May 2000).

Figure 9.6 Guatemala: All Categories of Contentious Political Activities and Deaths by Repression in Central Area by Quarter, 1973–1980

property (only a few here) of security forces, public officials, owners of large businesses and landholdings, and family members of leading figures in any of these categories.[27] *Bombings* is another variable like street vandalism where actual occurrences can be counted when there are few but not when "many" are reported. The trend for the overall measure of violent activities is a gradual increase from the beginning of the period until a sharp increase at the end of 1978 and then a much higher peak in early 1980 – with the same trend for armed attacks.

Figure 9.6 plots the three types of contentious political activities together, along with deaths from repression. Although the three – nonviolent, illegal, and violent political activities – generally show the same peaks, the shape of their overall curves are quite different. In particular, nonviolent activities reach their peak at an earlier stage in the contention cycle and the other two later. Earlier in the period, illegal activities always run below nonviolent activities; but from the beginning of 1979 on, they run closely together. In the final quarter of 1978, nonviolent activities are the most numerous, whereas in the mobilization of early 1980 they run behind the

---

[27] In many cases, attribution is unclear and some might have been nonpolitical in nature, although an effort was made to eliminate these. For example, armed attacks against police are included, but the shooting of a police officer when a robbery is interrupted is not.

other two categories while violent activities reach their highest peak at this point.

These patterns are to be expected from the literatures on both protest cycles and on Guatemala. One consequence of regime violence, especially when challengers are already mobilized, is that it provokes increased violence from challengers. Because repression reaches such incredible highs in some of the periods charted here, the visual impact of the lower scores of other periods might be minimized. For example, in Figure 9.6 it appears that there was very little regime killing in 1976, whereas in reality there were sixty-three deaths by repression in just that one year.

At the same time, it is important not to overlook another striking feature that emerges from Figure 9.6. Both illegal and violent activities reached their highest point for the entire period prior to early 1980, right at the end of the lowest period of repression in the Central Area during these years.[28] That is, with the October 1978 mobilization, all three forms of contentious activities jump, along with repression. Radicalization in challenger objectives and tactics at this point, then, cannot be fully explained as a response to repression. Repression during the late 1970s certainly radicalized many protesters. However, other challengers were already members of the revolutionary organizations and already undertaking illegal and violent activities. Yet they cannot be separated out from the data because who is responsible for armed attacks by challengers is often not indicated by sources. These data then can portray trends in the use of violence by challengers; but when violence increases, it cannot accurately distinguish whether that increase is an indication of radicalization of individuals or instead is a greater frequency of armed attacks by those who are already radicalized.

6. *Massive repression by authoritarian regimes, including the indiscriminate murder of protesters and nonprotesters alike, will normally end the protest cycle, reducing nonviolent contentious activities to a minimal level or even eliminating them altogether.*

As is clear from several of the prior figures, the February 1980 movement took place in the midst of the worst repression that the Central Area had experienced. The 246 deaths in January and February almost equalled the total for all of the prior year and surpassed the total in the Central Area for all of the four years before 1979 combined. In March and April of 1980, twenty-four people were killed just among the university community

---

[28] But do recall that the Panzós massacre occurred at the end of this period.

at San Carlos.[29] This huge escalation of state terrorism under Lucas García continued month after month, and protest collapsed. The last major nonviolent mass action in the Central Area occurred on May 1, 1980.[30] Some 5,000 brave souls marched that day, many with their faces covered. Radicalization was apparent – many called for an overthrow of the regime, to replace it with a democratic revolutionary government. Revolutionary propaganda was prevalent. Soon shots were fired at the marchers, who ran and dispersed. Thirty-two people disappeared that day, with twenty-eight of their tortured bodies recovered in the following days. The remaining leadership of the aboveground opposition was then decimated by two further violent actions. On June 21, twenty-seven labor leaders who gathered for an emergency meeting were seized; on August 24, seventeen more labor leaders disappeared from their "secret" meeting.[31] No one from the two groups was ever seen again. The database includes eighty-four labor leaders murdered and disappeared in 1980 (not counting the disappearances that occurred on May 1). At just the south coast sugar mills, some twenty-eight unionists were killed between the strike of early 1980 and 1983. In the face of this onslaught, in 1984 only 2 percent of the economically active population of Guatemala was organized in unions (CEH 1999 4:106–107).

Labor had been in the forefront of the mass movements of this period. Figure 9.7 portrays its contentious activities, along with the murder that was directed against its leadership. The data for demonstrations include those where press reports identify labor as key organizers – admittedly an inexact measure since it is often difficult to identify which group predominates in a demonstration. Occupations is a more accurate measure because most occupations in this database are clearly conducted by one group. The high point for labor demonstrations is the period from late 1977 through early 1980, with the peak in late 1978. In contrast, the peak for the more contentious tactic of occupations does not occur until early 1980. Almost all of the remaining occupations are clumped into two periods, early 1977 and late 1978. The decimation of labor's leadership is vividly captured here with the immense spike that occurs in the second quarter of 1980 following the broad mobilization of February.

The mass mobilization that began developing in Guatemala in the mid-1970s had become large enough and broad enough by June 1977 to be

[29] CEH (1999, 4:117).

[30] There was still another agricultural strike to come in September 1980, this time by coffee finca workers.

[31] CEH (1995, 1:191; 6:183–192).

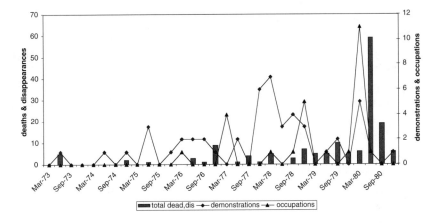

Source: Author's database.

Figure 9.7 Guatemala: Nonviolent Contentious Activities by Labor and Regime Violence against Labor in Central Area by Quarter, 1973–1980

classified as a protest cycle, one that continued with peaks and lulls through February 1980. As the movement became more successful in mobilizing large numbers of protesters and as it became more radical, the regime reacted with sufficient ferocity to bring this protest cycle to an end. Guatemala in 1980 provides clear evidence for the fact that massive repression does bring nonviolent protest to an end.[32] It would be some years before there would again be protest marches down the streets of Guatemala City. "The terror created a climate of generalized fear. Before the magnitude and cruel character of the violence, silence imposed itself as a new law of life" (CEH 1999, 3:35; see, more generally, pp. 14–37).

> 7. *Violent revolutionary organizations challenging authoritarian regimes experience rapid growth in both new participants and supporters during and immediately following the period when indiscriminate mass murder by the state kills the protest cycle.*

---

[32] This sequence appears similar to what Schock reports for Burma during the summer of 1988, when popular mobilization was facilitated by an apparent division within the regime and then "violent and often indiscriminate repression had the effect of mobilizing more people into the movement." However, after "the regime had reorganized and re-unified," sufficient repression was applied to successfully demobilize challengers (Schock 1998a, 368). Also see Deng 1997 on China in 1989.

The threat to the Guatemalan regime, however, was far from over. As revolutionary organizers hoped, increased repression radicalized increasing numbers of people, some of whom joined the guerrilla ranks. Others joined for nonideological reasons ranging from a desire for revenge to a hope to gain their safety.[33] Violent revolutionary organizations fighting authoritarian regimes normally experience rapid growth during and immediately following a period when indiscriminate repression ends a protest cycle. The more mobilized the population and the more indiscriminate the repression, the greater will be this effect. This study cannot provide direct evidence for this growth in the Guatemalan revolutionary ranks, but all accounts of Guatemala during this period are in agreement that this is exactly what did happen. And, the data collected do include two relevant indirect indicators of this growth: armed occupations of towns and fincas by guerrilla groups and their armed encounters resulting in deaths to state security personnel.

One of the first ways guerrilla organizations made their presence public was by occupying for an hour or so a town or a finca, gathering the local people together for a meeting to explain their objectives. If a town, this might include releasing prisoners and burning the jail; if a finca, it might include burning buildings and machinery. Sometimes, local police and finca administrators resisted and were shot. The records collected show the first such guerrilla occupation in 1976, another in 1977, two each in 1978 and 1979, and then six in just January 1980 alone, followed by six more in the next six months.

Armed confrontations are harder to tabulate. The records show many attacks on police and military personnel through the 1970s, but it is often unclear whether the assailants were guerrillas or nonpolitical. Counted here are only those attacks where it is reasonably clear that they were revolutionaries. There were four such attacks in 1977, eleven in 1978, twelve in 1979, and forty-one counted in 1980. In terms of total deaths, in 1977 five people were killed by guerrilla attacks on security officials. One of the 1978 attacks was in revenge for the massacre in Panzós – a military truck was bombed in Guatemala City with twenty killed. There were 14 other such deaths in 1978, 25 in 1979, and 102 counted in 1980.

---

[33] For differing interpretations, see Stoll 1993, 1999 and responses such as Rus 1999 and Streeter 2000.

8. *When authoritarian regimes have the capacity and propensity for massive repression in areas where violent revolutionary organizations operate, including the indiscriminate murder of noncombatants, the regime will normally defeat its revolutionary challenge.*

As the leftist challenge in Guatemala City dissipated and the rural guerrilla challenge grew through 1981, the regime further escalated its repression in the countryside, especially in the indigenous areas of the western highlands, where the guerrillas were most active. The violence expanded from the targeting of activists to including suspected supporters to finally indiscriminately attacking whole villages. A scorched-earth counterinsurgency campaign unfolded, with over six hundred massacres that destroyed over four hundred villages and in just 1982 left over eighteen thousand documented state murders (CEH 1999 3:256, 273; Schirmer 1998). This onslaught by the Guatemalan military – just like its counterinsurgency campaign in the east in the 1960s – is especially chilling evidence for the terrible truth that when authoritarian regimes have the capacity and propensity for massive repression in areas where armed revolutionary organizations operate, including the indiscriminate murder of thousands – even tens of thousands – of innocents, the regime will normally defeat its revolutionary challenge. Although the armed conflict continued until 1996, as a threat to the regime the guerrillas were isolated by the end of 1983. Many of the survivors of the counterinsurgency were angry at the guerrillas for abandoning them, leaving them defenseless in the face of the military's scorched-earth campaign (CEH 1999, 3:44).

9. *When repression lightens and other political opportunities open in authoritarian societies, popular movements will reemerge. The pace and intensity of movement emergence will be related to the prior level of contention achieved in the past, on the one hand, and the ferocity and length of the repression recently experienced, on the other.*

This is a restatement of the second proposition, now taking into account the impact of prior cycles of contention and repression on the reemergence of contentious political activities. It is extraordinary, given the level of state violence in Guatemala in the early 1980s, that when the configuration of political opportunities began to improve, civil society reemerged as quickly as it did. Death as the penalty for activism was not just a horrible memory but continued into the 1990s, as Figure 7.3 shows. Yet contentious popular movements did reappear.

Leading the way were a few activists. Some urban labor leaders, for example, were ready to resume organizing work whenever slight changes in political opportunities hinted encouragement. Their courage and dedication is notable given that these efforts continued in the face of continuing violence and that the overwhelming majority of their constituency had been demobilized by fear. Speaking of the Lucas period coming into 1982, labor leaders interviewed by a Guatemalan research team in the late 1980s indicated that up to 90 percent of the labor unions were fully inactive, with fear dominating the membership. Having lost their leaders, no one wanted to step forward to take their place (ASIES 1995, 4:3). Only three strikes occurred in Guatemala from 1981 to 1985 (Goldston 1989, 8).

When the regime of General Efraín Ríos Montt replaced Lucas with the coup of March 1982, some saw signs of hope and a few of the surviving leaders began meeting again. True, in its rhetoric the new government did make some encouraging statements, but this also was a government that banned all strikes and any demonstrations. Indeed, its eight-months-long state of siege was the first one since before 1945 to explicitly suspend all union activities. Nonetheless, after the coup some labor leaders returned from exile, soon beginning organizational efforts, albeit they were cautious and their efforts limited.

Not surprisingly, the most successful during this period were the most moderate. Critical for them were pressures applied by the U.S. labor movement, both through the international arms of the AFL-CIO and indirectly through its influence in Washington, D.C. Financial resources also were provided. This led to a new labor confederation formed on May 1, 1983, the Confederación de Unidad Sindical de Guatemala (CUSG), which would be the largest in Guatemala from this point on. Clearly, there was permission from the Ríos Montt government, and the new labor central had to struggle with charges that it was too close to the government. Equally clear, no labor organization could function during this time without accepting the narrow limits imposed by the military on its activities (ASIES 1995, 4:4–22; Goldston 1989, 21).

And the violence did continue, with the murders and disappearances of labor leaders and advisers reported throughout the Ríos Montt period continuing when he was replaced by General Oscar Mejía Víctores in August 1983. Still, the few remaining leaders from the more radical labor movement of the 1970s (FASGUA and CNT) began meeting by the end of 1983. An early effort at formally reconstituting the movement in early 1984 proved premature, in part as several of the leaders were murdered. But their work continued, leading to the formation of the Unión Sindical de Trabajadores de Guatemala (UNSITRAGUA) in February 1985 (ASIES 1995, 4:46–49, 326–327; Goldston 1989, 21).

Given the repression that brought the mobilization peak of October 1978 to an end and then the horrendous levels of violence directed at the popular sector in the years that followed, it is extraordinary that even before the long period of military rule ended in Guatemala those events were replicated in 1985. As in 1978, the burst of contentious activity in 1985 was provoked by an increase in the urban bus fare. Decreed in late August, the fare increase took place at the beginning of September. The reaction was at first cautious: Various groups issued their denunciations. Then on August 26, students at all levels initiated strikes at their centers of study. The next day, student groups halted their first buses, and on the night of August 28 the first bus was burned. The next morning, the first demonstration was held – in front of the National Palace with student protesters asking to speak to the military president. Later that day, vandalism spread throughout the streets and a number of buses were burned. Some 265 people were detained by the authorities (ASIES 1995, 4:88).

After a quiet weekend, the movement broadened on September 2. Spontaneous actions were taken throughout the metropolitan area by virtually all social groups. Explicit grievances broadened from the fare increase to larger economic difficulties and to the very nature of the government itself. There were more bus burnings and other forms of street vandalism. By the end of the day, 516 people were detained. Protests were even more intense the next day. Prominently, university students marched from San Carlos to the national palace, demanding the resignation of the military president (ASIES 1995, 4:88–89).

That night, the military responded promptly. About five hundred soldiers followed a tank onto the San Carlos campus, occupying it for four days. They looted and destroyed buildings, including the administration building, the Asociación de Estudiantes Universitarios's (AEU) headquarters, and the union offices of campus workers, as well as stealing irreplaceable human rights archives. Altogether, it was the gravest violation of university autonomy in Guatemala since 1944 (Kobrak 1999, 98). It also intensified the grievances of protesters and their contentious activities the next day. The government backed down. The fare increase was cancelled, with a government subsidy awarded to bus companies instead (ASIES 1995, 4:89).

In this changed and charged circumstance, public employees seized their opening. Public school teachers in the capital went on strike on September 1 and were soon followed by teachers throughout the country. Even as the bus fare protests ended, their demonstrations continued, growing larger well into the month. They were soon joined by others. Workers went on strike at a number of federal agencies, such as the Social Security Institute, National Bank, and Finance Ministry, as well as did municipal workers. The government response, though, was intransigence. Strikes ended in the third week of September as police evicted workers from their buildings and threatened military intervention of their agencies if they did not return to work. At the same time, some 2,000 police blockaded schools from their teachers, but their strike – unsuccessful in the end – continued well into October (ASIES 1995, 4:89–94).

Organized labor was back in Guatemala. It publicly rejoined the world observance of International Workers Day in 1986 as some 3,000 to 5,000 unionists and their supporters marched once again through the capital. Violence directed at its leadership continued – and continues (Goldston 1989, 53–71). Too many on the right and in the elite continued to agree with the words written by a leading newspaper columnist at the start of 1986, accusing the union movement of being an "arm of subversion and of international communism."[34] With the opening provided by the end of the military regime and the coming to office of an elected civilian in January 1986, organizing efforts redoubled. At the start of the administration of Vinicio Cerezo, there were 166 active unions in Guatemala. At the end of his term in 1990, another 220 unions were functioning (ASIES 1995, 4:320–321). At least formally, their efforts were now protected by the new constitution of 1986 recognizing the rights to organize and to strike by all workers, both public and private.

Conclusion

The Guatemalan truth commission estimates up to 200,000 deaths in thirty-six years of violent conflict in Guatemala, overwhelmingly at the hands of the state and its allied death squads. With repression at such a ferocious level, it would be understandable to assume that people would be deterred from any public protest activities, that the only avenue available to them would be covert revolutionary violence. But this was not the case. As much as by death, the history of contemporary Guatemala is marked by a courageous

---

[34] The columnist was Oscar Clemente Marroquín of *La Hora* (quoted in ASIES 1995, 4:118; translation by author).

insistence on the part of popular forces that they be allowed to assert their interests and their rights in public spaces. They have done so again and again, often in the face of extraordinary risks.

However, the level of popular contentious political activities certainly has been affected by the level of repression. The evidence provided in this study is that the curvilinear hypothesis for the relationship between repression and protest is accurate, at least for authoritarian societies that feature substantial variations in the level of repression across the years. Recent Guatemalan history shows that when repression lightens people organize and they protest. When sufficient political space allows the development of widespread, sustained mobilization to the level of what is termed a protest cycle, renewed repression does not automatically deter protest. Instead, repression is an additional grievance, one that is often powered by very strong emotions of anger on the one hand and solidarity on the other. The stronger the protest cycle, the more repression that is required to eliminate the challenge to the regime. Some regimes lack either the capacity or willingness to do so and fall before radicalized revolutionary forces. Other regimes, though, kill to the level required (and beyond) to end the challenge. But, of course, in doing so they have created new and powerful grievances.

The next chapter determines whether the propositions concerning the protest-repression relationship that were substantiated for the Guatemalan case apply as well to that of El Salvador. After that analysis, the explanation developed here for the relationship between protest and repression is pushed further. In particular, attention will be given to this relationship as it is experienced at the level of the individual.

10

Contention and Repression

EL SALVADOR

Few Latin American countries have witnessed a cycle of contention as lengthy and as intense as that of El Salvador in the late 1970s going into the early 1980s. Nor have many witnessed a sharper confrontation between a highly mobilized mass movement and a state willing to kill unarmed civilians as necessary in order to defeat its challengers. What is less well known is that within just a few years of the crushing of El Salvador's non-violent contentious movement, a new protest cycle developed again in the mid-1980s in the capital. And, of course, throughout the 1980s, a civil war raged that even after a decade of fighting found neither side able to defeat the other. This chapter will give close attention to the relationship between contention and repression in El Salvador, utilizing datasets for both sides of the relationship that, while not as complete as those used for Guatemala, are far better than those commonly utilized for such studies. The final section of this chapter then closes the study by analyzing the contention/repression relationship at the level of the individual.

Precursor Movements

This analysis of the relationship between cycles of contention and repression in El Salvador is organized by the same hypotheses utilized in the prior chapter on Guatemala. As with its larger neighbor, this analysis will show that there is a close fit between these hypotheses and the Salvadoran experience, as seen both with events data and with conventional accounts of the periods under examination.

> 1. *Repression by authoritarian regimes – along with other means of limiting access to the political system – normally keeps nonviolent protest at a minimal level.*

Seldom in its history did El Salvador have anything but repressive authoritarian regimes. There had been a political opening in the late 1920s/early 1930s, and predictably popular mobilization grew. But this challenge to the system from below led to a military takeover in late 1931 and then the massacre of January 1932 when thousands – or possibly even tens of thousands – of citizens were murdered. Except for the other crack in the system that occurred with the overthrow of dictator Maximiliano Hernández Martínez in 1944, repression kept nonviolent protest in El Salvador to a minimum.

>   2. *For social movements to emerge in authoritarian regimes, not only must other political opportunities open, but repression must be held at a sufficiently low level to provide potential protesters hope that they will not be immediately repressed.*

The next political opening in El Salvador did not occur until the 1960s, when urban popular forces were allowed into the electoral arena. Organizing along the center and left of the political spectrum picked up pace, especially at the national university and in factories. Although urban challengers faced harassment from police and occasional arrests, murder was not an instrument of state policy during this period. Given the success of the Partido Demócrata Cristiano (PDC) in winning the San Salvador mayor's office during the 1960s, the electoral process had gained credibility among challengers. Consequently, electoral politics was the focus of their activities; and as the February 1972 election approached, it was seen by many as a real opportunity to replace the military regime with a center-left civilian government.

>   3. *When authoritarian regimes increase repression against nonviolent activities that occur outside of a protest cycle, the lower the level of overall mobilization the more quickly and fully protest will be reduced (given similar levels of repressive capacity and propensity).*

The military regime responded to the electoral challenge of 1972 with fraud in the counting rooms and then repression on the streets. The regime was able to quiet oppositional activity quickly and with relative ease. There are few reports of political deaths in the month after the electoral fraud and prior to the March 25 uprising by a dissident group within the military. In smashing the revolt, an estimated one hundred were killed and an additional two dozen or more in the days that followed.[1] Putting the revolt from within

---

[1] NY Times (Mar. 27, 1972, 1); IDHUCA (1988, 23–24); Hernández (1973, 94, 139, 143); Webre (1979, 175).

the military aside, popular mobilization was repressed successfully in 1972 with little political violence, especially compared to the tragedy that would unfold later in the decade.

Two reasons stand out to explain this difference. First, in the years leading up to the 1972 election most challengers were active in institutionalized politics but were not engaged yet in other more contentious forms of political activity. The major exception was the teachers' union, the Asociación Nacional de Educadores Salvadoreños (ANDES), whose strike and related protest activities dominated the middle four months of 1971. Yet that campaign ended almost six months prior to the fraud. A primary lesson from the cases of El Salvador and Guatemala is that it is unlikely for a significant nonviolent contentious movement to emerge at the point when a committed regime applies repression as necessary to eliminate contention. There are situations when increasing repression does lead to greater contention, but this occurs when there is already a substantial contentious movement in existence.

Second, the campaign of the late 1960s/early 1970s was an urban affair. Life had been improving economically and politically for urban groups and certainly when compared to the still quiescent peasantry, as well as to what would be the situation for all of them later in the 1970s. Urban popular forces did have their grievances, but these lacked the intensity going into 1972 compared to what they would be after the fraud that was to come, and particularly the intensity that would develop later in the decade. Most importantly, at the time of the 1972 fraud and consequent repression, few activists had been affected directly by regime violence. Later in the decade, when their numbers were growing rapidly, the grief and rage that attended this grievance would motivate many to a heightened intensity in their challenge to the regime.

The fraud and repression of 1972 were crucial to the development of El Salvador's revolutionary movements, as explained in Chapter 3. But given the relationship between grievances, level of prior mobilization, and severely closing political opportunities, it did not result in further nonviolent contention at the time.

The Cycle of the Late 1970s/Early 1980s

Before long, though, a nonviolent popular movement began to reemerge by stops and starts. The beginning can be best traced to the activities in the region of Aguilares and Suchitoto north of the capital described in Chapter 5, including the birth in spring 1974 of the first of the mass organizations, the Frente de Acción Popular Unificada (FAPU). The next stage came with events in San Salvador and Santa Ana in July 1975 around the Miss Universe pageant and then the emergence that August of the Bloque Popular Revolucionario (BPR), the most important of the mass organizations. Contention continued to build, but it is difficult due to data limitations to estimate when a protest cycle could be said to have started. Accordingly, the focused examination of the relationship between repression and this all-important protest cycle begins in 1978, with the cycle already under way.

> *4. Once a protest cycle is underway in authoritarian regimes, gradually escalating repression will not deter contention. Instead, gradually escalating repression usually will ignite a more radicalized and perhaps an even higher level of contentious activities, often creating a crisis for the regime. The stronger the protest cycle is prior to the intensification of repression and the more gradual and inconsistent the escalation of repression, the greater the probability that repression will have this counterproductive impact.*

It was hard to develop a nonviolent contentious movement in El Salvador given the repressive military regime. For example, when some 1,000 protestors marched on May 1, 1977, they did so without the necessary authorization. Police confronted their defiance with violence: Estimates are of eight killed, sixteen wounded, and a hundred arrested.[2] Still, the mass organizations were persistent, and their activities mounted. Although their numbers were often small, a BPR-organized march on November 10, 1977 had up to 10,000 participants, according to supporters. This march accompanied a two-day occupation of the Labor Ministry in support of strikes at two textile factories, all occurring within the larger context of an ongoing campaign of farm takeovers by peasants. Two days later, a sixty-five-year-old industrialist was kidnapped by revolutionaries, yet another in what seemed to the right as a far too long line of terrorist actions.[3] Rightist pressures on the president mounted, and on November 24, 1977 General Carlos Romero promulgated his Law of Defense and Guarantee of Public Order. The intent, as he stated, was "to energetically repress violence and terrorism" (Morales and González 1988, 50).[4] Invariably described as draconian

---

[2] ECA (#342, 326–327); *El Imparcial* (May 3, 1977, 1); NY Times (May 3, 1977, 7).
[3] Harneker (1990a, 227; 1993, 141); Inforpress (Nov. 17, 1978, 6); NY Times (Nov. 13, 1977, 42); Véjar (1979, 516–517).
[4] Author's translation.

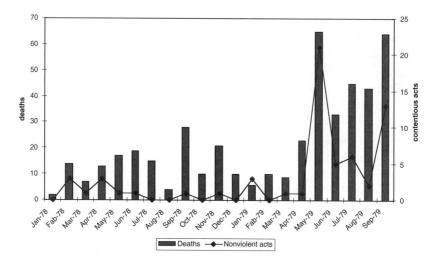

Source: Deaths: Socorro Jurídico as reported in Morales (1988, 189-201). "Identified urban civilians" is obtained by removing both unidentified victims and peasants.

Figure 10.1 El Salvador: Urban Civilian Deaths by Repression and Nonviolent Contentious Activities in San Salvador by Month, Jan. 1978–Sept. 1979

in scope and application, it did bring down contentious activities. But not as much as desired. Although less frequent and with smaller numbers, challengers pressed on, notably with a series of building occupations in late April 1978, with occupants held as hostages, and then a march on May 1, 1978 by "thousands" that proceeded without incident.[5] The relentless repression, though, took its toll, as indicated by Figure 10.1. There are few contentious activities recorded in the database after June 1978 until the Public Order Law was lifted at the end of February 1979 (see the Appendix to Chapter 8 for an explanation of the repression data).

Reviewing the rise of the contentious movement in El Salvador through the mid-1970s, it is apparent that it had little to do with expanding political opportunities at this stage. To the contrary, challengers faced growing repression and violence across this period, especially after Romero became president in July 1977. The emergence and persistence of this movement instead must be credited to the motivation, organizational competence, and strategic skill of challengers. The nonviolent contentious activities of this period were carried out by the mass organizations, notably the BPR and

[5] LPG (May 2, 1978, 2; May 8, 1978, 2; May 11, 1978, 2); Véjar (1979, 519).

FAPU. Behind them were the revolutionary organizations. Based on the limited knowledge that we have of the links between the two types of challenger organizations during this period, it appears to me that it was the organizational and strategic abilities of the revolutionary leadership that were most responsible for the emergence of this contentious movement – along with the dedication and courage of the thousands of activists who put themselves at serious risk to carry out their challenge to the military regime.

Despite the commitment and courage of challengers, this protest cycle undoubtedly would have ended in this early phase had the Romero repression continued in a consistent fashion or especially had it consistently intensified. Instead, Romero reversed course several times, beginning at the end of February 1979 when he revoked the Public Order Law under pressure from the Carter administration in the United States and moderate forces within El Salvador. It is at this point and for the rest of the year that expanding political opportunities were crucial to the full development of this protest cycle, as it soon took off, reaching a historic peak of contention.

It took the movement a little while to reemerge from the draconian period, but reemerge it soon did. Mass contention – and state violence – dominated May 1979, as well captured by Figure 10.1, making it the bloodiest month the country had suffered in decades. A number of BPR leaders had been arrested in late April, and their release was the major BPR demand in that year's May First parade, one notable for the level of disorganization between participating organizations. On May 4, the BPR seized the embassies of Costa Rica and France, as well as the National Cathedral. Three police were killed in the actions, and in the beginning some seventy hostages were taken. The same day, guerrillas attacked rural security and paramilitary forces, leaving an unknown number of casualties and suffering at least a dozen deaths among their own.[6]

Four days later, greater tragedy followed. The police opened fire on a BPR rally at the Cathedral on May 8, leaving an estimated twenty-three dead and another seventy wounded.[7] In response, over the next several days some 20,000 marched in protest, the BPR seized the Venezuelan embassy and then churches in at least five different towns, and the electrical union

---

[6] ECA (#368, 450; #403, 343); NY Times (May 5, 1979, 5); Véjar (1979, 521).
[7] ECA (#368, 451); IDHUCA (1988, 46); NY Times (May 9, 1979, 7; May 11, 1979, 2; May 14, 1979, 8).

turned the country's power off for twenty-three hours.[8] Guerrillas also were active during the same period, with the FPL killing three police in an attack on the South African embassy and two other, unidentified groups killing five police and sailors.[9]

These actions were followed once again by massacre. On May 22, activists tried to bring supplies to the group occupying the Venezuelan Embassy. Police fired into the crowd of protesters outside the embassy, killing at least fourteen. The next day, the FPL murdered the Minister of Education and his chauffeur in revenge. The government slapped down a state of siege for the next two months. Incredibly, after two massacres of nonviolent protesters in just two weeks, on May 25 some 10,000 brave souls defied the state of siege and walked in the funeral procession of those slain at the embassy. The embassy occupations continued, but the same day those at the Cathedral and other churches were brought to an end. On June 1, the embassy occupations ended, with the twenty-five participants given safe passage to Cuba.[10]

However, the first day of June also saw the FPL slay the mayor of Santa Tecla, which lies just west of the capital, and a soldier. The following day, a priest was killed in retaliation. During the month of June, as many as 123 people were killed throughout the country (recall that Figure 10.1 covers just the central urban area), including over thirty teachers, thought by many to be retaliation for the murder of the education minister.[11] With the state of siege and escalating repression, mass protest slackened again. And again, the brutal crackdown might have broken the nonviolent movement had it intensified as needed. But the Nicaraguan Revolution triumphed in mid-July in the face of tremendous regime violence, giving encouragement to Salvadoran challengers and increasing U.S. concerns that Romero was creating conditions for the same outcome in El Salvador. By September, with the state of siege ended, challengers initiated another round of marches, strikes, occupations of churches, factories and farms, and burnings of urban buses and hacienda offices. Once again, their contention continued in the face of certain repression, which as Figure 10.1 indicates, remained at high levels from May on. Marchers were attacked repeatedly by the authorities, leaving four dead and thirty wounded after a BPR march on

---

[8] ECA (#403, 343); IDHUCA (1988, 47); NY Times (May 11, 1979, 2; May 12, 1979, 3).

[9] ECA (#368, 451); NY Times (May 16, 1979, 5; May 19, 1979, 2).

[10] ECA (#368, 452); NY Times (May 23, 1979, 3; May 24, 1979, 8; May 26, 1979, 3; May 27, 1979, iv:3; June 2, 1979, 2).

[11] ECA (#369, 623); NY Times (June 20, 1979, 11).

September 14, two dead and twenty-one wounded a week later, and then four more killed at a march a week after that.[12]

Too repressive for many Salvadorans and for the Carter administration, yet unable to contain either the mass movements or the guerrillas and with revolution now successful in Nicaragua, Romero's government was finished. On October 15, progressive junior military officers installed a new government in collaboration with moderate civilians. Despite their hopes to bring civil peace, the new government was hit from both sides. On the left, the day after the coup, the ERP called for a national insurrection. Both it and the FPL attacked security forces in several locations with casualties on both sides. Three days after the coup, the three leading mass organizations denounced the new government.[13] Meanwhile, the hard right in and outside the military remained intransigent and continued to kill.

State killing of activists climbed from August into September and then tripled in October, as shown by Figure 10.2 (notice the change in values on the left axis), and remained high through the end of the year. Nonetheless, this was a period of intense nonviolent contention in the central area, and killings might have continued to climb further except for a truce arranged in November by Archbishop Oscar Romero between the mass organizations and the government. Under the continuing state violence, though, the truce broke down and contention began building again in December, especially in the countryside. At year's end, the U.S. embassy portrayed "radical groups" (especially the BPR affiliate FECCAS-UTC) "occupying or otherwise harassing agricultural operations" in the past few weeks on an "unprecedented scale." Although exact information was not available, the embassy cited one agricultural group's claim that "fifty coffee plantations, twenty-five cotton farms, and fifteen cattle ranches had been 'attacked' by 'mobs of extremist fanatics'" (USDS/NSA1 1979c). Similarly, guerrilla groups were described as "operating almost at will in [the] countryside of El Salvador," although not yet willing to engage the military in direct combat (USDS/NSA1 1979d).

---

[12] ECA (#372, 1001); NY Times (Sept. 11, 1979, 1; Sept. 15, 1979, 3; Sept. 22, 1979, 4; Oct. 5, 1979, 4).

[13] ECA (#372, 1001–1008; #403, 343); NY Times (Oct. 18, 1979, 3). Captured former FMLN leader Napoleón Romero García claimed that the mission of the BPR after the October coup through the next year was "to unmask the new Revolutionary Military Junta, to show the people that the Junta was not responding to popular demands, but that the Junta was just a strategy to readapt imperialism" (quoted in Prisk 1991, 22).

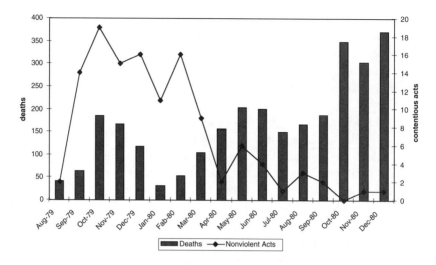

Source: Deaths: Socorro Jurídico as reported in Morales (1988, 189-201). "Identified urban civilians" is obtained by removing both unidentified victims and peasants.

Figure 10.2   El Salvador: Urban Civilian Deaths by Repression and Nonviolent Contentious Activities in San Salvador by Month, Aug. 1979–Dec. 1980

The nonviolent movement's emotional peak came on January 22, 1980, when the biggest demonstration in the country's history occupied the streets of the capital. Somewhere between 100,000 and 200,000 people marched – peasants, professionals, labor, students – many shouting their belief that victory was imminent. To increase its effectiveness, the sprawling movement began to unify, overcoming long-standing differences. The mass organizations drew themselves together in January 1980 with a coordinating directorate and then three months later joined with just about every organization left of center to form the Frente Democrático Revolucionario (FDR).[14]

5. *As repression increases during a protest cycle in authoritarian regimes, the frequency of illegal and violent acts by challengers increases.*

Illegal contentious acts were virtually eliminated during the Law of Public Order period, as shown in Figure 10.3, which portrays both illegal

---

[14] Not included in the FDR were the armed revolutionary movements, which were involved in their own process of unification. They formed the Frente Farabundo Martí de Liberación Nacional (FMLN) in October 1980, but, as discussed in Chapter 3, effective coordination was a longer process. The FDR and FMLN announced their formal alliance in January 1981, on the eve of the guerrillas' major offensive.

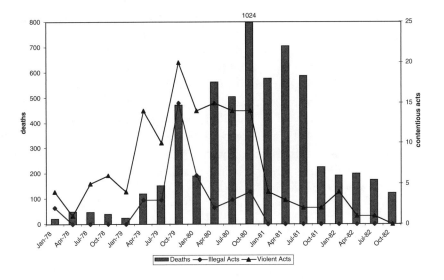

Source: Deaths: Socorro Jurídico as reported in Morales (1988, 189-201). "Identified urban
civilians" is obtained by removing both unidentified victims and peasants. Data for the last
quarter of 1982 is missing for urban civilians. A score for these months was created by using an
average of three months of actual scores (i.e., October is average of the prior three months;
December the average of September along with January and February).

Figure 10.3 El Salvador: Urban Civilian Deaths by Repression and Illegal and
Violent Contentious Activities in San Salvador by Quarter, 1978–1982

and violent acts for the 1978–1982 period, but only within the central area
of San Salvador City and Department. With the removal of the Law of
Public Order and yet a four-fold increase in state violence against identified urban civilians, illegal acts such as street barricades and burning buses
appear during the two middle quarters of 1979 and then quintuple to reach
their peak in the last quarter of 1979. This occurs as repression triples and
the protest cycle hits its peak. As the protest cycle is smashed in 1980, illegal
acts disappear with the end of the year.

Violent acts are represented in Figure 10.3 by a number of assassinations,
kidnappings, and bombings throughout 1978 and into 1979. As with illegal
acts, their number jumps substantially in the second quarter of 1979, peaks
at the end of the year, and maintains a higher than "normal" plateau for seven
quarters altogether before falling sharply in early 1981. The jump in violent
acts earlier in the protest cycle and its long plateau go against the hypothesis
for increasing challenger violence as an expression of radicalization and
frustration as a protest cycle nears its end.

301

The explanation here is apparent. El Salvador had a set of well-organized and active armed revolutionary organizations prior to the take-off of the protest cycle. When political opportunities opened for nonviolent and illegal contention in the central area, they also facilitated revolutionary violence. For example, the day after the October 1979 coup the FPL killed six National Guard in an attack near Zacatecoluca. The next day, the ERP and LP-28 issued their call for a national insurrection, reportedly passing out weapons at the national university in San Salvador. Before the month was over, top officials in both the military and national guard had been assassinated. In the following months, soldiers, guardsmen, and police were killed in attacks, as were local officials, members of ORDEN, and bodyguards to the elite. Bombings were frequent, and a noted member of the economic elite was kidnapped, as was the South African ambassador.[15] However, as state terrorism intensified in San Salvador during 1980 and remained at extraordinary levels through 1981, safe havens disappeared. Revolutionaries fled the city. The revolutionary movement in El Salvador had now become a rural insurgency.

> 6. *Massive repression by authoritarian regimes, including the indiscriminate murder of protesters and nonprotesters alike, will normally end the protest cycle, reducing nonviolent contentious activities to a minimal level or even eliminating them altogether.*

The Salvadoran military might have been more divided in 1979–1980 than its counterpart in Guatemala, but those in control in El Salvador still were able to escalate their violence in urban areas to whatever levels it might take to eliminate the challenge that they faced from popular forces. For three of the four quarters beginning at the end of 1979, around five hundred identified urban civilians were killed each quarter, as shown by Figure 10.3. At the end of 1980, the number killed doubled to over 1,000 for just that quarter. Among the dead were six key leaders of the recently formed FDR, who were kidnapped in November from a meeting, tortured, and murdered. The next month, it was four U.S. churchwomen who met the same horrible fate (Betancur et al. 1993, 55–65).

The peak of the protest cycle was the last quarter of 1979, as Figure 10.4 shows for total nonviolent contentious acts (and also true for each form of

---

[15] ECA (#372; #374; #403, 343), NY Times (Oct. 18, 1979, 3; Oct. 20, 1979, 3; Mar. 1, 1979, 3).

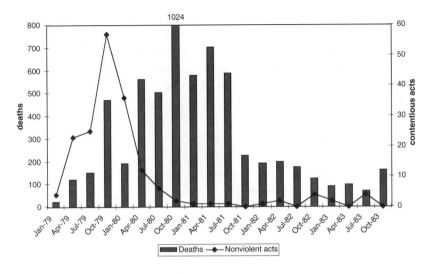

Source: Deaths: Socorro Jurídico as reported in Morales (1988, 189-201). "Identified urban civilians" is obtained by removing both unidentified victims and peasants. Data for the last quarter of 1982 are missing for urban civilians. A score for these months was created by using an average of three months of actual scores (i.e., October is the average of the prior three months; December is the average of September along with January and February).

Figure 10.4 El Salvador: Urban Civilian Deaths by Repression and Nonviolent Contentious Activities in San Salvador by Quarter, 1979–1983

nonviolent contention). The mass movement was able to withstand the high level of state violence in the final quarter of 1979 and continue with a high level of protest in the following quarter; but as the violence relentlessly continued, the movement was broken, as also portrayed by Figure 10.4, which presents the quarterly trend for murders of identified urban civilians as well. Nonviolent contention declines precipitously going into the second quarter of 1980. Any form of nonviolent contentious activity largely disappears through 1981, remaining only very occasional through 1983. As the U.S. embassy explained in September 1980, "It has become evident that the [urban] masses are no longer willing to support the . . . [leftist] organizations because they are exhausted by the extended violence and frightened of getting caught between the terrorists and the security forces" (USDS/NSA2 1980c).

Despite the elimination of the nonviolent movement in 1980, the ferocious urban state violence continued at the same levels through 1981. Finally, it was cut back by half in the last quarter of 1981, but state urban killing remained at levels higher than they had been back during the middle quarters of 1979 until the very last quarter of 1982. State murder continued to fall during 1983 but jumped back up again during the last quarter of 1983. It was at this point that the Reagan administration finally acted. Three and a half years after the nonviolent movement had been broken, U.S. President Reagan finally had Vice President George Bush and U.S. Ambassador Thomas Pickering state clearly and firmly to Salvadoran leaders that the killing of civilians must stop.

> 7. *Violent revolutionary organizations challenging authoritarian regimes experience rapid growth in both new participants and supporters during and immediately following the period when indiscriminate mass murder by the state kills the protest cycle.*

As clandestine organizations, the revolutionary groups could continue their violent acts in the San Salvador central area beyond the point where the collapse of open political space eliminated nonviolent and illegal forms of contention (compare Figure 10.3 to Figure 10.2). Violent acts continued into the first quarter of 1982 before largely disappearing until 1984 as the site of confrontation between the government and guerrillas changed from the larger San Salvador area to the countryside. Indeed, once urban repression dropped after 1983, life in San Salvador returned to a degree of normalcy for most inhabitants.[16] Although the civil war continued through 1991, it was largely absent in the capital until the guerrilla offensive of November 1989.

As revolutionaries left the capital in 1980 under the terrible repression to regroup with their comrades who had been organizing in rural areas, they took with them large numbers of recruits. Although it cannot be documented from the data collected for this study, by all reports the guerrilla organizations grew in size only slowly through the 1970s until the rapid escalation of repression in late 1979 and especially in 1980 led to an explosion in its recruiting. The revolutionary forces grew so rapidly that at least some of their leaders and foreign supporters believed that their "final offensive" of 1981 could succeed in bringing them to power (Prisk 1991).

---

[16] As one observer explained, "Life in San Salvador, the capital, is 'tranquilo' and becoming more so every day, aside from routine power and telephone blackouts caused partly by guerrilla sabotage and partly by faulty equipment.... Even political assassinations and kidnappings within the city have been limited" (Americas Watch 1986, 131).

8. *When authoritarian regimes have the capacity and propensity for massive repression in areas where violent revolutionary organizations operate, including the indiscriminate murder of noncombatants, the regime will normally defeat its revolutionary challenge.*

Rural people by the thousands were indiscriminately killed by El Salvador's military each year from 1980 through 1985. This brutality had its intended effect on most, terrorizing them into passivity or leaving their homes and even the country. As in Guatemala, there was a series of massacres, notably the more than five hundred civilians "deliberately and systematically" executed, including many children, in the El Mozote area of Morazán in December 1981 (Betancur 1993, 118–125; Binford 1996).[17] But as horrible as the indiscriminate rural violence was in El Salvador, it did not reach the levels of the scorched-earth campaign in Guatemala. This undoubtedly was due less to internal constraints on what the military would consider doing and more on external constraints from the United States and the guerrillas themselves.

The government and military of El Salvador needed the United States in order to fight the civil war, and they received extraordinary levels of support, as indicated in Chapter 8. But this support came with constraints. The U.S. Congress was reluctant through 1984 in its financing of the war, especially in the face of the rampant human rights abuses. Responsibility for the slaying of urban civilians could be passed off for some as the work of "unknown" death squads, but responsibility for massacres of large numbers of unarmed villagers during military offensives could not be so easily sidestepped. The violence against the rural population was horrible, but the military was limited in how far it could take its counterinsurgency strategy. The military's violence was able to deter even more peasants from joining or supporting the revolutionaries but insufficient to prevent many others from still doing so, especially in those areas that came under the control of the guerrillas.

[17] The El Mozote massacre was notable not only because of the number of victims involved but also because of the strong denials by both the Salvadoran and U.S. governments that a massacre had occurred and their consequent efforts to undermine the credibility of the journalists who had first reported the massacre. Crucial to the conclusions of the truth commission was an exhumation by an international team of experts of the human remains in a building next to the El Mozote church. There they identified the skeletal remains of 131 children, with their average age about six years (p. 116). The reports of the forensic investigation, as well as a photographic report, are available in Volume I of the Annexes to the commission's report (Betancur, Planchart, and Buergenthal, 1993).

The revolutionary opposition also proved to be a more tenacious foe in El Salvador than in Guatemala. Why this was so is beyond the scope of this inquiry. What is relevant is that the guerrillas were better able to protect the peasantry in their core areas than were their counterparts in Guatemala. Once the Guatemalan military was able to get its counterinsurgency act together in 1982, it soon had the guerrillas on the run and largely eliminated as a meaningful threat by the end of 1983. It took the Salvadoran military longer to develop an effective approach, but even then the best it could do was reach a draw with the guerrillas, with the revolutionary opposition in effective control of a significant portion of the countryside.

The Cycle of the Mid to Late 1980s

Consequently, a real civil war continued on in El Salvador through the entire decade of the 1980s and the first year of the next. In November 1989, the guerrillas were even able to bring the war into the capital, including to some of its exclusive residential neighborhoods and luxury hotels. Yet even with this civil war continuing and with the memory of the horrendous violence of the early 1980s still fresh, nonviolent contention returned to the capital.

> 9. *When repression lightens and other political opportunities open in authoritarian societies, popular movements will reemerge. The pace and intensity of movement emergence will be related to the prior level of contention achieved in the past, on the one hand, and the ferocity and length of the repression recently experienced, on the other.*

During the peak of the mass mobilization of the late 1970s and into 1980, the most important source of activists was the radicalized peasants of the Federación Cristiana de Campesinos Salvadoreños (FECCAS) and the Unión de Trabajadores del Campo (UTC). As the repression escalated, they also were the most frequent victims of the violence, with the survivors a leading source of new recruits into the guerrilla armies. When nonviolent mass mobilization resumed, peasants were in the forefront again, but this time led by the centrist Unión Comunal Salvadoreña (UCS). The largest peasant organization all along, its members were the primary beneficiaries of an agrarian reform instituted by the U.S.-brokered provisional government that came to power in March 1980. At the same time that one arm of the state unleashed massive violence against the peasantry, another arm implemented one of Latin America's most far-reaching agrarian reforms by a nonrevolutionary government.[18] When control of the government was taken by the right through the elections of March 1982, the reform was jeopardized. Despite the considerable risks to their lives, reform beneficiaries through the UCS and other new organizations, such as the more leftist Confederación de Asociaciones Cooperativas (COACES), acted to protect their gains.

The major vehicle for this renewed peasant contentious activity was the Unidad Popular Democrática (UPD), which united the UCS with fifteen civic and labor organizations, including some of the most important from the industrial sector. On April 29, 1982, the UPD mounted a demonstration in the capital in support of the agrarian reform. The following year in March, thousands of UCS/UPD peasants gathered around the assembly building, successfully putting pressure on the legislature's consideration of a renewal of one segment of the reform. In September 1983, the first significant opposition march since the worst days of the violence was held, with about 11,000 UPD demonstrators and another 4,000 from the PDC in support of agrarian reform. Although there was much apprehension among participants, few uniformed security forces were present and no incidents occurred. Some observers saw the strong connections of the UCS to the PDC and (indirectly the United States) as providing it with a cloak of protection at this point, one not available to protesters further to the left.[19]

In February 1984, the UPD formalized its alliance with the PDC, signing a Social Pact that pledged UPD support for Duarte's presidential campaign and both sides to their mutual reform objectives.[20] Once the victorious

---

[18] For an assessment of the Salvadoran agrarian reform, including comparison to other Central American reforms, see Brockett (1998, 141–146, 219–223). Also see the debate among Diskin 1996; Paige 1996; and Seligson 1995, 1996; as well as Thiesenhusen 1995.

[19] This is the explanation of ECA (1984, 153). Predating the agrarian reform, UCS-PDC ties were further strengthened by the reform, as were ties to the American Institute for Free Labor Development (AIFLD) of the AFL-CIO. Agrarian reform was central to the objectives of the United States in El Salvador, and much U.S. financial assistance was given to it, to the UCS, and to the UPD (Casper 1986); also see ECA (#413, 557; #420, 887; #403, 343); NY Times (Sept. 28, 1983, 6); and Garcia 1983.

[20] U.S. financial support for Duarte's campaign was largely funneled through the UPD's constituent organizations, which allowed the Reagan administration to disingenuously deny having taken sides in the election but rather having provided "assistance to democratic institutions" (NY Times May 11, 1984, 8).

Duarte took office on June 1, though, tensions within the alliance began to develop, and by September the UPD was publicly denouncing the PDC administration's failure to follow through on the reform agenda. By the end of November, it was threatening to break the alliance altogether. In office Duarte's reform and peace objectives were constrained both by an economic crisis that plagued his tenure to its very end and by pressures from those to his right within both the Salvadoran military and the Reagan administration. Consequently, Duarte continued the war and moved to the right on socioeconomic policy.[21] Given these policy failures from a government now of the center right rather than the far right, the locus of mass contentious activity shifted further to the left.

The traditional labor federations of the left, the Federación Nacional Sindical de Trabajadores Salvadoreños (FENASTRAS) and the Federación Unitaria Sindical de El Salvador (FUSS), pulled together in late 1982 along with several other labor organizations into the Movimiento Unitario Sindical y Gremial de El Salvador (MUSYGES). In part, they were motivated by the heightened economic grievances the continuing civil war brought their memberships and larger constituencies. At the same time, many of these groups had been constituent members of the Frente Democrático Revolucionario (FDR), which had been the unified voice of the nonviolent left in 1980. Soon after the FDR's leadership was tortured and murdered by security forces in November 1980, the FDR went into exile, allied publicly with the Frente Farabundo Martí de Liberación Nacional (FMLN), and served throughout the 1980s as the FMLN's international voice. From the beginning, consequently, MUSYGES was suspected of maintaining covert ties with the FMLN; indeed, from the beginning even sympathetic observers noted close similarities in their positions.[22] With

---

[21] See Casper 1986 and ECA (#434, 924–927). AIFLD unsuccessfully utilized its considerable financial leverage to try to keep UPD leaders from going public with their discontent but primarily succeeded in aggravating the severe factionalization in the UPD and in each of its constituent groups (Casper 1986, 212–220). On the other side, FMLN defector Romero García claims that the revolutionaries did what they could to break the UPD away from the Duarte coalition (Prisk 1991, 78).

[22] As an example, see ECA (#425, 154). Romero García claims that indeed they were connected and that the short life of MUSYGES was due to an FMLN decision to create other vehicles for its influence, such as the Comité Primero de Mayo (Prisk 1991, 77). Having worked as a covert revolutionary organizing popular groups in the 1970s, Romero was once again working in this area when he was arrested in 1985. General confirmation is provided by Marta Harneker's (1990b) interview in 1989 with Facundo Guardado. A top FPL leader, Guardado was the head of the BPR in the 1970s and closely involved with the resurrection of the mass movement in the 1980s.

such suspicions especially prevalent among the security apparatus, the left of the labor movement could return to contentious activities only slowly.

Their way was opened, as it so often has been in Central America, by protesting public employees. Due to the repression, labor conflict had virtually disappeared in the country. There were only four strikes in all of 1982, carried out by a total of only 373 participants (Béjar 1990, 876). In April of that year, both public works employees and public school teachers had talked of strikes over failures to receive their salaries on time. In November, the Asociación Nacional de Acueductos y Alcantarillado (ANDA) actually planned a strike, but it was preempted by the militarization of its workplace. The first important labor action came a few days later, in November 1982, when all of the Agriculture Ministry employees walked out with PDC support, demanding higher wages. A new phase of labor activity began later in 1983 as the configuration of political opportunities improved while the economic situation deteriorated further. For example, in the second half of 1983 workers at the urban housing institute went on strike for about two and half months. Contentious activities by public employees then took off with the Duarte presidency.[23]

Postal employees struck three days before Duarte's inauguration, and it took close to two months of intense negotiations to reach an agreement. While UPD took no position on the strike, MUSYGES gave it all of the support that it could. Encouraged by the postal strike, numerous other strikes and work stoppages followed, both in solidarity with postal workers and over salary issues specific to each group. And the strikes continued, such as at public works in October 1984; the Coffee Institute in November; the telephone company in December; by public school teachers in March 1985 for one day, three days in June, and again in October; and a particularly contentious strike at public hospitals in June. Strikes were to average fifty-nine a year between 1984–1986, with twice as many occurring in the public sector in the first two years as in the private sector.[24]

Increasing activism also was registered on other fronts, such as the annual May First commemoration. Overt protests were deemed too risky in 1983; instead, labor declared it a "national day of mourning." The following year, MUSYGES bravely mounted a demonstration with about 2,500 participants. In contrast, May First of 1985 featured the largest labor showing

[23] ECA (#405, 708; #410, 1145; #420, 887, 898), NY Times (Nov. 20, 1982, 5).
[24] Béjar (1990, 883); ECA (#428, 428; #429, 581; #434, 930, 933; #435, 95; #439, 418; #441, 546; #445, 853); NY Times (June 3, 1985, 3).

in recent years with some 10,000 to 15,000 demonstrators under combined sponsorship. Several demonstrations followed the next month in support of the public hospital strike and in protest of the government's eviction of strikers, the largest reaching perhaps 5,000 protesters. Demonstrations grew much bigger in 1986, with the largest march since 1980 taking place in February as somewhere between 20,000 and 60,000 participants challenged Duarte's economic program of austerity. Similar demonstrations followed on May First (25,000 to 50,000) and in October (up to 40,000).[25] This was true on the other side as well, as some 20,000 to 40,000 marched in support of Duarte in March 1986.[26]

The development of this new cycle of contention is vividly portrayed by Figure 10.5. After having disappeared for the first third of the decade, nonviolent contentious activities increase fairly steadily across the middle of the decade, with two prominent peaks: the third quarters of 1986 and especially 1987. By just about any standard, deaths by repression remain high; but in comparison to the immediately preceding years in El Salvador itself, they drop significantly and continue to do so as nonviolent protest activities surge.

The contentious activities of 1986 and the years that followed were led by a new umbrella organization that united many traditional allies of Duarte with his traditional opponents on the labor left. In helping to create the Unidad Nacional de los Trabajadores Salvadoreños (UNTS) in early February 1986, the UPD formally broke its ties with the PDC and its president. Other members were the confederation of cooperative members (COACES), the union representing the Treasury Ministry, and a coalition of leftist organizations.[27] The proximate cause bringing them together was Duarte's new economic program, which he announced on January 21, 1986 as "a new socioeconomic model that has the objective

---

[25] See Casper 1986; ECA (#428, 446; #429, 583; #441, 546; 552; #447, 94, 112; #450, 342; #451, 457, 472; #457, 1037); NY Times (May 2, 1983, 3; June 5, 1985, 5; Feb. 22, 1986, 5; Mar. 16, 1986, 4; May 2, 1986, 3); Garcia (1983, 504).

[26] Opponents claimed that many of the pro-Duarte marchers were shipped in from the countryside by the government. This demonstration was the first appearance of the Unidad Nacional Obrero Campesina (UNOC), an AIFLD/PDC creation intended to rival the mass organization forming to its left, UNTS (as discussed below). See Casper (1996, 222–226); ECA (# 450, 342); NY Times (Mar. 16, 1986, 4).

[27] In addition to the UPD, these were the Confederación de Asociaciones Cooperativas de El Salvador (COACES), Asociación General de Empleados del Ministerio de Hacienda (AGEMHA), and the seventy-five leftist groups of the Comité Primero de Mayo. Casper 1986; See ECA (#447, 93, 111; #457, 1023–1026).

310

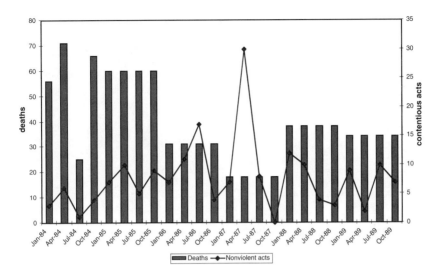

Source: 1984 Deaths: Socorro Jurídico as reported in Morales (1988, 189-201). "Identified urban civilians"
is obtained by removing both unidentified victims and peasants.
　　1985-1989: Tutela Legal as reported by Americas Watch (1987, 7-8 for 1985 and 1986; 1990, 199-200,
for 1988 and 1989) and McClintock (1998, 117) for 1987. Urban victims are Tutela Legal's category
"targeted killings by the military and death squads." Because the categories used
by Americas Watch and McClintock differ, the average ratio between their data for 1986
and 1988 was used to calculate a comparable 1987 score from McClintock's score
for assassinations for that year.

Figure 10.5　El Salvador: Urban Civilian Deaths by Repression and Nonviolent
Contentious Activities in San Salvador by Quarter, 1984–1989

of the well-being of all Salvadorans" (ECA #447, 105). Following negotiations with the International Monetary Fund (IMF), this model actually
was a stabilization program seen as necessary to hold the war economy
together: some small salary increases but also reductions in public spend-
ing (with staff reductions), along with tax increases. The UNTS demonstrations of 1986 denounced the austerity package for its impact on the
impoverished majority. The mass movement also played the war-economy
connection but in the opposite direction: If it was the war that mandated
the economic assault on the people, then this was another reason to halt the
war.

　　Certainly, these themes resonated with popular concerns. Real wages fell
considerably across the 1980s for both rural and urban workers, as shown
by Table 10.1. At the same time, unemployment soared, from 16.1 percent
in 1980 to 30 percent in 1984 and 33.7 percent in 1985 (IDH 1988, 193).
A national survey in the third trimester of 1986 of urban adults found that

Table 10.1 *El Salvador: Change in Real Minimum Wage,*
1980–1987*

	1980	1982	1983	1984	1987	Change
Agriculture						
general**	2.82	2.20	1.94	1.74	2.02	–28%
coffee***	7.66	5.97	5.28	4.73	3.53	–54%
cotton***	5.01	3.91	3.46	3.09	2.02	–60%
sugar***	5.29	4.12	3.65	3.27	2.02	–62%
Urban+	5.96	4.65	4.11	4.35	3.79	–36%

Notes:
* Colones per hour in 1975 prices.
** Male.
*** Combines separate wage scales for harvesting and processing.
+ Combines manufacturing/service with commerce (both the same).
Source:
Official data reported in IDHUCA (1988, 192).

84 percent portrayed the situation in the country as bad or very bad.[28] Certainly, there was the civil war, but the worse problem facing the country was the economic crisis, according to 69 percent of the respondents in the 1986 survey,[29] 66 percent in a 1987 survey of metropolitan San Salvador,[30] and 76 percent in a 1990 national survey.[31]

The UNTS coalition, however, was too broad ideologically, and by the end of 1986 the UPD broke away while other noneconomic groups from the left, such as students, human rights, and families of the disappeared, were soon added. This had three important consequences for the movement. First, the UPD took with it about half of the membership, which the new groups added could not match. With the exception of a demonstration of perhaps 35,000 in mid-January 1987 protesting further austerity measures announced by Duarte the month before (ECA #459, 119), UNTS's contentious activities never again reached the participation levels of its first year. Second, UNTS was now more purely a movement of the left and therefore

[28] Martín-Baró (1986, 766). This poll, as well as others referred to in this section, was conducted by the highly respected Instituto Universitario de Opinión Pública (IUDOP) at the Universidad Centroamericana (UCA).

[29] The war was selected by 41 percent as the worst problem, and the lack of employment was selected by 37 percent (Martín-Baró 1986, 766).

[30] The war was selected by 36 percent as the worst problem, as was the lack of employment (IUDOP 1987, 303).

[31] In 1990, the war and violence was selected by 59 percent as the worst problem, and the lack of employment was selected by 24 percent (IUDOP 1990, 514).

less representative of public opinion. When UNTS called for settling the war through negotiations between the government and the FMLN, it invariably sharply criticized the government but not the revolutionaries, with calls for Duarte's resignation a frequent theme. In contrast, the 1986 survey of urban adults found 63 percent of respondents thought the government had been seriously pursuing dialogue across the prior two years, but only 38 percent said the same of the FDR-FMLN.[32]

A third and especially dangerous consequence was that with a greater tilt to the left UNTS was more vulnerable to charges that it was a front for the FMLN.[33] As with their predecessor mass organizations of the 1970s, MUSYGES and then UNTS were frequently attacked by the Duarte administration and by the military as a front for the FMLN. The same was true for other protesters; for example, Duarte claimed of the June 1985 strikes, "All of these strikes, except for one or two small ones, are by the unions managed by the communists," a view reiterated by other top PDC officials (NY Times June 16, 1985, iv:5).[34] Major UNTS actions, such as the large 1986 demonstrations, were invariably attacked as either planned by the FMLN or infiltrated by the rebels.[35] As protests grew more contentious in 1987 and 1988, with increasing acts of street vandalism (somewhat captured

---

[32] Martín-Baró (1996, 768). The 1987 survey of metropolitan San Salvador found respondents split on the contentious form of the UNTS demonstrations (40 percent approving, 39 percent not) but still seeing UNTS demands as just (45 percent as just opposed to 22 percent unjust) (IUDOP 1987, 304).

[33] See Béjar (1990, 884–885); Casper 1987; ECA 1986. A 1986 CIA report portrays UNTS as "under FMLN influence but not direct FMLN control," whereas an early November 1988 report claimed all of UNTS's executive committee members were FMLN activists (USDS/NSA2 1986, 1988). According to former FMLN leader Romero García, the revolutionaries had been trying to revitalize the mass movement in the capital and decided in 1984 to redouble that effort. It was, he says, not so important that popular movements be directly tied to the FMLN but rather that once they were initiated they would destabilize the government by demanding "more than the Government could give, and if in the beginning the Government acquiesced, then ask for double, always go asking for more" (quoted in Prisk 1991, 73–74).

[34] Also see Casper (1986, 218); ECA (#441, 546); LeoGrande (1998, 279–280). As FPL leader Salvador Sánchez Cerén later explained about Duarte's predicament, since "the government had to present a democratic face" it had to allow the challenger activities. "So we applied ourselves to the legal struggle using union instruments and combined these with confrontations with the government" (quoted in Harnecker 1990a, 229; translation by author). Also see Harnecker's interview of Communist Party leader Schafik Jorge Handal (Harnecker 1990a, 229, 244–247).

[35] See, for example, ECA (#447, 94, 112; #451, 457); NY Times (Feb. 22, 1986, 5). For a good discussion of the nature of these links between the FMLN and specific popular organizations formed later in the 1980s, see Wood (2003, 165–177).

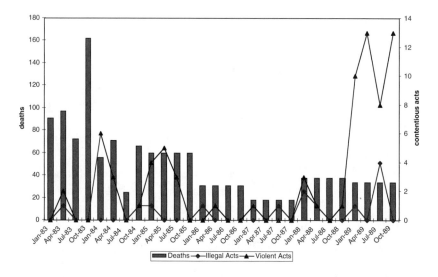

Source: 1983-1984 Deaths: Socorro Jurídico as reported in Morales (1988, 189-201). "Urban civilians" is obtained by removing both unidentified victims and peasants from source.

1985-1989, Tutela Legal as reported by Americas Watch (1987, 7-8, for1985 and 1986; 1990, 199-200, for 1988 and 1989) and McClintock (1998, 117) for 1987. Urban victims are Tutela Legal's category "targeted killings by the military and death squads." Because the categories used by Americas Watch and McClintock differ, the average ratio between their data for 1986 and 1988 was used to calculate a comparable 1987 score from McClintock's score for assassinations for that year.

Figure 10.6 El Salvador: Urban Civilian Deaths by Repression and Violent Contentious Activities in San Salvador by Quarter, 1983–1989

by Figure 10.6),[36] warnings from the military grew stronger. Rightist forces also perceived a more permissive climate. ARENA regained control of the congress in 1988 and the presidency in 1989. Also thought to be important was approval in October 1987 of an amnesty that Americas Watch charged sent a signal "that even the most heinous crimes can be forgiven by a sleight of hand" (Americas Watch 1988, 7).

---

[36] See, for example, NY Times (July 17, 1987, 3), which portrays the same group of some five hundred to one thousand committed student and union activists as behind the most contentious activities of the period; also see ECA (#465, 494; #473, 252; #475, 383, 415). According to a 1988 CIA report, "Captured FMLN documents from April 1987 clearly showed that the FMLN was attempting to increase violence during demonstrations and rallies and to promote simultaneous *masas* [front organization] and military action.... Numerous reports from August and September 1987 indicated that the FMLN was concerned because its demonstrations were not attracting large numbers of participants" (USDS/NSA2 1988).

The two most notorious cases of violent attacks on nonviolent progressive leaders came in the fall of 1989. On October 31, the FENAS-TRAS headquarters was bombed, destroying the building while a meeting of leaders from various organizations was under way. Among the ten dead was Febe Elizabeth Velaquez, one of the most dynamic popular leaders at this time; close to three dozen people were injured.[37] A few days later, the FMLN launched its most important offensive since January 1981, bringing heavy fighting into the capital for the first time. In the midst of the combat, the military murdered, at night in their home, six Jesuit priests affiliated with the Universidad Centroamericana (UCA), as well as their housekeeper and her daughter. Several of the priests had long been among the most powerful voices for nonviolent and progressive change in the country and a negotiated end to the war, often speaking through UCA's journal, *Estudios Centroamericanos*.[38]

With the increasing repression and then the eventual defeat of the FMLN offensive, the mass movement was paralyzed – but only for several months. By March 1990, it had renewed its activities, protesting President Alfredo Cristiani's economic measures (citing over 4,500 public employees discharged in just the first three months of the year) and the state of siege and calling for a reactivation of peace talks. With the government having moved back to the right, the popular movement was able to forge again a broader coalition. UNTS and the PDC-affiliated Unidad Nacional Obrero Campesina (UNOC) issued their first joint denunciation of government policy in August 1989 and in the next year found increasing opportunities for collaboration. On May 1, 1990, the combined opposition mounted the largest demonstration of the past decade as some 80,000 marched, calling for a peaceful settlement of the war (Solís 1990). Finally, a little over a year later, peace came to the war-weary country.

Contention, Repression and the Individual

The analysis of the last four chapters demonstrates a significant relationship between the configuration of political opportunities – and especially repression – with the emergence and trajectories of contentious movements.

---

[37] The same day Comité de Familiares de Presos, Desaparecidos y Asesinados Políticos's headquarters was bombed, and another four people were injured (ECA #492, 867; NY Times Nov. 1, 1989, 7).

[38] Betancur, Planchart, and Buergenthal (1993, 44–50); ECA (#493, 1140); NY Times (Nov. 16, 1989, 1).

In societies like those of El Salvador and Guatemala that feature high levels of grievances, the opening of political opportunities invariably produces contentious movements. But the opposite relationship is more complex. As indicated in these chapters, the closing of opportunities does not necessarily result in declining mass contention, even when state violence is increasing against challengers.[39] In order to understand this more complex relationship, it is necessary to move the analysis to the level of individuals and the nature of their grievances existing within the broader configuration of political opportunities.

Challengers do rationally calculate the risks they face, but this provides us with only a partial explanation for their behavior and not necessarily the most important. Critical, too, will be the type of grievances they hold and especially the emotional intensity of those grievances.[40] To be a powerful motivational force, grievances need to grow not only from a grave injustice but also have a clear agent who is held responsible. This is not always the case with socioeconomic grievances, which is one reason why organizing around them often can be so difficult. But that is often the case with repression. Furthermore, for victims of repression and those close to them the injustice could be no more grave: the rape of young daughters, the torture of parents, the murder of spouses. For survivors, rage is intense. But whether emotions will motivate contention or contention will be sustained or even radicalized depends on a multiplicity of factors.

Many of these factors are summarized by the concept of the cycle of contention. When potential challengers are largely unmobilized and facing a closed configuration of political opportunities, repression – and especially consistently escalating repression – prevents the emergence of mass movements. For example, the widespread and arbitrary murders of thousands

---

[39] Goldstone and Tilly point out that the literature on contentious politics gives insufficient attention to "threat," improperly regarding it "as merely the flip side of opportunity, a negative measure of the same concept." To the contrary, they argue, "'threat' is an independent factor whose dynamics greatly influence how popular groups and the state act in a variety of conflict situations. If this is true, much more needs to be said about how 'opportunity' and 'threat' combine to shape contentious action" (Goldstone and Tilly 2001, 181).

[40] Jasper and Goodwin appropriately ask, "Will we ever understand the diverse effects of state repression . . . without grasping subtle psychological and emotional dynamics – fear, inspiration, intimidation, revenge?" (Jasper and Goodwin 1999, 124). Booth and Richard 1999 provide an innovative effort to examine the relationship empirically for Central America using survey data (Booth 1980 was one of the first quantitative analyses of Central American political violence). Also on repression and fear in Latin America, see the essays in Corradi, Fagen, and Garretón 1992.

of noncombatant peasants and of a large number of urban activists in Guatemala in the last half of the 1960s and in Nicaragua in the mid-1970s did not provoke mass mobilization among the survivors. The revolutionary guerrilla organizations in their midst (which were the "justifications" for these campaigns of state terror) were small and isolated from other political forces. Indeed, society itself was largely demobilized – certainly the peasantry was. Under these circumstances, survivors had limited opportunities for collective action. No matter how sharp their grief nor how strong their rage, the configuration of political opportunities offered little hope for justice or possibilities for revenge.

Later, though, the political context changed. Space for political organizing and contentious action opened for a variety of reasons in each country: in urban El Salvador in the late 1960s and again in the late 1970s; in Guatemala in the mid-1970s; and in Nicaragua in the last third of the 1970s. Mass collective action, significantly including the previously passive peasantry, was greatly assisted by the appearance of numerous support groups and by changed domestic and international elite alliances. In this more supportive context, intermittent regime violence provoked not just grief and anger in each country, but also determination and resistance. Mass organizations grew in number, in size, and in assertiveness. Vigorous cycles of contention were initiated in each country.

Faced with this sustained threat from below, the regimes of each country turned to even more violence. Although this violence became increasingly widespread, brutal, and arbitrary, initially it did not deter mass mobilization but provoked even greater popular opposition. Already active opponents redoubled their efforts, and some turned to violence. Growing numbers gave their support to the expanding revolutionary armies, many becoming recruits themselves. Previously passive regime opponents were activated. And new opponents were created as the indiscriminate violence delegitimized regimes, on the one hand, and created new motivations for opposition, such as protection, revenge, and justice, on the other.

In his account of the nationalist movement that ended Soviet domination of Lithuania, Petersen places "strategic calculations and sensitivity to risk at the center" of his analysis yet finds this approach insufficient for understanding the behavior of "first actors" under situations of high risk (Petersen 2001, 278–280). To explain the behavior of these critical actors, he makes good use of the following insight by Stanley Benn: "Political activity may be a form of moral self-expression ... because one could not seriously claim ... to be on that side without expressing the attitude by the action most appropriate to it in the paradigm situation" (p. 284). Similarly in her study of peasant involvement in the Salvadoran insurgency, Wood emphasizes as part of her explanation the importance of participation, defiance, and pleasure in agency to the participants (Wood 2003, 231–237). Peasant revolutionaries valued "participation in activities that reflect moral commitments" (p. 232), that "expressed defiance and asserted a claim to dignity and personhood" (p. 233), and that provided "pleasure in together changing unjust social structures through intentional action" (p. 235).

Such desires – be they for justice, for living out one's commitments, for asserting one's dignity through defiance, or for revenge – can find an outlet through contentious action in this ascendant phase of the protest cycle even as state violence is increasing for at least two reasons, one rational calculating and the other emotional. First, there is hope of winning. Despite the brutality of the regime's indiscriminate violence, the active opposition of large numbers of people and of many organizations from many different sectors of society sustains the belief that the regime will be defeated.[41] This belief was widespread among popular forces in Nicaragua during the insurrections of 1978–1979 and in El Salvador and Guatemala at the peak of their cycles of contention.[42]

Second, when indiscriminate repression is directed against challengers during a strong cycle of contention, many activists are likely to continue their opposition for reasons that go beyond rational calculation. Although indiscriminate violence increases the dangers of further collective action and perhaps diminishes calculations of the probability of success, the rage and indignation engendered by that violence provides additional motivation for action, perhaps more than enough to offset increased danger.[43] Since challengers are already mobilized, the momentum of their involvement can

---

[41] Models emphasizing "thresholds," "critical-mass," and/or "tipping," such as Granovetter 1978, Kurzman 1996, and Moore 1995b, respectively, are useful for understanding this process as a cycle of contention grows. They are less helpful for understanding contention outside of cycles or the actions of "early risers."

[42] As the U.S. embassy pointed out in September 1980, after the peak of the Salvadoran cycle, "The fact that the Sandinistas were able to carry out a successful revolution in neighboring Nicaragua just one year ago in circumstances similar to those existing in El Salvador must serve as a great morale builder for the DRU [radical] groups. It is likely that this is an important factor in keeping the revolutionaries here going despite their inability to bring off the revolution that they thought they were so close to achieving" (USDS/NSA2 1980c).

[43] Gurr points out that "aggression is self-satisfying for angered" people. If regime coercion "is massive and sanctions severe, retaliation may become more salient [to challengers] than the economic and participatory values for which" they originally acted (Gurr 1970, 259).

carry them on into additional contentious activities, perhaps even including clandestine and violent forms of resistance and retaliation as the regime closes down nonviolent channels of protest.

Most importantly, mobilized individuals are not isolated. Instead, they are integrated into groups and organizations. These social networks provide the leadership and opportunities for continuing activity, as well as the solidarity bonds and obligations and the role models that encourage continuing involvement. For some individuals, commitment to a cause is primarily to abstract ideals, but for many others ideological commitment is heavily reinforced by solidarity ties and loyalties among group members. As one long-time Guatemalan labor activist explained concerning the continuing involvement by himself and his colleagues, "We all have problems, and we consult with each other. We try to share solutions so that we can continue the struggle. When one looks to his or her *compañeros* and finds unconditional support and friendship, there's a wonderful feeling of solidarity. We give each other that kind of support" (quoted in Reed and Brandow 1996, 48). It seems safe to postulate that when repression escalates and therefore fear, these are the individuals most likely to remain active.[44] In addition, since many already had preexisting ties or contacts with revolutionary organizations, they also are the most likely to join the violent insurgency when nonviolent contention is eliminated by repression.

Similarly, previously inactive individuals are more likely to become mobilized during the periods when a peak of contention is met by increasing repression than they are at other times. If and when the inactive are affected by repression personally, this new, intense grievance is generated in a context where they are more likely to be tied through their social networks to already active individuals and their organizations than during other periods. They are therefore more likely to became active themselves during a peak of a cycle of contention than during other periods.[45]

When a loved comrade or friend is mutilated by state actors in a slow death, this can be received primarily by survivors as a warning of the risks

---

[44] In one of the few efforts to take emotions seriously in an analytically useful way, Goodwin and Pfaff 2001 identify eight "encouragement mechanisms" that helped people to manage fear in order to act. Each is group related.

[45] For scholars who (appropriately) emphasize the mobilizing impact of repression, the examples are invariably of cases occurring within a cycle of contention. See, for example, McClintock (1998, 268–271, 284) and Wood (2003, 115–120) on El Salvador and Kurzman 1996 on Iran. It is important to emphasize that outside of a cycle widespread repression does not provoke an effective opposition.

they also face, but it also can recommit survivors to their struggle out of loyalty to the dead. Peterson, for example, quotes a widow who said, "I had to continue what my husband did. . . . I had to continue doing what he was doing when they killed him. His courage gave me strength to continue" (Peterson 1997, 141).

In their response to the costs of repression, survivors react not only based on their social ties and loyalties but also out of their worldviews. For contentious movements in Central America in the 1970s and 1980s, progressive Catholicism provided a powerful narrative for interpreting the dangers faced and for encouraging dedication to the cause.[46] Peterson has written about this important role of religious belief as insightfully as anyone, focusing especially on martyrdom and the belief by many Salvadorans "that the martyrs of their communities gave their lives not only in witness to Christ but in his image" (Peterson 1997, 13).[47] In the progressive Catholicism of the time, believers not only identified with Jesus' commitment to struggle for the liberation of the poor (pp. 76–77) but did so with the knowledge that "Jesus continued his struggle even though he knew the powerful would probably kill him for threatening their privileges" (p. 83). Peterson adds: "According to this view, contemporary Christians should adopt Jesus' attitude in the struggle against evil: neither a morbid search for death nor a fatalistic acceptance of it, but a clear-eyed knowledge of the likelihood of death and its role in the battle for justice" (Peterson 1997, 83).

In El Salvador, the Christian passion story was made real again through Archbishop Oscar Romero, assassinated in March 1980 while saying mass the day after giving especially strong, clear voice to the people's demand that the repression end. Peterson paraphrases a Salvadoran woman, "Because his faith was genuine . . . Romero chose to follow Christ and not to turn back even though he knew he would be killed" (p. 126). Importantly, the narrative does not end on the cross but instead with resurrection: "The

---

[46] Aminzade and Perry point out that although religious-based and secular-based movements have much in common, they also differ in important features, including "the unusual institutional legitimacy of religious-based organizations, which creates distinctive threat and opportunity structures, and the ability of religious movements to appeal to an other-worldly, transcendental ontology, which has implications for commitment processes, challenges to authority, and logics of action" (Aminzade and Perry 2001, 158).

[47] Petersen 2001 finds the same symbolic system working in the Lithuanian case, but he labels the mechanism "pseudomartyrdom" since in this case, unlike in Central America, there was actually only a small risk of martyrdom (Petersen 2001, 284–292).

sacrifices of contemporary martyrs, like Jesus' passion, transform pain into victory, death into life" (p. 85).[48]

With such commitments, loyalties, and models, activism continued for many beyond the point where escalating repression deterred those motivated more by rational calculations of risk.[49] Peterson gives the example of a Salvadoran activist who explained, "You shouldn't just be celebrating and admiring what the martyrs did, but rather emulating it. If they can do it, so can you" (Peterson 1997, 139). Similary, Pearce quotes a BPR-affiliated peasant activist, "The martyrs of history have always given me strength to confront this type of situation. . . . If they could struggle, then why couldn't I risk my life, and so I did" (Pearce 1986, 177).[50]

Such religious convictions and examples are powerful motivational forces. Levenson-Estrada found them as well within the Guatemalan labor movement, pointing out that "Those who were assassinated or disappeared now became martyrs who belonged to a labor movement that represented them as spiritual leaders" (Levenson-Estrada 1994, 157). For trade unionists "Their cult of martyrdom sustained them in the face of deaths that they did not seek" (p. 158). Similar commitments grow from more secular sources as well. How else to explain the continuing willingness of university students in Guatemala to take public leadership in the Asociación de Estudiantes Universitarios (AEU), even as the martyrdom that began with the October 1978 murder of AEU President Oliverio Castañeda de León continued on into the 1990s? Similarly, following the murder of a labor leader in October 1978, a fellow leader promised at his funeral: "your blood will not run in vain. Today more than ever, because of your blood, we will not be intimidated. Your murder has turned panic to anger" (Levenson-Estrada 1994, 159).

---

[48] Aminzade and Perry explain: "A transcendental ontology that includes belief in an afterlife allows leaders to make extraordinary demands on followers, whose interpretations of opportunities, threats, successes, and failures may not be firmly grounded in 'objective' political conditions. The altered sense of costs, benefits, and possibilities made possible by a transcendental ontology and supernatural powers can create intensely committed followers willing to sacrifice for the cause, including willing martyrs with altered understandings of obstacles and opportunities" (Aminzade and Perry 2001, 161).

[49] Similarly, Aminzade and Perry argue: "The means-ends calculations that scholars often assume inform the behaviors of actors may not be applicable to those whose logics of action privilege the existence of nonmaterial, or spiritual, forces and domains" (Aminzade and Perry 2001, 162).

[50] Relevant here is research on altruistic behavior both in psychology on the impact of situational factors such as imitation/modeling (Soule 2001) and in sociology on the importance of interactive processes within groups of activists (Tilly, 2001).

Conclusion

But even if convictions, commitments, and courage sustain contentious movements beyond where most rational calculators seek safety, state terrorism if sustained will usually succeed. So it was in El Salvador and Guatemala. The tens of thousands of civilian murders in each country in the early 1980s were sufficient to destroy most mass organizations or drive them underground, to restore fear and passivity to much of the countryside and in cities as well, and to contain the revolutionary forces (more successfully in Guatemala with the latter than in El Salvador). The fact is, successful rebellions and revolutions are rare. Although indiscriminate violence might escalate regime opposition under the circumstances described above, there are limitations to a people's ability to withstand ferocious regime violence. The difference in the outcomes between these two countries and Nicaragua, where the popular forces succeeded in overthrowing the murderous Somoza regime in 1979, in part resulted from a broader multiclass opposition to Somoza than in the other two. However, in addition, Somoza did not have nearly the same capacity for state terrorism as his neighbors. And the Guatemalan and Salvadoran regimes had the willingness to use their greater capacity to the extent necessary to ensure their survival.

Class polarization had been greater historically in El Salvador and Guatemala than in Nicaragua, making any multiclass antiregime coalition more difficult to forge in the first two than in Nicaragua.[51] This historical difference in class polarization was then reinforced by differing patterns of repression, in at least two ways. First is the radicalizing effect of state violence, especially on those who are targets or believe they are likely future targets. This radicalizing effect is especially important when these targets are leaders of popular organizations because leadership radicalization means that the organizations they lead are more likely to radicalize as well, both ideologically and tactically. From the secondary literature, it appears that urban mass organization leaders were more likely to be targeted for assassination by the state in Guatemala and El Salvador than in Nicaragua prior to the latter's insurrectional stage. This radicalizing effect in turn reinforced the differences between the two sets of countries in the challenges they confronted to building a multiclass alliance. Second, this alliance emerged in Nicaragua prior to the onslaught of indiscriminate state violence. Under this shared experience, indiscriminate repression seems to

---

[51] See Brockett 1998 for the relevant argument and bibliography.

have unified the broad opposition further. The class scope of regime opposition was less in El Salvador and even less so in Guatemala at the point when the state indiscriminately escalated its violence than it was in Nicaragua. The radicalizing impact of this state violence made all the more unlikely that a broad multiclass opposition would be created in either country, especially Guatemala.

11

Conclusion

The relationship between popular contention and political opportunities generally, and repression specifically, has been of interest to political observers going back centuries, including some of the great theorists of the past. De Tocqueville, for example, in seeking explanations for the European upheavals initiated with the French Revolution, noted the paradox that carries his name; "it often happens that when a people which has put up with an oppressive rule over a long period without protest suddenly finds the government relaxing its pressure, it takes up arms against it.... Only consummate statecraft can enable a king to save his throne when after a long spell of oppressive rule he sets out to improve the lot of his subjects" (quoted in Oberschall 1995, 155).

One option open to the "king" when popular mobilization ignites following the opening of political opportunities is to reapply repression. Indeed, often this has been the response of rulers. Sometimes, this heightened repression has succeeded from the viewpoint of "the throne." But at other times, it has aroused even higher levels of opposition and even an overturning of the throne itself. In the face of this repression-protest paradox, rulers have been advised by Machiavelli (paraphrasing): "if high coerciveness is applied, it should be applied consistently."[1]

This study has sought to build on such astute ages-old observations, as well as the findings of more recent scholarship, in order to bring a fuller

---

[1] The source is Zimmerman (1980, 197) who is quoting Feierabend, Nesvold, and Feierabend (1970, 115). Zimmerman, adds (p. 198), quoting now Tilly (1969, 42): "A large portion of the European disturbances we have been surveying turned violent at exactly the moment when the authorities intervened to stop an illegal but nonviolent action."

understanding to these paradoxical relationships. The best explanations, it has been argued here, are not to be found in one set of variables or one theoretical approach. Instead, we need to bring together individuals and their grievances with the broad set of political variables aggregated into the concept of "the configuration of political opportunities."

Motivation

Bringing humans in their fullness into the analysis has been crucial to the resolution offered here of the political contention paradoxes. For certain types of behavior, rational actor models might be sufficient. But not for political contention under situations of dire need and acute risk. The disadvantaged have an accumulation of long-term grievances. But their mobilization is often sparked by their emotional response to new socioeconomic grievances – such as the loss of access to land described in Chapter 2 – and intensified by new sociopolitical grievances – such as the lack of government responsiveness and even state violence that greets their contention. Furthermore, emotion, as with cognition, is not the product of atomized individuals but rather of people embedded in emotionally charged relationships who interpret and respond drawing on the socially constructed material at hand. How the individual will then act follows from this shifting emotional/cognitive processing of information, including perceptions of changing configurations of opportunities and threats in the world around them.

The Configuration of Political Opportunities

Are increasing political opportunities necessary for the emergence of social movements? Perhaps not in the sense of a limited appearance. But if we mean the emergence of movements that grow and persist long enough to present significant challenge to authorities in at least noninstitutionalized democracies, then the answer is yes. There are, as always, qualifications. It would be a mistake to posit a direct linear relationship between political opportunities and the strength of movement challenge to authorities. Other variables drive mobilization, notably the intensity of grievances. Nonetheless, the Central American cases analyzed here demonstrate that changes in the configuration of political opportunities are crucial for the emergence, trajectory, and certainly outcomes of contentious movements living under such regimes. This is true both for understanding dynamics within an individual country as well as comparatively.

For the mobilization of the poor and powerless, the assistance of allies and support groups is critical, as demonstrated repeatedly in the Salvadoran and Guatemalan cases. Concerning this dimension of political opportunities, perhaps the most important contribution of this study has been demonstrating the importance of the underground revolutionary movements to the organization and leadership of aboveground nonviolent popular movements prior to the onset of significant armed conflict.

The opening and closing of access to the political system is important to all groups, from the numerous electoral frauds and states of siege in each country to the more infrequent periods when political freedoms were honored. The relationship of access to contentious movements, though, is complex. Deteriorating access and governmental responsiveness are in themselves new and often intense grievances, but at the same time they limit chances for policy success for contentious movements and even for mobilization itself. Conversely, expanding access dissipates dissatisfaction among some groups yet provides the necessary political space for the successful mobilization of others. This complexity is especially vivid with the frequent changes in the Salvadoran government's behavior toward protesters throughout 1979 under General Romero and then the October reform junta.

Fluctuating access is often associated with changes in another key dimension of the configuration of political opportunities: the cohesion/fragmentation of elites. Fissures among domestic elites – and especially between the state and upper-sector groups – creates significant opportunities for contentious movements, such as seen in the late 1970s with Nicaragua compared to Guatemala. Important as well in the Central American cases were cross-national elite relations, especially with the U.S. government. Fluctuations in the relationship with Washington, DC were important particularly for the Salvadoran case, from the late 1970s through the end of the civil war in the early 1990s.

Finally, there is the central focus of this study. The capacity and willingness of the state to repress challengers has been crucial to the fate of contentious movements in Central America. Although the relationship is conditioned by other factors, the emergence, trajectory, and outcomes of contentious movements in Central America have been closely tied to the state's use of violence against challengers and other citizens.

Conclusion

Cycles of Contention and Repression

How individuals will respond to increasing repression is substantially influenced both by whether one is already a member of a contentious movement and by the already existing level of mass contention in society. For contentious movements, too, the relationship between the two sets of variables associated with grievances and opportunities/threats is highly conditioned by the preexisting level of mass mobilization. Repression generally succeeds in smothering contention if the prior level of mobilization was low. However, if state violence is increased after a protest cycle/cycle of contention is well underway, this repression is more likely to provoke even higher levels of challenge, both nonviolent and violent, rather than deter contention. This provocation is especially likely if state violence is inconsistent. But revolutionary toppling of thrones such as Nicaragua in 1979 are rare events. El Salvador and Guatemala are extreme examples of the more usual outcome: When regimes are willing to repress as necessary and have the capacity to do so, they usually succeed in eliminating popular contention as a threat to their regime and often to their own rule as well.

The capacity and willingness of the regime to repress does not stand alone. Often a key issue fragmenting elites and aggravating elite conflict is precisely the use of repression in the face of mass mobilization. Good strategists among challengers understand this and seek to heighten elite fragmentation and conflict (both domestic and international), generally and especially over reliance on repression. This is also a key divide among challengers: Nonviolent strategists hope to bolster the position of elites who would reduce repression while at least some violent challengers seek to provoke greater repression, believing it would further fragment elites and promote greater mass mobilization and radicalization.

Commitment

As much as for their violence, Guatemala and El Salvador are impressive examples of the continuing insistence by activists in the face of great personal risks that they be allowed to struggle in public spaces for a better world for their constituents. Despite the horrific levels of violence directed at nonviolent challengers in both countries in the early 1980s, as soon as levels of state violence fell activists were again challenging authorities. Tragically, violence against activists continued in both countries even after their peace settlements of the 1990s, most notably in Guatemala. As recently as the first twenty-eight months of the new century, some 150 incidents of violence against challengers were reported in Guatemala. A United Nations representative investigating the situation concluded that credible evidence connects the clandestine groups responsible for this violence to the army and national police.[2] As with their courageous counterparts in the past, activists still continue their struggle in Guatemala, even though the connection of the security forces to this violence carries with it the ever present threat of a new round of escalating repression.

Of all the subjects treated in this work, what is most striking to me is precisely this: the willingness of challengers to carry on their struggle, not only against heavily unfavorable odds of success, but also in the face of great risks to themselves. Perhaps urban protesters in Guatemala in the late 1950s and early 1960s did not feel that they were at great risk, nor their counterparts in El Salvador up through the mid-1970s. But after the first waves of state murders of nonviolent urban challengers intensified in both countries, there could only be an acute awareness of the high degree of risk, including to one's own life, that any political contentious activities brought. And yet contention continued as the waves of violence built, resumed once the waves of repression waned, and continues today.

In our social scientific treatment of contention and opportunities, of protest and repression, we identify variables and relationships. We elaborate and test hypotheses. As well we should. But in the end, we are dealing with the tenacity of the human spirit and the astonishing complexity of each unique individual. Beyond self-interest and rational calculation, political contention in situations of intense grievances and high risks is finally determined by uniquely individual configurations of hope and fear, conviction and doubt, anger and love.

---

[2] NotiCen 2002.

References

I. Central American newspapers and journals

ECA. *Estudios Centroamericanos*. San Salvador monthly

El Imparcial. Guatemala City daily

Inforpress. Guatemala City weekly

LPG. *La Prensa Graphica*. San Salvador daily

II. Central American archives

A. El Imparcial *clipping archive*

The clipping file of a major Guatemala City newspaper, which also includes clippings from other newspapers, covering 1954 into the early 1980s. Clippings are stored in envelopes, identified by general subjects (and within, specific topics). Given below are the codes used in the text for the corresponding subjects and topics. The archive is maintained at the Centro de Investigaciones Regionales de Mesoamérica (CIRMA) in Antigua, Guatemala.

Code	Subject/Topic
	I. EDUCACIÓN
IMP1	A. Manifestaciones
	II. TRABAJO
	A. Huelga
IMP2	banco
IMP3	maestros
IMP4	camineros
IMP5	CIDASA

Code	Subject/Topic
IMP6	tribunales
IMP7	empleados jd
IMP8	hospitales
IMP9	finca xata
IMP10	1978
IMP11	costa sur 1980
IMP12	1977–1979
IMP13	telefonos
IMP14	1970
IMP15	1973
IMP16	municipal
IMP17	varios 1955–1979
	B. Conflictos
IMP18	varios
IMP19	IRCA
IMP20	camioneteros
IMP21	[blank]
IMP22	pamarco
IMP23	camineros
IMP24	1979
IMP25	[blank]
	C. Dia del trabajo
IMP26	[blank]
IMP27	[blank]
IMP28	varios
IMP29	1968–1970
IMP30	1979
	D. Sindicales
IMP31	varios 1956
IMP32	1960–1961
IMP33	1962
IMP34	1963
IMP35	1979
	E. Sindicato
IMP36	periodistas
IMP37	1979
IMP38	municipal
IMP39	varios
IMP40	varios 1979

III. POLÍTICA
A. Disturbios

IMP41	varios 1962A
IMP42	varios 1962B

References

Code	Subject/Topic
IMP43	1962
	B. Manifestación
IMP44	campesino orient
IMP45	noctornos
IMP46	Castro
IMP47	alto costo
IMP48	entierro simbólico
IMP49	1 de mayo 1974
IMP50	solicitada
IMP51	catedral
IMP52	Ydígoras
IMP53	1960
IMP54	1961A
IMP55	1961B
IMP56	1961C
IMP57	1962
IMP58	varias 1962
IMP59	varias 1963
IMP60	varias 1964–1965
IMP61	varias 1966
IMP62	varias 1967
IMP63	1970–1978
IMP64	varios
	IV. JUDICIALES
	A. Desaparecidos
IMP65	1966
IMP66	1954–1967
IMP67	1968–1969
IMP68	1970–1971
IMP69	1972 (Tapachula)
IMP70	1973–1978
IMP71	1979–1984
	B. Desordenes
IMP72	atropellos
IMP73	varios 1960–1973
IMP74	1977
IMP75	1978
IMP76	1979
IMP77	varios, estud.
IMP78	huelga
	C. Asesinatos
IMP79	1975
IMP80	famosas

B. Inforpress *clipping file*

The clipping file of a weekly newsletter on Central America published in Guatemala City. An exhaustive file of clippings from numerous Central American – and especially Guatemalan – newspapers, it covers 1973 into the early 1980s. Clippings are taped on pages gathered in volumes of several hundred pages each. Given below are the codes used in the text and their corresponding set of volumes. The archive is maintained at the Centro de Investigaciones Regionales de Mesoamérica (CIRMA) in Antigua, Guatemala.

IPEE   Política de Guatemala/Eventos Electorales/Política Presidencial
            (volumes organized by date)
IPSET   SocioEconómicas – Trabajo
            (volumes organized alphabetically by subject)
IPV   Política de Guatemala/Violencia
            (volumes organized by date)

III. United States State Department Documents

A. Documents stored at the U.S. National Archives in College Park, Maryland. Record Group 59

USDS. 1954a. Desp. #144 from AmEm. Guat.: "Guatemalan Labor Situation Deteriorates." 814.06/8–2054. August 20.
   1954b. Desp. #512 from AmEm. Guat.: "Joint Week." 714.00(w)/12–1754. December 17.
   1954c. Outgoing telegram to multiple embassies. 714.00/7-1754. July 17.
   1955. Memoradum of Meeting: "Current Situation in Guatemala." Lot 57 D 295, Box 3; file: Guat. 1955. April 28–29.
   1956a. Dept of State from Guatemala. 714.501/7-1356. July 13.
   1956b. Incoming Telegram #370 from Guat. City. 714.00/6-2856. June 28.
   1956c. Sec of State from Guat. 714(W)/3-2856. March 28.
   1956d. Sec of State from Guatemala. 714 May Day/5-456. May 4.
   1957. Outgoing Telegram #254 to AmEm Guat. 714.5-MSP/11-1457. November 14.
   1959. Office Memorandum: "Current Political Situation in Guatemala." 714.00/9-2359. September 23.

B. Documents available from National Security Archives, Georgetown University, Washington. D.C.

1. El Salvador 1977–1984 Collection

USDS/NSA1. 1979a. "After the Lights Went Out: An Overview of Salvadoran Labor Situation After Events of March 19–20." Embassy cable, San Salvador, March 20. Collection #121.
   1979b. "General Uneasiness of Salvadoran Political Scene: An Assessment." Embassy cable, San Salvador, December 4. Collection #307.

1979c. "Guerrilla Occupation of Rural Communities in El Salvador." Embassy cable, San Salvador, December 11. Collection #313.

1979d. "Heavy BPR Involvement in Recent Labor Disturbances." Embassy cable, San Salvador, July 19. Collection #176.

1979e. "Labor Dispute at 'La Constancia' and 'La Tropical' Bottling Plan[t]s Spreads to Other Firms." Embassy cable, San Salvador, March 13. Collection #104.

1979f. "Seizure of Town and Other Terrorist Acts." Embassy cable, San Salvador, December 14. Collection #319.

2. El Salvador 1980–1994 Collection

USDS/NSA 2. 1979a. "Appraisal of the Terrorist/Political Situation in El Salvador." C.I.A. cable, San Salvador, May 29. Collection #003.

1979b. "Threat Assessment – El Salvador." C.I.A. memorandum, March 1. Collection #002.

1980a. "Growth and Prospects of Leftist Extremists in El Salvador." Interagency intelligence memorandum, January. Collection #019.

1980b. "The Guerrillas in the Salvadoran Equation." C.I.A. intelligence report, July. Collection #034.

1980c. "Strength of the Revolutionary Forces in El Salvador As of Late September 1980." C.I.A. cable, September 24. Collection #038.

1986. "Organization of a New Salvadoran Opposition Labor Union and Efforts to Gain Support for It in Mexico." C.I.A. cable, March 20. Collection #205.

1988. "Advisory 26–88 – Role of Front Groups and Masas in FMLN Strategy." D.I.A. cable, November 10. Collection #445.

IV. Secondary Sources

Abercrombie, Nicholas. 1980. *Class, Structure and Knowledge: Problems in the Sociology of Knowledge.* New York: New York University Press.

Abercrombie, Nicholas, Stephen Hill, and Bryan S. Turner. 1980. *The Dominant Ideology Thesis.* London: Allen & Unwin.

Ackerman, Peter, and Jack DuVall. 2000. *A Force More Powerful: A Century of Nonviolent Conflict.* New York: St. Martin's Press.

Adam, Barry D. 1995. *The Rise of a Gay and Lesbian Movement*, rev. ed. New York: Twayne Publishers.

Adams, Richard N. 1970. *Crucifixion by Power: Essays on Guatemalan National Social Structure, 1944–1966.* Austin: University of Texas Press.

Aguilera Peralta, Gabriel. 1979. "The Massacre at Panzós and Capitalist Development in Guatemala." *Monthly Review* 31 (7): 13–24.

Aguilera Peralta, Gabriel, et al. 1981. *Dialectica del Terror en Guatemala.* San José, Costa Rico: EDUCA.

Akram-Lodhi, A. Haroon. 1992. "Peasant and Hegemony in the Work of James C. Scott." *Peasant Studies* 19 (3&4): 179–201.

Albizures, Miguel Angel. 1980. "Struggles and Experiences of the Guatemalan Trade-Union Movement, 1976–June 1978." *Latin American Perspectives* 7 (2&3): 145–159.

———. 1987. *Tiempo de Sudor y Lucha*. Mexico City: n.p.

Alvarez, Sonia E., Evelina Dagnino, and Arturo Escobar, ed. 1998. *Cultures of Politics, Politics of Cultures: Re-Visioning Latin American Social Movements*. Boulder, CO: Westview Press.

Amenta, Edwin, Neal Caren, Tina Fetner, and Michael P. Young. 2002. "Challengers and States: Toward a Political Sociology of Social Movements." *Research in Political Sociology* 10: 47–83.

Amenta, Edwin, Bruce G. Carruthers, and Yvonne Zylan. 1992. "A Hero for the Aged? The Townsend Movement, the Political Mediation Model, and U.S. Old-Age Policy, 1934–1950." *American Journal of Sociology* 98 (2): 308–339.

Amenta, Edwin, and Yvonne Zylan. 1991. "It Happened Here: Political Opportunity, the New Institutionalism, and the Townsend Movement." *American Sociological Review* 56 (2): 250–265.

Americas Watch. 1982. *U.S. Reporting on Human Rights in El Salvador: Methodology at Odds with Knowledge*. New York: Americas Watch.

———. 1984. *Protection of the Weak and Unarmed: The Dispute Over Counting Human Rights Violations in El Salvador*. New York: Americas Watch.

———. 1986. *Settling into Routine: Human Rights Abuses in Duarte's Second Year*. New York: Americas Watch Committee.

———. 1988. *Nightmare Revisited 1987–88: 10th Supplement to the Report on Human Rights in El Salvador*. New York: Americas Watch Committee.

———. 1990. *A Year of Reckoning: El Salvador a Decade after the Assassination of Archbishop Romero*. New York: Americas Watch Committee.

———. 1991. *El Salvador's Decade of Terror: Human Rights since the Assassination of Archbishop Romero*. New Haven: Yale University Press.

———. 1993. *El Salvador. Accountability and Human Rights: The Report of the United Nations Commission on the Truth for El Salvador*. New York: Americas Watch.

Aminzade, Ronald. 1984. "Capitalist Industrialization and Patterns of Industrial Protest: A Comparative Urban Study of Nineteenth-Century France." *American Sociological Review* 49 (August): 437–453.

Aminzade, Ronald and Doug McAdam. 2001. "Emotions and Contentious Politics." Pp. 14–50. In *Silence and Voice in the Study of Contentious Politics*, ed. Ronald R. Aminzade et al. New York: Cambridge University Press.

Aminzade, Ronald, and Elizabeth J. Perry. 2001. "The Sacred, Religious, and Secular in Contentious Politics: Blurring Boundaries." Pp. 155–178. In *Silence and Voice in the Study of Contentious Politics*, ed. Ronald R. Aminzade, et al. New York: Cambridge University Press.

Amnesty International. 1981a. *"Disappearances": A Workbook*. New York: Amnesty International.

———. 1981b. *Guatemala: A Government Program of Political Murder*. New York: Amnesty International.

References

Anderson, Leslie E. 1990. "Post-Materialism from a Peasant Perspective: Political Motivation in Costa Rica and Nicaragua." *Comparative Political Studies* 23 (1): 80–113.

1994. *The Political Ecology of the Modern Peasant: Calculation and Community*. Baltimore: Johns Hopkins University Press.

Anderson, Leslie E., and Mitchell A. Seligson. 1994. "Reformism and Radicalism among Peasants: An Empirical Test of Paige's Agrarian Revolution." *American Journal of Political Science* 38 (4): 944–972.

Anderson, Thomas P. 1971. *Matanza: El Salvador's Community Revolt of 1932*. Lincoln, NE: University of Nebraska Press.

Andrews, Kenneth T. 1997. "The Impacts of Social Movements on the Political Process: The Civil Rights Movement and Black Electoral Politics in Mississippi." *American Sociological Review* 62 (5): 800–819.

Arias, Arturo. 2001a. "La Quema de la Embajada de España en Guatemala: La Versión de Maximo Cajal y la Construcción Ideológica de la Versión Defendida por Stoll." *Meeting of the Latin American Studies Association, Washington D.C., September 6–8.*

ed. 2001b. *The Rigoberta Menchú Controversy*. Minneapolis, MN: University of Minnesota Press.

Arnson, Cynthia J. 1993. *Crossroads: Congress, the President, and Central America, 1976–1993*, 2nd ed. University Park: Pennsylvania State University Press.

ASIES. 1995. *Más de 100 Años del Movimiento Obrero Urbano en Guatemala, v. 3: Reorganización, Auge y Desarticulación del Movimiento Sindical (1954–1982)*. Guatemala City: Asociación de Investigación y Estudios Sociales Guatemala.

1995. *Más de 100 Años del Movimiento Obrero Urbano en Guatemala, v. 4: Recomposición y Busqueda de Unidad del Movimiento Sindical (1982–1990)*. Guatemala City: Asociación de Investigación y Estudios Sociales Guatemala.

Astorga Lira, Enrique. 1975. *Evaluación de las Asentamientas y Cooperativas Campesinas en Honduras*. Tegucigalpa: Instituto Nacional Agrario.

AWC/ACLU. 1982. *Report on Human Rights in El Salvador*. New York: Random House.

Aya, Rod. 1979. "Theories of Revolution Reconsidered." *Theory and Society* 8: 39–99.

Babb, Sarah. 1996. "A True American System of Finance: Frame Resonance in the U.S. Labor Movement, 1866 to 1886." *American Sociological Review* 61 (6): 1033–1052.

Ball, Patrick. 1999. *AAAS/CIIDH Database of Human Rights Violations in Guatemala (ATV20.1)*. http://hrdata.aaas.org/ciidh/data.html (downloaded May 2000).

Ball, Patrick, Paul Kobrak, and Herbert F. Spirer. 1999. *State Violence in Guatemala, 1960–1966: A Quantitative Reflection*. Washington, DC: American Association for the Advancement of Science.

Baloyra, Enrique. 1982. *El Salvador in Transition*. Chapel Hill: University of North Carolina Press.

Barkey, Karen. 1991. "Rebellious Alliances: The State and Peasant Unrest in Early Seventeenth-Century France and the Ottoman Empire." *American Sociological Review* 56 (6): 699–715.

Barkey, Karen, and Ronan Van Rossem. 1997. "Networks of Contention: Villages and Regional Structure in the Seventeenth-Century Ottoman Empire." *American Journal of Sociology* 102 (5): 1345–1388.

Barndt, Deborah. 1985. "Popular Education." Pp. 317–345. In *Nicaragua: The First Five Years*, ed. Thomas W. Walker. Boulder, CO: Praeger.

Barnes, Samuel, Barbara G. Farah, and Felix Heunks. 1979. "Personal Dissatisfaction." Pp. 381–408. In *Political Action: Mass Participation in Five Western Democracies*, ed. Samuel H. Barnes and Max Kaase. Beverly Hills: Sage.

Bastos, Santiago, and Manuela Camus. 1996. *Quebrando el Silencio: Organizaciones del Pueblo Maya y Sus Demandas*. Guatemala City: FLACSO.

Beissinger, Mark R. 2002. *Nationalist Mobilization and the Collapse of the Soviet State*. New York: Cambridge University Press.

Béjar, Rafael G. 1990. "El Movimiento Sindical después de la Segunda guerra Mundial en El Salvador." *Estudios Centroamericanos* 45 (504): 871–892.

Benford, Robert D., and David A. Snow. 2000. "Framing Processes and Social Movements: An Overview and Assessment." *Annual Review of Sociology* 26: 611–639.

Benn, Stanley. 1979. "The Problematic Rationality of Political Participation." In *Philosophy, Politics and Society*, ed. Peter Laslett and James Fishkin. New Haven: Yale University Press.

Berejikian, Jeffrey. 1992. "Revolutionary Collective Action and the Agent-Structure Problem." *American Political Science Review* 86 (3): 647–657.

Berger, Peter L. 1975. "The False Consciousness of 'Consciousness Raising.'" *Worldview* 33–38.

Berryman, Phillip. 1984. *The Religious Roots of Rebellion: Christians in Central American Revolutions*. Maryknoll, NY: Orbis Books.

Betancur, Belisario, Reinaldo Figueredo Planchart, and Thomas Buergenthal. 1993. *From Madness to Hope: The Twelve-Year War in El Salvador; Truth for El Salvador*. New York: United Nations.

Billings, Dwight B. 1990. "Religion as Opposition: A Gramscian Analysis." *American Journal of Sociology* 96 (1): 1–31.

Binford, Leigh. 1996. *The El Mozote Massacre*. Tucson: University of Arizona Press.
    1997. "Grassroots Development in Conflict Zones of Northeastern El Salvador." *Latin American Perspectives* 24 (2): 56–79.

Black, George. 1981. *Triumph of the People*. London: Zed Press.
    1983a. "Garrison Guatemala." *NACLA Report on the Americas* 17: 1.
    1983b. "Guatemala – The War Is Not Over." *NACLA Report on the Americas* 17: 2.

Blacklock, Cathy, and Laura Macdonald. 1998. "Human Rights and Citizenship in Guatemala and Mexico: From 'Strategic' to 'New' Universalism." *Social Politics* 5: 2.

Blasier, Cole. 1976. *The Hovering Giant: U.S. Responses to Revolutionary Change in Latin America*. Pittsburgh: University of Pittsburgh Press.

Booth, John A. 1980. "A Guatemalan Nightmare: Levels of Political Violence, 1966–1972." *Journal of Interamerican Studies and World Affairs* 22 (2): 195–220.

References

1982. *The End and the Beginning: The Nicaraguan Revolution*, 2nd ed. Boulder, CO: Westview Press.

1991. "Socioeconomic and Political Roots of National Revolts in Central America." *Latin American Research Review* 26 (1): 33–74.

Booth, John A., and Patricia Bayer Richard. 1999. "The Effects of Repression, Political Violence, and Pain and Loss on Social Capital in Central America." Paper presented at Annual Meeting of the American Political Science Association., September 1–5, Atlanta.

Boswell, Terry, and William J. Dixon. 1990. "Dependency and Rebellion: A Cross-National Analysis." *American Sociological Review* 55 (4): 540–559.

1993. "Marx's Theory of Rebellion: A Cross-National Analysis of Class Exploitation, Economic Development, and Violent Revolt." *American Sociological Review* 58 (5): 681–702.

Boudreau, Vincent. 1996. "Northern Theory, Southern Protest: Opportunity Structure Analysis in Cross-National Perspective." *Mobilization* 1 (2): 175–189.

Bowen, Gordon. 1985. "The Political Economy of State Terrorism: Barrier to Human Rights in Guatemala." In *Human Rights and Third World Development*, ed. George W. Shepherd Jr. and Ved P. Nanda. Westport, CT: Greenwood Press.

Bracamonte, José Angel Moroni, and David E. Spencer. 1995. *Strategy and Tactics of the Salvadoran FMLN Guerrillas: Last Battle of the Cold War, Blueprint for Future Conflicts*. Westport, CT: Praeger.

Brams, Steven J. 1997. "Game Theory and Emotions." *Rationality and Society* 9 (1): 91–124.

Brett, Edward T., and Donna W. Brett. 1988. "Facing the Challenge: The Catholic Church in Honduras." In *Central America: Historical Perspectives on the Contemporary Crises*, ed. Ralph Lee Woodward Jr. New York: Greenwood Press.

Brintnall, Douglas E. 1979. *Revolt against the Dead: The Modernization of a Mayan Community in the Highlands of Guatemala*. New York: Gordon and Breach.

Brockett, Charles D. 1991a. "Sources of State Terrorism in Central America." Pp. 59–76. In *State Organized Terror: The Case of Violent Internal Repression*, ed. P. Timothy Bushnell et al. Boulder, CO: Westview Press.

1991b. "The Structure of Political Opportunities and Peasant Mobilization in Central America." *Comparative Politics* 23 (3): 253–274.

1992. "Measuring Political Violence and Land Inequality in Central America." *American Political Science Review* 86 (1): 169–176.

1995. "A Protest-Cycle Resolution of the Repression/Popular-Protest Paradox." Pp. 117–144. In *Repertoires and Cycles of Collective Action*, ed. Mark Traugott. Durham: Duke University Press.

1998. *Land, Power, and Poverty: Agrarian Transformation and Political Conflict in Central America*, 2nd. ed. Boulder, CO: Westview Press.

2002. "An Illusion of Omnipotence: U.S. Policy toward Guatemala, 1954–1960." *Latin American Politics and Society* 44 (1): 91–126.

2003. "The Quantitative Study of Domestic Political Violence and Measurement Error." Unpublished manuscript.

Brown, Cynthia, ed. 1985. *With Friends Like These: The Americas Watch Report on Human Rights and U.S. Policy in Latin America*. New York: Pantheon Books.

Bruner, Jerome. 1994. "The View from the Heart's Eye: A Commentary." Pp. 269–286. In *The Heart's Eye: Emotional Influences in Perception and Attention*, ed. Paula M. Niedenthal and Shinobu Kitayama. San Diego: Academic Press.

Brush, Stephen G. 1996. "Dynamics of Theory Change in the Social Sciences: Relative Deprivation and Collective Violence." *Journal of Conflict Resolution* 40 (4): 523–545.

Burgos Debray, Elizabeth, ed. 1984. *I, Rigoberta Menchú: An Indian Woman in Guatemala*. London: Verso.

Burstein, Paul. 1998. "Interest Organizations, Political Parties, and the Study of Democratic Politics." Pp. 39–56. In *Social Movements and American Political Institutions*, ed. Anne N. Costain and Andrew S. McFarland. New York: Rowman & Littlefield.

Bwy, Douglas P. 1968. "Political Instability in Latin America: The Cross-Cultural Test of a Causal Model." *Latin American Research Review* 3 (2): 17–66.

Cabarrús, Carlos R. 1983a. "El Salvador: De Movimientos Campesinos y Revolución popular, v. 2." In *Historia Política de los Campesinos Latinoamericanos*, ed. Pablo González Casanova. 77–115. Mexico: siglo veintiuno editores.

    1983b. *Génesis de una Revolución: Análisis del Surgimiento y Desarrollo de la Organización campesina en El Salvador*. Mexico, City: Ediciones de la Casa Chata.

Cacioppo, John T., and Wendi L. Gardner. 1999. "Emotion." *Annual Review of Psychology* 50: 191–214.

Calhoun, Craig. 1982. *The Question of Class Struggle: Social Foundations of Popular Radicalism during the Industrial Revolution*. Chicago: University of Chicago Press.

    1988. "The Radicalism of Tradition and the Question of Class Struggle." Pp. 129–175. In *Rationality and Revolution*, ed. Michael Taylor. New York: Cambridge University Press.

Calvert, Randall. 2000. "Rationality, Identity, and Expression." Paper presented at Annual Meeting of the American Political Science Association, Aug. 30–Sept. 3, Washington, DC.

Campos, Jose E. L., and Hilton L. Root. 1995. "Markets, Norms, and Peasant Rebellions: A Rational-Choice Approach with Implications for Rural Development." *Rationality and Society* 7 (1): 93–115.

Campos, Tomás R. 1979. "El Papel de las Organizaciones Populares en la Actual Situación del País." *Estudios Centroamericanos* 34 (372–373): 923–946.

Cardenal, Rodolfo. 1987. *Historia de una Esperanza: Vida de Rutilio Grande*. San Salvador: UCA Editores.

Carmack, Robert M. 1988. "The Story of Santa Cruz Quiché." Pp. 39–69. In *Harvest of Violence: The Maya Indians and the Guatemala Crisis*, ed. Robert M. Carmack. Norman: University of Oklahoma Press.

Carpio, Salvador Cayetano. 1993. "La Huelga General Obrera de Abril de 1967." In *Siembra de Vientos: El Salvador 1960–69*, ed. Victor Valle. San Salvador: Centro de Investigación y Acción Social.

References

Carranza, Salvador. 1977. "Aguilares: Una Experiencia de Evangelización Rural Parroquial (Septiembre de 1972–Agosto de 1974)." *Estudios Centroamericanos* 32 (348–349): 838–853.

Carter, W. E. 1969. *New Lands and Old Traditions: Kekchi Cultivators in the Guatemalan Lowlands*. Gainesville: University of Florida Press.

Casper, Norman. 1986. "El IADSL y la Corrupción del Movimiento Sindical de El Salvador." *Estudios Centroamericanos* 40 (449): 205–229.

Castro Torres, Carlos Felipe. 1978. "Crecimiento de las luchas campesinas en Guatemala, Febrero 1976–Mayo 1978." *Estudios Centroamericanos* 33 (356–357): 462–477.

CEH. 1999. *Informe de la Comisión para el Esclarecimiento Histórico*. Guatemala City: UNOPS.

Chirot, Daniel, and Charles Ragin. 1975. "The Market, Tradition, and Peasant Rebellion: The Case of Romania in 1907." *American Sociological Review* 40: 428–444.

Colburn, Forrest D. 1994. *The Vogue of Revolution in Poor Countries*. Princeton: Princeton University Press.

Collins, Randall. 2001. "Social Movements and the Focus of Emotional Attention." Pp. 27–44. In *Passionate Politics: Emotions and Social Movements*, ed. Jeff Goodwin, James M. Jasper, and Francesca Polletta. Chicago: University of Chicago Press.

Corbin, David. 1981. *Life, Work, and Rebellion in the Coal Fields: The Southern West Virginia Miners, 1880–1922*. Urbana: University of Illinois Press.

Corr, Edwin G. 1991. "Preface." Pp. xiii–xix. In *The Comandante Speaks: Memoirs of an El Salvadoran Guerrilla Leader*, ed. Courtney E. Prisk. Boulder, CO: Westview Press.

Corradi, Juan E., Patricia Weiss Fagen, and Manuel Antonio Garretón, ed. 1992. *Fear at the Edge: State Terror and Resistance in Latin America*. Berkeley: University of California Press.

Costain, Anne N. 1992. *Inviting Women's Rebellion: A Political Process Interpretation of the Women's Movement*. Baltimore: Johns Hopkins University Press.

Costain, Anne N., and Andrew S. McFarland, ed. 1998. *Social Movements and American Political Institutions*. New York: Rowman & Littlefield.

Crane, George T. 1994. "Collective Identity, Symbolic Mobilization, and Student Protest in Nanjing, China, 1988–1989." *Comparative Politics* 26 (4): 395–413.

Cuzán, Alfred G. 1990. "Resource Mobilization and Political Opportunity in the Nicaraguan Revolution: The Theory." *American Journal of Economics and Sociology* 49 (4): 401–412.

Davenport, Christian. 2000. "Introduction." Pp. 1–24. In *Paths to State Repression: Human Rights Violations and Contentious Politics*, ed. Christian Davenport. Lanham, MD: Rowman & Littlefield.

Davies, James C. 1962. "Toward a Theory of Revolution." *American Sociological Review* 27 (1): 5–19.

Davis, David R., and Michael D. Ward. 1990. "They Dance Alone: Deaths and Disappeared in Contemporary Chile." *Journal of Conflict Resolution* 34 (3): 449–475.

Davis, Shelton H. 1983a. "The Social Roots of Political Violence in Guatemala." *Cultural Survival Quarterly* 7 (1): 4–11.

1983b. "State Violence and Agrarian Crisis in Guatemala." Pp. 155–171. In *Trouble in Our Backyard: Central America and the United States in the Eighties*, ed. Martin Diskin. New York: Pantheon.

Debray, Régis. 1967. *Revolution in the Revolution? Armed Struggle and Political Struggle in Latin America*. New York: Grove Press.

della Porta, Donatella. 1992. "Introduction: On Individual Motivations in Underground Political Organizations." *International Social Movement Research* 4: 3–28.

1995. *Social Movements, Political Violence, and the State: A Comparative Analysis of Italy and Germany*. New York: Cambridge University Press.

Denardo, James. 1984. *Power in Numbers: The Political Strategy of Protest and Rebellion*. Princeton: Princeton University Press.

Deng, Fang. 1997. "Information Gaps and Unintended Outcomes of Social Movements: The 1989 Chinese Student Movement." *American Journal of Sociology* 102 (4): 1085–1112.

Diacon, Todd A. 1991. *Millenarian Vision, Capitalist Reality: Brazil's Contestado Rebellion, 1912–1916*. Durham: Duke University Press.

Diani, Mario. 1996. "Linking Mobilization Frames and Political Opportunities: Insights from Regional Populism in Italy." *American Sociological Review* 61 (6): 1053–1069.

Diskin, Martin. 1995. "El Salvador: Reform Prevents Change." Pp. 429–450. In *Broken Promises: Agrarian Reform and the Latin American Campesino*, ed. William C. Thiesenhusen. Boulder, CO: Westview Press.

1996. "Distilled Conclusions: The Disappearance of the Agrarian Question in El Salvador." *Latin American Research Review* 31 (2): 111–126.

Dixon, William J., Edward N. Muller, and Mitchell A. Seligson. 1993. "Inequality and Political Violence Revisited." *American Political Science Review* 87 (4): 983–994.

Dobyns, Henry F., Paul L. Doughty, and Harold D. Lasswell. 1971. *Peasants, Power, and Applied Social Change: Vicos as a Model*. Beverly Hills: Sage.

Dodson, Michael, and Laura Nuzzi O'Shaughnessy. 1990. *Nicaragua's Other Revolution: Religious Faith and Political Struggle*. Chapel Hill: University of North Carolina Press.

Duberman, Martin. 1993. *Stonewall*. New York: Dutton.

Dunkerley, James. 1982. *The Long War: Dictatorship and Revolution in El Salvador*. London: Junction Books.

Earle, Duncan. 2001. "Menchú Tales and Maya Social Landscapes: The Silencing of Words and Worlds." Pp. 288–308. In *The Rigoberta Menchú Controversy*, ed. Arturo Arias. Minneapolis, MN: University of Minnesota Press.

Ebel, Roland H. 1988. "When Indians Take Power: Conflict and Consensus in San Juan Ostuncalco." Pp. 174–191. In *Harvest of Violence: The Maya Indians and the Guatemala Crisis*, ed. Robert M. Carmack. Norman: University of Oklahoma Press.

References

ECA. 1978. "Los Sucesos de San Pedro Perulapán." *Estudios Centroamericanos* 33 (354): 223–247.

    1987. "La Cuestión de las Masas (editorial)." *Estudios Centroamericanos* 42 (465): 415–434.

Eckstein, Susan, ed. 2001. *Power and Popular Protest: Latin American Social Movements*, 2nd ed. Berkeley: University of California Press.

Eisinger, Peter K. 1973. "The Conditions of Protest Behavior in American Cities." *American Political Science Review* 67 (1): 11–28.

Elster, Jon. 1999. *Alchemies of the Mind: Rationality and the Emotions*. New York: Cambridge University Press.

Emirbayer, Mustafa. 1997. "Manifesto for a Relational Sociology." *American Journal of Sociology* 103 (2): 281–317.

Emirbayer, Mustafa, and Jeff Goodwin. 1994. "Network Analysis, Culture, and the Problem of Agency." *American Journal of Sociology* 99 (6): 1411–1454.

Escobar, Arturo, and Sonia E. Alvarez, ed. 1992. *The Making of Social Movements in Latin America: Identity, Strategy, and Democracy*. Boulder, CO: Westview Press.

Evans, Peter, Dietrich Rueschemeyer, and Theda Skocpol, ed. 1985. *Bringing the State Back In*. New York: Cambridge University Press.

Evans, Sara M. and Harry C. Boyle. 1986. *Free Spaces: The Sources of Democratic Change in America*. New York: Harper.

Eyerman, Ron. 1981. *False Consciousness and Ideology in Marxist Theory*. Atlantic Highlands, NJ: Humanities Press.

Falla, Ricardo. 1978. *Quiché Rebelde*. Guatemala City: Editorial Universitaria de Guatemala.

    2001. *Quiché Rebelde: Religious Conversion, Politics, and Ethnic Identity in Guatemala*. Translated by Phillip Berryman. Austin: University of Texas Press.

Feierabend, Ivo K., Betty Nesvold, and Rosalind L. Feierabend. 1970. "Political Coerciveness and Turmoil: A Cross-National Inquiry." *Law and Society Review* 5 (1): 93–118.

Femia, Joseph. 1975. "Hegemony and Consciousness in the Thought of Antonio Gramsci." *Political Studies* 23 (1): 29–48.

Fernández, Damián. 2000. *Cuba and the Politics of Passion*. Austin: University of Texas Press.

Fernández, José M. 1988. *El Comité de Unidad Campesina: Origen y Desarrollo*. Guatemala, City: Centro de Estudios Rurales Centroamericanos.

Ferree, Myra Marx. 1992. "The Political Context of Rationality: Rational Choice Theory and Resource Mobilization." Pp. 29–52. In *Frontiers in Social Movement Theory*, ed. Aldon D. Morris and Carol McClurg Mueller. New Haven: Yale University Press.

Figueroa Ibarra, Carlos. 1991. *El Recurso del Miedo: Ensayo Sobre el Estado y El Terror en Guatemala*. San José, Guatemala: EDUCA.

Fine, Gary A. and Kent Sandstrom. 1993. "Ideology in Action: A Pragmatic Approach to a Contested Concept." *Sociological Theory* 11 (1): 21–38.

Finkel, Steven E., Edward N. Muller, and Karl-Dieter Opp. 1989. "Personal Influence, Collective Rationality, and Mass Political Action." *American Political Science Review* 83: 885–903.

Finkel, Steven E., and James B. Rule. 1986. "Relative Deprivation and Related Psychological Theories of Civil Violence: A Critical Review." *Research in Social Movements, Conflicts and Change* 9: 47–69.

Fireman, Bruce, and William A. Gamson. 1979. "Utilitarian Logic in the Resource Mobilization Perspective." Pp. 8–44. In *The Dynamics of Social Movements: Resource Mobilization, Social Control, and Tactics*, ed. Mayer N. Zald and John D. McCarthy. Cambridge, MA: Winthrop.

Flam, Helena. 1996. "Anxiety and the Successful Oppositional Construction of Societal Reality: The Case of KOR." *Mobilization* 1 (1): 103–121.

Foley, Michael W. 1990. "Organizing, Ideology, and Moral Suasion: Political Discourse and Action in a Mexican Town." *Comparative Study of Society and History* 455–487.

Foroohar, Manzar. 1989. *The Catholic Church and Social Change in Nicaragua*. Albany: State University of New York Press.

Francisco, Ronald A. 1995. "The Relationship between Coercion and Protest: An Empirical Evaluation in Three Coercive States." *Journal of Conflict Resolution* 39 (2): 263–282.

Frank, Robert H. 1988. *Passions within Reason: The Strategic Role of the Emotions*. New York: Norton.

——— 1990. "A Theory of Moral Sentiments." Pp. 71–96. In *Beyond Self-Interest*, ed. Jane J. Mansbridge. Chicago: University of Chicago Press.

Freire, Paulo. 1970a. *Cultural Action for Freedom*. Cambridge, MA: Center for the Study of Development and Social Change.

——— 1970b. *Pedagogy of the Oppressed*. New York: Seabury Press.

——— 1973. *Education for Critical Consciousness*. New York: Seabury Press.

Friedan, Betty. 1963. *The Feminine Mystique*. New York: Dell.

Gallardo, Aria Eugenia, and José Roberto López. 1986. *Centroamérica: La Crisis en Cifras*. San José, Costa Rica: Instituto Interamericano de Ciencias Sociales.

Gamson, William A., Bruce Fireman, and Steven Rytina. 1982. *Encounters with Unjust Authority*. Homewood, IL: Dorsey Press.

García, Juan José. 1983. "Las Fuerzas Laborales ante el Nuevo Proyecto Norteamericano." *Estudios Centroamericanos* 38 (415–416): 501–506.

Garson, G. David. 1973. "Automobile Workers and the Radical Dream." *Politics and Society* 3: 163–179.

Gaventa, John. 1980. *Power and Powerlessness: Quiescence and Rebellion in an Appalachian Valley*. Urbana: University of Illinois Press.

Gelb, Joyce. 1989. *Feminism and Politics: A Comparative Perspective*. Berkeley: University of California Press.

Gilly, Adolfo. 1965. "The Guerrilla Movement in Guatemala I." *Monthly Review* 17 (May): 9–40.

Giugni, Marco G., Doug McAdam, and Charles Tilly, ed. 1998. *From Contention to Democracy*. 1998. Lanham, MA: Rowman & Littlefield.

——— 1999. *How Social Movements Matter*. Minneapolis: University of Minnesota Press.

References

Gleijeses, Piero. 1991. *Shattered Hope: The Guatemalan Revolution and the United States, 1944–1954*. Princeton: Princeton University Press.

Goldston, James A. 1989. *Shattered Hope: Guatemalan Workers and the Promise of Democracy*. Boulder, CO: Westview Press.

Goldstone, Jack A. 1994. "Is Revolution Individually Rational? Groups and Individuals in Revolutionary Collective Action." *Rationality and Society* 6 (1): 139–166.

    1998a. "Initial Conditions, General Laws, Path Dependence, and Explanations in Historical Sociology." *American Journal of Sociology* 104 (3): 829–845.

    1998b. "Social Movements or Revolutions? On the Evolution and Outcomes of Collective Action." Pp. 125–145. In *From Contention to Democracy*, ed. Marco G. Giugni, Doug McAdam, and Charles Tilly. Lanham, MD: Rowman & Littlefield.

    2001. "Toward a Fourth Generation of Revolutionary Theory." *Annual Review of Political Science* 4: 139–187.

    2003. "Introduction: Bridging Institutionalized and Noninstitutionalized Politics." Pp. 1–24. In *States, Parties, and Social Movements*, ed. Jack A. Goldstone. New York: Cambridge University Press.

Goldstone, Jack A., and Charles Tilly. 2001. "Threat (and Opportunity): Popular Action and State Response in the Dynamics of Contentious Action." Pp. 179–194. In *Silence and Voice in the Study of Contentious Politics*, ed. Ronald R. Aminzade et al. New York: Cambridge University Press.

Goodwin, Jeff. 2001. *No Other Way Out: States and Revolutionary Movements, 1945–1991*. New York: Cambridge University Press.

Goodwin, Jeff, and James M. Jasper. 1999. "Caught in a Winding, Snarling Vine: The Structural Bias of Political Process Theory." *Sociological Forum* 14, (1): 27–54.

Goodwin, Jeff, James M. Jasper, and Francesca Polletta. 2001a. "Introduction: Why Emotions Matter." Pp. 1–24. In *Passionate Politics: Emotions and Social Movements*. Chicago: University of Chicago Press.

    2001b. *Passionate Politics: Emotions and Social Movements*. Chicago: University of Chicago Press.

Goodwin, Jeff, and Steven Pfaff. 2001. "Emotion Work in High-Risk Social Movements: Managing Fear in the U.S. and East German Civil Rights Movements." Pp. 282–302. In *Passionate Politics: Emotions and Social Movements*, ed. Jeff Goodwin, James M. Jasper, and Francesca Polletta. Chicago: University of Chicago Press.

Goodwin, Jeff, and Theda Skocpol. 1989. "Explaining Revolutions in the Contemporary Third World." *Politics and Society* 17(4): 489–509.

Gott, Richard. 1972. *Guerrilla Movements in Latin America*. Garden City, NY: Doubleday Anchor Books.

Gould, Deborah. 2001. "Rock the Boat, Don't Rock the Boat, Baby: Ambivalence and the Emergence of Militant AIDS Activism." Pp. 135–157. In *Passionate Politics: Emotions and Social Movements*, ed. Jeff Goodwin, James M. Jasper, and Francesca Polletta. Chicago: University of Chicago Press.

Gould, Jeffry. 1990. *To Lead As Equals: Rural Protest and Political Consciousness in Chinandega, Nicaragua, 1912–1979*. Chapel Hill: University of North Carolina Press.

Gould, Roger V. 1991. "Multiple Networks and Mobilization in the Paris Commune, 1871." *American Sociological Review* 56 (6): 716–729.

Gramsci, Antonio. 1971. *Selections from the Prison Notebooks*. London: Wishart.

Grandin, Greg. 1997. "To End with All These Evils: Ethnic Transformation and Community Mobilization in Guatemala's Western Highlands, 1954–1980." *Latin American Perspectives* 24 (2): 7–34.

Granovetter, Mark. 1978. "Threshold Models of Collective Behavior." *American Journal of Sociology* 83 (6): 1420–1443.

Grenier, Yvon. 1999. *The Emergence of Insurgency in El Salvador: Ideology and Political Will*. Pittsburgh: University of Pittsburgh Press.

Gupta, Dipak K., Harinder Singh, and Tom Sprague. 1993. "Government Coercion of Dissidents: Deterrrence or Provocation." *Journal of Conflict Resolution* 37 (2): 301–339.

Gurney, Joan, and Kathleen Tierney. 1982. "Relative Deprivation and Social Movements: A Critical Look at Twenty Years of Theory and Research." *Sociological Quarterly* 23 (1): 33–47.

Gurr, Ted R. 1970. *Why Men Rebel*. Princeton: Princeton University Press.

    1986. "The Political Origins of State Violence and Terror: A Theoretical Analysis." In *Government Violence and Repression: An Agenda for Research*, ed. Michael Stohl and George A. Lopez. New York: Greenwood.

    1993. "Why Minorities Rebel: A Global Analysis of Communal Mobilization and Conflict since 1945." *International Political Science Review* 14 (2): 161–201.

Gurr, Ted R., and Raymond Duvall. 1973. "Civil Conflict in the 1960s: A Reciprocal Theoretical System with Parameter Estimates." *Comparative Political Studies* 6 (2): 135–170.

Haines, Gerald K. 1995. *CIA and Guatemala Assassination Proposals 1952–1954*. Washington, DC: Center for the Study of Intelligence, Central Intelligence Agency.

Hammond, John L. 1998. *Fighting to Learn: Popular Education and Guerrilla War in El Salvador*. New Brunswick, NJ: Rutgers University Press.

Handy, Jim. 1984. *Gift of the Devil: A History of Guatemala*. Boston: South End Press.

Hannigan, John A. 1991. "Social Movement Theory and the Sociology of Religion: Toward a New Synthesis." *Sociological Analysis* 52 (4): 311–331.

Harnecker, Marta. 1984. *Pueblos en Armas*. Mexico City: Ediciones Era.

    1990a. *America Latina: Izquierda y Crisis Actual*. Mexico City: Siglo Veintiuno Editores.

    1990b. *El Salvador: Movimiento de las Masas Urbano antes y durante la Guerra*. Pub. unk.

    1993. *Con la Mirada en Alto: Historia de las Fuerzas Populares de Liberación Farabundo Martí a Través de Entrevistas con sus Dirigentes*. San Salvador: UCA Editores.

Hatfield, Elaine, John T. Cacioppo, and Richard L. Rapson. 1994. *Emotional Contagion*. New York: Cambridge University Press.

References

Hechter, Michael. 1987. *Principles of Group Solidarity.* Berkeley: University of California Press.

Hernández Pico, Juan, César Jerez, Ignacio Ellacuria, Emilio Baltodano, and Roman Mayorga Q. 1973. *El Salvador: Año Político 1971–72.* San Salvador: Universidad Centro Americana.

Hibbs Jr., Douglas A. 1973. *Mass Political Violence: A Cross-National Causal Analysis.* New York: Wiley Interscience.

Hipsher, Patricia L. 1998. "Democratic Transitions as Protest Cycles: Social Movement Dynamics in Democratizing Latin America." Pp. 153–172. In *The Social Movement Society: Contentious Politics for a New Century*, ed. David S. Meyer and Sidney Tarrow. Lanham, MD: Rowman & Littlefield.

Hirsch, Eric L. 1990. "Sacrifice for the Cause: Group Processes, Recruitment, and Commitment in a Student Social Movement." *American Sociological Review* 55 (2): 243–254.

Hobsbawm, Eric. J. 1959. *Primitive Rebels: Studies in Archaic Forms of Social Movement in the 19th and 20th Centuries.* Manchester: Manchester University Press.

Hogan, R., and N. Emler. 1981. "Retributive Justice." Pp. 125–44. In *The Justice Motive in Social Behavior: Adapting to Times of Scarcity and Change*, ed. M. Lerner and S. Lerner. New York: Plenum Press.

Hoover, Dean, and David Kowalewski. 1992. "Dynamic Models of Dissent and Repression." *Journal of Conflict Resolution* 36 (1): 150–182.

Huizer, Gerrit. 1972. *The Revolutionary Potential of Peasants in Latin America.* Lexington, MA: Lexington Books.

Human Rights Watch. 1994. *Honduras: The Facts Speak for Themselves (The Preliminary Report of the National Commissioner for the Protection of Human Rights in Honduras).* New York: Human Rights Watch.

IADS (International Agricultural Development Service). 1978. *Agricultural Development Indicators.* New York: IADS.

IDHUCA (Instituto de Derechos Humanos). 1988. *La resistencia no violenta ante los regímenes salvadoreños que ha utilizado el terror institucionalizado en el período 1972–1987.* San Salvador: IDHUCA, Universidad Centroamericana.

ILO (International Labour Organization). 1975, 1985, 1995. *Year Book of Labour Statistics.* Geneva, Switzerland: ILO.

Isaacs, Kenneth S. 1998. *Uses of Emotion: Nature's Vital Gift.* Westport, CT: Praeger.

IUDOP (Instituto Universitario de Opinión Pública). 1987. "Tres años de política gubernamental y el incremento de las movilizaciones populares de protesta." *Estudios Centroamericanos* 42 (463–468): 283–304.

(Instituto Universitario de Opinión Pública). 1989. "La Opinión Pública ante los Primeros Cien Días del Gobierno de Cristiani." *Estudios Centroamericanos* 44 (490/491): 715–726.

1990 "La Opinión Pública a un Año del Gobierno de Cristiani." *Estudios Centroamericanos* 45 (500–501): 507–516.

IWGIA (International Work Group for Indigenous Affairs). 1978. *Guatemala 1978: The Massacre at Panzós.* Copenhagen: IWGIA.

Jasper, James M. 1997. *The Art of Moral Protest.* Chicago: University of Chicago Press.

1998. "The Emotions of Protest: Affective and Reactive Emotions in and around Social Movements." *Sociological Forum* 13 (3): 397–424.

Jasper, James M., and Jeff Goodwin (Jaswin). 1999. "Trouble in Paradigms." *Sociological Forum* 14 (1): 107–127.

Javeline, Debra. 2003. "The Role of Blame in Collective Action: Evidence from Russia." *American Political Science Review* 97 (1): 107–121.

Jenkins, J. Craig. 1983a. "Resource Mobilization Theory and the Study of Social Movements." *Annual Review of Sociology* 9: 527–553.

1983b. "Why Do Peasants Rebel? Structural and Historical Theories of Modern Peasant Rebellions." *American Journal of Sociology* 88 (3): 487–514.

1985. *The Politics of Insurgency: The Farm Worker Movement in the 1960s*. New York: Columbia University Press.

Jenkins, J. Craig, and Charles Perrow. 1977. "Insurgency of the Powerless: Farm Worker Movements (1946–1972)." *American Sociological Review* 42 (2): 249–268.

Jenkins, J. Craig, and Kurt Schock. 1992. "Global Structures and Political Processes in the Study of Domestic Political Conflict." *Annual Review of Sociology*: 18 161–185.

Jessop, Bob. 1982. *The Capitalist State: Marxist Theories and Methods*. New York: New York University Press.

Johnson, Kenneth F. 1973. "On the Guatemalan Political Violence." *Politics and Society* 4 (1): 55–83.

Johnston, Hank, and Carol Mueller. 2001. "Unobtrusive Practices of Contention in Leninist Regimes." *Sociological Perspectives* 44 (3): 351–375.

Jonas, Susanne. 1991. *The Battle for Guatemala: Rebels, Death Squads, and U.S. Power*. Boulder, CO: Westview Press.

Joseph, Gilbert. 1986. *Rediscovering the Past at Mexico's Periphery*. Birmingham: University of Alabama Press.

Kerbo, Harold R. 1982. "Movements of 'Crisis' and Movements of 'Affluence.'" *Journal of Conflict Resolution* 25 (4): 645–663.

Khawaja, Marwan. 1993. "Repression and Popular Collective Action: Evidence from the West Bank." *Sociological Forum* 8 (1): 47–71.

Kincaid, Douglas. 1985. "We Are the Agrarian Reform: Rural Politics and Agrarian Reform." Pp. 135–147. In *Honduras: Portrait of a Captive Nation*, ed. Nancy Peckenham and Annie Street. New York: Praeger.

Kingdon, John W. 1984. *Agendas, Alternatives, and Pubic Policies*. Boston: Little, Brown.

Kitayama, Shinobu, and Paula M. Niedenthal. 1994. "Introduction." Pp. 1–13. In *The Heart's Eye: Emotional Influences in Perception and Attention*, ed. Paula M. Niedenthal and Shinobu Kitayama. San Diego: Academic Press.

Kitschelt, Herbert P. 1986. "Political Opportunity Structures and Political Protest: Anti-Nuclear Movements in Four Democracies." *British Journal of Political Science* 16 (1): 57–85.

Klandermans, Bert. 1984. "Mobilization and Participation: Social-Psychological Expansions of Resource Mobilization Theory." *American Sociological Review* 49: 583–600.

References

1986. "New Social Movements and Resource Mobilization: The European and the American Approach." *International Journal of Mass Emergencies and Disasters* 4 (2): 13–37.

1990. "Linking the 'Old' and the 'New': Movement Networks in the Netherlands." P.p.122–136. In *Challenging the Political Order: New Social and Political Movements in Western Democracies*, ed. Russell J. Dalton and Manfred Kuechler. New York: Oxford University Press.

1992. "The Social Construction of Protest and Multiorganizational Fields." Pp. 77–103. In *Frontiers in Social Movement Theory*, ed. Aldon D. Morris and Carol McClurg Mueller. New Haven: Yale University Press.

1997. *The Social Psychology of Protest*. Cambridge: Blackwell.

Klandermans, Bert, and Sidney Tarrow. 1988. "Mobilization into Social Movements: Synthesizing European and American Approaches." Pp. 1–38. In *From Structure to Action: Comparing Social Movement Research across Cultures*, ed. Bert Klandersman, Hanspeter Kriesi, and Sidney Tarrow. Greenwich, CT: JAI.

Knoke, David. 1990. *Organizing for Collective Action: The Political Economics of Associations*. New York: Aldine de Gruyter.

Kobrak, Paul. 1997. *Village Troubles: The Civil Patrols in Aguacatán, Guatemala*. Unpublished Ph. D. dissertation, University of Michigan.

1999. *Organizing and Repression in the University of San Carlos, Guatemala, 1944 to 1996*. Washington, DC: American Association for the Advancement of Science.

Koopmans, Ruud. 1993. "The Dynamics of Protest Waves: West Germany, 1965 to 1989." *American Sociological Review* 58 (5): 637–658.

1998. "The Use of Protest Event Data in Comparative Research: Cross-National Comparability, Sampling Methods and Robustness." Pp. 90–110. In *Acts of Dissent: New Developments in the Study of Protest*, ed. Dieter Rucht, Ruud Koopmans, and Friedhelm Neidhardt. Berlin: Edition Sigma.

1999. "Political Opportunity Structure: Some Splitting to Balance the Lumping." *Sociological Forum* 14 (1): 93–105.

2001. "Better Off by Doing Good: Why Antiracism Must Mean Different Things to Different Groups." Pp. 111–131. In *Political Altruism? Solidarity Movements in International Perspective*, ed. Marco Giugni and Florence Passy. New York: Rowman & Littlefield.

Koopmans, Ruud, and Dieter Rucht. 1999. "Introduction to Special Issue: Protest Event Analysis – Where to Now?" *Mobilization* 4 (2): 123–130.

Krain, Matthew. 1997. "State-Sponsored Mass Murder: The Onset and Severity of Genocides and Politicides." *Journal of Conflict Resolution* 41 (3): 331–360.

2000. *Repression and Accommodation in Post-Revolutionary States*. New York: St. Martin's Press.

Kselman, Thomas A. 1986. "Ambivalence and Assumption in the Concept of Popular Religion." Pp. 24–41. In *Religion and Political Conflict in Latin America*, ed. Daniel H. Levine. Chapel Hill: University of North Carolina Press.

Kuper, Leo. 1981. *Genocide: Its Political Use in the Twentieth Century*. New Haven: Yale University Press.

Kuran, Timur. 1989. "Sparks and Prairie Fires: A Theory of Unanticipated Political Revolution." *Public Choice* 61 (1): 41–74.

———. 1995. *Private Truths, Public Lies: The Social Consequences of Preference Falsification.* Cambridge, MA: Harvard University Press.

Kurian, George T. 1982. *Encyclopedia of the Third World.* New York: Facts on File.

Kurzman, Charles. 1996. "Structural Opportunity in Social-Movement Theory: The Iranian Revolution of 1979." *American Sociological Review* 61 (1): 153–170.

Lachmann, Richard. 1997. "Agents of Revolution: Elite Conflicts and Mass Mobilization from the Medici to Yeltsin." Pp. 73–101. In *Theorizing Revolutions*, ed. John Foran. New York: Routledge.

Lancaster, Roger N. 1988. *Thanks to God and the Revolution: Popular Religion and Class Consciousness in the New Nicaragua.* New York: Columbia University Press.

Laqueur, Walter. 1976. *Guerrilla: A Historical and Critical Study.* Boston: Little, Brown.

Law, Kim S., and Edward J. Walsh. 1983. "The Interaction of Grievances and Structures in Social Movement Analysis: The Case of JUST." *Sociological Quarterly* 24: 123–136.

Lears, T. J. Jackson. 1985. "The Concept of Cultural Hegemony: Problems and Possibilities." *American Historical Review* 90 (3): 567–593.

Le Bot, Yvon. 1995. *La Guerra en Tierras Mayas: Comunidad, Violencia y Modernidad en Guatemala (1970–1992).* Translated by María Antonía Neira Bigorra. México City: Fondo de Cultura Económica.

Lee, Chris, Sandra Maline, and Will H. Moore. 2000. "Coercion and Protest: An Empirical Test Revisited." Pp. 127–147. In *Paths to State Repression: Human Rights Violations and Contentious Politics*, ed. Christian Davenport. Lanham, MD: Rowman & Littlefield.

LeGrand, Catherine. 1986. *Frontier Expansion and Peasant Protest in Colombia, 1850–1936.* Albuquerque: University of New Mexico Press.

Leiken, Robert S. 1984. "The Salvadoran Left." Pp. 111–130. In *Central America: Anatomy of Conflict*, ed. Robert S. Leiken. New York: Pergamon.

Lemarchand, René. 1990. "Burundi: Ethnicity and the Genocidal State." Pp. 89–112. In *State Violence and Ethnicity*, ed. Piere L. van den Berghe. Niwot: University Press of Colorado.

LeoGrande, William M. 1998. *Our Own Backyard: The United States in Central America, 1977–1992.* Chapel Hill: University of North Carolina Press.

Lernoux, Penny. 1980. *Cry of the People.* New York: Doubleday.

Levenson-Estrada, Deborah. 1994. *Trade Unionists Against Terror: Guatemala City, 1954–1985.* Chapel Hill: University of North Carolina Press.

Levine, Daniel H. 1990a. "How Not to Understand Liberation Theology, Nicaragua, or Both (Review Essay)." *Journal of Interamerican Studies and World Affairs* 32 (3): 229–246.

———. 1990b. "Popular Groups, Popular Culture, and Popular Religion." *Comparative Studies in Society and History* 32 (4): 718–764.

Lichbach, Mark I. 1987. "Deterrence or Escalation? The Puzzle of Aggregate Studies of Repression and Dissent." *Journal of Conflict Resolution* 31, (2): 266–297.

References

1989. "An Evaluation of 'Does Economic Inequality Breed Political Conflict?' Studies." *World Politics* 41 (4): 431–470.

1995a. "The 5% Rule." *Rationality and Society* 7 (1): 126–128.

1995b. *The Rebel's Dilemma*. Ann Arbor: University of Michigan Press.

1997. "Contentious Maps of Contentious Politics." *Mobilization* 2 (1): 87–98.

1998. "Contending Theories of Contentious Politics and the Structure-Action Problem of Social Order." *Annual Review of Political Science* 1: 401–424.

Lichbach, Mark I., and Ted R. Gurr. 1981. "The Conflict Process: A Formal Model." *Journal of Conflict Resolution* 25 (1): 3–30.

Lindo-Fuentes, Hector. 1981. "El Salvador: Inflación y Salarios." *Estudios Centroamericanos* 36 (395): 899–901.

Lindstrom, Ronny, and Will H. Moore. 1995. "Deprived, Rational or Both? 'Why Minorities Rebel' Revisited." *Journal of Political and Military Sociology* 23 (2): 167–190.

Lofland, John.1985. *Protest: Studies of Collective Behavior and Social Movements*. New Brunswick, NJ: Transaction Books.

Lopez, George A. 1986. "National Security Ideology as an Impetus to State Violence and State Terror." Pp. 73–95. In *Government Violence and Repression: An Agenda for Research*, ed. Michael Stohl and George A. Lopez. New York: Greenwood Press.

1988. "Terrorism in Latin America." Pp. 497–524. In *Terrible Beyond Endurance? The Foreign Policy of State Terrorism*, ed. Michael Stohl and George A. Lopez. New York: Greenwood Press.

López Larrave, Mario. 1976. *Breve Historia del Movimiento Sindical Guatemalteco*. Guatemala City: Editorial Universitaria.

López Vallecillos, Italo. 1979. "Rasgos Sociales y Tendencias Políticas en El Salvador (1969–1979)." *Estudios Centroamericanos* 34 (372–373): 863–884.

López Vallecillos, Italo, and Víctor A. Orellana. 1980. "La Unidad Popular y el Surgimiento del Frente Democrático Revolucionario." *Estudios Centroamericanos* 35 (377–378): 183–206.

Luciak, Ilja A. 1995. *The Sandinista Legacy: Lessons from a Political Economy in Transition*. Gainesville: University Press of Florida.

Lungo Uclés, Mario. 1996. *El Salvador in the Eighties: Counterinsurgency and Revolution*. Translated by Amelia F. Shogan. Philadelphia: Temple University Press.

Lupsha, Peter A. 1971. "Explanation of Political Violence: Some Psychological Theories Versus Indignation." *Politics and Society* 2 (1): 89–104.

Magagna, Victor V. 1991. *Communities of Grain: Rural Rebellion in Comparative Perspective*. Ithaca: Cornell University Press.

Mann, Michael. 1973. *Consciousness and Action among the Western Working Class*. London: Macmillan.

Mansbridge, Jane J. 1990. "The Rise and Fall of Self-Interest in the Explanation of Political Life." Pp. 3–22. In *Beyond Self-Interest*, ed. Jane J. Mansbridge. Chicago: University of Chicago Press.

Marcus, George E. 2000. "Emotions in Politics." *Annual Review of Political Science* 3: 221–250.

Marcus, George E., W. Russell Neuman, and Michael MacKuen. 2000. *Affective Intelligence and Political Judgment*. Chicago: University of Chicago Press.

Markoff, John. 1997. "Peasants Help Destroy an Old Regime and Defy a New One: Some Lessons from (and for) the Study of Social Movements." *American Journal of Sociology* 102 (4): 1113–1142.

Marks, Gary, and Doug McAdam. 1999. "On the Relationship of Political Opportunities to the Form of Collective Action: The Case of the European Union." Pp. 97–111. In *Social Movements in a Globalizing World*, ed. Donatella della Porta, Hanspeter Kriesi, and Dieter Rucht. New York: St. Martin's Press.

Martin, JoAnn. 1992. "When the People Were Strong and United: Stories of the Past and the Transformation of Politics in a Mexican Community." Pp. 177–189. In *The Paths to Domination, Resistance, and Terror*, ed. Carolyn Nordstrom and JoAnn Martin. Berkeley: University of California Press.

Martin, Joanne, and Alan Murray. 1984. "Catalysts for Collective Violence: The Importance of a Psychological Approach." In *The Sense of Injustice: Social Psychological Perspectives*, ed. Robert Folger. New York: Plenum Press.

Martín-Baró, Ignacio. 1973. "Psicología del Campesino Salvadoreño." *Estudios Centroamericanos* 28 (297–298): 476–495.

1990. "Religion as an Instrument of Psychological Warfare." *Journal of Social Issues* 46 (3): 93–107.

Marx, Karl. 1959. "Excerpt from 'Toward the Critique of Hegel's Philosophy of Right.'" In *Marx and Engels: Basic Writings on Politics and Philosophy*, ed. Lewis S. Feuer. New York: Doubleday Anchor Books.

Mason, T. David. 1989. "Nonelite Response to State-Sanctioned Terror." *Western Political Quarterly* 42: 467–492.

Mason, T. David, and Dale A. Krane. 1989. "The Political Economy of Death Squads: Toward a Theory of the Impact of State-Sanctioned Terror." *International Studies Quarterly* 33: 175–198.

McAdam, Doug. 1982. *Political Process and the Development of Black Insurgency 1930–1970*. Chicago: University of Chicago Press.

1988. "Micro-mobilization Contexts and Recruitment to Activism." Pp. 243–297. In *From Structure to Action: Comparing Social Movement Research Across Cultures*, ed. Bert Klandermans, Hanspeter Kriesi, and Sidney Tarrow. Greenwich, CT: JAI Press.

1994. "Culture and Social Movements." Pp. 36–57. In *New Social Movements: From Ideology to Identity*, ed. Enrique Laraña, Hank Johnston, and Joseph R. Gusfield. Philadelphia: Temple University Press.

1996. "Conceptual Origins, Current Problems, Future Directions." Pp. 23–40. In *Comparative Perspectives on Social Movements: Political Opportunities, Mobilizing Structures, and Cultural Frames*, ed. Doug McAdam, John D. McCarthy, and Mayer N. Zald. New York: Cambridge University Press.

1998. "On the International Origins of Domestic Political Opportunities." Pp. 251–267. In *Social Movements and American Political Institutions*, ed. Anne N. Costain and Andrew S. McFarland. New York: Rowman & Littlefield.

References

McAdam, Doug, John D. McCarthy, and Mayer N. Zald, ed. 1996. *Comparative Perspectives on Social Movements: Political Opportunities, Mobilizing Structures, and Cultural Frames*. New York: Cambridge University Press.

McAdam, Doug, and Ronnelle Paulsen. 1993. "Specifying the Relationship between Social Ties and Activism." *American Journal of Sociology* 99 (3): 640–667.

McAdam, Doug, and William H. Sewell Jr. 2001. "It's About Time: Temporality in the Study of Social Movements and Revolution." Pp. 89–125. In *Silence and Voice in the Study of Contentious Politics*, ed. Ronald R. Aminzade, et al. New York: Cambridge University Press.

McAdam, Doug, Sidney Tarrow, and Charles Tilly. 1996. "To Map Contentious Politics." *Mobilization* 1 (1): 17–34.

1997. "Toward an Integrated Perspective on Social Movement and Revolution." Pp. 142–173. In *Comparative Politics: Rationality, Culture, and Structure*, ed. Mark I. Lichbach and Alan S. Zuckerman. New York: Cambridge University Press.

2001. *Dynamics of Contention*. New York: Cambridge University Press.

McCamant, John F., and Ernest A. Duff, with Waltraud Q. Morales. 1976. *Violence and Repression in Latin America: a Quantitative and Historical Analysis*. New York: Free Press.

McCarthy, John D., and Mayer N. Zald. 1977. "Resource Mobilization and Social Movements: A Partial Theory." *American Journal of Sociology* 82: 1212–1241.

McClintock, Cynthia. 1984. "Why Peasants Rebel: The Case of Peru's Sendero Luminoso." *World Politics* 37 (1): 48–84.

1998. *Revolutionary Movements in Latin America: El Salvador's FMLN and Peru's Shining Path*. Washington DC: U.S. Institute of Peace.

McClintock, Michael. 1985a. *The American Commentary: Volume 1: State Terror and Popular Resistance in El Salvador*. London: Zed Books Ltd.

1985b. *The American Commentary: Volume 2: State Terror and Popular Resistance in Guatemala*. London: Zed Books Ltd.

McElhinny, Vincent, and Mitchell A. Seligson. 2001. "From Civil War to Civil Violence: The Impact of Agrarian Inequality in El Salvador." Paper presented at Annual Meeting of the American Political Science Association, Washington DC, September 6–8.

McPhail, Clark, and David Schweingruber. 1998. "Unpacking Protest Events: A Description Bias Analysis of Media Records with Systematic Direct Observations of Collective Action – The 1995 March for Life in Washington, D.C." In *Acts of Dissent: New Developments in the Study of Protest*, ed. Dieter Rucht, Ruud Koopmans, and Friedhelm Neidhardt. Berlin: Edition Sigma.

Meléndez, Mario. 1997. "Entrevista: Fernando Hoyos." Pp. 185–202. In *Fernando Hoyos? Donde Estás?*, ed. María Pilar Hoyos de Asig. Guatemala City: Fondo de Cultura Editorial.

Menjivar, Rafael. 1979. *Formación y Lucha del Proletariado Industrial Salvadoreño*. San Salvador: UCA Editores.

Merton, Robert K. 1996. *On Social Structure and Science*, ed. Piotr Sztompka. Chicago: University of Chicago Press.

Meyer, David S. 1990. *A Winter of Discontent: The Nuclear Freeze and American Politics*. New York: Praeger.

1999. "Tending the Vineyard: Cultivating Political Process Research." *Social Forum* 14 (1): 72–92.

Meyer, David S., and Sidney Tarrow, ed. 1998. *The Social Movement Society: Contentious Politics for a New Century*. Lanham, MD: Rowman & Littlefield.

Midlarsky, Manus I. 1988. "Rulers and the Ruled: Patterned Inequality and the Onset of Mass Political Violence." *American Political Science Review* 82 (2): 491–510.

Midlarsky, Manus I., and Kenneth Roberts. 1985. "Class, State, and Revolution in Central America." *Journal of Conflict Resolution* 29 (2): 163–193.

Migdal, Joel S. 1974. *Peasants, Politics, and Revolution: Pressures toward Political and Social Change in the Third World*. Princeton: Princeton University Press.

Miller, D. and N. Vidmar. 1981. "The Social Psychology of Punishment Reactions." Pp. 145–172. In *The Justice Motive in Social Behavior: Adapting to Times of Scarcity and Change*, ed. M. Lerner and S. Lerner. New York: Plenum Press.

Millett, Richard. 1977. *Guardians of the Dynasty*. Maryknoll, NY: Orbis Books.

Minkoff, Debra C. 1997. "The Sequencing of Social Movements." *American Sociological Review* 62 (5): 779–799.

Moaddel, Mansoor. 1992. "Ideology as Episodic Discourse: The Case of the Iranian Revolution." *American Sociological Review* 57 (3): 353–379.

Moise, Edwin E. 1982. "The Moral Economy Dispute." *Bulletin of Concerned Asian Scholars* 14 (1): 72–77.

Monroe, Kristen R. 1991a. "John Donne's People: Explaining Differences between Rational Actors and Altruists through Cognitive Frameworks." *Journal of Politics* 53 (2): 394–453.

1991b. "The Theory of Rational Action: Origins and Usefulness for Political Science." Pp. 1–31. In *The Economic Approach to Politics: A Critical Reassessment of the Theory of Rational Action*, ed. Kristen R. Monroe. New York: Harper Collins.

2001. "Paradigm Shift: From Rational Choice to Perspective." *International Political Science Review* 22 (2): 151–172.

Monroe, Kristen R., Michael C. Barton, and Ute Klingemann. 1991. "Altruism and the Theory of Rational Action: An Analysis of Rescuers of Jews in Nazi Europe." Pp. 317–352. In *The Economic Approach to Politics: A Critical Reassessment of the Theory of Rational*, ed. Kristen R. Monroe. New York: Harper Collins.

Montes, Segundo. 1980. *El Agro Salvadoreño (1973–1980)*. San Salvador: Universidad Centroamericana.

Montgomery, Tommie Sue. 1982–1983. "Cross and Rifle: El Salvador and Nicaragua." *Journal of International Affairs* 36 (2): 209–221.

1995. *Revolution in El Salvador*, 2nd ed. Boulder, CO: Westview Press.

Moore, Barrington. 1978. *Injustice: The Social Basis of Obedience and Revolt*. White Plains, NY: M. E. Sharpe.

References

Moore, Will H. 1995a. "Action-Reaction or Rational Expectations?" *Journal of Conflict Resolution* 39 (1): 129–167.

1995b. "Rational Rebels: Overcoming the Free-Rider Problem." *Political Research Quarterly* 48 (2): 417–454.

1998. "Repression and Dissent: Substitution, Context, and Timing." *American Journal of Political Science* 42: 851–873.

2000. "The Repression of Dissent: A Substitution Model of Government Coercion." *Journal of Conflict Resolution* 44 (1): 107–127.

Morales Velado, Oscar A. et al. 1988. *La Resistencia No Violenta ante los Regimenes Salvadoreños que Han Utilizado el Terror Institucionalizado en el Periodo 1972–1987*. San Salvador: Universidad Centroamericana.

Morris, Aldon D. 1993. "Birmingham Confrontation Reconsidered: An Analysis of the Dynamics and Tactics of Mobilization." *American Sociological Review* 58 (5): 621–636.

1996. "The Black Church in the Civil Rights Movement: The SCLC as the Decentralized, Radical Arm of the Black Church." Pp. 29–46. In *Disruptive Religion: The Force of Faith in Social-Movement Activism*, ed. Christian Smith. New York: Routledge.

Morris, Aldon D., and Carol McClurg Mueller, ed. 1992. *Frontiers in Social Movement Theory*. New Haven: Yale University Press.

Morris, James, and Steve C. Ropp. 1977. "Corporatism and Dependent Development, a Honduran Case Study." *Latin American Research Review* 12 (2): 27–68.

Morrissey, James A. 1978. "A Missionary Directed Resettlement Project among the Highland Maya of Western Guatemala." Unpublished Ph.D. dissertation, Stanford University.

Muller, Edward N. 1972. "A Test of a Partial Theory of Potential for Political Violence." *American Political Science Review* 66 (3): 928–959.

1979. *Aggressive Political Participation*. Princeton: Princeton University Press.

Muller, Edward N., S. Finkel, and H. Dietz. 1991. "Discontent and the Expected Utility of Rebellion: The Case of Peru." *American Political Science Review* 85 (4): 1261–1283.

Muller, Edward N., and Karl-Dieter Opp. 1986. "Rational Choice and Rebellious Collective Action." *American Political Science Review* 80 (2): 471–487.

Muller, Edward N., and Mitchell A. Seligson. 1987. "Inequality and Insurgency." *American Political Science Review* 81 (2): 425–452.

Muller, Edward N., Mitchell A. Seligson, and Hung-der Fu. 1989. "Land Inequality and Political Violence." *American Political Science Review* 83 (2): 577–586.

Muller, Edward N., and Erich Weede. 1990. "Cross-National Variation in Political Violence: A Rational-Action Approach." *Journal of Conflict Resolution* 34 (4): 624–651.

1994. "Theories of Rebellion: Relative Deprivation and Power Contention." *Rationality and Society* 6 (1): 40–57.

Munck, Gerardo L. 1990. "Identity and Ambiguity in Democratic Struggles." Pp. 23–42. In *Popular Movements and Political Change in Mexico*, ed. Joe Foweraker and Ann L. Craig. Boulder, CO: Lynne Rienner.

Munro, Dana. 1918. *The Five Republics of Central America.* New York: Oxford University Press.

Nardin, Terry. 1971. *Violence and the State: A Critique of Empirical Political Theory.* Beverly Hills: Sage.

Nepstad, Sharon E. 1996. "Popular Religion, Protest, and Revolt: The Emergence of Political Insurgency in the Nicaraguan and Salvadoran Churches of the 1960s–80s." Pp. 105–124. In *Disruptive Religion: The Force of Faith in Social-Movement Activism*, ed. Christian Smith. New York: Routledge.

Nisbett, Richard E., and Timothy D. Wilson. 1977. "Telling More Than We Can Know: Verbal Reports on Mental Processes." *Psychological Review* 84 (3): 231–259.

NotiCen. 2002. "Guatemala: Government Accused of Complicity in Threats and Abuses Against Human Rights Defenders, Other Social Activists." *Central American and Caribbean Political and Economic Affairs* (Latin American Data Base, University of New Mexico) 7 (23): June 27.

Oberschall, Anthony R. 1994. "Rational Choice in Collective Protests." *Rationality and Society* 6 (1): 79–100.

1995. *Social Movements: Ideologies, Interests, and Identities.* New Brunswick, NJ: Transaction Press.

O'Donnell, Guillermo. 1973. *Modernization and Bureaucratic-Authoritarianism: Studies in South American Politics.* Berkeley: University of California.

Oliver, Pamela. 1984. "'If You Don't Do It, Nobody Else Will': Active and Token Contributors to Local Collective Action." *American Sociological Review* 49 (5): 601–610.

1993. "Formal Models of Collective Action." *Annual Review of Sociology* 19: 271–300.

Olson, Mancur. 1965. *The Logic of Collective Action.* Cambridge, MA: Harvard University Press.

Opp, Karl-Deiter. 1988. "Grievances and Participation in Social Movements." *American Sociological Review* 53: 853–864.

1989. *The Rationality of Political Protest: A Comparative Analysis of Rational Choice Theory.* Boulder, CO: Westview Press.

1994. "Repression and Revolutionary Action: East Germany in 1989." *Rationality and Society* 6 (1): 101–138.

Opp, Karl-Deiter, and Christiane Gern. 1993. "Dissident Groups, Personal Networks, and Spontaneous Cooperation: The East German Revolution of 1989." *American Sociological Review* 58 (5): 659–680.

Opp, Karl-Deiter, and Wolfgang Roehl. 1990. "Repression, Micromobilization, and Political Protest." *Social Forces* 69 (2): 521–547.

Paige, Jeffery M. 1975. *Agrarian Revolution: Social Movements and Export Agriculture in the Underdeveloped World.* New York: Free Press.

1983. "Social Theory and Peasant Revolution in Vietnam and Guatemala." *Theory and Society* 12 (6): 699–737.

1985. "Cotton and Revolution in Nicaragua." Pp. 91–114. In *State versus Market in the World-System*, ed. Peter Evans et al. Beverly Hills: Sage.

References

1996. "Land Reform and Agrarian Revolution in El Salvador: Comment on Seligson and Diskin." *Latin American Research Review* 31 (2): 127–139.

Parkman, Patricia. 1988. *Nonviolent Insurrection in El Salvador: The Fall of Maximiliano Hernández Martínez*. Tucson: University of Arizona Press.

Parks, Craig D., and Anh D. Vu. 1994. "Social Dilemma Behavior of Individuals from Highly Individualist and Collectivist Cultures." *Journal of Conflict Resolution* 38 (4): 708–718.

Parsa, Misagh. 2000. *States, Ideologies, and Social Revolutions: A Comparative Analysis of Iran, Nicaragua and the Philippines*. New York: Cambridge University Press.

Payeras, Mario. 1983. *Days of the Jungle: The Testimony of a Guatemalan Guerrillero, 1972–1976*. New York: Monthly Review Press.

Pearce, Jenny. 1986. *Promised Land: Peasant Rebellion in Chalatenango El Salvador*. London: Latin America Bureau.

Perera, Victor. 1993. *Unfinished Conquest: The Guatemalan Tragedy*. Berkeley: University of California Press.

Petersen, Roger D. 2001. *Resistance and Rebellion: Lessons from Eastern Europe*. New York: Cambridge University Press.

2003. *Understanding Ethnic Violence: Fear, Hatred, and Resentment in Twentieth-Century Eastern Europe*. New York: Cambridge University Press.

Peterson, Anna L. 1997. *Martyrdom and the Politics of Religion: Progressive Catholicism in El Salvador's Civil War*. Albany: State University of New York Press.

Pion-Berlin, David. 1989. *The Ideology of State Terror: Economic Doctrine and Political Repression in Argentina and Peru*. Boulder, CO: Lynne Rienner.

Piven, Frances Fox, and Richard A. Cloward. 1977. *Poor People's Movements: Why They Succeed, How They Fail*. New York: Vintage Books.

1995. "Collective Protest: A Critique of Resource-Mobilization Theory." Pp. 137–167. In *Social Movements: Critiques, Concepts, Case-Studies*, ed. Stanford M. Lyman. New York: New York University Press.

Poblete Troncoso, Moisés, and Ben G. Burnett. 1962. *The Rise of the Latin American Labor Movement*. New Haven, CT: College & University Press.

Polletta, Francesca. 1999. "Snarls, Quacks, and Quarrels: Culture and Structure in Political Process Theory." *Sociological Forum* 14 (1): 63–70.

Polletta, Francesca, and Edwin Amenta. 2001. "Conclusion: Second That Emotion? Lessons from Once-Novel Concepts in Social Movement Research." Pp. 303–316. In *Passionate Politics: Emotions and Social Movements*, ed. Jeff Goodwin, James M. Jasper, and Francesca Polletta. Chicago: University of Chicago Press.

Popkin, Samuel L. 1979. *The Rational Peasant*. Berkeley: University of California Press.

1988. "Political Entrepreneurs and Peasant Movements in Vietnam." Pp. 9–62. In *Rationality and Revolution*, ed. Michael Taylor. New York: Cambridge University Press.

Porpora, Douglas V. 1985. "The Role of Agency in History: The Althusser-Thompson-Anderson Debate." *Current Perspectives in Social Theory* 6: 219–241.

Prisk, Courtney E., ed. 1991. *The Comandante Speaks: Memoirs of an El Salvadoran Guerrilla Leader*. Boulder, CO: Westview Press.

Prosterman, Roy L., and Jeffrey M. Riedinger. 1987. *Land Reform and Democratic Development*. Baltimore: Johns Hopkins University Press.

Ramírez, Chiqui. 2001. *La Guerra de los 36 Años: Vista con Ojos de Mujer de Izquierda*. Guatemala: Editorial Palacios.

Rasler, Karen. 1996. "Concessions, Repression, and Political Protest in the Iranian Revolution." *American Sociological Review* 61 (1): 132–152.

Raudales, Walter, and Juan Ramón Medrano. 1994. *Ni Militar Ni Sacerdote*. San Salvador: Ediciones Arcoiris.

Reed, Thomas F., and Karen Brandow. 1996. *The Sky Never Changes: Testimonies from the Guatemalan Labor Movement*. Ithaca: Cornell University Press.

REMHI. 1999. *Guatemala Never Again! The Official Report of the Human Rights Office, Archdiocese of Guatemala*. Maryknoll, NY: Orbis Books.

Richards, Michael. 1985. "Cosmopolitan World View and Counterinsurgency in Guatemala." *Anthropological Quarterly* 58 (3): 90–107.

Robinson, Thomas D., and Bruce London. 1991. "Dependency, Inequality, and Political Violence: A Cross-National Analysis." *Journal of Political and Military Sociology* 19 (1): 119–156.

Rochon, Thomas R. 1988. *Mobilizing for Peace: The Antinuclear Movements in Western Europe*. Princeton: Princeton University Press.

Roeder, Philip G. 1984. "Legitimacy and Peasant Revolution: An Alternative to Moral Economy." *Peasant Studies* 11, 149–168.

Ropp, Steve C. 1974. "The Honduran Army in the Sociopolitical Evolution of the Honduran State." *The Americas* 30 (4): 504–528.

Rucht, Dieter, and Friedhelm Neidhardt. 1998. "Methodological Issues in Collecting Protest Event Data: Units of Analysis, Sources and Sampling, Coding Problems." Pp. 65–89. In *Acts of Dissent: New Developments in the Study of Protest*, ed. Dieter Rucht, Ruud Koopmans, and Friedhelm Neidhardt. Berlin: Edition Sigma.

Rucht, Dieter, and Thomas Ohlemacher. 1992. "Protest Event Data: Collection, Uses and Perspectives." Pp. 76–106. In *Studying Collective Action*, ed. Mario Diani and Ron Eyerman. London: Sage.

Rudé, George. 1980. *Ideology and Popular Protest*. New York: Pantheon Books.

Rus, Jan. 1999. "Introduction: If Truth Be Told: A Forum on David Stoll's *Rigoberta Menchú and the Story of All Poor Guatemalas*." *Latin American Perspectives* 26 (6): 5–14.

Sanford, Victoria. 2003. *Buried Secrets: Truth and Human Rights in Guatemala*. New York: Palgrave Macmillan.

Sassoon Showstack, Anne. 1982. "A Gramsci Dictionary." Pp. 12–17. In *Approaches to Gramsci*, ed. Anne Showstack Sassoon. London: Writers and Readers.

Scheff, Thomas J. 1983. "Toward Integration in the Social Psychology of Emotions." *Annual Review of Sociology* 9: 333–354.

    1990. *Microsociology: Discourse, Emotion, and Social Structure*. Chicago: University of Chicago Press.

    1992. "Rationality and Emotion: Homage to Norbert Elias." Pp. 101–119. In *Rational Choice Theory: Advocacy and Critique*, ed. James S. Coleman and Thomas J. Fararo. Newbury Park, CA: Sage.

References

1994. *Bloody Revenge: Emotions, Nationalism, and War*. Boulder, CO: Westview Press.

Scheper-Hughes, Nancy. 1992. *Death Without Weeping: The Violence of Everyday Life in Brazil*. Berkeley: University of California Press.

Schipani, Daniel S. 1984. *Conscientization and Creativity: Paulo Freire and Christian Education*. Lanham, MD: University Press of America.

Schirmer, Jennifer. 1998. *The Guatemalan Military Project: A Violence Called Democracy*. Philadelphia: University of Pennsylvania Press.

Schock, Kurt. 1996. "A Conjunctural Model of Political Conflict: The Impact of Political Opportunities on the Relationship between Economic Inequality and Violent Political Conflict." *Journal of Conflict Resolution* 40 (1): 98–133.

——— 1999a. "People Power and Political Opportunities: Social Movement Mobilization and Outcomes in the Philippines and Burma." *Social Problems* 46 (3): 355–375.

——— 1999b. "The Pro-Democracy Movement in Thailand: Political Opportunities and the 1992 Uprising." Unpublished paper, Weatherhead Center for International Affairs, Harvard University.

Schoultz, Lars. 1981. *Human Rights and United States Policy toward Latin America*. Princeton: Princeton University Press.

——— 1983. "Guatemala: Social Change and Political Conflict." In *Trouble in Our Backyard: Central America and the United States in the Eighties*, ed. Martin Diskin. New York: Pantheon.

Schulz, Markus S. 1998. "Collective Action Across Borders: Opportunity Structures, Network Capacities, and Communicative Praxis in the Age of Advanced Globalization." *Sociological Perspectives* 41 (3): 587–616.

Scott, James C. 1976. *The Moral Economy of the Peasant: Rebellion and Subsistence in Southeast Asia*. New Haven: Yale University Press.

——— 1977. "Hegemony and the Peasantry." *Politics and Society* 7 (3): 267–296.

——— 1979. "Revolution in the Revolution: Peasants and Commisars." *Theory and Society* 7 (1): 97–134.

——— 1985. *Weapons of the Weak: Everyday Forms of Peasant Resistance*. New Haven: Yale University Press.

——— 1990. *Domination and the Arts of Resistance: Hidden Transcripts*. New Haven: Yale University Press.

Selbin, Eric. 1993. *Modern Latin American Revolutions*. Boulder, CO: Westview Press.

——— 1997a. "Contentious Cartography." *Mobilization* 2 (1): 99–106.

——— 1997b. "Revolution in the Real World: Bringing Agency Back In." Pp. 123–136. In *Theorizing Revolutions*, ed. John Foran. New York: Routledge.

Seligson, Mitchell A. 1995. "Thirty Years of Transformation in the Agrarian Structure of El Salvador, 1961–1991." *Latin American Research Review* 30 (3): 43–74.

——— 1996. "Agrarian Inequality and the Theory of Peasant Rebellion." *Latin American Research Review* 31 (2): 140–157.

Seligson, Mitchell A., and Vincent McElhinny. 1996. "Low-Intensity Warfare, High-Intensity Death: The Demographic Impact of the Wars in El Salvador and Nicaragua." *Canadian Journal of Latin American and Caribbean Studies* 21 (42): 211–241.

Sennett, Richard, and Jonathan Cobb. 1972. *The Hidden Injuries of Class*. New York: Vintage Books.

Serra, Luis H. 1986. "Religious Institutions and Bourgeois Ideology in the Nicaraguan Revolution." Pp. 43–116. In *The Church and Revolution in Nicaragua*, ed. Laura Nuzzi O'Shaughnessy and Luis H. Serra. Athens: Ohio University.

Shin, Gi-Wook. 1994. "The Historical Making of Collective Action: The Korean Peasant Uprisings of 1946." *American Journal of Sociology* 99 (6): 1596–1624.

Sider, Gerald M. 1980. "The Ties That Bind: Culture and Agriculture, Property and Propriety in the Newfoundland Village Fishery." *Social History* 5 (1): 1–39.

Singelmann, Peter. 1981. *Structures of Domination and Peasant Movements in Latin America*. Columbia: University of Missouri Press.

Skocpol, Theda. 1979. *States and Social Revolutions: A Comparative Analysis of France, Russia and China*. Cambridge: Cambridge University Press.

   1982. "What Makes Peasants Revolutionary?" *Comparative Politics* 14 (3): 351–375.

Smelser, Neil J. 1998. "The Rational and the Ambivalent in the Social Sciences." *American Sociological Review* 63 (1): 1–16.

Smith, Christian. 1991. *The Emergence of Liberation Theology: Radical Religion and Social Movement Theory*. Chicago: University of Chicago Press.

   1996a. "Correcting a Curious Neglect, or Bringing Religion Back In." Pp. 1–25. In *Disruptive Religion: The Force of Faith in Social-Movement Activism*, ed. Christian Smith. New York: Routledge.

   ed. 1996b. *Disruptive Religion: The Force of Faith in Social-Movement Activism*. New York: Routledge.

Snow, David A., and Robert D. Benford. 1988. "Ideology, Frame Resonance, and Participation Mobilization." Pp. 197–217. In *From Structure to Action: Social Movement Participation across Cultures*, ed. Bert Klandermans, Hanspeter Kriesi, and Sidney Tarrow. Greenwich, CT: JAI Press.

Snow, David A., Daniel M. Cress, Liam Downey, and Andrew W. Jones. 1998. "Disrupting the 'Quotidian': Reconceptualizing the Relationship between Breakdown and the Emergence of Collective Action." *Mobilization* 3 (1): 1–22.

Snow, David A., and Pamela E. Oliver. 1995. "Social Movements and Collective Behavior: Social Psychological Dimensions and Considerations." Pp. 571–599. In *Sociological Perspectives on Social Psychology*, ed. Karen S. Cook, Gary A. Fine, and James S. House. Boston: Allyn and Bacon.

Snow, David A., E. Burke Rochford, Steven Worden, and Robert D. Benford. 1986. "Frame Alignment Processes, Micromobilization, and Movement Participation." *American Sociological Review* 51: 464–481.

Snow, David A., Louis A. Zurcher Jr., and Sheldon Ekland-Olson. 1980. "Social Networks and Social Movements: A Microstructural Approach to Differential Recruitment." *American Sociological Review* 45 (5): 787–801.

Solís, Claudia. 1990. "La dinámica socio-laboral en el Primer Año del Gobierno de ARENA." *Estudios Centroamericanos* 45 (500–501): 465–477.

References

Somers, Margaret R. 1998. "'We're No Angels': Realism, Rational Choice, and Relationality in Social Science." *American Journal of Sociology* 104 (3): 722–784.

Spilka, Bernard, Phillip Shaver, and Lee A. Kirkpatrick. 1985. "A General Attribution Theory for the Psychology of Religion." *Journal for the Scientific Study of Religion* 24 (1): 1–20.

Stanley, William. 1996. *The Protection Racket State: Elite Politics, Military Extortion, and Civil War in El Salvador*. Philadelphia: Temple University Press.

Stokes, Susan C. 1991. "Hegemony, Consciousness, and Political Change in Peru." *Politics and Society* 19 (3): 265–290.

Stoll, David. 1993. *Between Two Armies in the Ixil Towns of Guatemala*. New York: Columbia University Press.

1999. *Rigoberta Menchú and the Story of All Poor Guatemalans*. Boulder, CO: Westview Press.

2001. "The Battle of Rigoberta." In *The Rigoberta Menchú Controversy*, ed. Arturo Arias. Minneapolis: University of Minnesota Press.

Streeter, Stephen M. 2001. "David Stoll." Paper presented at International Congress of the Latin American Studies Association in Washington DC, September 6–8.

Stryker, Sheldon. 1981. "Symbolic Interactionism: Themes and Variations." Pp. 3–29. In *Social Psychology: Sociological Perspectives*, ed. Morris Rosenberg and Ralph H. Turner. New York: Basic Books.

Suh, Doowon. 2001. "How Do Political Opportunities Matter for Social Movements? Political Opportunity, Misframing, Pseudosuccess, and Pseudofailure." *Sociological Quarterly* 42 (3): 437–463.

Tarrow, Sidney. 1988. "National Politics and Collective Action: Recent Theory and Research in Western Europe and the United States." *Annual Review of Sociology* 14, 421–440.

1989. *Democracy and Disorder: Protest and Politics in Italy 1965–1975*. New York: Oxford University Press.

1992. "Mentalities, Political Cultures, and Collective Action Frames: Constructing Meaning through Action." Pp. 174–202. In *Frontiers in Social Movement Theory*, ed. Aldon D. Morris and Carol McClurg Mueller. New Haven: Yale University Press.

1998a. *Power in Movement, 2nd. ed.* New York: Cambridge University Press.

1998b. "Studying Contentious Politics: From Event-ful History to Cycles of Collective Action." Pp. 33–64. In *Acts of Dissent: New Developments in the Study of Protest*, ed. Dieter Rucht, Ruud Koopmans, and Friedhelm Neidhardt. Berlin: Edition Sigma.

Taylor, Charles L., and David A. Jodice. 1983. *World Handbook of Political and Social Indicators*, 3rd ed., v. 2. New Haven: Yale University Press.

1985. *World Handbook of Political and Social Indicators III, 1948–1982*. ICPSR Study 7761. Ann Arbor: Inter-University Consortium for Political and Social Research.

Taylor, Michael. 1988. "Rationality and Revolutionary Collective Action." Pp. 63–97. In *Rationality and Revolution*, ed. Michael Taylor. New York: Cambridge University Press.

Thiesenhusen, William C. 1995. *Broken Promises: Agrarian Reform and the Latin American Campesino.* Boulder, CO: Westview Press.

Thoits, Peggy A. 1989. "The Sociology of Emotions." *Annual Review of Sociology* 15: 317–342.

Thompson, E. P. 1971. "The Moral Economy of the English Crowd in the Eighteenth Century." *Past and Present* 50: 76–136.

1978. "Eighteenth-Century English Society: Class Struggle Without Class." *Social History* 3 (2): 137–165.

Thompson, Kenneth. 1986. *Beliefs and Ideology.* New York: Tavistock.

Tilly, Charles. 1969. "Collective Violence in European Perspective." Pp. 4–45. In *Violence in America: Historical and Comparative Perspectives*, ed. Hugh D. Graham and Ted R. Gurr. New York: Bantam Books.

1978. *From Mobilization to Revolution.* Reading, MA: Addison-Wesley.

1997. "Kings in Beggars' Raiment." *Mobilization* 2 (1): 107–111.

2001. "Do Unto Others." Pp. 27–47. In *Political Altruism? Solidarity Movements in International Perspective*, ed. Marco Giugni and Florence Passy. New York: Rowman & Littlefield.

2003. *The Politics of Collective Violence.* New York: Cambridge University Press.

Time. 1968. "Guatemala: Caught in the Crossfire." *Time* January 26, 23.

Trudeau, Robert H. 1993. *Guatemalan Politics: The People Struggle for Democracy.* Boulder, CO: Lynne Rienner.

Tullock, Gordon. 1995. "Comment: Rationality and Revolution." *Rationality and Society* 7 (1): 116–120.

Turner, Bryan S. 1983. *Religion and Social Theory: A Materialist Perspective.* London: Heinemann.

Turner, Ralph H., and Lewis M. Killian. 1987. *Collective Behavior*, 3rd ed. Englewood Cliffs, NJ: Prentice-Hall.

Tutino, John. 1986. *From Insurrection to Revolution in Mexico: Social Bases of Agrarian Violence 1750–1940.* Princeton: Princeton University Press.

UCA. 1971. *Análisis de una Experiencia Nacional.* San Salvador: Universidad Centroamericana.

U.S. House, U.S. 1982. *Presidential Certification of El Salvador (Volume 1): Hearings before the Subcommittee on Inter-American Affairs, 97th Cong, 2nd Sess.* Washington, DC: U.S. Government Printing Office.

1984. *The Situation in El Salvador. Hearings before the Committee on Foreign Relations, 98th Congress, 2nd. Sess.* Washington DC: U.S. Government Printing Office.

U.S. State. 1982. "A Statistical Framework for Understanding Violence in El Salvador (AmEmbassy San Salvador, January 15, 1982)." Pp. 74–95. In *Presidential Certification of El Salvador (Volume 1): Hearings before the Subcommittee on Inter-American Affairs, 97th Cong, 2nd Sess*, ed. U.S. House. Washington, DC: U.S. Government Printing Office.

Useem, Bert. 1980. "Solidarity Model, Breakdown Model, and the Boston Anti-Busing Movement." *American Sociological Review* 45: 357–369.

1998. "Breakdown Theories of Collective Action." *Annual Review of Sociology* 24: 215–238.

References

Valle, Victor. 1993. *Siembra de Vientos: El Salvador 1960–69*. San Salvador: Centro de Investigación y Acción Social.

Véjar, Rafael G. 1979. "La Crisis Política en El Salvador, 1976–1979." *Estudios Centroamericanos* 34 (369–370): 507–526.

Waddington, David, Karen Jones, and Charles Critcher. 1989. *Flashpoints: Studies in Public Disorder*. New York: Routledge.

Walsh, Edward J. 1981. "Resource Mobilization and Citizen Protest in Communities around Three Mile Island." *Social Problems* 29 (1): 1–21.

Wang, T. Y. 1995. "Dependency, World System Position and Political Violence in Developing Countries." *Journal of Political and Military Sociology* 23 (1): 25–42.

Warren, Kay B. 1978. *The Symbolism of Subordination: Indian Identity in a Guatemalan Town*. Austin: University of Texas.

  1998. *Indigenous Movements and Their Critics: Pan-Maya Activism in Guatemala*. Princeton: Princeton University Press.

Warren, Mark. 1990. "Ideology and the Self." *Theory and Society* 19: 599–634.

Webb, Keith, et al. 1983. "Etiology and Outcomes of Protest: New European Perspectives." *American Behavioral Scientist* 26 (3): 311–331.

Webre, Stephen. 1979. *José Napoleón Duarte and the Christian Democratic Party in Salvadoran Politics 1960–1972*. Baton Rouge: Louisiana State University Press.

Weede, Erich. 1981. "Income Inequality, Average Income, and Domestic Violence." *Journal of Conflict Resolution* 25 (4): 639–654.

  1986. "Income Inequality and Political Violence Reconsidered." *American Sociological Review* 51 (3): 438–445.

White, Christine Pelzer. 1986. "Everyday Resistance, Socialist Revolution and Rural Development: The Vietnamese Case." *Journal of Peasant Studies* 13 (2): 49–63.

White, Robert A. 1977. "Structural Factors in Rural Development: The Church and the Peasant in Honduras." Unpublished Ph.D. dissertation, Cornell University.

Wickham-Crowley, Timothy P. 1991. *Exploring Revolution: Essays on Latin American Insurgency and Revolutionary Theory*. Armonk, NY: M. E. Sharpe.

  1992. *Guerrillas and Revolutions in Latin America: A Comparative Study of Insurgents and Regimes since 1956*. Princeton: Princeton University Press.

  1997. "Structural Theories of Revolution." Pp. 38–72. In *Theorizing Revolutions*, ed. John Foran. New York: Routledge.

Wilkinson, Daniel. 2002. *Silence on the Mountain: Stories of Terror, Betrayal, and Forgetting in Guatemala*. Boston: Houghton Mifflin.

Williams, Philip J., 1989. *The Catholic Church and Politics in Nicaragua and Costa Rica*. Pittsburgh: University of Pittsburgh Press.

Williams, Philip J., and Knut Walter. 1997. *Militarization and Demilitarization in El Salvador's Transition to Democracy*. Pittsburgh: University of Pittsburgh Press.

Willams, Raymond. 1977. *Marxism and Literature*. Oxford: Oxford University Press.

Williams, Robert G. 1986. *Export Agriculture and the Crisis in Central America*. Chapel Hill: University of North Carolina Press.

Wilson, Kenneth L., and Anthony M. Orum. 1976. "Mobilizing People for Collective Political Action." *Journal of Political and Military Sociology* 4 (2): 187–202.

Wolf, Eric R. 1969. *Peasant Wars of the Twentieth Century*. New York: Harper & Row.

Wood, Elisabeth J. 2001. "The Emotional Benefits of Insurgency in El Salvador." Pp. 267–281. In *Passionate Politics: Emotions and Social Movements*, ed. Jeff Goodwin, Jim Jasper, and Francesca Polletta. Chicago: University of Chicago Press.

2003. *Insurgent Collective Action and Civil War in El Salvador*. New York: Cambridge University Press.

Zaid, Gabriel. 1982. "Enemy Colleagues: A Reading of the Salvadoran Tragedy." *Dissent* Winter: 13–40.

Zhao, Dingxin. 1998. "Ecologies of Social Movements: Student Mobilization during the 1989 Prodemocracy Movement in Beijing." *American Journal of Sociology* 103 (6): 1493–1529.

Zimmerman, Ekhart. 1980. "Macro-Comparative Research on Political Protest." Pp. 167–237. In *Handbook of Political Conflict: Theory and Research*, ed. Ted R. Gurr. New York: Free Press.

Zolberg, Aristide R. 1972. "Moments of Madness." *Politics and Society* 183–207.

Index

363

Index

365

Index

Index

Index